Successful Patents and Patenting for Engineers and Scientists

Successful Patents and Patenting for Engineers and Scientists

Edited by
Michael A. Lechter
Meyer, Hendricks, Victor,
Osborn & Maledon

Earl C. Clifford
Clifford & Clifford

Robert B. Famiglio
Lipton, Famiglio & Stapler

R. J. Joenk

The Institute of Electrical and Electronics Engineers, Inc., New York

This book may be purchased at a discount from the publisher when
ordered in bulk quantities. For more information, contact:

IEEE PRESS Marketing
Attn: Special Sales
P.O. Box 1331
445 Hoes Lane
Piscataway, NJ 08855-1331
Fax: (908) 981-8062

Printed in the United States of America

10   9   8   7   6   5   4   3   2   1

ISBN 0-7803-1086-1
IEEE Order Number: PP4478

Library of Congress Cataloging-in-Publication Data

Successful patents and patenting for engineers and scientists / edited
   by Michael A. Lechter.
         p.   cm.
   Includes bibliographical references and index.
   ISBN 0-7803-1086-1
   1. Patent laws and legislation—United States.   2. Intellectual
property—United States.   3. Patent laws and legislation.   4. Patent
searching.   I. Lechter, Michael A.
KF3114.8.E54S83   1995
346.7304'86—dc20
[347.306486]   94-46193
                                                                    CIP

CONTENTS

CONTENTS

PREFACE

Not so long ago, we entered the age of personal computing. Many people believe that the new age was in large part due to a particular visionary spreadsheet program. However, once the market was established, conceptually identical competing spreadsheet programs appeared, placed on the market by other companies. The other companies had, perhaps, greater resources, and the pioneering program was soon supplanted in the marketplace by the competing programs. Recently one of the developers of the original spreadsheet program was asked, during an interview, if it had made a difference that his company had not pursued patent protection for its product. He thought for a moment and replied, "only several hundreds of millions of dollars."

Some people, invariably those who do not understand the patent system, argue that patents are an impediment to progress and competition. They are wrong.

The patent system in the United States finds its roots in the Constitution. Our founding fathers recognized the need for some form of legal protection that would prevent innovations from being appropriated when introduced to the marketplace. In the absence of such protection, there would be no incentive to invest the time and money in innovating, and to the extent there was innovation it would be kept secret, and unavailable for the public to build upon. Every company would have to reinvent the wheel, without the benefit of the prior work by others. Hence, the patent system was created by constitutional design "to promote the progress of science and the useful arts."

In addition to protecting the investment required to develop new technology and products, by those who know how to access it, the patent system provides a wealth of information. Information is made available to the public to build upon and improve. The nature of the exclusive right afforded by a patent provides an incentive to make improvements to patented technology, to patent those improvements and enter into some form of cross-licensing arrangement with the basic patent holder. Technology is advanced.

The patent system also fosters competition. Like the Colt 45 in the pulp novel *Old West,* patents can function as an "equalizer." A patent is often the only thing that permits an emerging company to compete against larger, established competitors with vastly more marketing power. Patents are also demonstrative evidence of expertise and the worth of technology. A patent can provide an emerging company the necessary credibility to compete in the marketplace, and it can be invaluable in winning a contract or obtaining financing.

Intellectual property law and the patent system, however, are not intuitive. There are catastrophic pitfalls for the unwary. Without at least some familiarity with the basics of intellectual property law and the patent system, significant resources can be wasted in "reinventing the wheel," valuable potential patent rights can be irretrievably lost through inadvertence, and third-party rights can be unwittingly infringed.

This book is intended to provide an overview of intellectual property law and the patent system that will hopefully permit the reader to avoid those pitfalls.

ACKNOWLEDGMENTS

I gratefully acknowledge the dedicated efforts of Sharon Lechter (my lovely wife), CJ Thompson and Jan Rossetti, as well as the patience and support of my colleagues at Meyer, Hendricks, Victor, Osborn & Maledon, without which this book would never have come together.

I also acknowledge the valuable assistance of Dr. Rudolph J. Joenk, Dr. Geoffrey Gates, Earl Clifford, Esq., and Robert Famiglio, Esq.

Michael A. Lechter
Coordinating Editor

BACKGROUND AND PERSPECTIVE

The best place to start is typically at the beginning. The articles of this section place patents in the overall scheme for protecting intellectual property and provide some philosophical and historical perspectives on the patent system. MAL

AN OVERVIEW OF THE BASIC PROTECTION MECHANISMS

Michael A. Lechter

Michael A. Lechter, a member of the law firm Meyer, Hendricks, Victor, Osborn & Maledon in Phoenix, Arizona, and specializing in intellectual property law, is the coordinating editor of this book. A more complete biography is provided at the end of the book.

Abstract

The bulk of this book is devoted to patents and patenting. It is important to keep in mind, however, that patents are only one element, albeit an important element, of an overall system of laws designed to protect *intellectual property* rights and to promote advancement of science and technology. There is a framework of five basic legal mechanisms available for protecting rights in the various aspects of a product. This article reviews that framework, and attempts to provide perspective for patent protection in that context.

1.1 INTRODUCTION

At long last, after countless hours of research and development, InventCo Incorporated is ready to bring its revolutionary new product to the market. It was a costly endeavor, the result of much blood, sweat, and tears by InventCo's engineers and scientists. Extensive market and consumer studies have been performed. New packaging has been designed. Advertising and promotional materials have been developed. All of this was at great expense. In all, InventCo invested tens of millions of dollars in the product, with the expectation that it will take the market by storm.

But what is to prevent the competition from merely copying the product once it is placed on the market, and competing against InventCo without having to recoup the expense of development? Can the competition be prevented from simply appropriating the benefits of InventCo's investment?

In a word, yes. InventCo's investment CAN be protected; the legal system provides a framework of five basic protection mechanisms to protect InventCo's intellectual property rights in its product: trade secret; patent; copyright; *mask work*; and trademark.

One thing, however, is clear—in order to protect its investment in the product, InventCo must be cognizant of the basic precepts of intellectual property law. In general, (excepting copyrights) protection is not automatic. It must be consciously pursued, and certain improvident acts can preclude certain forms of protection. For example, failure to restrict access to information or disclosure to a third party that is not obligated to keep the information in confidence can preclude trade secret status; and premature publication or exploitation of an invention can preclude patent protection. (This topic will be dealt with in detail later in this book.)

The particular approach to protecting a given product must be tailored to the specific characteristics and form of the product, and the particular marketing approach and distribution scheme adopted for the product. A product has many different aspects. Each of those aspects may be valuable and worthy of protection in its own right. For example, a microprocessor-based product includes functional (what the product does), system, component, hardware, and software aspects. The software itself also has many aspects: functional (what the software does), the context of the software in the overall system, the software architecture, algorithms and implementation techniques employed in the software, the code implementing the software, data bases operated upon by the software, and documentation. The documentation includes instruction or users' manuals and promotional materials associated with the product. In addition, the product has marketplace aspects that factor into the value of product—the goodwill and recognition developed in the marketplace, as well as trademarks and trade dress (packaging) used in connection with the product.

Each of the five basic legal protection mechanisms has distinct advantages and disadvantages and provides differing scopes of protection when applied to the various aspects of a product. The nature and scope of each of the protection mechanisms will be separately discussed below. The basic rule, however, is simple: absent an express or implied contractual obligation, a third party is at liberty to use and copy any unpatented, uncopyrighted aspect of a product that comes into its possession legally as long as there is no likelihood that the public would be deceived or confused as to the source of a product.

1.2 TRADE SECRET PROTECTION

Trade secret protection is the most basic and ancient form of protection for technology. As the name implies, information or technology is kept secret from the competition. If the competition is prevented from obtaining access to the technology, it cannot copy or appropriate it. Accordingly, assuming it is capable of doing so, it must take the time and go to the expense of developing the technology on its own. The technology is thus "protected" until the competition can independently develop it or it becomes otherwise known. If the competition is unable to develop the technology on its own, a trade secret strategy can potentially provide infinite protection.

Any proprietary information or technology that is not accessible to the public can be a *trade secret*. However, to have a trade secret right that is enforceable against third parties the information or technology must: (1) derive economic value from being kept secret (provide a commercial advantage); (2) not be generally known or readily accessible from publicly available information; and (3) be subject to *reasonable measures* to maintain secrecy.

It must be appreciated, however, that a trade secret is no protection whatsoever against independent development of the technology by others. In fact, it is possible that the independent developer, even though developing the technology subsequent to the trade secret owner, could obtain exclusive proprietary rights to the technology. It must also be appreciated, that a trade secret will not stop copying or reverse engineering of the technology, if technology or information is obtained legally and the copier is not under any express or implied contractual obligation not to use it.

Clearly, some aspects of a product are totally unsuited to being maintained as a trade secret. Any information or technology that must be disclosed to the public in order to market the product, or which is embodied in a product that is sold to the public and can be reverse engineered, simply cannot be maintained effectively as a trade secret. For example, the functionality of mass-marketed software typically cannot, as a practical matter, be maintained as a trade secret. In order to market the software, potential end-users must be made aware of what it does.

Other aspects of the product, however, need not be disclosed in order to market the product, and can sometimes be maintained as trade secrets. A common example is the particular code used in the software to implement functionality. These aspects can successfully be maintained as trade secrets through an appropriate licensing program. Basically, the customer enters a license agreement under which the customer is permitted to use the trade secret in return for, among other things, a promise not to disclose the trade secret (and, of course, to pay a fee).

Trade secret licensing is commonplace in the software industry. However, as a practical matter, it is often difficult to police and enforce trade secret licenses, particularly when there are a substantial number of licensees, or where there is no direct contact between the software developer and the end-user of the software.

1.3 COPYRIGHT PROTECTION

Copyright protection is available for the form of expression of an idea (as opposed to the idea itself). Copyright protection is available for *works of authorship,* including booklets, advertising brochures, artistic designs, maps and architectural blueprints, audio tapes, and records, and, at least to a limited extent, computer programs. However, ideas, methods, systems, mathematical principles, formulas, and equations are not copyrightable.

Copyright protection is essentially automatic and, while not potentially infinite, is still of relatively long duration (at least 50 years). A registration is not required to preserve the copyright. As to works originating in the United States, the copyright need only be registered before bringing an infringement action. With respect to works originating outside of the United States, even that is not necessary. (However, registration does provide certain procedural advantages, and certain remedies are available only if the copyright is registered prior to commencement of an infringement or within three months of publication.)

5

Copyrights were created to protect artistic expression. A copyright protects only the form of the expression of an idea, not the substance of an idea and, thus, provides very limited scope of protection. For example, assume that a copyrighted article is published describing InventCo's newest product. Notwithstanding the copyright, the competition could read the article and use all of the information disclosed. Assuming no applicable patents, the competition can copy or reverse engineer the product described. Basically, the copyright merely precludes them from copying and marketing the article.

This expression versus idea dichotomy gives rise to some particularly interesting questions when an attempt is made to apply copyright protection to non-textual aspects of a work (product). For example, which aspects of an audio-visual work—a television commercial—are copyrightable expression, and which are uncopyrightable idea? Which non-literal aspects of a software program are copyrightable expression, and which are uncopyrightable idea? The issue must be reviewed on a case-by-case basis.

Infringement of a copyright requires copying; a copyright is no protection whatsoever against independent development by others. Even if a work of authorship is identical to the copyrighted work, there is simply no infringement if the work was created independently.

1.4 TRADEMARK PROTECTION

Trademark protection prevents the competition from trading on a company's reputation. A trademark (or service mark) is used to identify the source or origin of a product (or service). Anything (word, symbol, non-functional aspect of trade dress, packaging, design, shape, sound, or smell) that is capable of distinguishing the goods or services of one company from those of another can be a trademark.

Under the law, a competitor is prevented from capitalizing on a company's reputation and goodwill by passing off possibly inferior goods as those made by the trademark owner. Thus, in a manner of speaking, proper use of a trademark can protect the sales value of the reputation of the company and the product as well as protecting investments in advertising and other promotional activities used to develop that goodwill.

In the United States, rights in a trademark can be acquired (1) through actual use of the mark with goods or services in commercial transactions; or (2) by filing an application for trademark registration based upon a bona fide intent to use.

In general, the first to use a given mark in connection with particular goods in a given geographical area obtains the exclusive rights to the mark for use with those goods in that area. Federal registration prevents someone in a geographical area where the mark is not currently being used from subsequently obtaining rights in the mark. In that way, federal registration can effectively expand the geographic scope of the rights. It also provides additional remedies. When an application for trademark registration based upon a *bona fide intent to use* is filed, and the registration is later granted, it is as if use of the mark on a nationwide basis began on the date of the application.

The laws in other countries vary significantly from the United States. Some countries require registration and, in some cases, various other formalities as a prerequisite to any exclusive right in the trademark. In fact, a few countries require that a mark be registered with the government before it is used in that country.

A trademark provides protection of potentially infinite duration and protects against competition trading on a company's reputation. However, a trademark provides no protection whatsoever against independent development of technology or, for that matter, copying the technology, so long as there is no likelihood that the public will be confused as to the source or origin of the goods.

1.5 MASK WORK PROTECTION

Mask work protection under the Semiconductor Chip Protection Act is available for semiconductor chip mask works (a "series of related images, however fixed or encoded" that represent three dimensional patterns in the layers of a semiconductor chip). In essence, mask work protection precludes the use of reproductions of mask works in the manufacture of competing chips. However, the law makes it absolutely clear that competitors are not precluded from reverse engineering the chip for purposes of analysis or from using any (unpatented) idea, procedure, process, system, method of operation, concept, principle or discovery embodied in the mask work.

1.6 PATENT PROTECTION

Patent protection is available for inventions embodied in a product and prevents others from making, using, or selling any product embodying the patented inventions. In a nutshell, a patent is an agreement between an inventor and the government: the inventor teaches the public how to make and use the invention and, in return, is given the right to preclude the public from making, using, or selling the invention for a period of up to 17 years from the date that the patent is granted. At the end of that time, the public is free to use the invention.

A utility patent provides the broadest scope of legally available protection. The utility patent can be used to protect novel and unobvious aspects of the product, for the life of the patent (up to 17 years). A patent is the only protection against independent development of the product by others and, if properly drafted can sometimes secure the exclusive right to the functionality of the product (what the product does). Of course, in return for this, the details of the product, or at least the details of the product relating to the inventive concepts, must be disclosed to the public and become the property of the public when the patent expires.

Not everything, of course, is patentable. To be patentable, an invention must fall within certain broad categories of subject matter (*e.g.,* be other than merely abstract information or a law of nature or merely printed matter) and must be novel and objectively nonobvious for the perspective of the typical person practicing in the relevant area of technology. *Novelty* is defined in the patent statute by describing certain circumstances, referred to as statutory bars, which preclude patentability. Under those circumstances the invention is, in effect, considered to have already passed into the public domain or to already be the property of another, and therefore unpatentable.

The nature, use, interpretation, and process of obtaining patents are discussed at length in the following sections of this book.

1.7 CONCLUSION

The various forms of protection are not necessarily mutually exclusive. In many cases, different forms of protection can be used concurrently with respect to a given product. With a little bit of forethought, an appropriate strategy using each of the various protection mechanisms to its best effect can be developed to protect a given product.

Article

2

APPLICATION OF THE INTELLECTUAL PROPERTY LAWS: A NOT ATYPICAL HYPOTHETICAL CASE*

Michael A. Lechter

Michael A. Lechter, a member of the law firm Meyer, Hendricks, Victor, Osborn & Maledon in Phoenix, Arizona, and specializing in intellectual property law, is the coordinating editor of this book. A more complete biography is provided at the end of the book.

The following article provides a somewhat light-hearted treatment of the travails of Joe Unsophistico in his efforts to belatedly protect his intellectual property. In this case, (thanks to literary license) Joe was lucky. In the real world, the good guys don't always win, particularly when they fail to take timely actions to protect their intellectual property.   MAL

Joe Unsophistico, president and majority stockholder of Unsophistico Software Incorporated (USI) had finally decided that it was necessary for USI to consult with an attorney. He appointed himself the liaison and met with a well publicized attorney specializing in domestic relations and personal injury litigation. (Joe had seen his advertisement on television.) Joe laid out the following scenario for the attorney:

> USI is an up and coming player in the personal computer industry. The bulk of our business is sales of IBM compatible computers, and associated after-market and peripheral product lines. Our flagship product is the *Hi-Bird* 3-D display system. It's revolutionary—it generates real 3-D images on a conventional color monitor. We first introduced it just under a year ago; in fact, it will be a year next week, and it has absolutely taken over the market.
>
> We market the *Hi-Bird* and our other products through independent distributors. We give the distributors extensive technical training, documentation, and a master disk of the code, including the source code for the products, so they can customize the system for individual customers. Then they go out and solicit orders from customers, and submit them to us. We ship the hardware to the distributor—or directly to the customer, if they ask us to. The distributor does whatever customization on the software that's necessary,

sets up the hardware and installs the customized software in object code on a hard disk in the hardware. The distributor pays us a discounted price, and keeps whatever's actually received from the customer—for the system, installation, and customization services. That's the way a lot of companies are doing it.

We took on Copy-Co as our exclusive distributor in the Midwest. They're in Chicago.

Those crooks took all our training courses, got all our materials, got our code—then they tell us they're no longer going to distribute our products. And now I find out that they've come out with their own version of *Hi-Bird.* It looks like they're using the same basic hardware set up as *Hi-Bird,* but they're getting the components from different manufacturers than we use. And they're using our software. There's no way they could have developed the software on their own in a couple of months. They knew squat when they started our training course.

Here's the thing. We make about 80 percent of our annual sales at the Mon-Dex show next week in Chicago. We've got to stop Copy-Co from pitching their new system at the show. Man, it's a commercial necessity! We were going to sell out of Copy-Co's booth. It's a prime booth. We don't have any other booths—they were our exclusive distributor, for cripe's sake!

I'm supposed to be the keynote speaker at the technical program. But I'm supposed to give a technical presentation on our new technology. We've got a brand new product coming out. We call it the Big-Bird. It's an educational aid system for children. It's totally different from the *Hi-Bird* system. That's what I'm supposed to talk about. It won't help with the sales of *Hi-Bird.*

It's more than just lost sales of *Hi-Bird.* If customers buy the Copy-Co hardware instead of ours, we'll lose the customers for not only *Hi-Bird,* but also for our after-market and peripheral product lines.

So here's what I want. I want to stop those buzzards from even displaying their product at the show, and I want to stop them from marketing a competing system, period.

How can we do it?

The attorney sat back in his chair, looking thoughtfully into space for a moment. "Trade secrets. They stole your trade secrets. I'll start preparing the complaint right away. Just give me two days, and we'll bring suit in Chicago." Then he went on to assure Joe that he was more than capable of "handling the case"; he was a very experienced litigator, and Joe couldn't find better representation.

Joe, however, was not sure. He was troubled by the attorney's constant misuse of jargon (he used software and peripheral interchangeably, and kept referring to the system "CPA"). Joe told the attorney to hold off unless he got back to him.

Troubled by the experience, Joe called an old classmate who was now an attorney, in-house counsel to a software company in the Southeast. He told his friend about the meeting and asked for his advice. Joe's friend was quite candid:

"Look, Joe, you need to go to a bona fide intellectual property attorney—a patent attorney. Not every attorney is a patent attorney. In fact, not every attorney calling themselves an IP—intellectual property—attorney, or a computer law specialist is a patent attorney.

"Patent attorneys have technical backgrounds and they are licensed by the Patent and Trademark Office. They are required to take an additional bar exam—the *patent bar.* As a prerequisite to even taking that exam, they have to prove to the Patent and Trademark Office that they have a technology or science background. That typically means having a degree in engineering or a *hard* science.

"The courts will let non-patent attorneys litigate intellectual property cases in the courtroom. But most non-patent attorneys simply won't be able to counsel you on patent matters, let alone actually do non-litigation patent work. A lot of the time, non-patent intellectual property attorneys don't fully understand the patent law. They're just not sensitized to all of the traps. Most attorneys will admit it when they recognize that they're not competent to take on a matter. But some will tend, albeit unconsciously, to try to 'force fit' the matter into the legal cubbyholes that they are competent to handle, ignoring potential application of aspects of intellectual property law with which they are less familiar.

"Look, in all candor, going to a non-patent attorney on an IP issue is like hiring a carpenter who has a saw, but no hammer. Patent protection may or may not be the solution, but it clearly should be considered as part of an overall strategy for protecting your IP assets.

"And, Joe, don't be penny-wise but dollar foolish in protecting your intellectual property. IP protection is an area where you clearly get what you pay for. Intellectual property protection, by its nature, will be scrutinized by adverse, and sometimes hostile, third parties looking for a chink in your IP armor. Developing a strategy for protecting the company's intellectual property assets should be a thorough and analytical process. You want lots of interaction and *think tanking* with your patent attorney. This is true in spades for any patent protection to be employed in implementing the strategy. Preparing a patent application should be a cooperative and extremely interactive process between the company and its patent attorney. That's the only way to ensure that the patent, when you get it, is valid and meets your business goals to the fullest possible extent."

Joe thanked his friend profusely. He, like many other business people, did not appreciate the need for a coordinated strategy for intellectual property protection, or the role a patent attorney could play in developing and implementing that strategy.

Off Joe went, to set up an appointment with a patent attorney his friend had recommended. Before long, Joe was sitting at a conference table, next to the patent attorney. They spoke at length, and during the conversation the patent attorney's questions elicited a number of facts Joe hadn't thought to mention on his own.

- *Hi-Bird* uses USI hardware and USI proprietary software. The software is revolutionary, and, while all of the individual components are commercially available, the combination of hardware components used in the system is novel.
- There were no explicit obligations of confidentiality imposed on Copy-Co, with respect to the master disk or source code in the distributorship agreement. In fact, USI has never actually requested return of the materials.
- USI has not employed any sort of end-user agreements with respect to the software, or even any proprietary legends in the software or user documentation. They simply sell the system outright.

- The software displays a log-on screen that includes a *Hi-Bird* logo, and what purports to be a copyright notice:

  © 1990 USI software.

- The date on the screen is indeed 1990; it was used in the screen because USI wanted the user to know that *Hi-Bird* was a really new product. Sales of *Hi-Bird* systems, with the software included, had commenced some 11 months earlier in 1989.
- No copyrights have actually been registered with respect to the software.
- USI does not hold any patents.
- The system does not employ any custom integrated circuits that might be subject to mask work protection, but USI does have trademark registrations on its name and the word *Hi-Bird;* and, for various reasons, Copy-Co, as a former distributor, is clearly aware of those registrations.
- Joe had faxed Copy-Co and demanded that they cease and desist. Copy-Co, however, had less than respectfully declined. Copy-Co contended:

  That the software has become public domain and, in any event, it's only using the *Hi-Bird* software until it completes development of its own improved version.

  That the brand of the hardware is clearly marked so no one will think that it is a USI product; and

  That Copy-Co advises all of its customers that it is no longer associated with USI and that Copy-Co will have a sign to that effect prominently displayed at its booth at the show.

After the attorney had finished questioning Joe, Joe looked him in the eyes. "Okay, counselor, what do we do?"

The patent attorney met Joe's gaze.

"O.K., Joe. First of all I need to point out to you that there are a number of issues here. Copy-Co is not your only problem.

"I suggest that you consider a name other than "Big-Bird" for your new product. 'The "Big-Bird" education aid system for children.' I don't know if you are aware of Children's Television Workshop? Sesame Street? Big Bird from Sesame Street?"

"Of course I've heard of Sesame Street. That's why I picked the name. I thought it was a great play on words. Hi-Bird. Big-Bird for Kids . . ."

"Joe, if you use Big-Bird on an education aid for children, you're just asking to be sued. And you'll get hammered. Probably would end up paying CTW's attorney's fees. We can come back to this later. There are some other issues we need to address.

"Let me just touch on one so I don't forget. If you are interested in patent protection outside of the United States on the education system, we should have an application on file before your talk next week. Unfortunately, it's too late for any foreign patents on *Hi-Bird.* I'll explain later.

"With respect to Copy-Co, there is a possibility that we can effectively shut them down at the show. We may be able to prevent them from running your software by pursuing a trademark infringement claim since the software displays your registered *Hi-Bird* trademark.

"Long term though, the only thing that might be able to prevent them from developing their own analogous product is a patent on some strategic aspect of *Hi-Bird.*"

Joe was a little puzzled. "Well, what about suing them for stealing my trade secrets?"

The attorney replied. "Joe, based on what you've told me, they didn't steal any trade secrets from you. Unfortunately, it looks like you gave them away."

"Huh?"

"Joe, if we could show that Copy-Co had misappropriated a valid trade secret, we would have a pretty formidable arsenal of remedies available to us, including injunctive relief, as well as damages, unjust enrichment, and, if the misappropriation can be shown to be willful, punitive damages and reasonable attorney's fees.

"The problem is that you have to take reasonable measures to maintain confidentiality. With respect to the object code, you haven't taken any. You don't have any enforceable trade secret rights in *Hi-Bird.*

"You can enforce trade secret rights only against an entity that is subject to an obligation of confidentiality and/or knowingly obtained the trade secret through improper channels. Copy-Co could easily have been made subject to an obligation of confidentiality in a distributorship or other agreement, or perhaps even by implication, if there had been agreements imposing confidentiality on end-users—but there were none.

"The bottom line is that the *Hi-Bird* object code has, in effect, been published and trade secret protection simply is not applicable to published material or anything that is readily ascertainable from it."

One of Joe's oxen had just been gored. "But, what about Copy-Co's use of my source code? Could that be misappropriation of a trade secret?"

The attorney replied. "Frankly, based on what you told me, it's extremely doubtful that under these circumstances the source code could be established as a trade secret. It was released to the distributors without any obligation of confidentiality and, on top of that, in view of the commercial availability of decompilers that will generate a source code from an object code—in effect translate the object code—the publication of the object code may well be enough to destroy any trade secret rights in the source code."

"Okay, I guess a trade secret action is out. So you say to yourself; well, there's still copyright protection—right?"

"It would be great if it is. If a case of copyright infringement can be made: injunctive relief is available, as well as, depending on the circumstances, impoundment; actual damages and profits or statutory damages; and discretionary costs and attorney's fees to the prevailing party.

"But there are a couple of problems. There may be a problem with the copyright notice. Under copyright law applicable to programs first published after March 1, 1989, a copyright notice is no longer a requirement—but the program was first published before that. That being the case, the notice could be problematical. The © is not statutory, and more important, the date in the notice is improper—and that would negate the notice.

"We would have to proceed under the omitted notice provisions of section 405 of the Copyright Act, and I'm not sure that you can qualify. Probably not; quite a few copies were distributed with the improper notice.

"What do you mean that the copyright is improper?"

"The copyright statute specifies three specific forms of notice. © is not one of them, and some courts have found it not to be an effective notice.

"Look, we don't need to get into that. Let's ignore those issues for now. The real problem is that even assuming that you have a valid copyright, it is not registered—and registration of the copyright is a prerequisite to an infringement suit."

"Okay," said Joe, "we can just register the copyright now, can't we?"

"Sure. Preparing a copyright application involves filling out the appropriate copyright office form, and filing it, together with deposit materials and a fee at the copyright office. So, assuming we have blank originals of the appropriate copyright office forms—the Copyright Office won't accept photocopies—and appropriate listings and copies of the program for use as deposit materials, we could probably have the application on file with the Copyright Office in a day or so."

"O.K. So you file the application."

"Well, we can get it on file, but then the ball is in the Copyright Office's court. Registration is not instantaneous. You can request special handling by the Copyright Office—I think they're charging about $100 or so—but the earliest you can realistically expect to get the registration in hand is probably sometime the week after next. That won't help for Mon-Dex."

"Could we get away with filing a copyright action before obtaining the registration, based on having an application for registration on file?"

"Maybe, but probably not. Anyway, I am not comfortable with it and strongly advise against it. Most courts require that a certificate of registration, or Copyright Office denial of registration, be in hand, as a threshold of jurisdiction, and if the issue arises, the suit would be dismissed. This is probably the present state of the law in the Seventh Circuit—that's the law that would apply in Chicago.

"This is a typical problem encountered with respect to copyright protection of software—the practice of delaying registration of a copyright until an infringement situation arises is prevalent in the software industry—primarily in an attempt to avoid questions as to the trade secret status of the software. This tends to delay filing of copyright actions and, more important, limits the available remedies. Again, attorney's fees and statutory damages are generally not available if infringement commences prior to registration."

"Okay—it looks like my copyrights won't stop Copy-Co from displaying at the show, but what about long-range protection?"

"You're asking how effective a copyright will be against the Copy-Co developed version of the software, presupposing that USI has a valid, registered copyright? The answer is: it depends. It depends on just what aspects of the *Hi-Bird* program are reflected in the Copy-Co program.

"We would have to prove actionable copying. This is typically done by showing access and substantial similarities to copyrightable aspects of the respective programs. The problem is that a copyright is intended to protect artistic expression—it protects the expression of an idea, not the idea itself. So if the only similarity between the respective programs is that they perform the same functions, there would be no copyright infringement.

On the other hand, if Copy-Co lifts substantial blocks of code from *Hi-Bird,* it probably would be a copyright infringement.

"Infringement might be shown if the structure, code sequence, and organization of the respective programs were the same—but that's a huge question mark.

"What is clear though, is that Copy-Co could get around any claim of copyright infringement by proving it employed a clean room scheme to develop its program. A first set of programmers dissect *Hi-Bird* and provide a functional specification to a second group of programmers that have never had direct access to the *Hi-Bird* software. The second group of programmers then develop the Copy-Co program from the functional specification.

"If this can be credibly shown, notwithstanding any similarities between the programs, a copyright infringement claim would be defeated. So, depending upon the extent to which the ultimate Copy-Co program incorporates aspects or portions of *Hi-Bird,* there may or may not be a copyright infringement."

Joe was beginning to get queasy; his understanding of software protection was being severely shaken. "Okay, how about patent protection?"

"Let's assume that some of the aspects of *Hi-Bird* that make it work are patentable. We don't know that, but based on what you said it's probably a safe bet. Again, we don't know, but it's conceivable that we could get a patent that covered the functions of the *Hi-Bird* program. Copying is not a requisite for patent infringement—a patent can protect against independent development of competing software by others. So, Copy-Co couldn't avoid patent infringement by setting up a clean room.

"If we prove patent infringement, injunctive relief is available, and from recent cases it appears that lost profits may be obtainable—based not only on sales of the *Hi-Bird* program, but also convoyed sales of the hardware, and aftermarket and peripheral products.

"Given the equities here and the strong presumption of validity that now attaches to patents, if there is an enforceable patent, preliminary relief might be a possibility with respect to the Copy-Co product that actually uses the *Hi-Bird* software.

"The thing is, you told me that you didn't have any applicable patents."

"Can you patent software?" Joe queried.

"You can in the United States and many other countries, as long as the software doesn't merely implement some mathematical algorithm—$x + y = 2$. By and large patent protection is available for software just like anything else. As long as it meets the other requisites for patentability."

"But is *Hi-Bird* patentable?"

"I am not in a position to say, for sure. To do that I'd have to investigate what else is already out there. For an aspect of the program to be patentable, the aspect has to be *novel* and *unobvious.* From what you said, and what I have heard from others, the *Hi-Bird* program is revolutionary—it does something that no previous product has ever done. It's clearly new and not obvious. . . ."

"So," Joe piped in, "that means it's patentable—right?"

The attorney smiled. "Well, it's not quite that simple. Novelty is defined by statute, 35 U.S.C. § 102. Under a portion of that statute, you can lose rights by prematurely publishing or exploiting an invention. Basically, in the United States, you're given a one-year grace period to file an application. The one-year clock starts with the first publication describing the invention, or the first U.S. public use or offer for sale of a product employing the invention. After that year the patent is barred.

"You told me the *Hi-Bird* system was introduced almost a year ago. Sometimes products are offered for sale before there is an actual roll out of the product. We need to determine whether there were any offers for sale more than a year ago."

"There weren't. Can a patent application still be filed?"

"Yes, in the United States. The *Hi-Bird* system is still within the one-year grace period. I need to point out, however, that most foreign countries have no grace period. That's why it's too late for patent protection in most, if not all, foreign countries."

Now Joe was enthused. "So, what do you think? Can you throw together a patent application and get it on file before Tuesday?

Now, the attorney chuckled. "Frankly, it would take an heroic effort. A patent application is not a matter of merely filling out forms. It's really in the nature of a proposed patent. If things go well in the Patent and Trademark Office, the patent will be word for word what's in the application. You have to include a description that's sufficiently detailed to permit someone to actually make and use the invention—in this case, to develop software that would perform the functions performed by *Hi-Bird*. But it could be done as long as you can get me the information that I would need, and the inventors are available to work with me. And, we're talking an around-the-clock proposition here."

"Okay, but let's take a step back here. Exactly what will getting the application on file before Mon-Dex get us?"

"Well, if it's not filed by then, you will be barred from filing because the one year grace period will clearly have run. So if you want to pursue a patent, we have to get the application on file. But, just filing the application isn't going to stop Copy-Co at Mon-Dex. You don't get any enforceable rights until the patent is actually granted, and on the average, that takes on the order of two years from the date of filing. Once the patent is filed, a patent pending notice can be placed on the software and this does have an *ad terrorem* effect on—scares off—potential copiers, but it does not create any enforceable right."

Joe just shook his head. "Okay. It looks like patent protection provides no help with respect to stopping the display at Mon-Dex, but may well be the long-term answer for preventing Copy-Co from developing a competing product."

The patent attorney nodded affirmatively.

Joe was perplexed. "So where are we with respect to the show? What I hear you telling me is that a trade secret action is out—we didn't do what we had to for the software to qualify as a trade secret. The likelihood of obtaining timely relief based on copyrights is pretty dismal. A patent action is out. So, what can we do?"

"Like I said, we sue for trademark infringement and request a temporary restraining order against Copy-Co displaying at the show. Essentially anything that's capable of indicating the source of the software can be a trademark, and exclusive rights are acquired immediately through use. In this case, *Hi-Bird* displays registered trademarks on the screens of the software. Use of a mark that is likely to cause confusion as to source, affiliation, or sponsorship, is a trademark infringement under the common law, and under the Lanham Act.

"If we can show a trademark, under these circumstances, we can get injunctive relief, as well as destruction orders, defendant's profits plus damages and costs, and in exceptional cases, reasonable attorney's fees—and more if it's an instance of counterfeiting.

"The primary drawback of trademark protection is that infringement does require a showing of likelihood of confusion. So trademarks don't look promising for preventing Copy-Co from developing its own version of the *Hi-Bird* system. The technology of the software can be appropriated without trademark infringement by merely adopting a different mark and excising the original mark from the software. But in the initial product, Copy-Co didn't do that—it's using unauthorized copies of the *Hi-Bird* software—which displays the screens featuring USI's trademarks.

"The only issue is whether, under the circumstances, use of the unauthorized copies displaying the trademarks—will create a likelihood of confusion as to source, affiliation, or sponsorship."

"Wait a minute!" Joe blurted out. "They've got a disclaimer. How can anyone be confused? How can consumers be confused if Copy-Co tells them that Copy-Co is not affiliated with USI, and we didn't make the copy of the software, they did?"

Once more the patent attorney chuckled. "There can be confusion based on what happens after the sale—aftermarket confusion—post-sale confusion. That comes into play. Confusion doesn't have to occur at the point of sale—a likelihood of aftermarket or post-sale confusion is actionable. There have been a number of cases like this that have involved Levi jeans and Rolex watches.

"In those cases, point of sale disclaimers, packaging, or both, precluded any confusion on the part of the initial purchaser—but the courts, nonetheless, found trademark infringement based on the potential for post-sale confusion.

"You see, potential purchasers who observe the counterfeits in use will not necessarily be privy to the disclaimers or packaging, and they may well tend to associate any observed defects or problems in the counterfeit with the genuine goods. If there is a potential that the use of the unauthorized copies will be observed by individuals who were not advised that the copy is unauthorized, a likelihood exists that those potential consumers would believe that the software was an authorized copy. And, this could, in fact, have an adverse impact on USI's reputation.

"For example, the unauthorized copy might not have been updated with a program fix—and the observer would be exposed to an apparent bug in the program—that had actually been cured. Or, the observer may be exposed to an operator having difficulties that would be cured by a quick call to USI's support services, if an authorized copy had been involved.

"So, there is clearly an actionable likelihood of confusion. The use by Copy-Co of the *Hi-Bird* marks in the screens displayed by the unauthorized copies presents a potential trademark action. In fact, the infringement arguably comes within the anti-counterfeiting provisions of the Lanham Act—the trademark statute. In any event, it's entirely feasible that a TRO—a temporary restraining order—could be obtained, preventing Copy-Co from displaying *Hi-Bird* at the show.

"So, the bottom line is this. Nothing is guaranteed, we've got a shot at a TRO to stop Copy-Co at the show. Hopefully, that will take care of the short-term problem. To stop Copy-Co from developing analogous software, it looks like we should get a patent application on file with respect to *Hi-Bird*, post haste. If we get that patent, and the claims are broad enough, that will take care of the United States. We should also go ahead and register the copyright on *Hi-Bird* software. At this point, it doesn't look like there is any chance of establishing trade secret status for the software, so there is no reason to delay. Unfortunately, it looks like it's too late for patent protection on *Hi-Bird* outside of the United States. And, if you are going to want to patent your new technology outside of the United States, we'll have to get an application filed on it by the day you give your speech, either that or cancel or change the subject of the talk. I'm also counseling you to choose something other than "Big-Bird" to call the new product. If you use "Big-Bird", you're just going to end up paying me a bunch of money and still get hammered. Speaking of money, we really should talk about what it's going to cost you to have me do all this work. . . ."

Now Joe really began to feel nervous.

* * *

So, in our hypothetical example, the good guys ultimately prevail. More important, however, the example illustrates that the different protection mechanisms will be applicable to a greater or lesser degree depending upon the individual circumstances, and that all of the protection mechanisms should be considered when developing a protection strategy.

Article	# HISTORY OF THE U.S.
# 3	# PATENT SYSTEM

Robert A. Walsh

Robert A. Walsh is the Patent Counsel for AlliedSignal Inc.,
located in Phoenix, Arizona. He is a retired Colonel with the USAF
Reserve, Office of the Judge Advocate General Patent Operation.

*The basic premise of the patent system in the United States is somewhat
different than in most other countries. The U.S. patent system was created to
provide an incentive for inventors to advance "science and useful arts". In most
other countries a patent grant originated as a gift or favor from the sovereign.
In fact, many of the early* patents *granted in Europe had nothing to do with
invention—they related to exclusive trading rights within a geographic region or
to ownership of land. In part because of the differing origins, the philosophy
of the U.S. patent system and the patent systems of most other countries are sub-
tly different.*

The U.S. system exacts a detailed description of the best mode *of the invention
contemplated by the inventor, in return for the patent grant. Most other countries do
not require a description of the* best mode, *the disclosure requirements tend to be
much less stringent.*

Most countries, have adopted what is known as first to file *patent systems—
the first to file an application on an otherwise patentable invention is awarded the
patent. This is not necessarily the case in the United States. The United States has
adopted what is known as a* first to invent *system. To be entitled to a patent in the
United States, the applicant must be the first to have "made", and not abandoned,
suppressed, or concealed the invention in the United States. The U.S. law also requires that a patent be granted in the name of the actual inventor. This is not the case
in most other countries. (Of course, the owner, or assignee, of a U.S. patent can be
someone other than the inventor.)*

These differences find their origins in history.

The following article provides a bit of historical perspective. MAL

3.1 BASIS AND PHILOSOPHY

The patent system of the United States finds its basis in Article I, Section 8, of the
Constitution. One of the enumerated powers of Congress is to:

Promote the Progress of Science and Useful Arts, by securing for limited times to authors and inventors the exclusive right to their respective writings and discoveries.

This language has been interpreted to require that all patents be issued in the name of the actual inventor, and to require that the inventor contribute to the progress of science and the useful arts. This contribution is in the form of the publication of a detailed description of the best mode (version) of the invention contemplated by the inventor at the time the application is filed. The basic philosophy is that the inventor is provided an exclusive right to the invention for a limited time in return for making the contribution to the progress of science. Only the first to make an invention which is revealed to the public, and not suppressed or concealed, contributes to progress; latecomers add nothing to the store of public knowledge. Hence, a patent can be awarded only to the first person to make, and not abandon, suppress, or conceal an invention. Likewise, there is no contribution if the invention is not new to the public or is obvious in view of what the public already knows.

This philosophy of awarding rights to the individuals that contribute to progress, in return for that contribution, must be contrasted with the historical basis for the patent systems in many other countries—grants by the sovereign to a privileged class. The United States remains the only country in the world that grants an exclusive right to individuals who are the first to invent. These rights enable inventors to start up successful and innovative businesses.

3.2 HISTORY

The first U.S. Patent Act became law on April 10, 1790. The 1790 Act required inventors to file a specification in writing, a drawing and, if feasible, a model. The State Department was assigned the administrative responsibility for granting patents and establishing a board of examiners. The first board of examiners consisted of the Secretary of State (Thomas Jefferson), the Secretary of War (Henry Knox), and the Attorney General (Edmund Randolph). A majority of the patent board was required to agree to the grant. On July 31, 1790, the first U.S. patent was granted to a man named Samuel Hopkins for "Making Pot and Pearl Ashes".

However, the original law was found to be overly burdensome, and on February 21, 1793, the Patent Law was revised. The patent board was abolished and a registration system created. Patents were granted without examination, and the issue of patentability was left for determination by litigation in the courts. In 1802, a Patent Office was established to administer the registration of patents, with a superintendent and clerical staff under the auspices of the Secretary of State.

Although the new law liberalized the patent system and was well received by many, several prominent statesmen including Thomas Jefferson [1] were concerned about the possible abuse of a registration system. Nevertheless, the registration system stayed in place for over forty years.

Ultimately, because of the proliferation of patent litigation in the courts (resulting from the registration system), a formal examination procedure to determine if an invention were new and useful before a patent was granted was established by the Patent Act of July 4, 1836. The 1836 Act also established an examination Corps and the office of Commissioner of Patents under the Secretary of State. Later the Patent Office was moved under the auspices of the Department of Commerce, where it continues today.

The 1836 Act required that copies of issued patents be available and that each patent include a short description of the invention and a statement specifying what was claimed. The examination procedure of 1836 Act became the standard for the world to emulate.

During this period, the Patent Office used a *flash of genius* test to determine if the applicant was to receive a patent. This standard was difficult to apply and was eliminated with the passage of the 1952 Patent Act in favor of the *Novelty* and *Nonobviousness* tests for patentability that have carried through into the present law.

A strong patent system is essential for a strong and vibrant economy. History has made this clear. Patents are enforced through litigation in the Federal District Courts. Prior to 1982, an appeal from the decision of a district court was taken to one of the eleven regional U.S. Circuit Courts of Appeals. During the 1970s, the patent system became the subject of express judicial hostility in a number of the regional circuits; they did not understand technology or the premise of the patent system and viewed patents as dangerous "monopolies". This difficulty was often compounded in litigation in that neither of the judges involved, at the trial or appellate level, had any background in technology or in the patent system. In addition, each of the different appeals circuits had its own body of law interpreting the patent statutes, some less hospitable to the patentee than others. This led to the incongruous result that a patent could be found valid and infringed under the laws of one circuit, but not under the laws of another. Forum shopping and races to the courthouse to find the least inhospitable forum were rampant. Most significantly, the inability to enforce patents in the courts was one of the primary contributing factors for the decline in innovation experienced by the United States in the late 1970s [2].

This led to the creation, in 1982, of a special court of appeals, the U.S. Court of Appeals for the Federal Circuit (CAFC), to provide consistency in the interpretation and application of patent law and to restore the incentive for technological innovation. Since October of 1982, all appeals in patent cases are heard by the U.S. Court of Appeals for the Federal Circuit, rather than the individual circuit courts of appeals. The judges in the CAFC are, in general, familiar with the patent laws, and either have technical backgrounds themselves, or have technical advisers available to them. Enforcement of patents has become more uniform across the nation. A strong patent system to provide the necessary incentive for technological innovation has indeed been restored.

This was the charter of the Court of Appeals for the Federal Circuit. As stated by former Chief Judge Helen Nies:

> Our society is dependent on the self-generated efforts of individual businesses to create the goods and jobs which we enjoy. The change of direction around the world from wholly government-directed economies to increased private enterprise confirms that our forefathers selected the right course. How remarkable that the drafters of the Constitution foresaw the benefit of encouraging individual initiative by providing in the Consti-

tution itself, among the short list of specific powers of Congress that Congress shall have power to secure to authors and inventors the exclusive right to their respective writings and discoveries for a limited time. (Article I, section 8.) By this power and the statutes dependent on the power, our society has expressed its philosophical view that individual creativity *can* be stimulated with material rewards and that society as a whole will thereby be benefitted. Only by maintaining a strong and vigorous economy can the ultimate objective of personal liberty be achieved. The Federal Circuit lives daily with the responsibility to carry out this societal decision [3].

NOTES

[1] *The Smithsonian Book of Invention* distributed by W.W. Norton & Co., 1978.

[2] *The United States Court of Appeals for the Federal Circuit—A History* Published by authorization of the United States Judicial Conference Committee on the Bicentennial of the Constitution of the United States, 1991.

[3] *Id.* at page xii.

THE PATENT SYSTEM AS A SOURCE OF INFORMATION

The patent system holds a wealth of information for those who know how to access it. This portion of the book contains articles that discuss how the U.S. patent system is organized, and the various media available for information retrieval from the U.S. and other patent systems. MAL

THE U.S. PATENT CLASSIFICATION SYSTEM AND SUBJECT MATTER SEARCHES OF U.S. PATENTS

Kendall J. Dood

Kendall J. Dood is a Supervisory Patent Classifier in the U.S. Department of Commerce Patent and Trademark Office in Washington, DC.

Abstract

The U.S. Patent Classification is a system for finding patents pertaining to specific technical subject matter. The system includes a classified file, search tools, and rules to facilitate searches. Searching is an iterative process involving the searcher, the search tools, and the patent file.

4.1 THE U.S. PATENT CLASSIFICATION SYSTEM (USPCS)

> The specification shall contain a written description of the invention . . . in such . . . terms as to enable any person skilled in the art to which it pertains . . . to make and use the same.
>
> Title 35, United States Code, Section 112.

This requirement—which has appeared in the U.S. patent statutes continuously since 1790—has made U.S. patents a unique source of historical information about practical solutions to technical problems of all kinds. Such information should be of particular interest to engineers who need to know not only what solutions to technical problems already exist but to what extent a solution of their own may constitute a patentable invention. But with over five million U.S. patents now in existence, how does one find just those pertinent to one's own interests? Or, to put the question in more general terms, how does one do a subject matter search of the patent file?

Over the years, the Patent and Trademark Office (PTO) has developed the U.S. Patent Classification System (USPCS) specifically for storing and retrieving patents according to their subject matter. It consists of an arrangement of classes and subclasses of processes, apparatus, articles of manufacture, and compositions according to which each U.S. patent is classified. Classes and subclasses within the system can be found in the Manual of

Classification which currently contains over 400 classes. Figure 1, discussed in more detail below, is a listing of some of these classes. Figures 2 and 3 are parts of a typical listing— or *schedule*—of subclasses within a class. Because the arrangement of subclasses within a class is hierarchical, their order and indentation levels are significant. The subclass numbering system does not necessarily reflect this, however, since revisions of classes sometime require new subclasses to be inserted into a class or old ones to be moved or canceled which precludes strict sequential numbering.

Each class and its subclasses are *defined*, class by class, in a separately published document. Each definition consists of a detailed description of the contents of the class or subclass, usually with cross-reference notes to other classes or subclasses where similar or related subject matter may be found. Since the basic subject matter specifically provided for in one class will not be specifically provided for in another, its definition must stand alone without reference to any other class. Subclass definitions, on the other hand, explicitly reflect the fact that each must satisfy not only the definition of the class but also that of each subclass from which it depends. Figure 4 is a page of the definition of Class 360, "Dynamic Magnetic Information Storage or Retrieval." The basic subject matter of this class is delineated in section I-A as "apparatus and corresponding processes for the storage and retrieval of information based on relative movement between a magnetic record carrier and a transducer." Figure 5 contains selected subclass definitions from the same class. Note that the definition of subclass 34.1, for example, depends on the definition of subclass 33.1 which, in turn, depends on the class definition.

4.2 USING THE CLASSIFICATION SYSTEM

To find a particular subject matter in the USPCS, one begins by identifying the most appropriate class. This can be done by scanning the list titled "Classes Within the U.S. Classification System Arranged by Related Subjects" at the beginning of the manual. In this list, the classes are arranged in three main groups: chemical, electrical, and mechanical/miscellaneous. Figure 1 is a page from the electrical portion of this list. Although there is no strict hierarchy amongst classes as there is amongst subclasses, the relationships between classes, as spelled out in the class definitions, do suggest some logical ordering, and this has been followed in this list. Class 360, for example, is shown indented under Class 369, "Dynamic Information Storage or Retrieval," because the subject matter of the former class is considered a species of the subject matter of the latter. In this case, a box on the Class 360 schedule (see Figure 2), as well as notes in the class definitions of both classes, make their relationship explicit. According to the box, Class 360 is to be thought of as actually part of Class 369.

Once a class has been selected, the search is continued by scanning the left-most coordinate subclasses listed in the subclass schedule of that class, starting from the top and working down until a subclass is arrived at whose title explicitly designates some feature of the object of the search. The same process is applied to the subclasses indented under that subclass, *i.e.,* the next level of coordinate subclasses is scanned from the top down un-

Class	Subject
505	SUPERCONDUCTOR TECHNOLOGY-APPARATUS, MATERIAL, PROCESS (See subclass 1 involving material superconducting above 30° Kelvin and Subclasses 800-933 for art collections on superconductor technology.)
376	INDUCED NUCLEAR REACTIONS, SYSTEMS AND ELEMENTS
380	CRYPTOGRAPHY
340	COMMUNICATIONS, ELECTRICAL
358	PICTORIAL COMMUNICATION; TELEVISION
382	IMAGE ANALYSIS
342	COMMUNICATIONS, DIRECTIVE RADIO WAVE SYSTEMS AND DEVICES (E.G., RADAR, RADIO NAVIGATION)
343	COMMUNICATIONS, RADIO WAVE ANTENNAS
370	MULTIPLEX COMMUNICATIONS
381	ELECTRICAL AUDIO SIGNAL PROCESSING SYSTEMS, AND DEVICES
379	TELEPHONIC COMMUNICATIONS
178	TELEGRAPHY
375	PULSE OR DIGITAL COMMUNICATIONS
455	TELECOMMUNICATIONS
341	CODED DATA GENERATION OR CONVERSION
367	COMMUNICATIONS, ELECTRICAL: ACOUSTIC WAVE SYSTEMS AND DEVICES
334	TUNERS
332	MODULATORS
329	DEMODULATORS
116	SIGNALS AND INDICATORS
	CALCULATORS. COMPUTERS OR DATA PROCESSING SYSTEMS
371	ERROR DETECTION/CORRECTION AND FAULT DETECTION/RECOVERY
*364/737	ARITHMETICAL ERRORS
*235/375	REGISTERS (Systems Controlled by Data Bearing Records)
400	(Ordnance or Weapon System Computers) (Record Controlled Calculators)
364	ELECTRICAL COMPUTERS AND DATA PROCESSING SYSTEMS
395	INFORMATION PROCESSING SYSTEM ORGANIZATION
377	ELECTRICAL PULSE COUNTERS, PULSE DIVIDERS OR SHIFT REGISTERS: CIRCUITS AND SYSTEMS
902	ELECTRONIC FUNDS TRANSFER
*235/61	REGISTERS (Mechanical Calculators)
	INFORMATION STORAGE
369	DYNAMIC INFORMATION STORAGE OR RETRIEVAL
360	DYNAMIC MAGNETIC INFORMATION STORAGE OR RETRIEVAL
365	STATIC INFORMATION STORAGE AND RETRIEVAL
*235/435	REGISTERS (Coded Sensors)
346	RECORDERS
	MEASURING, TESTING, PRECISION INSTRUMENTS (See also Group I, Class 436, Chemistry: Analytical and Immunological Testing)
73	MEASURING AND TESTING
324	ELECTRICITY, MEASURING AND TESTING
*250/250	WAVEMETERS
356	OPTICS, MEASURING AND TESTING
368	HOROLOGY: TIME MEASURING SYSTEMS OR DEVICES
374	THERMAL MEASURING AND TESTING
177	WEIGHING SCALES
33	GEOMETRICAL INSTRUMENTS
*250	RADIANT ENERGY (See also Group I, Class 204, Chemistry, Electrical and Wave Energy)

Figure 1 A page from the Table of Contents of the *Manual of Classification*

```
CLASS 360 IS TO BE CONSIDERED AS AN INTEGRAL PART OF CLASS 369 (AFTER
SUBCLASS 18) AND FOLLOWS THE SCHEDULE HIERARCHY, RETAINING ALL PERTINENT
DEFINITIONS AND CLASS LINES OF CLASS 369.
```

1	RECORDING ON OR REPRODUCING FROM AN ELEMENT OF DIVERSE UTILITY	34.1	.Inverting polarity of alternate periods
		35.1	.Single field or frame recording
2	Card	36.1	.Time correction
3	.Motion picture film	36.2	..Digital techniques
4	MANUAL INPUT RECORDING	37.1	.Synchronization signal modifying
5	RECORDING FOR SELECTIVE RETENTION OF A SPECIAL OCCURRENCE	38.1	.Drop-out correction
		39	GENERAL PROCESSING OF A DIGITAL SIGNAL
6	RECORDING COMBINED WITH METERING OR SENSING	40	.In specific code or form
		41	..Nonreturn to zero
7	RECORDING FOR MONETARY DELAY OF AN ANALOG SIGNAL	42	..Phase code
		43	.Multi-frequency[sic]
8	RECORDING FOR CHANGING DURATION, FREQUENCY OR REDUNDANT CONTENT OF AN ANALOG SIGNAL	44	..Intra-cell transition
		45	.Pulse crowding correction
		46	.Head amplifier circuit
9.1	.Television signal	47	.Redundant or complimentary tracks
10.1	..Fast, slow, or stop reproducing	48	.Data in specific format
10.2	...Scan locus or tracking control	49	.Address coding
10.3	...Tape	50	.Inter-record gap processing
11.1	..Field or frame skipping	51	.Data clocking
12	RECORDING OR REPRODUCING FOR AUTOMATIC ANNOUNCING	52	..With incremental movement between record and head
13	RECORD EDITING	53	.Data verification
14.1	.Television	54	.Data recirculation
14.2	..Control track	55	GENERAL RECORDING OR REPRODUCING
14.3	...Numerical code	57	.Selective erase recording
15	RECORD COPYING	58	.Boundary displacement recording or transducers
16	.Contact transfer	59	.Thermomagnetic recording or transducers
17	..With magnetic bias	60	.Recording-or erasing-prevention
18	RECORDING OR REPRODUCING PLURAL INFORMATION SIGNALS ON THE SAME TRACK	61	.Signal switching
19.1	.Audio and video	62	..Record-reproduce
20	.Frequency multiplex	63	..Between plural stationary heads
21	.Head gap azimuth multiplex	64	..Between heads in alternate engagement with medium
22	SPLITTING ONE INFORMATION SIGNAL FOR RECORDING ON PLURAL DISTINCT TRACKS OR REPRODUCING SUCH SIGNAL	65	.Specifics of equalizing
		66	.Specifics of biasing or erasing
23	.Time division	67	.Specifics of the amplifier
24	SPLITTING, PROCESSING AND RECOMBINING ONE INFORMATION SIGNAL FOR RECORDING OR REPRODUCING ON THE SAME TRACK	68	..Recording amplifier
		69	AUTOMATIC CONTROL OF A RECORDER MECHANISM
25	CHECKING RECORD CHARACTERISTICS OR MODIFYING RECORDING SIGNAL FOR CHARACTERISTIC COMPENSATION	70	.Synchronizing moving-head moving-record recorders
26	ELECTRONICALLY CORRECTING PHASING ERRORS BETWEEN RELATED INFORMATION SIGNALS	71	.Controlling the record
		72.1	..Locating specific areas
27	RECORDING OR REPRODUCING AN INFORMATION SIGNAL AND A CONTROL SIGNAL FOR CONTROLLING ELECTRONICS OF REPRODUCER	72.2	...Responsive to recorded address
		72.3	...Responsive to tape transport
		73.01	..Speed
28	.Reference carrier to control demodulator	73.02	...Control of relative speed between carriers
29	MODULATING OR DEMODULATING	73.03	...Rotary carrier
30	.Frequency	73.04	...Linear carrier
31	MONITORING OR TESTING THE PROGRESS OF RECORDING	73.05	....Plural speed transport
32	CONVERTING AN ANALOG SIGNAL TO DIGITAL FORM FOR RECORDING; REPRODUCING AND RECONVERTING	73.06	.....Automatic change between fixed speeds
		73.07	.....Automatic selection of carrier or track speed
33.1	GENERAL PROCESSING OF A TELEVISION SIGNAL	73.08	.....Variable speed

Figure 2   The first page of the subclass schedule for Class 360

```
          HEAD MOUNTING
107       .For moving head during transducing
108       ..Signal transfer to and from head
109       .For adjusting head position
110       HEAD
111       .Flux gate
112       .Hall effect
113       .Magnetoresistive or magnetostrictive
114       .Magneto-optic
115       .Flux scanning
116       .Cathode ray
117       .Hand-held
118       .Erase
119       .Gap structure details
120       ..Spacer material
121       ..Plural gaps
122       .Head surface structure
123       .Head winding
124       ..For cross-talk prevention
125       .Head core
126       ..Laminated
127       ..Nonmetallic
128       .Head accessory
129       ..Housing
130.1     ..Record separator
130.2     ..Record guide
130.21    ...Tape record
130.22    ....Rotating head
130.23    .....Helical scan
130.24    ......Head drum details
130.3     ..Pressure element
130.31    ...Tape record
130.32    ....Element mounting details
130.33    ....Element in tape container
130.34    ...Disc record
131       RECORD MEDIUM
132       .In container
133       ..For disk
134       .Tape
135       .Disk
136       .Drum
137       MISCELLANEOUS
          ******************************

          CROSS-REFERENCE ART COLLECTIONS
          ******************************
900       DISK DRIVE PACKAGING
901       .Access time
902       .Storage density (e.g., bpi, tpi)
903       .Physical parameter (e.g., form factor)
904       ..Weight
```

Figure 3 The last page of the subclass schedule for Class 360

CLASS 360, DYNAMIC MAGNETIC INFORMA-
TION STORAGE OR RETRIEVAL

CLASS DEFINITION

I. GENERAL STATEMENT OF THE CLASS SUB-
JECT MATTER

   A. This class is an integral part of
Class 369, Dynamic Information Storage or Retrieval, following subclass
18 and is the specific class for apparatus and corresponding processes
for the storage and retrieval of information based on relative movement
between a magnetic record carrier
and a transducer.

   B. This class also includes apparatus
and corresponding processes for making copies or editing of records
falling within the above definition.

   C. A magnetic record carrier within the
meaning of this class is an element
which consists of a magnetizable material or is comprised of a coating or
impregnation of magnetizable material
which is intended for the storage of
more than a single bit of information.
Storage elements which include dis-
crete magnetic areas, inserts, spots,
etc. each intended for the storage of
single bits of information, whether or
not relative motion is used in trans-
ducing that information, are not included in the above definition. See
Class 235, Registers, subclasses 449+
and 493 for the use of such elements.

II. SUBCOMBINATIONS OF DYNAMIC MAGNETIC
RECORDERS OR REPRODUCERS

   A. This class includes elements forming
subcombinations specific to apparatus within the class definition such
as record carriers, transducers, etc.

   B. Electrical circuits not specific
to magnetic recording or reproducing
which may constitute subcombinations
of such apparatus are classified in
the appropriate class for such
circuits.

   C. Mechanisms forming subcombinations of
apparatus within the class definition

are classified in the appropriate
mechanical class providing for such
subject matter unless claimed in
significant combination with specific recorder structure.

III. COMBINATIONS OF OTHER APPARATUS
WHICH INCLUDE APPARATUS OF THIS
CLASS

   A. Significantly claimed apparatus external to this class, claimed in combination with apparatus under the class
definition, which records or repro-
duces some quality or quantity related
to such external apparatus or its
function, is classified in the class
appropriate to the external apparatus.

   B. Nominally claimed apparatus external
to this class, claimed in combination with apparatus under the class
definition, is classified in this
class unless provided for in the appropriate external class.

   C. Because of the placement of Class 360
into the Class 369 schedule, this
class is no longer exhaustive of dynamic magnetic storage or retrieval,
as to the art now classified in subclasses 1-18 of Class 369.

IV. ORGANIZATION OF THIS CLASS

   A. Special Purpose Devices: Subclasses
1-17 are provided for devices where
the major significance of the device
is in its use or the result which it
produces.

   B. Signal Processing Subclasses 18-54
are provided for devices which are
basically electronic in nature and
are used to modify, correct or in-
sure the efficient storage or retrieval of information signals.

   C. General Recording or Reproducing Subclasses 55-68 are provided for methods
or devices which are concerned with
the physics of recording or reproducing or are electronic in nature and
not limited to the types of signal
processing provided for in section
B above.

Figure 4 The first class of the Class Definition of Class 360

30.   Subject matter under subclass 29 including specific frequency modulation
or demodulation of a signal.

31.   Subject matter under the class definition wherein, during recording, the
recorded information signal is reproduced in whole or in part for quali-
tative analysis of the operation of
the recorder system or a part thereof.

SEARCH THIS CLASS, SUBCLASS:
25,   for record carrier characteristic determination and
compensation.
53,   for digital data error checking.

32.   Subject matter under the class definition including producing a digital
equivalent of a nondigital signal for
recording, or producing a nondigital
equivalent of a reproduced digital
signal.

SEARCH CLASS:
235,   Registers, subclasses 321+,
for analog-digital converters.

33.1   GENERAL PROCESSING OF A TELEVISION
SIGNAL:
Subject matter under the class definition of specific utility in treating a
noncolor television signal for dynamic
magnetic recording or reproducing.

(1)   Note. This subclass is the
residual area for devices and
methods concerned with processing television signals in a manner not provided for above.
Subject matter properly classi-
fiable above should not, as a
matter of course, be cross-
referenced here.

(2)   Note. Although specific mechanical apparatus may be included in
the subject matter of this and
indented subclasses, the subject
matter remains mainly electronic
in nature and its utility is
in distinctive handling of a
noncolor television signal.

SEARCH THIS CLASS, SUBCLASS:
9.1+,   for recording for changing the
duration, frequency, or redun-
dant content of a television
signal, subclasses 14.1+ for

television signal recording or
reproducing both audio and video
signals in the same track.
55+,   for generally usable recording
or reproducing techniques.
69+,   for automatically controlling
recorder or reproducer mechanisms which includes synchro-
nizing such mechanisms to a
television signal.
81+,   88+ and 101, for recorder or
reproducer mechanisms.
102+,   104+, 110+ and 131+, for
recorder or reproducer elements.

SEARCH CLASS:
358,   Pictorial Communication; Television, subclasses 310+ for dynamic recording and reproducing
of color television signals including the use of magnetic
record media; subclasses 335+
for nonmagnetic dynamic recording and reproducing of noncolor television signals.

34.1   Inverting polarity of alternate
periods:
Subject matter under subclass 33.1
for inverting the polarity of alternate dots, lines, fields or frames of
a television signal.

35.1   Signal field or frame recording:
Subject matter under subclass 33.1
for gating a single field or frame
from a television signal of indeter-
minate duration for recording such
field or frame.

SEARCH THIS CLASS, SUBCLASS:
5,   for surveillance recorders
which may include single field
or frame gating of television
signals.
10.1,   for still reproduction of
television signals.
14.1,   for editing television signal
records.

36.1   Time correction:
Subject matter under subclass 33.1 for
correction of timing errors introduced
during recording or reproducing.

SEARCH CLASS:
358,   Pictorial Communication; Television, subclasses 320+ for
time control in a color television signal recording or

Figure 5   A page of subclass definitions for class 360

til one—if any—is found that designates a further feature of the object of the search. This process is reiterated until one can go no further. Referring to Figure 2, for example, if one were searching for video recorders in general without any of the features expressly provided for in subclasses 1, 4–8, 12, 13, 15, 18, 22, 24–27, 29, 31 or 32, one would arrive appropriately at subclass 33.1, "GENERAL PROCESSING OF A TELEVISION SIGNAL." Then, the next level of indented subclasses—subclasses 34.1 to 36.1 and 37.1 and 38.1— would be considered, starting with 34.1. If the object of the search includes none of the features designated by these subclass titles, the search ends at subclass 33.1. If, however, a subclass such as 36.1 is arrived at that does provide for another feature of the search object, the process is repeated on subclasses indented under it. In the case of subclass 36.1, there is only one that needs to be considered.

In deciding whether a subclass is appropriate, one should always consult its definition. The definition of subclass 33.1 together with its notes, for example, indicates that it contains only black and white television recording and that color television recording is currently found in Class 358, "Pictorial Communication; Television" (see Figure 5).

Note also that, even though one is searching for video recorders, the word "video" or "television" need not be in the title of an appropriate subclass. Suppose one were searching for an apparatus for recording one video cassette onto another. One would correctly stop at subclass 15, "RECORD COPYING," even though the title says nothing about television specifically. One would, of course, find patents pertaining to the copying of audio and other kinds of recordings in this subclass as well as to the copying of television recordings. This suggests that the best search strategies are based not solely on an analysis of the search object but on such an analysis in the light of the subclass schedule of the class most likely to provide for the object of the search.

In general, subclasses providing for the basic subject matter of the class are located near the middle of the schedule. Subclasses providing for combinations of the basic subject matter with other types of subject matter or for special or peculiar embodiments of the basic subject matter are found near the beginning. Subclasses for subcombinations of the basic subject matter are generally located near the end. In Class 360, television recording is considered a special kind of recording, and subclasses for it are found above those for general recording or reproducing (subclasses 55 through 68), the basic subject matter of the class. Patents pertaining merely to structural details of recording heads, on the other hand, will be found in subclasses 110 to 134.34 near the end (see Figure 3). If, therefore, the object of one's search were a complex device with something unique about one of its parts, a double search path might be desirable. For example, if the object of our search is a video recorder with a novel record head, we might choose to scan the subclasses indented under subclass 110, "HEAD," as well as those indented under subclass 33.1.

But suppose one were searching only for a particular recording head for a video recorder. Would one have to consider subclass 33.1 and all those indented under it as well as subclass 110 and its indents? Usually not. When an *original* copy of a patent is classified into a specific subclass following the rules outlined above, if that patent also contains significant details of subject matter provided for by a subclass lower in the schedule, a *cross-reference* copy of the patent is placed in that subclass as well. In some cases, however, a reference under "SEARCH THIS CLASS, SUBCLASS:" in a subclass definition may direct a searcher to subclasses higher in the schedule. The references under that heading in the definition of subclass 35.1 of Class 360 (see Figure 5), for example, refer the searcher to superior subclasses 5, 10.1, and 14.1 for the subject matter of that subclass in specific use environments.

Besides shortening some searches, cross-reference copies, like the search notes of class and subclass definitions, can be useful in broadening the search field. For instance, if one were searching primarily for a particular recording head but also wished to see complete recorders of which similar heads were a part, the classifications of the *original* copies of pertinent cross-reference copies might provide useful leads. The *cross-reference art collections* found in some subclass schedules are particularly useful for this purpose. See, for example, subclasses 900 to 904 of Class 360 in Figure 3. These subclasses differ from the others in not being restricted by the class definition or by subclass hierarchy. They are, therefore, especially useful in searching for technologies that cut across class or subclass lines.

4.3 THE INDEX TO THE U.S. PATENT CLASSIFICATION SYSTEM

Another useful search aid is the Index to the U.S. Patent Classification System. It contains nearly 60,000 terms and provides the searcher with one entry into the system for each term. However, there may be other relevant classifications, and the one cited may not be the most relevant to a specific search query. The Index is intended to be used only as a first step and in conjunction with the schedules and definitions. Figure 6 is a portion of the Index that refers to "Recording and Recorders". Note that under "television" there is only one reference to Class 360, the others being to Class 358 for color television recording.

4.4 THE PTO'S AUTOMATED PATENT SYSTEM (APS)

Another useful aid is the PTO's Automated Patent System (APS). It permits computerized text and classification searches of all U.S. patents issued after 1970. Searches can be tightly focused by combining USPCS classifications with terms relevant to the object of the search in search queries. Terminals are accessible to the public in the PTO's Public Search Room in Arlington, Virginia, as well as in some of the Patent and Trademark Depository Libraries located throughout the country.

4.5 PATENT AND TRADEMARK DEPOSITORY LIBRARIES

Patent and Trademark Depository Libraries are university, municipal, state, and special research institutions which receive and maintain collections of patents and trademark materials for public use. They also provide expert assistance to users of these collections.

	Class	Subclass
Paperbox box	229	100*
Paper type filling and closing	53	467*
Piano case music storing	84	181
Plant or flower	47	66*
Bio degradable	47	74*
Irrigator	47	79*
Terrarium	47	69*
Window box	47	68*
Plumbing for sink or bath	4	679*
Portable with burglar alarm	116	99
Racks	211	126*
Wall or window mounted	211	88
Relocatable with charging & discharging	414	332
Safe and vault type	109	
Sheet metal making	413	
Sifter type	209	233*
Sink	4	619*
Special or packages	206	
Spittoons	4	258*
Spool holder	242	137*
Static mold	249	117
Stratifiers	209	422*
Supports	248	128*
Bag holders	248	95
Bracket type	248	311.2*
Desk and inkwell combined	108	26.2
Inkstand dispensing	222	577
Paste tube type	248	108
Stand eg inkstand		
Movable receptacle	248	128
Stationary inkwell	248	146*
Suspended type	248	318
Testing	73	52
Textile washing machine	68	
Deformable for squeezer type	68	96
Tumbler type	68	139*
Twine holder	242	146
Wash tub	68	232*
With scrubbing surface	68	233
Water heating type	126	373*
Well	166	162*
Hoist bucket type	294	68.1*
Wheeled	280	
Barrows or trucks	280	47.17*
Wooden	217	
Reclaiming (See Recovery)		
Celluloid	536	38*
Cellulose ester film scrap	536	76*
Cotton waste	8	141
Apparatus	68	1
Fats and oils	554	175*
Lumber denailing	254	18
Paper	162	4*
Rubber	521	41*
Scrap metal salvaging	29	403.1*
Synthetic resin or natural rubber	521	40*
Tin scrap		
Hydrometallurgy	75	716
Metallurgy	75	401*
Tobacco	131	96
Recoil		
Checks (See shock)	188	266*
Ordnance	89	42.1*
Operated		
Firearms and guns	89	125*
Package retainer, recoil-type	206	825*
Pads for shoulder arms	42	74
Design	D22	111
Recombination (See Genetic Engineering)	435	172.3
X-art collection	935	
Record		
Changer	369	178*
Controlled calculator	235	419*
Disk for phonograph	369	272*
Disk holder	206	309*
Hand carrier	294	158
Forming sound grooves in	264	106*
Shaving	82	1.11
X-art collection	425	810*
Recording and Recorders	346	
Aerial projectile target	273	348.1*
Borehole indicator	33	304*
Burning	346	76R
Calculator	235	58R*
Charts	346	134*
Coating process	427	146
Crt	346	158
Electrical memories	365	118
Direction indicator	33	331

	Class	Subclass
Dispenser combined	222	30
Dynamometer	73	862.27
Electric spark	346	162
Electrolytic	346	165
Equipment design	D14	
Facsimile		
Optical	358	296*
Receiver	358	296*
Float gauge	73	312
Fluid pressure gauge	73	713*
Holograms	359	1*
Electrical circuits	365	125
Liquid purification or separation	210	85*
Lock position	70	433*
Magnetic bubbles	365	1*
Mail letter box	232	18
Music	84	461*
In notation form	984	254*
Pens	346	140R
Printing	101	
Pyrographic	346	76R
Radioactive	346	152
Railway		
Block signal	246	107
Cab signal or train control	246	185
Train position	246	123
Register combined	235	2*
Reproducer combined		
Electrical wave for measuring	324	111*
For electrical transient	324	102
Scale	177	2*
Sound	369	
Acoustic image	367	7
Cabinet	312	9.1*
Composition	106	37
Electric music instrument	84	600*
Electroforming process	205	68
Indexing devices	369	30
Magnetic tape or wire	360	88*
Manufacture	29	169.5
Molding device	425	406*
Molding process	264	106*
Phonograph electric	369	128*
Rack	211	40
Seismic mechanical	346	7
Talking picture apparatus	352	1*
Tape winding means	242	179*
Strip sprocket hole testing	73	157
Tape winding means	242	179*
Unidirectional	242	55.17*
Telegraphy		
Chemical & electrolytic	178	62
Page printing	178	28*
Photographic	178	15
Printing selector	178	34
Receiver	178	89*
Reed printer	178	48
Siphon	178	91
Transmitter	178	17R*
Type wheel printer	178	35
Telephone		
Calling number	379	142
Conversation time	379	114*
Telegraphophone	369	132*
Television	358	335*
Camera with recorder	358	906*
Color	358	310*
Magnetic	360	33.1*
Pause control	358	908*
Track skipper	358	907*
Television system combined	358	296*
Thermoplastic, storage retrieval of information	365	126
Thermoplastic, visual record	346	151
Television	358	344
Color	358	310
Facsimile	358	300
Time		
Plural recordings	346	45*
Printing or punching	346	80*
Transparency	365	127
Verifying	73	156
Voting machine	235	50R
Wire	346	150
Sound type	360	89
X ray photography	378	
Recovery (See Material Recovered)		
Coating excess	427	345
Dyes	8	440
Fats and oils	554	175*
Inorganic actinide compounds	423	249*

	Class	Subclass
Nuclear materials	376	189
Nuclear materials	376	201
Nuclear materials	376	308
Scrap metal salvaging	29	403.1*
Separation of solids	209	
Solvent apparatus	68	18R
Rectangular Proportioner	33	DIG. 9
Rectifiers and Rectifying	D13	110*
Beam power amplifier	313	298
With two cathodes	313	5
Distillation	203	
Apparatus	196	
Apparatus	202	
Liquids	203	
Mineral oil	208	350*
Doubler high vacuum	313	306*
With two cathodes	313	1
Electrical	363	13*
Barrier layer coating	437	
Barrier layer compositions	252	62.3 R
Electrolytes	252	62.2
Electrolytic devices	361	436
Full wave high vacuum	313	306
Lamp or electronic tube supply	315	200R*
Manufacture	29	25.1*
Process	437	
X ray circuit supply	378	101
Gas and liquid contact apparatus	261	
Gas liquefaction	62	42*
Process	62	32*
Process, plural separation	62	24*
Gas separation processes	55	36*
Half wave system	363	13*
Circuit interrupter for	200	
Dynamoelectric machine	310	10*
Electronic tube for	313	317*
Gas tube type	363	114*
Power packs	307	150
Vacuum tube type	363	114*
With filter	363	39*
With voltage regulator	363	84*
Mercury vapor system	363	114*
Rectifier control only	315	246*
Mineral oils	208	350*
Vacuum or gas tube	313	
Recuperator		
Distillation retort combined	202	111
Gas bench	202	148
Horizontal	202	140
Inclined	202	130
Vertical	202	122
Furnace		
Fuel burned in permeable mass	431	170
Gas heating furnaces	432	179
Red Lead	423	619
Redox Catalyst	526	915*
Reducer		
Commutation sparking	310	220*
Machines		
Cabinets	128	371*
Exercising	482	
Massage	128	24R*
Pipe joint	285	177
Screw	285	392
Pressure (See pressure, regulator)		
Socket wrench	81	185
Reduction (See Hydrogenation)		
Amines primary production by	564	415*
Apparatus for ores	266	168*
Catalysts treatment	502	100*
Chemical agents	252	188.1
Detergent	252	105
Hydrogen production by	423	648.1
Inorganic sulfide production by	423	
Iron and alloys electrothermic	75	10.1*
Of metal ores and metal compounds	75	
Separation distillation	203	32
Sulphur production by	423	567R
Thermit type	75	959
Reed		
Musical		
Accordion	84	376R
Harmonica	84	377*
Nonorgan reed instruments	84	375*
Organ reed pipes	84	350
Reed organs	84	351*
Toy	446	207*
Tuning reed for furnishing pitch	84	456
Wood winds	84	380R*
Station selective signalling	340	825.39
Telephone call type	379	360*

Figure 6 A page from the *Index to Classification*

For more information about them, contact The Patent and Trademark Depository Library Program, Crystal Plaza 2, Room 2C04, U.S. Patent and Trademark Office, Washington, D.C. 20231, (703)308–3924.

4.6 OBTAINING MANUALS AND DOCUMENTATION

Complete copies of the *Manual of Classification* and the *Index to the U.S. Patent Classification System* are available from The Superintendent of Documents, U.S. Government Printing Office, Mail List Section, Washington, D.C. 20402, (202)783–3238.

Copies of individual class and subclass definitions or class schedules are available from The Office of Classification Support, Editorial Division, U.S. Patent and Trademark Office, Crystal Mall 2, Room 309, Washington, D.C. 20231, (703)305–6101.

The *Manual of Classification,* class and subclass definitions, and other types of classification information are also available on CD-ROM (Compact Disk Read-Only Memory). For information about these products, contact the Office of Electronic Information Products and Services, U.S. Patent and Trademark Office, Crystal Plaza 2, Room 9D30, Washington, D.C. 20231, (703)308–0322.

Article

5

PATENT SEARCHING USING COMMERCIAL DATABASES

John T. Butler

John T. Butler is a Science and Engineering Reference Librarian and Bibliographer at the University of Minnesota-Twin Cities. Other recent writings include "A Current Awareness Service Using Microcomputer Databases and Electronic Mail", *College & Research Libraries* 54(2); 115–23 (March 1993) and "Current Awareness System: Delivering Customized Information to Faculty", *LibraryLine* 4(1) (January 1993).

5.1 INTRODUCTION

This article describes commercially available online and CD-ROM patent databases and provides a framework to guide their selection and use. Descriptive tables of the major patent databases for searching by subject, for legal status information, and for patent equivalencies are presented. Topics discussed include the characteristics of patent information, patent search objectives, database selection, and search techniques. A bibliography of further reading on patent database resources and searching techniques concludes the chapter.

Information lies at the heart of patents and patenting, fueling a cycle that fosters technological development in industrial society. The cycle begins with the patent itself as a reward for disclosing new and useful technological information. That information is, in turn, published to promote the development of new knowledge. From that base of knowledge, new technologies are cultivated and the cycle begins again. Over time, the effect is the continuous and efficient advancement of society's technological information base.

Through the world's patent offices flow an increasing volume of patent applications and published patent documents. This coincides with an apparent rise in the value placed on patent literature as a source of strategic technical and business-related information. For instance, large corporations turn to patent information for the purposes of competitor intelligence, market analysis and forecasting, current awareness, research and development, infringement avoidance, and other reasons. Academic institutions consult patents to explore licensing opportunities for technologies grown out of university research. And individual inventors access patent information to determine the novelty of prototypes or ideas on the drawing board, to identify potential licensors, or to seek existing solutions to technical problems.

Patent databases are fundamental tools for searching the vast stores of patent literature. In 1993, over 60 online and approximately 20 microcomputer-based CD-ROM patent databases were available commercially. Powerful search software, provided by online services and CD-ROM vendors, facilitates immediate and precise retrieval from enormous volumes of information.

5.2 CHARACTERISTICS OF PATENT INFORMATION

Although frequently regarded as the literature of technology, patents are set apart from other forms of technical literature. Like technical articles or reports, patents communicate new technical information. Unlike these other literature types, however, patents also must function as legal instruments. Being aware of this dual function is important when searching for patent information.

National patent laws and international conventions generally require that patent applications disclose a level of detail sufficient for someone "skilled in the art" to reproduce the proposed invention. Yet, in also being a legal document a patent application strives to seek the broadest possible protection or monopoly for the invention disclosed. The objective to establish robust property rights often influences the terminology used in a patent application. As a result, the clarity and straightforwardness of the technical disclosure can be obscured. An early lesson in patent searching is that patents are not written to aid in their retrieval. Rather, the text in patents is often written to keep the interpretation of the claims as broad or general as possible. For example, U.S. 4,227,805 discloses a device that uses holography to identify fingerprints. However, it is obliquely entitled "Finger Identification Apparatus and Method." A search of the patent's abstract and of all the patent's claims for the words "fingerprint" or "fingerprinting" finds nothing. However, "fingerprinting" is clearly what the patent is about. Pioneer patents, or those patents that introduce a new technology, raise a similar concern. Often, they precede the establishment of terminology that later becomes prevalent and useful in describing the technology.

Noting these linguistic obstacles, patent searches that rely solely on natural language (keyword or other word-matching strategies) cannot be trusted to provide comprehensive results. To circumvent the difficulties described here, experienced patent searchers supplement keyword strategies with use of indexing and coding assigned to patents by issuing patent offices or database producers. They also rely, whenever possible, on databases that have professionally written patent titles and abstracts that enhance subject retrieval.

The significant growth in the volume of patent literature also has implications for patent searching. The International Patent Documentation Centre, which registers patent documents published by 56 patent-issuing authorities worldwide, indicates a 37 percent increase in the number of patent documents published in the past ten years from 917,503 in 1982 to 1,258,996 in 1992 [1]. Closer to home, the U.S. Patent and Trademark Office (PTO) showed an increase of 71 percent in patents granted over the same period [2], and predicts that by 1995 it will receive nearly 250,000 applications annually [3].

Reflecting the increased attention given to international markets, transnational and international patenting activities are also increasing [4]. This, along with the increased volume of patent information, adds another dimension to the patent search. The plurality of patent laws and patent system protocols followed by the 100 national and four supranational patent-issuing authorities can magnify the complexity of a patent search.

5.3 DETERMINING PATENT SEARCH OBJECTIVES

Formulating effective patent search strategies begins by establishing clear search objectives. Most patent searches fall into one of the following categories:

- Novelty Search
- Infringement and Validity Searches
- Equivalency or Patent Family Search
- Business-Related Search

The following paragraphs describe each of these search types. [5]

5.3.1 Novelty Search

The novelty search, also known as a patentability, prior-art, or anticipatory search, is conducted to evaluate the newness of an invention before application for a patent. The novelty search is one of the most difficult searches to perform as it seeks to prove a negative—that the invention being searched has not existed previously [6]. The hope of someone conducting a novelty search is to find nothing. This lends confidence that an application will succeed. While the patent literature is often regarded as the first place where technology is disclosed, a novelty search should not be restricted to patents alone. All types of publications worldwide—including the journal and trade literature, manufacturers' catalogs, and other product literature—should also be searched.

5.3.2 Infringement and Validity Searches

The infringement search seeks to establish if the contemplated use, manufacture, or sale of specific devices, products, or processes would infringe upon the claims of unexpired patents. Typically, only the patents in countries where action is contemplated need be searched. If an infringement search identifies a relevant patent, a validity search may then be conducted to determine whether the claims of that patent were valid at the time of application. In this sense, the validity search is similar to the novelty search.

5.3.3 Equivalency or Patent Family Search

An equivalency search seeks to determine whether an invention patented (or published as an application) in one country has also been patented in another (a practice permitted under the property rights provision of the Paris Convention). Patents are *equivalent* or *corresponding* if they share the same priority data as published by different countries or issuing authorities. A *patent family* is the grouping of equivalent patents in a single database record. A few special databases report patent family information and these are used to conduct equivalency searches. One purpose for the equivalency or patent family search is to monitor a competitor's patenting activities. Patent family databases that cover fast-publishing patent offices, such as the European Patent Office (EPO), can be searched to determine if an equivalent U.S. application has claimed priority on a competitor's EPO publication. If it has, the published EPO patent (or other published equivalent) can serve to preview the competitor's pending U.S. application. Companies also use patent family searches to identify the countries in which their competitors intend to market a technology.

Equivalency searches can also identify English-language (or other language in which the user is literate) equivalents to foreign language patents, saving on the time and costs of translating original documents. Only a few databases, including DERWENT WORLD PATENTS INDEX, INPADOC, and EDOC, contain patent family data.

5.3.4 Business-Related Search

Patents are searched to support business-related purposes, such as competitor intelligence, market analysis and technological forecasting, identification of licensing opportunities, personnel recruitment, and to avoid costly duplication of research and development activities.

5.4 CRITERIA FOR SELECTING PATENT DATABASES

In selecting appropriate databases for a patent search, it is important first to understand the criteria used to define and evaluate individual patent databases. These criteria include:

- Functional Orientation
- Scope
- Text Elements
- Indexing and Classification
- Graphical Elements
- Timeliness

The following paragraphs discuss each of these criteria. To illustrate several of these criteria, three patent database records are presented and described at the end of this section.

5.4.1 Functional Orientation

Patent databases may be divided into two functional groups: those that represent patents as technical disclosures, and those that represent patents as legal documents. Databases that emphasize the technical content in patents typically include abstracts, text of patent claims, patent office classification, and indexing, coding, and other descriptions supplied by the database producer. These databases are primary choices for subject-oriented searches, such as novelty or infringement searches.

Databases representing patents as legal documents may contain information on the prosecution status of patents, litigation activity, or on post-issuance actions (*e.g.,* expirations, reexaminations, reissues, etc.). This category also includes databases that report patent family data, which is information linking equivalent patents.

Many databases are oriented strictly along one of these two functions. Others, like DERWENT WORLD PATENTS INDEX (WPI), bridge the gap and serve in both capacities. Nearly all patent databases contain bibliographic data, which is a type of information that uniquely identifies a document. Bibliographic data for patents include patent title, country code, patent number, inventor name(s), assignee(s), application number and date, and priority application data.

5.4.2 Scope

A database's scope characteristics include time period covered, technologies covered, and countries or patent-issuing authorities represented. Country coverage can be further defined by the kinds of patent documents an issuing authority publishes (*e.g.,* unexamined published applications, examined patents, both, etc.). Many databases provide coverage of all patents published by a single nation, regardless of subject matter. Several databases provide international and multinational coverage of patents but only in specialized subject areas. And a few databases cover multiple countries for all technologies.

5.4.3 Text Elements

Text elements in patent databases, such as the patent title, abstract, and claims, are important both for searching purposes and for determining the legal relevance of patent documents retrieved as a result of a search. The quantity of text included ranges from basic bibliographic data, to full *front-page* information (includes all text appearing on the front page of the original patent document including the abstract and/or exemplary claim), to front-page information plus text of all the patent's claims, to full-text, which is the complete text of the patent document. Many database producers load directly into their systems the raw data supplied by patent-issuing authorities with whom they have agreements. However, a few database producers, such as Derwent and Chemical Abstracts, employ technical experts to write an informative title and abstract for each patent record entering their respective databases. These professionally written titles and abstracts reflect the technical content and inventive features of patents and, as a result, facilitate more effective keyword or natural language retrieval. As a caveat, patent searchers must be aware that abstracting criteria or bias may cause aspects of a patent disclosure to be omitted from the title or abstract.

Several databases provide English language patent titles and abstracts for non-English language documents. Others, such as INPADOC, only provide information in the language of the original patent document.

5.4.4 Indexing and Classification

Select database producers add indexing to patent records to enhance subject retrieval. Indexing involves the review of each patent by a technical expert who assigns indexing terms and/or numeric coding to represent the patent's concepts, substances, functionality, and other technical content.

Of all areas of technology, chemical patents are the subject of the most advanced and intensive indexing practices. In recent years, a few producers have introduced databases for searching the Markush structures (a defined group of alternative components for which no generic term exists), or generically-defined structures often found in the claims of chemical patents [7]. Of great importance to the chemical and pharmaceutical industry, these databases aim for retrieval of all substances implied by a claimed Markush structure. In these databases, Markush structures are indexed topologically, a technique that enables graphical searching of variably-defined chemical structures or substructures. In some cases, the deep-chemical indexing described here is available only to subscribers to the database. Such subscriptions, which are quite expensive, are intended for large chemical and pharmaceutical companies.

Patent offices assign classification codes to patents as a way of providing standardized, non-verbal access points for subject-based searches. These codes aim to represent a patent's function, structure, substance, or field of use. The U.S. National Classification is a detailed, hierarchical, and ever-changing scheme containing over 120,000 specific categories (called subclasses). The International Patent Classification (IPC) is a less detailed scheme but one that is used internationally. The PTO assigns both U.S. National Classification and IPC codes to U.S. patents. As interpretation of the IPC varies, IPC codes have been applied inconsistently from country to country.

5.4.5 Graphical Elements

The graphical information in patents—drawings, schematics, chemical structures, and formulae—plays an essential role in disclosing a technology. It is of similar importance to the patent search. For many years now, several CD-ROM databases have provided scanned images from patents. Some of these databases provide the image of the front-page of a patent, while others provide facsimiles of the entire patent document, all graphical elements included. To date, the availability of patent images in online databases has been limited, but this is changing rapidly. Progress is particularly notable in the chemical patent area, where several online databases—such as MARPAT and PHARMSEARCH—now provide displayable and graphically searchable representations of the chemical structures appearing in patents. At least one major online database, WPI, now provides selected images from mechanical and electrical patents.

5.4.6 Timeliness

The timeliness or currency of a database largely depends on the speed with which the database producer processes newly received data from the national patent offices or other sources. Many databases are comprised of raw data coming directly from patent offices, and are not augmented in any way. These databases are generally current 0 to 14 days after patent publication. Databases that provide deep-indexing, translated titles or abstracts, or other intellectually-intensive enhancements are considerably slower and are generally current anywhere from 2 to 6 months after publication.

Another factor affecting database currency is the database's updating schedule. Most online databases are updated weekly. While some CD-ROM databases are updated weekly, most are updated monthly and some quarterly.

5.4.7 Sample Database Records

Presented in Figures 1, 2, and 3 are database records for U.S. 5,189,482 as represented by three of the foremost abstracting patent databases: CLAIMS™/U.S. Patent Abstracts, WPI, and INPADOC/Family and Legal Status, respectively.

CLAIMS™ covers U.S. patents only. The CLAIMS™ record (Figure 1) illustrates the inclusion of all front-page information including the patent's abstract. In addition, CLAIMS™ provides the text of all patent claims, a feature that is most valuable in searches where the legal scope of the patent is of concern. All text in the record is identical to that in the original patent document, as CLAIMS™ is generated from the PTO's full-text data tapes. This patent discloses a specialized laser device. However, it is not until the fifth and last claim that the "optical apparatus", referred to in the patent's title, abstract, and previously stated claim, is described as a laser. CLAIMS™ also provides both U.S. and IPC classification codes and cited references.

The WPI record (Figure 2) provides an informative patent title, which stands in favorable contrast to the more generic title provided in the CLAIMS™ record. Here, the title clearly states "laser". Both patent titles and abstracts in WPI are professionally written to reflect the content of the entire patent document, an attribute that greatly enhances retrieval. Another salient characteristic of WPI is its provision of extensive patent family data. Rep-

2336411 3310723
E/ OPTICAL APPARATUS FOR FINGERPRINT RECOGNITION SYSTEM
Document Type: UTILITY
Inventors: Yang Keun Y (KR)
Name and Address of Inventors: Yang, Keun Y, Seoul, KR
Assignee: Gold Star Co Ltd KR Assignee Code: 17157
Name and Address of Assignee: Goldstar Co, Ltd, Seoul, KR
Primary Examiner: McGraw, Vincent P

	Patent Number	Issue Date	Applic Number	Applic Date
Patent:	US 5189482	930223	US 704228	910522
Priority Applic:			KR 7896/1990	900530

Abstract:
An optical apparatus for a fingerprint recognition system utilizes a light source for emitting a spherical beam. A collimating hologram produces a plane beam upon receiving the emitted spherical beam from the light source. A diffuser generates a scattered beam by scattering the plane beam. A prism absorbs the light at ridges of a subject fingerprint and reflects the light at valleys of the subject fingerprint. An image producing hologram then processes the reflected spherical beam from the prism corresponding to the valleys and condenses the spherical beam upon an area CCD. The area CCD converts the produced fingerprint image into an electric signal. The fingerprint image producing hologram and a cutoff/absorption plate for cutting off and absorbing the beam are, respectively, mounted on a vertical surface of the prism.

Number of Claims: 005
Exemplary Claim:

DRAWING

1. An optical apparatus for fingerprint recognition system comprising: a light source for emitting a spherical beam; collimating hologram means for producing a plane beam upon receiving the emitted spherical beam from said light source; diffuser means for scattering the plane beam from said collimating hologram onto a subject fingerprint; prism means for absorbing the scattered beam encountering ridges in the subject fingerprint ridges and reflecting the scattered beam encountering valleys in the subject fingerprint; fingerprint image producing hologram means for converting the scattered beam encountering the valleys reflected by said prism into a reflected spherical beam and for condensing the reflected spherical beam representing the subject fingerprint; and a light sensitive area for converting the condensed reflected spherical beam of the fingerprint image into an electric signal; said prism means including a cutoff/absorption plate for cutting off and absorbing the scattered beam; said fingerprint producing hologram means being mounted on a surface of said prism means vertical to a surface receiving the plane beam.

Non-exemplary Claims:
2. The optical apparatus according to claim 1, wherein said collimating hologram means is mounted at an angle of theta 3 and a distance of Lo from said light source and at a center point C2 of said collimating hologram means, a spherical beam, as a reference beam emitted from a spherical beam scanning point P1 located at a distance of lo from said center point C2, crosses with a plane beam, as an object beam, at an angle of theta 4 and wherein theta 4 theta 3 and Lo lo.

.
.

4. The optical apparatus according to claim 3, wherein said fingerprint image producing hologram means is a hologram; at a center point C3 of said fingerprint image producing hologram means, a spherical beam, as a reference beam emitted from a spherical beam scanning point P2 and a distance of l1 from the center point C3, crosses at an angle of theta 5+ theta 6 with a condensed spherical beam condensed at a point P3 and a distance of l2 from the center point C3; and theta 1 theta 5, theta 2 theta 6, L1 nl1, L2 l2, 25*< theta 5, and theta 6<35*.
5. The optical apparatus according to claim 1, wherein said light source is a laser.

Class: 356073000
Class Cross Ref: 382004000
IPC: G06K-009/20
Field of Search: 356071000; 382004000
Art Unit: 255

U.S. References Cited:

Patent Number	Date YYYYMM	Class	Inventor
US 4728186	198803	356071000	Eguchi et al.
US 4924085	199005	356071000X	Kato et al.

Number of Figures in Patent: 7
Number of Drawing Sheets Issued: 3

Figure 1 CLAIMS™/U.S. Patent Abstracts (on Dialog) Database Record for U.S. 5,189,482

008851936 WPI Acc No: 91-355956/49
XRPX Acc No: N91-272424
    Laser optical apparatus for fingerprint recognition system - reflects scattered beam at valleys of fingerprint and detects reflected beam in area CCD producing image representation
Patent Assignee: (GOLD-) GOLDSTAR CO LTD
Author (Inventor): YANG K Y; YANG G
Number of Patents: 003
Number of Countries: 006
Patent Family:

CC Number	Kind	Date	Week	
EP 459712	A	911204	9149	(Basic)
US 5189482	A	930223	9310	
KR 9207329	B	920831	9312	

Priority Data (CC No Date): KR 907896 (900530)
Applications (CC,No,Date): EP 91304710 (910524); US 704228 (910522)
Language: English
EP and/or WO Cited Patents: NoSR.Pub
Designated States
 (Regional): DE; FR; GB; IT
Abstract (Basic): EP 459712
    A laser light source (1) emits a spherical beam (10) which is converted to a plane beam (11) in a collimating hologram (2). A diffuser (3) scatters the plane beam (11), producing a scattered beam (12). A triangular prism (4) absorbs the scattered beam (12) at ridges of a fingerprint, and reflects the scattered beam (12) at valleys of the fingerprint.
    A fingerprint image producing hologram (5) processes the reflected spherical beam (13) from the valleys and condenses a spherical beam representing the subject fingerprint upon an area CCD (6) to produce an electrical signal which is amplified and analysed in the amplifying and analysing circuit (19).
    USE/ADVANTAGE - In fingerprint recognition systems. Inexpensive system. Small size. @(6pp Dwg.No.3/7)@
Abstract (US): 9310 US 5189482 A
    The optical appts. uses a light source for emitting a spherical beam. A collimating hologram produces a plane beam upon receiving the emitted spherical beam from the light source. A diffuser generates a scattered beam by scattering the plane beam. A prism absorbs the light at ridges of a subject fingerprint and reflects the light at valleys of the subject fingerprint. An image producing hologram then processes the reflected spherical beam from the prism corresp. to the valleys and condenses the spherical beam upon an area CCD. The area CCD converts the produced fingerprint image into an electric signal.
    The fingerprint image producing hologram and a cutoff/absorption plate for cutting off and absorbing the beam are, respectively mounted on a vertical surface of the prism.
    ADVANTAGE - Uses holograms capable of mass prodn.
    Dwg.3/7
File Segment: EPI
Derwent Class: S05; T04; V07; R28;
Int Pat Class: G06K-009/20; G06K-009/58; G06K-009/74
Manual Codes (EPI/S-X): S05-D01C5; T04-D02; V07-M

Figure 2   DERWENT WORLD PATENTS INDEX (on Dialog) Database Record
          for Patent Family Containing U.S. 5,189,482

resented in this record is a patent family consisting of three equivalent patent publications, with the Korean patent (KR) claiming priority. If you review the publication dates for each equivalent patent (see the column labeled "Date"), you will notice that the Korean patent was published six months before the U.S. patent, and that the European patent (EP) was published fifteen months before the U.S. issue! For this reason, WPI and other databases that provide patent family data are often used to get a "first look" at U.S. patents when

10630667
Basic Patent (No,Kind,Date): EP 459712 A2 911204   <No. of Patents: 005>

PATENT FAMILY:
EUROPEAN PATENT OFFICE (EP)
  Patent (No,Kind,Date): EP 459712 A2 911204
    OPTICAL APPARATUS FOR FINGERPRINT RECOGNITION SYSTEM (English; French; German)
    Patent Assignee: GOLD STAR CO (KR)
    Author (Inventor): YANG KEUN YOUNG (KR)
    Priority (No,Kind,Date): KR 907896 A 900530
    Applic (No,Kind,Date): EP 91304710 A 910524
    Designated States: (National) DE; FR; GB; IT
    IPC: * G06K-009/74
    Derwent WPI Acc No: ; G 91-355956
    Language of Document: English
  Patent (No,Kind,Date): EP 459712 A3 930421
    OPTICAL APPARATUS FOR FINGERPRINT RECOGNITION SYSTEM (English; French: German)
    Patent Assignee: GOLD STAR CO (KR)
    Author (Inventor): YANG KEUN YOUNG (KR)
    Priority (No,Kind,Date): KR 907896 A 900530
    Applic (No,Kind,Date): EP 91304710 A 910524
    Designated States: (National) DE; FR; GB; IT
    IPC: * G06K-009/74
    Derwent WPI Acc No: * G 91-355956
    Language of Document: English

EUROPEAN PATENT OFFICE (EP)
  Legal Status (No,Type,Date,Code,Text):
    EP 459712   P   900530 EP AA   PRIORITY (PATENT APPLICATION)
                       (PRIORITAET (PATENTANMELDUNG))
                   KR 907896 A 900530
    EP 459712   P   910524 EP AE   EP-APPLICATION (EUROPAEISCHEANMELDUNG)
                   EP 91304710 A 910524
    EP 459712   P   911204 EP AK   DESIGNATED CONTRACTING STATES IN AN APPLICATION
WITHOUT SEARCH   REPORT (IN EINER ANMELDUNG OHNE RECHERCHENBERICHT
BENANNTE VERTRAGSSTAATEN)
                   DE FR GB IT
    EP 459712   P   911204 EP A2   PUBLICATION OF APPLICATION WITHOUT SEARCH REPORT
                       (VEROEFFENTLICHUNG DERANMELDUNG OHNE RECHERCHENBERICHT)
    EP 459712   P   930421 EP AK   DESIGNATED CONTRACTING STATES IN A SEARCH REPORT (IN
                   EINEM RECHERCHENBERICHT BENANNTE VERTRAGSSTAATEN)
                   DE FR GB IT
    EP 459712   P   930421 EP A3   SEPARATE PUBLICATION OF THE SEARCH REPORT (ART. 93)
                       (GESONDERTE VEROEFFENTLICHUNG DES RECHERCHENBERICHTS
                       (ART. 93))
JAPAN (JP)
  Patent (No,Kind,Date): JP 5073666 A2 930326
    Priority (No,Kind,Date): KR 907896 A 900530
    Applic (No,Kind,Date): JP 91125985 A 910529
    IPC: * G06F-015/64; A61B-005/117; G02B-005/32; G02B-027/00
    Derwent WPI Acc No: * G 91-355956
    Language of Document: Japanese

KOREA, REPUBLIC (KR)
  Patent (No,Kind,Date): KR 9207329 B1 920831
    OPTICAL APPARATUS FOR FINGER PRINTERS RECOGNITION (English)
    Patent Assignee: GOLD STAR CO (KR)
    Author (Inventor): YANG KUN-YONG (KR)
    Priority (No,Kind,Date): KR 907896 A 900530
    Applic (No,Kind,Date): KR 907896 A 900530
    IPC: * G06K-009/58
    Derwent WPI Acc No: * G 91-355956
    Language of Document: Korean

Figure 3   INPADOC/Family & Legal Status (on Dialog) Database Record for Patent Family
            Containing U.S. 5,189,482

```
UNITED STATES OF AMERICA (US)
   Patent (No,Kind,Date):  US 5189482  A  930223
   OPTICAL APPARATUS FOR FINGERPRINT RECOGNITION SYSTEM (English)
   Patent Assignee:  GOLD STAR CO  (KR)
   Author (Inventor):  YANG KEUN Y  (KR)
   Priority (No,Kind,Date):  KR 907896  A  900530
   Applic (No,Kind,Date):  US 704228  A  910522
   National Class: *  356073000; 382004000
   IPC: *  G06K-009/20
   Derwent WPI Acc No: *  G  91-355956
   Language of Document:  English

UNITED STATES OF AMERICA (US)
   Legal Status (No,Type,Date,Code,Text):
      US 5189482    P  900530  US AA      PRIORITY (PATENT)
                    KR 907896  A  900530
      US 5189482    P  910522  US AE      APPLICATION DATA (PATENT)
                    (APPL. DATA (PATENT))
                    US 704228  A  910522
      US 5189482    P  930223  US A       PATENT
```

Figure 3   Continued

equivalent applications have been issued by faster-publishing patent offices. WPI is a unique database coupling superb technical representation of patents with extensive patent family information.

The INPADOC/Family and Legal Status database (Figure 3) provides sweeping patent family coverage, and documents the history of each patent publication in a family from its application through potential post-issue actions. INPADOC is also very current. To illustrate its timeliness, note that INPADOC includes an equivalent unexamined Japanese patent, where it was not or at least not yet included in the WPI record (see previous paragraph). In contrast to the CLAIMS™ and WPI records, INPADOC does not provide information useful to subject searching, other than classification codes and patent titles. However, INPADOC is unsurpassed for its extensive bibliographic, patent family, and legal status information.

5.5 ONLINE AND CD-ROM PATENT DATABASES

An in-depth knowledge of patent databases is fundamental to effective searching. Table 5-1 presents descriptions of the major online patent databases. These databases meet the needs of the vast majority of patent searches, and in particular those which are subject-oriented. Table 5-2 briefly describes additional online databases for subject searching, including a number of specialty files focusing on pharmaceutical and biotechnology patents. Table 5-3 presents additional online databases that emphasize bibliographic, patent family, or legal status information. CD-ROM databases covering U.S. patents and those covering European Patent Office (EPO) and the World Intellectual Property Organization (WIPO) patents are presented in Tables 5-4 and 5-5, respectively. For the most current information on a database, always contact the appropriate database producer, online service, or CD-ROM vendor (see bibliography for more information).

Table 5-1 Major Online Patent Database

DATABASE (Producer)	Countries Covered	Technologies Covered	Period Covered	Description	Feature Codes*
DERWENT WORLD PATENTS INDEX (Derwent Publications Ltd.)	31 leading industrial countries. EPO and WIPO (1). *Defensive publications Research Disclosure* and *Int. Technology Disclosure* also covered.	Pharmaceuticals Agricultural chemicals Plastics and polymers All chemical patents All technologies (including mechanical and electrical; complete U.S. coverage begins here) Japanese electrical patents	1963- 1965- 1966- 1970- 1974- 1982-	• Bibliographic data with professionally written titles and abstracts; provides images of selected drawings of chemical patents from 1992, and of electrical/mechanical patents from 1988; updated weekly. The premier patent database for excellent subject access and international patent family data, representing the basic patent and corresponding equivalent patents in a single database record. Patent titles, abstracts and in-depth indexing all reflect the inventive features, uses, and advantages conveyed in the entire patent document. Intensive chemical indexing (searchable by Derwent subscribers only) includes molecular fragmentation coding for plastics, polymers, pharmaceuticals, agrochemicals, and general chemicals. This coding facilitates the searching the entire scope of compounds hypothesized in a chemical patent's claims by a generalized Markush structure. Companion database **WPIM** (WORLD PATENTS INDEX-Markush) facilitates graphical retrieval of both generically defined chemical structures and specific compounds found in patents from 1987 (Derwent subscribers only). Coding of electrical patents from 1980 is also available (Derwent subscribers only). Because of its informative text, excellent indexing, and international patent family data, the DERWENT WORLD PATENTS INDEX is the starting place for many searches and is often the "hub" for cross-file patent searching.	A C D E F G I K
INPADOC/FAMILY and LEGAL STATUS (European Patent Office, Vienna) The online service ORBIT offers the LEGAL STATUS database apart from INPADOC/FAMILY	Bibliographic information for 57 countries and patent issuing authorities (1). Legal status information for 12 countries including the U.S., Germany, EPO, and WIPO.	All technologies, including utility models.	Most countries: 1968- Japan (both examined and unexamined patents) and Eastern European countries: 1973-	• Bibliographic data with patent family and legal status data; abstracts are <u>not</u> available and patent titles are in the language of the original patent document; legal status information is in English; updated weekly. INPADOC is the most comprehensive bibliographic patent database available. Approximately 95% of patent documents published worldwide are included. INPADOC documents the complete progress of a patent application through each patent office to which it has been submitted. Equivalent patent documents can be retrieved as patent families (although expensive). With over 30 post-issue actions reported for U.S. patents (from 1983; reissues back to 1969), the LEGAL STATUS component provides the most extensive coverage of post-issue legal actions for U.S. patents. Note: LEGAL STATUS information regarding patent litigation is limited to notifications; resultant court actions are not reported. Having no abstracts and with patent titles frequently provided in foreign languages, INPADOC is not recommended for subject searching. But cross-file connections with other subject-strong databases can produce very comprehensive searches.	A B K
CA FILE / CA SEARCH (Chemical Abstracts Service)	27 countries including the United States and Japan; also covers EPO and WIPO (1).	Chemical and chemical engineering patents	1967-	• Bibliographic data with professionally written abstracts (abstracts are only available through STN International); updated biweekly. This renown chemistry and chemical engineering literature database adds over 500,000 records annually, 16% of which are patents. Its inclusiveness and international coverage makes a major source for chemical patent information. Note, however, that only one patent of a family of equivalent patents is entered into the database. Abstracts tend to reflect new chemical concepts, which are not necessarily the aspects of the invention claimed as new. Graphical structure searching of specific compounds, as well as protein/nucleic acid sequence searching is supported by companion file **REGISTRY** (compounds synthesized in the patent's examples are indexed here). Generic chemical patent searching is supported by companion database **MARPAT** (described below).	C E G H J K

Continued

Table 5-1 Major Online Patent Database, *continued*

DATABASE (Producer)	Countries Covered	Technologies Covered	Period Covered	Description	Feature Codes*
MARPAT (Chemical Abstracts Service)	26 countries including the United States and Japan, plus EPO and WIPO. Excludes former USSR.	All chemical patents indexed in *Chemical Abstracts* which contain Markush structures, excluding alloys, metal oxides, inorganic slats, intermetallics, and polymers.	1988-	• Provides searchable/displayable graphical representations of generic (Markush) chemical structures found in the patent's claims and often in the patent's disclosure. Search results display bibliographic information, abstracts, and the in-depth indexing of the original *Chemical Abstracts* record. Search results can be cross-filed to the CA FILE to expand or refine the search using other parameters such as keywords; updated biweekly. Enables the searching of the entire scope of prophetic chemical structures, those not actually synthesized, but hypothesized by a Markush structure in chemical patent claims. MARPAT is an excellent complement to **REGISTRY**, which provides access to specific synthesized chemical compounds (described above).	C E
APIPAT (American Petroleum Institute) **DERWENT WORLD PATENTS INDEX/API** (merged database by Derwent Publications Ltd. and the American Petroleum Institute)	28 industrial countries; before 1982 limited to 11 patent offices including the U.S., Japan, EPO and WIPO.	All technologies related to the petroleum industry, including petrochemicals, transportation, refining, waste disposal, synfuels, etc. Oil field chemicals	1964- 1981-	• Bibliographic data with professionally written abstracts (derived from Derwent and *Chemical Abstracts*); updated monthly. Noted for its superb hierarchical indexing scheme, making it possible to formulate search strategies which are both very inclusive and precise (objectives common to most patent searches). Provides exclusive coverage of important early 1960s patents on hydrocarbon polymers. Generic chemical structures are indexed by structural fragment codes. Role qualifiers can be linked to chemical compound information to determine its function or performance. Because APIPAT obtains its patent information from Derwent and *Chemical Abstracts*, the database suffers from a multiple indexing lag time and tends to be very slow to report new patents. The **DERWENT WORLD PATENTS INDEX/API** merged database (avail. to Derwent/API subscribers only) combines the country, technology, and period coverage, as well as the excellent indexing of both databases into one (see description of Derwent WORLD PATENTS INDEX above).	C D F H K
CLAIMS™/U.S. PATENTS **CLAIMS™/UNITERM** **CLAIMS™/COMPREHENSIVE** (IFI/Plenum Data Company) Note: Also known as IFI databases (e.g. IFIPAT, IFIUDB, IFICDB)	United States (contains equivalent patent numbers from select European countries to U.S. chemical patents through 1979).	Chemical patents General, Mechanical, and Electrical patents Design patents Statutory Invention Registrations (SIRs)	1950- 1963- 1980- 1985-	• Bibliographic data with applicant-written abstracts and the text of the main claim of each patent document. The online services Dialog, Orbit, Questel, and STN International offer complete front-page information and the text of all claims since 1971; updated weekly; U.S National Classification codes in patent records are updated annually in accordance with changes made in the classification scheme. Noted for its exclusive retrospective depth of U.S. chemical, electrical, and mechanical patents. The **UNITERM** and **COMPREHENSIVE** versions carry the same bibliographic and text data as CLAIMS™/U.S. PATENT ABSTRACTS, but also offer deep-indexing for chemical patents. **UNITERM** adds a minimum of 40 chemical indexing terms to each patent record. To that, **COMPREHENSIVE** adds precise chemical fragmentation coding, enabling chemical substructure and generic chemical patent searching. Role indicators are also added. COMPREHENSIVE is only avail. to IFI subscribers.	D F I J K
U.S. PATENTS (Derwent Publications Ltd.)	United States	Utility patents -- all technologies Design patents Plant patents:	1971- Jul. 1975- Dec. 1976-	• Complete front-page information, with applicant-written abstracts and the text of all claims; updated weekly; U.S National Classification codes in patent records are updated regularly in accordance with changes made in the classification scheme. Although no longer an exclusive feature among bibliographic patent databases, U.S. PATENTS' ability to search and display all claims in U.S. patent documents remains an outstanding feature and one that's key to infringement and validity searches.	I J K

Continued

Table 5-1 Major Online Patent Database, *continued*

DATABASE (Producer)	Countries Covered	Technologies Covered	Period Covered	Description	Feature Codes*
U.S. PATENTS FULLTEXT (Dialog Information Services, Inc.)	United States	Utility patents -- all technologies; design, plant, and reissue patents; defensive publications and	1971-73 (partial cover.) 1974-	• Complete text verbatim of all U.S. patents, including all front page information, all claims, background/field of invention, summary of invention, description or embodiment, description of drawings (if present), and examples (if present). Images of patent drawings are not included as of 1993; updated weekly.	I J
		Statutory Invention Registrations	1985-	The 1993 introduction of U.S. PATENTS FULLTEXT gives Dialog the advantage of being the only online service to offer a full-text component to its patent database cluster. Because of enhanced possibilities for cross-file searching to and from other patent databases in the cluster, this database is perhaps of greater utility than the otherwise comparable full-text database LEXPAT (see below).	K
				Note: full-text patent databases are both a blessing and a curse. They are invaluable to patent attorneys who must search the text for all claims, disclosures and specifications of patent documents. They are also useful when searching for trade names or other specialized scientific terminology which may appear in the body of the patent document, but not in its abstracts or claims. Because of the power of full-text databases, however, search results can often become often cluttered with irrelevant references while still not guaranteeing the retrieval of all relevant references.	
LEXPAT (Mead Data Central, Inc.; available as a NEXIS database)	United States	Utility patents -- all technologies	1971- Dec. 1974 (partial cover.) Dec. 1974-	• Complete text verbatim of all U.S. patents, including all front page information, all claims, background/field of invention, summary of invention, description or embodiment, description of drawings (if present), and examples (if present). Images of patent drawings are not included; updated weekly.	B J
		Design and plant patents	Dec. 1976-	LEXPAT is regularly updated to include revised status information regarding corrections, reclassifications, reassignments, reissues, disclaimers, and litigation notices. This is a feature not offered by U.S. PATENTS FULLTEXT. Also, see the note regarding full-text databases in the entry on U.S. PATENTS FULLTEXT (above).	K
JAPIO (Japan Patent Information Organization)	Japan	Published unexamined Japanese patent applications (Kokai Tokkyo Koho) for all technologies. Not included are examined patents, utility models, and design patents.	Oct. 1976-	• Bibliographic, with translated English language titles and abstracts for about 65% of the database; updated monthly.	C K
				Provides exclusive database coverage of unexamined Japanese patents for certain periods of times (especially 1976-82 for non-chemical patents). In many cases it is the only source for English language abstracts of Japanese patents. The database is slow to report new patents with a typical 5-6 month lag time between patent publication and entry in the database.	

Notes
(1) Country coverage varies with both period and technologies covered.

* Feature Codes

A = Patent family data available (current records)
B = Legal Status data available
C = Provides informative, enhanced, or translated titles and abstracts
D = Access to part or all of the database may be restricted to database subscribers
E = Markush graphical structure searching available (directly/companion database)
F = Searchable by chemical codes (directly/companion database)
G = Searchable by protein and/or nucleic acid sequences (directly/companion database)
H = Searchable by Chemical Abstracts Registry number (current records)
I = Searchable by cited references (directly or through companion database)
J = Searchable by U.S. National Patent Classification codes
K = Searchable by International Patent Classification codes (IPC)

Table 5-2 Additional Online Patent Databases: For Subject Searching

International / Multinational Coverage

CURRENT PATENTS FAST ALERT -- a fast reporting, current awareness database of selected pharmaceutical, agrochemical and biotechnology patents from published EPO, World PCT, and United Kingdom applications, U.S. granted patents, and German Offenlegungsschrift documents (for agrochemicals); abstracts include therapeutic classification and examples of preferred compounds; from 1989; produced by Current Patents Ltd.

DRUG PATENTS INTERNATIONAL -- provides evaluative information on pharmaceutical patents either in the market or in active research and development. Selective coverage emphasizes top-selling or "most promising" drugs, especially in the area of anti-cancer, anti-inflammatory, and cardiovascular therapeutic agents. Product patent families are searchable by trade names, generic names, therapeutic class or laboratory codes; no abstracts; produced by IMSWorld Publications LTD.

GENESEQ -- indexes protein sequences and nucleic acids indicated in published patent applications and granted patents of 14 patent issuing authorities, including the U.S., EPO, and JAPIO (Japan Patent Information Organization); each sequence is assigned an accession number for cross-referencing with DERWENT WORLD PATENTS INDEX; produced by Derwent Publications Ltd.; available through Intelligenetics.

IMSWorld PATENTS INTERNATIONAL -- provides evaluated product patent family data from over 1000 commercially significant drugs; products are searchable by generic or trade names; produced by IMSWorld Publications Ltd.; available through online services Dialog and Data-Star.

PHARMSEARCH / MPHARM -- covers pharmaceutical patents, including peptide patents, issued by the U.S., France, Germany and the EPO from 1986 (coverage from 1978 for U.S. and EPO patents and from 1961 for French patents is planned). Contain displayable images from European, French, and WIPO patent documents published since 1989 and from U.S., British, and German documents published since 1992. Chemical structures presented in patents, including Markush structures, are graphically searchable using companion database MPHARM; is relatively fast to report new patents (approx. 6 weeks after publication); produced by Institut National de la Propriété Industrielle.

U.S. Coverage

PATDATA -- covers U.S. utility patents, with abstracts, from 1975; provides searchable cited references; updated weekly; produced and made available by the online service BRS Information Technologies.

Foreign National Coverage

CHINESE PATENT ABSTRACTS -- covers all patents published by the Patent Office of the People's Republic of China (PRC) since its inception in April 1985; includes English-language titles and abstracts and patent numbers of equivalent patents published in other countries; produced by the Patent Documentation Service Centre of the PRC and provided by the EPO.

5.5.1 Online Databases and Services

Online databases are accessed through commercial online services. These services provide interactive access to a multitude of databases and are, in a sense, analogous to shopping malls where many "stores" of information (databases) are readily available. Large computers in various locations around the U.S., Europe, and Japan store these databases, and users connect to them remotely via modem or the Internet. Each online service offers a unique array of databases, and uses its own search command language.

Table 5-3 Additional Online Patent Databases: For Bibliographic, Patent Family, or Legal Status Information

<u>International Coverage</u>

EDOC -- the European Patent Office's (EPO) documentation database of published applications and granted patents from 18 major industrialized countries, and those of the EPO, international PCT applications, and the African Intellectual Property Organization (OAPI); EDOC is the only online source covering granted Japanese patents; the database provides minimal bibliographic data with which patent families can be identified; period covered varies with country with some data going back to the 1870s; in French; produced by the EPO and the Institut National de la Propriété Industrielle.

EPAT -- provides bibliographic, administrative, and legal status information on all European and EURO-PCT (European Patents Convention) patents and published applications since June 1978; abstracts and main claims added to patent records from 1994; very current as the database is updated weekly on the day of patent publication; in French, German, and English; produced by the Institut National de la Propriété Industrielle.

PATOSEP -- represents patent applications and granted patents published by the EPO since 1978 with legal status data for each entry; includes the patent's exemplary claim which may be in English, French, or German; produced by Wila Verlag.

PATOSWO --covers international patent applications published by the World Intellectual Property Organization since 1983; in English with abstracts; produced by Wila Verlag.

PCTPAT -- contains information on Patent Cooperation Treaty (PCT) and European PCT patent applications published in the *PCT Gazette* since 1978; produced by Institut National de la Propriété Industrielle and the World Intellectual Property Organization (WIPO).

<u>U.S. Coverage</u>

CLAIMS™ REASSIGNMENT AND REEXAMINATION -- tracks four post-issue actions of U.S. patents: registered reassignments from 1980; reexamined patents from 1981; expired patents from September 1985; and extended patents from April 1986; produced by IFI/Plenum Data Corp.

LitAlert -- a patent litigation database which documents U.S. patent and trademark infringement and validity cases filed in U.S. District Courts; cases are tracked from notices of filing through to the record of actions taken by the courts; coverage is from 1970; produced by Research Publications Inc.

PATENT STATUS FILE (PAST) -- tracks over twenty post-issue actions on U.S. patents as printed in the PTO's *Official Gazette*; actions covered include requests for reexaminations, reissues, withdrawals, expirations due to failure to pay maintenance fees, and certificate of corrections; includes actions taken since 1973 (affecting patents dating back to 1969); produced by Research Publications Inc.

<u>Foreign National Coverage</u>

FPAT (French Patent Registry) -- covers published French patents, with bibliographic information, abstracts, and legal status data from 1966 (from 1961 for French pharmaceutical patents); in French; very current as the database is updated weekly on the day of patent publication; produced by Institut National de la Propriété Industrielle.

ITALPAT -- contains bibliographic on all Italian patent applications (brevetti), utility model applications (modello utilita) and design patent applications (modello ornamentale) from 1983; produced by JUSTINFO Ltd.

PATDD -- contains bibliographic information and abstracts (in German) of patent publications of the former German Democratic Republic from 1982 to October 2, 1990 and by the German Patent Office since October 3, 1990; produced by Deutsches Patentamt.

PATDPA / PATGRAPH -- covers German patent documents and utility models since 1968, with thorough legal status information for all published applications; in German; related graphics database, PATGRAPH, displays images patent drawings, chemical structures, complex mathematical equations for German first patent publications issued by the German Patent Office from 1983; both produced by Deutsches Patentamt.

PATOSDE -- covers publications of the German Patent Office including patent applications and examined patent applications from 1968; granted patents from 1980 and utility models from 1983; produced by Wila Verlag.

Table 5-4   Major CD-ROM Databases: U.S. Coverage

Databases Providing Bibliographic/Front Page Information

U.S. PatentSearch (MicroPatent)-- provides bibliographic information on all U.S. utility, design, and reissued patents with searchable front-page information, abstracts, and exemplary claims; avail. from 1975; updated monthly; 1 disc/year.

Patent Scan (Research Publications) -- contains bibliographic information for all U.S. patents since 1974 on a single disc; **Patent Scan Update** contains bibliographic information plus abstracts and exemplary claims for U.S. patent for the current year, and is updated monthly; **Patent Scan Plus** provides the text of abstracts and claims of U.S. patents for the past twenty years, with each disc containing two years of data.

OG/Plus™ (Research Publications) -- a compilation of the following three databases which together provides bibliographic data and information on legal status and litigation activity of U.S. patents for the current year; updated weekly or monthly: 1) PATENTS ISSUED -- provides facsimiles of entries from the *Official Gazette*, including, drawings, equations, chemical formulae, and searchable bibliographic data, exemplary claims, and abstracts (abstracts which are not included in the *Official Gazette*); 2) PATENT STATUS FILE -- a subset of the online database of the same name (described previously) which tracks post-issue actions affecting U.S. patents and; 3) LitAlert -- provides citations with abstracts to litigation in the U.S. District Courts involving U.S. patent violations of the current year; a subset of the online database by the same name (described previously).

Patent History™ (Research Publications) -- a compilation of the following three databases which together provides complementary retrospective coverage to that of **OG/Plus**™ (described above); updated annually: 1) PATENTS BACKFILE -- contains minimal bibliographic and classification data, such as patent title, number, assignee name, and assigned U.S. National Classification codes, for U.S. patents issued during the past 17 years; 2) PATENT STATUS FILE -- covers over 20 post-issue actions on U.S. patents, including withdrawals, reassignments, reissues and reexaminations and; 3) LitAlert -- contains citations to U.S. District Court cases involving U.S. patent violations, such as infringement, from 1972.

CASSIS/BIB (U.S. Patent and Trademark Office) -- provides bibliographic information for all U.S. utility patents from 1969, and for other U.S. patent documents (design and plant patents, reissues, defensive publications, etc.) since 1977; includes abstracts for the most recent 3 years; updated bimonthly.

BIOTECH PatentSearch (MicroPatent) -- covers all U.S. biotechnology patents since 1980 with searchable front-page information, abstracts, and exemplary claims; also includes coverage of Patent Cooperation Treaty (PCT) biotechnology-related applications since 1992; updated monthly; cumulated on 1 disc.

Databases Providing Full-Text/Full-Images

FullText (MicroPatent) -- provides complete searchable text (with no images) of all U.S. patents; avail. from 1990; updated monthly; 12 discs/year.

U.S. PatentImages™ (MicroPatent) -- scanned facsimile images of all U.S. utility and design patents with searchable front-page information and abstracts; available from 1976; weekly updates; approx. 100 discs/year.

PatentView™ (Research Publications) -- scanned facsimile images of all U.S. utility, design, plant, and re-issue patents with searchable front-page information, abstracts, and exemplary claims; weekly updates; approx. 100 discs/year; database subsets for General/Mechanical patents, and for Electrical patents are also available.

Chemical PatentImages™ (MicroPatent) -- scanned facsimile images of all U.S. chemical patents with searchable front-page information and abstracts; avail. from 1976; biweekly updates; approx. 30 discs/year.

BIOTECH PatentImages™ (MicroPatent) -- scanned facsimile images of all U.S. biotechnology-related patents with searchable front-page information and abstracts; avail. from 1980; biweekly updates; approx. 4 discs/year.

Table 5-5   Major CD-ROM Databases: International Coverage (including EPO/WIPO)

<u>Databases Providing Bibliographic/Front Page Information</u>

ESPACE-Access (European Patent Office) -- an index to EPO patent applications with searchable bibliographic information and abstracts; from 1978; updated quarterly; cumulated on 2 discs.

ESPACE-First (European Patent Office) -- contains facsimile images of the first page of all European Patent applications and published PCT International applications; with searchable bibliographic information; updated bimonthly; avail. from 1988; 5 discs/year.

PCT PatentSearch (World Intellectual Property Organization) -- provides searchable front-page information with abstracts on international patent applications published by WIPO under the Patent Cooperation Treaty (PCT); avail. from 1992; updated monthly.

ESPACE-Bulletin (European Patent Office) -- provides bibliographic and legal status data on all European Patent applications filed since 1978; updated quarterly; cumulated on 1 disc.

<u>Databases Providing Full-Text/Full-Images</u>

ESPACE EP-A (European Patent Office) -- scanned facsimile images of European Patent Applications ('A' publications), with 13 searchable bibliographic elements; updated weekly; avail. from 1978; 85-90 discs/year.

ESPACE EP-B (European Patent Office) -- scanned facsimile images of granted European Patents ('B' publications), with 13 searchable bibliographic elements; updated weekly; avail. from 1988; 85-90 discs/year.

ESPACE-World (World Intellectual Property Organization) -- scanned facsimile images of international patent applications published by WIPO under the PCT (involving over 50 countries worldwide); text fields not searchable; facsimile documents are retrieved by number or by number lists generated by PCT PatentSearch (described above); updated semi-monthly; 35-40 discs/year.

Patents Preview + Specifications (Derwent Publications Ltd.) -- a current awareness database for pharmaceutical patents; database records contain professionally written patent abstracts and indexing , and can be linked to facsimiles of complete pharmaceutical patent publications from patent offices in the U.K., U.S., Japan, France, Germany, the EPO and the Patent Cooperation Treaty (PCT); database records are created within 5-10 days of the patent document's publication date; coverage backdates to August 1993; issued every two weeks.

Two objectives guide the selection of an online service for patent searching. First, if you intend to conduct exhaustive patent searching, as is necessary for novelty and infringement studies, select a service that offers a complementary *cluster* of patent databases. The utility of any single database may be appreciably enhanced if searched in an online database cluster using techniques such as *cross-file* and multiple database searching (see Search Strategy and Techniques section below for more details). Table 6 presents the patent database clusters of the major online services—STN International, Orbit, Questel, Dialog and Mead/NEXIS. From this, you can compare the strengths and weaknesses of the various clusters in areas such as international and domestic coverage, or coverage of patent family and legal status information. All databases listed in Table 6 are described in this article.

Second, because searches often require looking beyond the patent literature (*e.g.,* novelty searches), consider the selection of relevant non-patent databases that an online service offers. For example, if it is important to search not only the most recent patents by XYZ Communications Co. on multicarrier modulation systems, but also related product an-

Table 5-6| Online Patent Coverage (including EPO/WIPO)

Databases for Subject Searching (1)

Online Database Services (2)

International Coverage	STN	ORBIT	QUESTEL	DIALOG	MEAD/NEXIS
DERWENT WORLD PATENTS INDEX †	X	X	X	X	
DERWENT WORLD PAT. IND. / API†		X			
CA FILE/CA SEARCH (Chem. Abstracts)	X	X	X	X	
MARPAT	X				
APIPAT	X			X	
PHARMSEARCH / MPHARM			X		
CURRENT PATENTS		X			
DRUG PATENTS INTERNATIONAL		X			

U.S. Coverage	STN	ORBIT	QUESTEL	DIALOG	MEAD/NEXIS
CLAIMS™ /U.S. Patents	X	X	X	X	
CLAIMS™ /UNITERM	X	X	X	X	
CLAIMS™ /COMPREHENSIVE	X	X		X	
U.S. PATENTS FULLTEXT				X	
U.S. PATENTS		X			
LEXPAT					X

Foreign National Coverage	STN	ORBIT	QUESTEL	DIALOG	MEAD/NEXIS
CHINESE PATENT ABSTRACTS (PRC)†		X		X	
JAPIO (Japan)		X	X	X	

Databases for Bibliographic, Patent Family, or Legal Status Information (3)

International Coverage	STN	ORBIT	QUESTEL	DIALOG	MEAD/NEXIS
INPADOC/Family and Legal Status	X	X		X	
EDOC (EPO Documentation File)			X		
EPAT (European Patent Registry)			X		
PATOSEP (European Patent Office)	X				
PATOSWO (World Intell. Property Org.)	X				
PCTPAT (PCT Applications)			X		

Foreign National Coverage	STN	ORBIT	QUESTEL	DIALOG	MEAD/NEXIS
FPAT (French Patent Registry)			X		
ITALPAT (Italy)			X		
PATDD (Form. E. Germ. and Germany)	X				
PATDPA/PATGRAPH (Germany)	X				
PATOSDE (Germany)	X				

U.S Coverage	STN	ORBIT	QUESTEL	DIALOG	MEAD/NEXIS
CLAIMS™ Reassignmt. and Reexamin.	X	X		X	
LitAlert		X			
PATENT STATUS FILE (PAST)		X			

General Note:

Database listed are accessible to all subscribers of the specified online services except DERWENT WORLD PATENTS INDEX / API (merged database) and CLAIMS COMPREHENSIVE which to access require additional subscriptions with their respective database producers.

(1) Includes online databases which emphasize the technical information disclosed in patents. In addition to providing at least basic bibliographic information, records in the databases usually contain English language abstracts and one or more of the following: the text of patents claims; patent office classification; and indexing, coding, or other text enhancements supplied by the database producer. Subject-oriented databases which also provide current patent family data and /or legal status data are signified by (t).

(2) Consult the *Gale Directory of Databases* (see bibliography) for current information on these and other online database services.

(3) Includes online databases which provide bibliographic information, and either information on patent prosecution status, patent family data litigation activity, or reports of post-issuance actions. Many databases in this category also provide abstracts and/or text of patent claims, although some in non-English languages.

nouncements, technical journal literature, and industry standards, select a service that offers the range of databases meeting those requirements.

5.5.2 Costs of Searching Online Databases

To use a commercial online database, you must establish an account with an online service. For a nominal annual subscription fee, which is separate from the costs of searching the databases, an online service will provide you with a user *ID* and password. The cost of a database varies with each database as well as with each online service. Typically these costs are an aggregation of charges for 1) connect time to specific databases (ranging from approximately $100 to $300/hour); 2) display or print charges (typically ranging from $.40 to $1.50 per record, although full record displays in some databases go as high as $20/record), and 3) telecommunications charges (ranging from $8 to $15/hour). These rates, especially those related to connect time, may be intimidating at first glance. However, many search sessions can be completed in a matter of five, ten, or twenty minutes. To keep costs down, searches should be well-prepared before going online. Access to some databases, as well as access to the special indexing available on a number of databases, requires a subscription with the database producer. These subscription agreements, which are in addition to that with the online service, often entitle searchers to preferential searching rates.

5.5.3 CD-ROM Databases

CD-ROM is a high-capacity optical medium capable of storing 660 megabytes or the equivalent of approximately 330,000 typewritten pages on one 4.75 inch disc. CD-ROM patent databases are searched using a microcomputer with a CD-ROM drive and appropriate extensions software, or through a local area network (LAN) similarly equipped. In the late 1980s, several patent databases on CD-ROM were introduced, providing an alternative to online patent searching. Since then numerous patent CD-ROMs have emerged, including several using full-text and image data produced by the major patent offices and their automation projects.

The major patent offices, particularly the European Patent Office (EPO) and the World Intellectual Property Organization (WIPO) have for some time used CD-ROMs as an economical means to disseminate patent information. And most recently, the Japanese Patent Office, which processes over 500,000 applications per year, has made the unprecedented decision to publish patents solely on CD-ROM.

Patent databases on CD-ROM hold special appeal in two ways. First, searchers are freed from the beat-the-clock pressures of online searching as CD-ROM databases are typically leased from database vendors on fixed-rate annual subscription terms. Costs remain fixed no matter how often or much a database is used. Many searchers using CD-ROM databases claim that the completeness of their patent searches has improved because of the freedom to browse and execute multiple search strategies. Some searchers like the menu-driven interfaces or the report-generating capabilities that many of the CD-ROM products offer.

Second, CD-ROM has taken the lead over online databases in providing representation of the drawings, schematics, and other graphical elements found in patents. Today there are several *full-text/image* CD-ROM databases that contain scanned facsimiles of complete patent documents including all text, drawings, figures, tables, and charts. In many libraries and companies, full-text/image CD-ROM patent databases are replacing paper and microfilm files as a new generation, computerized document storage medium. To transmit documents to remote locations, software is available to fax copies of records or documents directly from the CD-ROM without making a paper copy.

But the CD-ROM medium for patent searching also has its disadvantages, some worth serious consideration. For many patent searches, comprehensive retrieval requires searching a complement of databases. Whereas the online environment facilitates combining the strengths of multiple databases using synergistic cross-file and multiple database searching techniques, a CD-ROM database is searched in isolation. A question also arises as to whether optical discs, even though a high capacity medium, are sufficiently capacious to contain some of the enormous patent files. For example, a full-text/image database of U.S. patents requires approximately 100 CD-ROM discs per year. Searching that many discs requires either a considerable amount of manual disc swapping or an expensive "juke-box" type CD-ROM player. These requirements may erode search efficiency. Annual subscription costs for CD-ROM patent databases vary widely (from approximately $350/year to $6000/year) depending on the database producer, the type of database (*e.g.,* bibliographic, full-text, etc.) and the updating frequency.

5.6 SEARCH STRATEGY AND TECHNIQUES

In the simplest view, patent searches are either bibliographic or subject-oriented. Bibliographic searches seek information about documents known or expected to exist, such as patents by a particular inventor, those assigned to a specific company, or patents equivalent to another. Because bibliographic searches begin with well-defined factual information, they are simpler and can usually be completed with greater certainty. Subject-oriented searches seek to determine if patents exist on a specific technology, and are conducted for such purposes as novelty, infringement, and validity studies. This type of search requires in-depth knowledge of the patent databases, searching experience, and a strong methodology.

Most search strategies, and especially those subject-oriented in nature, follow these steps:

1. Determine search objectives.
2. Select database(s) to search.
3. Define search strategy, using keywords, indexing terms and codes, or other appropriate search parameters such as assignee names, priority dates, etc.
4. Conduct preliminary search.
5. Modify search strategy based on preliminary results.

6. Conduct refined search.

7. For relevant results, retrieve full patent documents (either electronically or otherwise) for examination.

Along with practicing sound methodology, it helps to know specific search techniques. Patent searching authority Stuart Kaback offers some specific advice on patent search techniques in a 1991 article in *World Patent Information* [8]. The following recommendations include selected points from this article:

- Use the Simplest and Most Inclusive Strategy Possible. With patents, it is too easy to exclude relevant references by crafting too fine an initial search strategy. Broad strategies can always be made more precise, but at some time it is important to cast a wide net. In many online databases, patent titles and indexing from database records can be displayed or printed at no extra cost (other than for the connect time it takes to display them). A common technique when beginning a search is to execute a broad-based strategy in a database like Derwent WPI, which provides descriptive titles. From a list of titles, acquired at minimal costs, selected records can be displayed with complete information for further examination. Figure 4 presents an example of such an approach. Here, a preliminary search on the topic of "applications of holography in fingerprinting technology" is begun in the Derwent WPI online database. The search combines keywords and IPC codes, and results in a display of informative patent titles.

- Use Multiple Retrieval Parameters. When possible, use patent office classification coding, or database indexing and coding to supplement keyword strategies.

- Use Multiple Databases to Ensure Comprehensive Retrieval. The demanding nature of novelty and infringement searches underscores the need for comprehensiveness in patent searching. However, never assume that any one database is completely fit for the task at hand. Even some of the omnibus patent databases, those covering all technologies for a desired time frame and all countries of interest, cannot be relied on solely for exhaustive searching. To maximize the strengths that many databases offer and to ensure the most comprehensive retrieval possible, you should search *clusters* of complementary databases using cross-file or multiple database techniques.

  Cross-file techniques exploit the strengths of individual patent databases in a single search session. In *cross-filing*, the online service's software allows the transfer of data retrieved in one database for searching in another of complementary content. For example, the CLAIMS™/U.S. PATENTS database might be selected for a particular subject search because of its detailed U.S. classification codes. A hypothetical search on a specific subclass in CLAIMS™/U.S. PATENTS may retrieve 100 patent records. A command is then given to *capture* and store all patent numbers in that set of search results. The captured patent numbers can then be searched in another database, such as WPI, which does not index U.S. classification codes

File 351:DERWENT WORLD PATENTS INDEX-LATEST
1981+;DW=9324,UA=9317,UM=9244

Set Items Description

? s fingerprint? or (finger? or thumb?)(w)(print? or pattern?)

	561	FINGERPRINT?
	24320	FINGER?
	3032	THUMB?
	129977	PRINT?
	111666	PATTERN?
	367	(FINGER? OR THUMB?)(W)(PRINT? OR PATTERN?)
S1	811	FINGERPRINT? OR (FINGER? OR THUMB?)(W)(PRINT? OR PATTERN?)

> *Keywords/phrases representing "finger-printing" are searched in patent titles and abstracts; 811 database records are found.*

? s (finger? or thumb?) and ic=(a61b-005/117 or g06k-009?)

	24320	FINGER?
	3032	THUMB?
	45	IC=A61B-005/117
	7974	IC=G06K-009?
S2	228	(FINGER? OR THUMB?) AND IC=(A61B-005/17 OR G06K-009?)

> *International Patent Classification (IPC) codes are combined with keywords to form a set of related results.*

? s s1 or s2

	811	S1
	228	S2
S3	835	S1 OR S2

> *A union of the two preceding search statements is formed to yield 835 database records, broadening the search.*

? s hologra? or ic=g03h

	3198	HOLOGRA?
	1428	IC=G03H
S4	3355	HOLOGRA? OR IC=G03H

> *A keyword stem and IPC subclass code are searched for the concept of "holography/holograms," yielding 3355 records.*

? s s3 and s4

	835	S3
	3355	S4
S5	17	S3 AND S4

> *The search results representing "fingerprint-ing" and those representing "holography" are intersected yielding 17 records.*

? t5/6/all

> *Patent titles are displayed for further review. The full database record for title number 3 (in italics) is displayed in Figure1.2*

5/6/1
008977544 WPI Acc No: 92-104813/13
XRPX Acc No: N92-078378
  Holographic credit card with automatic authentication and verification - has matched optical filter that stores fingerprint of user as fourier hologram that can be read using coherent light

5/6/2
008897584 WPI Acc No: 92-024853/04
XRPX Acc No: N92-018994
  Line pattern identification system for finger prints - compares positive slide image of line pattern with positive and negative reference images

5/6/3
008851936 WPI Acc No: 91-355956/49
XRPX Acc No: N91-272424
  Laser optical apparatus for fingerprint recognition system - reflects scattered beam at valleys of fingerprint and detects reflected beam in area CCD producing image representation

5/6/4
008645907 WPI Acc No: 91-149936/21
XRPX Acc No: N91-115134
  Fingerprint recognition device - uses hologram, flat CCD and laser and produces distortion-free images
  .
  .
  .

Figure 4 Online Search Example: "Applications of Holography in Fingerprinting Technology" (DERWENT WORLD PATENTS INDEX on Dialog)

but does report patent family equivalents. The result, in this example, is the retrieval of patent family information from one database using the subject indexing of another. Cross-file capabilities are offered on STN International, Orbit (Print Select), Questel (MEMory command), and Dialog (MAPping).

Along with cross-file capabilities, many online services let you search multiple databases simultaneously. To maximize advantage and economy, some of these online services also allow you to remove duplicate records that may result in the overlapping coverage by the databases searched. Multiple database searching capability is available on STN International, Dialog (OneSearch) and Orbit (PowerSearch).

- Review the Indexing, Classification and Text Fields of Relevant References. Patent searching is an iterative process, wherein search strategies are modified in response to information gleaned from previous search results. For example, a relevant reference may reveal important International Patent Classification codes, index terms, or even other terminology, which were not included in the original search strategy.

  To help strengthen a revised (or even the original) search strategy, several online services offer statistical analysis capabilities. These capabilities allow you to analyze a set of search results by almost any field in any database. For example, search results obtained using keywords on a topic such as "fingerprint classification devices" could be statistically analyzed to determine high-incidence patent classifications. With the intent of making the search more inclusive, these classifications could then be reviewed and factored into the next iteration of the search. The following online services offer statistical analysis: Orbit (GET command), Dialog (RANK command), Questel (MEMSort command), and STN International (SmartSELECT).

- Conduct Citation Searches on the Most Relevant References You Retrieve. Patents cite earlier patents and literature deemed to be relevant prior art. For example, U.S. 4,301,536 (issued in 1981) cites six earlier U.S. patents as relevant prior art. A citation search also reveals that, since its issue in 1981, seven later patents have cited U.S. 4,301,536 as relevant prior art. Many patent databases now contain complete front-page information that facilitates the searching of both cited and citing references.

- Consult Experts. Make sure the patent search process benefits from the mutual consultation of a technical expert, legal counsel, and a patent information specialist.

5.7 THE FUTURE OF PATENT DATABASES

While the 1980s brought tremendous growth in access to bibliographic patent databases, all eyes are now on the mid-to-late 1990s. In this period the major patent offices—United States Patent and Trademark Office (PTO), the European Patent Office (EPO), and the Japanese Patent Office (JPO)—will become *paperless* as a result of long-term automation projects. The database products and services resulting from these efforts may profoundly affect public access to patent information, as well as the commercial database market.

Since 1982 and at a cost of nearly $900 million, the PTO has been developing its Automated Patent System (APS). The project, which is expected to be fully implemented by 2002, includes: 1) the APS Text search system, which already contains the full-text of nearly all U.S. patents since 1971 (the same data contained in commercial online databases U.S. PATENTS FULLTEXT and LEXPAT) and English language abstracts of all Japanese published applications from 1980; and 2) the APS Image system, which contains scanned facsimile images of all U.S. patents from 1791. In time, APS will also include an electronic application filing module, called the Patent Application Management System, which will further the PTO's progress to become a paperless patent system.

Since 1989, APS Text has been available to users of the PTO's Public Search Center in Arlington, Virginia. There, the APS Image system is also available for use on 10 terminals linked to high speed printing facilities. Since 1991, 14 of the most heavily used Patent and Trademark Depository Libraries (PTDLs), located in various cities around the country, have provided public access to the APS Text system via modem. Beginning in 1994, the PTO will begin efforts to provide all 78 PTDLs with a high-speed Internet connection to the APS Text system. Plans for extending similar access to other constituencies, such as government agencies, private industries, and individuals, are presently under discussion. Electronic deployment of the APS Image system to PTDLs awaits the implementation of the high-bandwidth national computer network, which is necessary to transmit the enormous volumes of digital information involved with image data. The very ambitious EPO automation program, which also has invested heavily in capturing patent image data, has a strong commitment to the dissemination of its patent data to the public and to industry [9].

Along with their own automation programs, the PTO, EPO, and the JPO agreed in 1983 to share scanned facsimiles of the front pages of patent documents filed and published in their respective offices since 1920. While each patent office has its own plan for product development and distribution, they share the goal of supporting a common search engine. MIMOSA is the name of the product the PTO is currently developing with the pooled data. It's anticipated that MIMOSA will provide searchable front-page data of PTO, EPO, and JPO patents from 1978 to the present. Initially, the plan is to distribute MIMOSA on CD-ROM (approximately 100 discs) beginning in 1995.

Commercial database producers and online services increasingly use data generated by the massive patent office automation programs to mount their own full-text, and selected- or full-image patent databases. Experience searching full-text databases makes evident the need for advanced search systems capable of producing precise and relevant search results from enormous quantities of text. One trend sees the development of search systems that use probabilistic algorithms to retrieve relevant search results while filtering unwanted or marginally relevant results. One such system, called the Patent Analyzer, uses statistical linguistics to first analyze the full text of a patent application, full patent specification, and/or an engineering memorandum. Based on that analysis, the system constructs a strategy using concepts rather than keywords or search codes. The concept-based strategy is then run against full-text U.S. patent information in all technologies since 1971 [10].

Both the major patent offices and commercial database producers bring important strengths to the quality of and accessibility to patent databases [11]. Whether the major patent offices with their monumental automated systems become competitors or partners to the commercial database sector remains to be seen. Whichever, it is hoped that the outcome will bring increased public access to patent information.

BIBLIOGRAPHY

For the most current information on any specific database or for search training purposes, contact the appropriate database producer, online service, or CD-ROM vendor. Database documentation produced by online services can be very informative as can the classes and workshops that several online services and database producers offer.

As a single comprehensive source providing basic information about databases, their producers, online services, and other database product vendors, the following is recommended:

Marcaccio, Kathleen Young, ed. *Gale Directory of Databases*. Vol. 1, *Online Databases*. Vol. 2, *CD-ROM, Diskette, Magnetic Tape, Handheld, and Batch Access Database Products*. Detroit: Gale Research, published semi-annually.

OVERVIEWS OF PATENT INFORMATION
AND PATENT DATABASES

Butler, John T. "Electronic Resources for Patent Searching," *Law Library Journal* 84 (Winter 1992): 121–157.

Raduazo, Dorothy M. "Online Patent Databases: A Review Article," *Government Publications Review* 13 (March–April 1986): 277–286.

Simmons, Edlyn S. "Patents," in: *Manual of Online Search Strategies*, ed. C.J. Armstrong and J.A. Large (New York: G. K. Hall, 1992, 2nd edition): 51–127.

Suhr, Claus. "Patent Information," in: *Ullmann's Encyclopedia of Industrial Chemistry*, ed. Gerhartz, Wolfgang (Weinheim, Germany: VCH, 1985, 5th completely rev. ed.); vol. B1: 12.28–12.44.

Thompson, N. J. "Intellectual Property Materials Online/CD-ROM: What and Where," *Database 15* (December 1992): 14–15+.

SPECIFIC ONLINE PATENT DATABASES
(NON-CHEMICAL)

Harwell, Kevin R. "Searching U.S. Patents: Core Collection and Suggestions for Service," RSR: *Reference Services Review* 21, no. 3 (Fall 1993):49–60. Reviews the print and electronic resources for patent searching available at the 78 U.S. Patent and Trademark Depository Libraries (PTDLs) located around the United States.

Lambert, Nancy. "After the Grant: Online Searching of Legal Status Information for U.S. Patents", *Database 14* (August 1991): 42–48. Compares four legal status patent databases: INPADOC/LEGAL STATUS, CLAIMS™ Reassignments and Reexaminations, LitAlert, and PAST (Patent Status File).

Simmons, Edlyn S. "JAPIO—Japanese Patent Applications Online," *Online 10* (July 1986): 51–58.

Simmons, Edlyn S. "Patent Family Databases," *Database 8* (February 1985): 49–55. Defines patent families, basic and equivalent patents and designated states of the transnational patent offices, and describes the databases used to search for patent family data.

CHEMICAL PATENT DATABASES

Ebe, Tommy; Sanderson, Karen A.; and Wilson, Patricia S. "The Chemical Abstracts Service Generic Chemical (Markush) Structure Storage and Retrieval Capability. 2. The MARPAT File", *Journal of Chemical Information and Computer Sciences* 31 (February 1991): 31–36.

Kaback, Stuart M. "WPI + APIPAT: The Sum of the Parts," *Database 13* (April 1990): 22–26. Discusses what is now known as DERWENT WORLD PATENTS INDEX / API, a database resulting from the merging of two long-standing patent databases.

Lambert, Nancy. "How to Search the IFI Comprehensive Database Online . . . Tips and Techniques," *Database 10* (December 1987): 46–59. The database explored here is also known as CLAIMS™ COMPREHENSIVE, produced by IFI/Plenum Data Corp.

Lambert, Nancy. "Online Searching of Polymer Patents: Precision and Recall", *Journal of Chemical Information and Computer Sciences* 31 (November 1991): 443–446.

O'Hara, Michael P., and Pagis, Catherine. "The PHARMSEARCH Database", *Journal of Chemical Information and Computer Sciences* 31 (February 1991): 59–63.

Patent Information from Chemical Abstracts Service: Coverage and Content. Chemical Abstracts Service, a division of the American Chemical Society; Columbus, Ohio, 1991.

Rieder, M. D. "The IFI Polymer Indexing System: its Past, Present, and Future", *Journal of Chemical Information and Computer Sciences* 31 (November 1991): 458–462. Assesses the unique polymer indexing system of IFI/Plenum Data Corp., producers of the CLAIMS™ family of patent databases.

Schmuff, Norman R. "A Comparison of the MARPAT and Markush DARC Software", *Journal of Chemical Information and Computer Sciences* 31 (February 1991): 53–59.

Tokuno, H. "Comparison of Markush Structure Databases", *Journal of Chemical Information and Computer Sciences* 33 (November/December 1993): 799–804. Evaluates the performance of the major Markush structure databases: WPIM (World Patents Index Markush), MPHARM (Markush Pharmsearch), and MARPAT.

PATENT SEARCHING TECHNIQUES

Kaback, Stuart M. "Crossfile Patent Searching: A Dream Come True", *Database 10* (October 1987): 17–30.

Kaback, Stuart M. "Online Patent Information. What's Beyond the Claims, or When Everything That's Claimed Just Isn't Enough", *World Patent Information* 13, no. 2 (1991): 101.

Ojala, Marydee. "A Patently Obvious Source for Competitor Intelligence: The Patent Literature", *Database 12* (August 1989): 43–49.

"Online Statistical Analysis: a Means of Unlocking Hidden Information", *Online & CD-ROM Review* 17, no. 2 (1993): 112–117. Profiles statistical analysis functions, offered by many online services to assist searchers in analyzing specific patent and other search results.

Van der Drift, J. "Effective Strategies for Searching Existing Patent Rights", *World Patent Information* 13, no. 2 (1991): 67–71.

Vijvers, W. G. "The International Patent Classification as a Search Tool", *World Patent Information* 12, no. 1 (1990): 26–30.

Weckend, Bernd-Ruediger. "Complementary Searching in Patent Databases", *World Patent Information* 9, no. 3 (1987): 140–146.

Wilson, R. M. "Patent Analysis Using Online Databases: Competitor Activity Monitoring", *World Patent Information* 9, no. 2 (1987): 73–78.

Wilson, R. M. "Patent Analysis Using Online Databases: Technological Trend Analysis", *World Patent Information* 9, no. 1 (1987): 18–26.

CD-ROM PATENT DATABASES

Claus, P. "CD-ROM Products of the World Intellectual Property Organization (WIPO)", *World Patent Information* 14 (August 1992): 195–197. Describes the ESPACE-WORLD, ESPACE-FIRST, and IPC: CLASS patent CD-ROM databases.

Hearle, E. "CD-ROM-a New Means of Searching and Storing Patent Information", *World Patent Information* 13, no. 3 (1991): 139–142.

Jackson, Kathy M. "CASSIS/CD-ROM: Makes Patent Searching Easier", *Laserdisk Professional* 3, no. 2 (1990): 60–66.

Lobeck, M. A. "Patent Information on CD-ROMs", *World Patent Information* 12, no. 4 (1990): 200–211.

Melvin, T. C. "Patent Information on Compact Disk: a Review of Four Products", *Science & Technology Libraries* 12 (Fall 1991): 35–54. Evaluates Research Publication's OG/PLUS, Micro-Patent's APS (a product now called PatentSearch), the PTO's CASSIS, and the now-discontinued CLAIMS/PATENT CD.

PATENT INFORMATION IN NON-PATENT DATABASES

Snow, Bonnie. "Patents in Non-Patent Databases: Bioscience Specialty Files", *Database* 12 (October 1989): 41–48.

Snow, Bonnie. "Patents in Non-Patent Databases: Food, Agriculture and Environment Files", *Database* 12 (December 1989): 115–119.

AUTOMATION OF THE U.S. PATENT AND
TRADEMARK OFFICE

Brown, L. J. "USPTO Automated Patent System: A Critical Discussion of APS and its Use for Full-Text Searching", *Special Publication—Royal Society of Chemistry* 120 (1993): 157– .

Lucas, J. "The Progress of Automation at the US Patent and Trademark Office", *World Patent Information* 14 (August 1992): 167–172.

Thieme, Bill and Smith, Harold. "Automating Search and Retrieval of Patents in the U.S. Patent and Trademark Office", *Government Publications Review* 13 (July/August 1986): 431–449.

NOTES

[1] Based on data obtained from the INPADOC database, produced by the International Patent Documentation Centre, an agency of the European Patent Office (EPO).

[2] Based on data obtained from the database CLAIMS™/U.S. Patent Abstracts, produced by IFI/Plenum Data Corp.

[3] U.S. Patent and Copyright Bicentennial Celebration Open House. *Patent Statistics: Applications for Patents.* Washington, DC: U.S. Patent and Trademark Office, 1990.

[4] Archibugi, Daniele. "Patenting as an Indicator of Technological Innovation: a Review", *Science and Public Policy* 19, no. 6 (December 1992): 357–368.

[5] Patent search objectives are explored in great detail by Lotz, John W. "Patents (Literature)", vol. 16, *Encyclopedia of Chemical Technology,* 3rd edition, ed. Martin Grayson (New York: John Wiley and Sons, 1981): 889–945.

[6] Simmons, Edlyn S. "The Paradox of Patentability Searching", *Journal of Chemical Information and Computer Sciences* 25 (November 1985): 379–386.

[7] A Markush structure is a generically-defined chemical structure that contains one or more structural variables defined by a list of substituents. Markush claims cover each compound that is implied by the generic structure and its variables, even though only one or two may have been synthesized in the laboratory. The generic description holds the potential to represent a large or even infinite number of implied structures under a single disclosure. The name is derived from Eugene Markush, an American scientist who brought a court case in 1925 that led to the acceptance of generic structures in patent claims by the U.S. Patent Office.

[8] Kaback, Stuart M. "Online Patent Information" *World Patent Information* 13, no. 3 (1991): 166–167.

[9] Michel, J. "The Future of Patent Information Products", *World Patent Information* 13, no. 2 (1991): 61–66.

[10] The Patent Analyzer, designed to serve large organizations and law firms, is produced jointly by Rapid Patent and Electronic Data Systems.

[11] Ilmaier, E. and Sibley, J. F. "The Moving Goal-Posts", *World Patent Information* 15, no. 1 (March 1993): 5–11.

Article
6

BENEFITS OF USING PATENT DATABASES AS A SOURCE OF INFORMATION

Debrah C. Marcus

Debrah C. Marcus is an Information Scientist with Dr. Reinhold Cohn & Partners in Tel Aviv, Israel.

Abstract

Patents serve as a valuable source of information. However, when in the form of online databases, the amount and inherent value of this information increases greatly, due, among other things, to the greater accessibility offered by this medium.

There are many types of patent databases available online: country specific databases (*e.g.,* Japan, United States, China, France); subject specific databases (*e.g.,* biotechnology related or petroleum related only); and more international, non-subject specific databases. These can be further classified as containing full text, or abstract, diagram or family and status details only.

There is also an ever increasing variety of CD-ROMs which cover individual countries, patenting bodies, and conventions. As CD-ROMs, they offer the user the added benefit of no time or cost restrictions over and above the actual purchase price. This is especially useful for the inexperienced searcher, but then again, not all countries are covered. Depending on what one wishes to achieve by searching, the CD-ROM may or may not be the answer.

Knowing where to search for which type of information is an art in itself, but the comments which follow are relevant for whichever database you may decide to use.

6.1 TYPES OF INFORMATION AVAILABLE

In general, patents provide a wonderful source for idea generation and can also serve as a source of inspiration when it comes to solving technological problems.

Apart from the obvious parameters, such as author's name, patent assignee, priority dates, family, etc., with a little bit of imagination, patent databases can be used to obtain a wide variety of commercially valuable information:

- Identify possible partners or clients
- Provide background information prior to a business meeting
- Identify trends in R&D, technologies, products

- Identify trends within companies
- Facilitate technology transfer or licensing in place of in-house R&D
- Prevent duplication of R&D
- Identify experts in a specific field
- Establish new applications for existing technologies or products
- Solutions to technological problems
- Idea generation
- Identify marketing trends
- Establish expiration date of a patent
- Identify potential competitors
- Monitor competitors
- Establish state of the art

The following is a selected list of patent databases available from the main online vendors.

DATABASE	COVERAGE	TYPE OF INFORMATION
Derwent World Patents Index	International	Abstract, diagram
Inpadoc	International	Patent family and status
Claims/US Patents	USA	Full text, claims
Claims/Reference	USA	US Manual of classification
Claims/Citation	USA	Cited and citing patent references
Claims/Reassignment and reexamination	USA	Reassigned and reexamined patents
US Patents full text	USA	Full text
Chinese Patent Abstracts in English	China	Abstract
Japio	Japan	Abstract
Current Patents Fast Alert	Pharmaceutical	Abstract
Current Patents Evaluation	Pharmaceutical	Abstract and evaluation
Apipat	Petroleum	Abstract
Drug Patents International	Pharmaceutical	Bibliographic
Epat	Europe	European Patent Abstracts
Fpat	France	Abstract
PCTpat	Patent Convention Treaty Countries	Abstract
Pharm	Pharmaceutical	Abstract

6.1.1 Identification of Possible Partners or Clients

Let's presume that Company X is active in a particular field of technology. Company X is interested (for any one of a variety of reasons) in locating suitable partners who are already active in the same field or a related field. For example, Company X may have a patent that it would like to sell or find an established firm in a specific field with which to go into partnership.

Potential buyer/partners can be identified by searching company directories using a SIC (Standard Industrial Classification) code or possibly keywords. This, however, would not give a realistic view of the technological strength of the prospective companies.

Alternatively, a search in a patent database will more than likely reveal several possible candidates. For example, by searching patent databases such as Derwent's World Patent Index (which contains patents from 33 patent issuing authorities, or IFI/Plenum's U.S. Claims—United States only) using keywords or patent classification, or preferably a combination of both, Company X could obtain a set of all patents in the specified field. Depending on the print format requested and the files searched, lists can be generated containing company names (patent assignee) along with selected information regarding the patent holdings of the companies, such as patent numbers and the title of the patent, or the abstracts and/or claims of the actual patents.

Again depending on the database searched and the vendor used, it is possible to rank the results in the set obtained by company and number of patents, and in this manner obtain a clear picture of which companies are the most active patent-wise in the field of interest. Needless to say, the more patents a company has, the greater its potential worth.

The same method could be used to identify possible clients for your company's products. For example, if your company manufactures or markets a component that could be used for a variety of applications, what better way to home in on likely clients than by searching patent databases. Relevant companies can be identified by searching company information files using SIC (Standard Industrial Classification) codes or keywords, but by searching the patent files one can actually "get a feel" for the company's technology. Prospective clients could be given concrete examples of how your component could be incorporated into their products.

A broad search in patent databases could be used to identify technologies in which your company's product could serve as an integral part. For example, if your company manufactures a ball-bearing which can be used, among other things, as a replacement or alternative to a certain type of valve, then anyone who uses this valve, for whatever purpose, could be a potential client. Alternately, if one of your engineers just happened to know all the uses or instances in which your product or alternative products are used, then the search could be made for these technologies. Again, a list of patent titles would give you an idea as to whether you were on the right track, and company names could then be printed out either with or without further details of the patents.

6.1.2 Providing Background Information Prior to a Business Meeting

The number and nature of patents held by a company can also serve as an indication of both past, present, or future areas of development of a company, and is generally considered to be a good indicator of R & D trends within the company. This type of information can be of great value at the negotiating table, or merely as background information prior to a business meeting. As mentioned in section 6.1.1, the more patents a company has, the greater its potential worth. One should be aware, however, that not all patents are actually commercialized.

6.1.3 Facilitating Technology Transfer or Licensing in Place of In-house R & D

R & D budgets are not infinite. Why use precious resources trying to reinvent the wheel, when an online database search can often reveal just the technology you need? With this information (and sometimes a bit of extra footwork in order to establish the address of the patent assignee), one can contact the company and purchase rights to this specific know how/technology. In most cases, this expenditure is justified by the manpower and time saved, enabling the R & D team to concentrate on the *real* issues.

6.1.4 Identification of Experts in a Specific Field

If your company wants to develop or implement a specific technology, process, or product, why not contact a proven expert in the field by locating him or her in the patent databases? In this case, the inventor or author would be the right person to contact. For such a search, the relevant keywords could be keyed in and the search results typed out initially as titles. The most relevant titles could then be selected and printed in full format, to obtain information regarding the inventor. If details (apart from the actual name) are not available in that specific database, other databases which provide more detailed information can be accessed. Examples of such databases include (depending on the patent country) U.S. Claims, Fpat, and Epat, to name but a few. Information regarding the inventor can also be obtained by ordering the actual patent specification, or by accessing a suitable patent CD-ROM containing the desired information. The patent specification typically includes the name and address of the patent agent who handled the filing, through whom you can contact the inventor.

Once you have established the inventor's name, it is also possible (and often advisable) to check to see how many patents the inventor has, either in total, or in a specific field, in order to assure that the person you approach really is an expert. Obviously, this is not the sole criteria for locating an expert, but may serve as a stepping stone.

6.1.5 Establishing New Applications for Existing Technologies or Products

Examining what methods exist for achieving "X" might just provide food for thought or even a *eureka* reaction apropos your company's product/technology. If you already know that "X" can be substituted for "Y", identifying the instances (patents) in which "Y" appears might just provide a whole new variety of applications.

6.1.6 Identification of Marketing Trends

The country coverage of a patent usually gives a reasonably good indication of marketing intentions. A company will usually not apply for a patent in outer Mongolia if they have no intention of marketing there. However, marketing is not the sole reason for requesting patent protection, and this should be kept in mind at all times.

If something has been patented in countries 1, 2, 3, and 4, but not in countries 5 and 6, then it would be possible to manufacture and market this item in the latter two countries, although a patent could not be granted in these two countries. However, it would be considered an infringement in countries 1, 2, 3, and 4 if anyone other than the patent assignee or licensee marketed this product. The product could not be legally imported into countries 1, 2, 3, and 4, if manufactured in countries 5 or 6. Should this occur, it would be considered an infringement.

6.1.7 Establishing the Expiration Date of a Patent

Patent protection is usually granted for approximately 20 years from the date of filing, varying slightly from country to country. (In the United States, the term is 17 years from date of grant.) This protection may on occasion be extended, but generally speaking, once a patent expires it becomes *public domain* and can be used by anyone without payment of fees. The expiration date of a patent may therefore be of great interest to certain companies, and this generally can be established by searching patent databases. A word of warning—extensions are not included in most databases and therefore anyone with a specific interest in this aspect should consult a patent attorney before proceeding.

6.1.8 Identifying Potential Competitors

If your company is contemplating entering a certain field, patent databases can be used to identify potential competitors well in advance. Knowing who your potential competitors are enables you to take the next logical step, namely, finding out more about these companies.

6.1.9 Monitoring of Competitors

It is quite a simple matter to subscribe to a service that automatically informs you via electronic mail each time competitor XYZ is granted a new patent (which subsequently appears in a patent database). This is, in fact, a wonderful way of keeping up-to-date with regard to all topics, and not only specific companies or patent-related items.

6.1.10 Establishing the State of the Art

A subject search will serve as a good indicator of the state of the art and is also of great use in establishing the prior art, before writing a patent application.

6.1.11 Avoiding Future Infringement Suits

Most countries have an opposition period of a few months. If you suspect that a specific company is infringing your patent, the online *alert* system, whereby you are automatically notified via electronic mail (as discussed in section 6.1.9) each time your stipulated profile is updated, enables you to keep within the opposition deadline, thus enabling you to avoid future infringement suits. This is possible as new patents usually appear in online databases within weeks of having appeared in a country's Gazette.

6.2 STATISTICS

Certain databases offer the possibility (either with or without post-processing software) of performing statistical analyses on the sets obtained during a search. It is then quite easy to analyze the results. This may range from identifying the top ten countries in patenting electronics, to establishing which patent assignees are the main movers in each of these countries. The variety is endless, and the possibility of limiting a search to a specific time period, *i.e.,* 1990–1994, is also of great value.

6.3 SUMMARY

None of the above should be treated as clear-cut, but rather as a loose indication of the multitude of information available both in patents and patent databases. As in so many cases, it is not a matter of simply having the information but rather of what you do with it!

Article

7

HOW TO READ A PATENT

Marc D. Schechter

Marc D. Schechter is a Senior Attorney in the Intellectual Property
& Licensing Services department at International Business
Machines Corporation in Stamford, Connecticut.

The search is now done. With the aid of the tools described in the previous articles, the patent system has been navigated, and a number of patents of interest found. Now the task of reading and deriving intelligence from those patents must be addressed . . . a daunting task to the uninitiated.

The patent specification includes a variety of information: bibliographic and technological information and information of particular legal significance. There is, however, a basic logic to the structure and organization of a patent. Depending on the purpose for reviewing the patents, the information sought may be found by reviewing only a particular portion of the patent, rather than a complete analysis of the entire patent. The task of "wading through a pile of patents" can often be simplified by applying a basic understanding of the structure and organization of a patent.

The logic of the organization of a U.S. patent is apparent when the "contract theory" of the patent system is recalled. A patent is, in effect, an agreement between the government and the inventor. The inventor teaches the public how to make and use the invention in its preferred form and, in return, is granted a right to preclude unauthorized manufacture, use, and sale of the invention for up to 17 years from the date the patent is granted. This is reflected in the organization of the patent specification. In addition to bibliographic data, there are two major parts: the written description of the invention and the claims.

- *The written description is the consideration provided by the inventor to the public for the patent grant—a description of the best version of the invention contemplated by the inventor, in sufficient detail that the average person working in the relevant field of technology can make and use the invention. As discussed in the following article, the written description typically includes a number of defined subparts.*
- *The claims define the rights of the inventor. In essence, a claim is a one sentence definition of the invention (or specific aspects of the invention). An unauthorized product infringes a patent if it includes the equivalent of each and every element of any of the claims.*

There are many reasons to read a patent. Depending on the reader's purpose, the written description or the claims will have primary significance. For example, if the is-

sue at hand is the patentability of an invention over a prior patent, the analysis should be focused on the teachings of the written description of the prior patent, not its claims. On the other hand, if the issue is whether a product might infringe the prior patent, the initial analysis would focus on the patent claims. The issue is not whether the product is the same as that described in the written description of the patent, but rather is whether the product includes the equivalent of each and every element of the claims.

A word of caution is in order. Patent infringement is serious business, the consequences potentially dire. Interpretation of patent claims is an arcane art. The claims must be interpreted in the light of the complete patent document and the history of correspondence with the Patent and Trademark Office leading to the grant of the patent. Technological distinctions that are very real to the engineer or scientist may not be reflected in the claims or might even be meaningless in a patent law context. If there is any inkling of a potential infringement problem, it cannot be ignored. Even if the company's employees are convinced in their own minds that there is in fact no infringement, it still may be necessary to have a formal opinion from patent counsel as to invalidity/noninfringement in the file, just in case. If a company is found to infringe a patent of which it is aware, and did not obtain the opinion of a competent patent attorney, the infringement will likely be considered willful, and the company could be liable for treble damages and the patentee's attorney's fees. The issue of infringement is discussed in later sections of the book.

The following articles provide a map to the typical patent specification, and to the interpretation of patent claims, and discuss the nature of the exclusive rights afforded by a patent grant.   MAL

Abstract

In addition to defining the scope of exclusive rights to an invention, patents also provide a source of valuable technical information. This article will describe the types of information that can be found in U.S. patents and will introduce the reader to interpreting claims and the scope of the patent grant.

7.1 WHY READ A PATENT?

It has been said that reading a patent is about as enjoyable as reading the fine print in your homeowner's insurance policy. Some have chimed in that reading a patent is about as exciting as reading a quarterly financial statement. Household budgeteers have observed that browsing a patent is nearly as relaxing as perusing the pages of your monthly credit card statement.

Couch potatoes have been heard complaining that understanding a patent is more difficult than understanding the operating instructions for their video cassette recorders. On the other hand, supporters contend that a patent is easier to comprehend than the instructions for filling out a federal income tax return. Not to be forgotten, literary critics have alleged that studying a patent is about as intellectually stimulating as poring over an eye chart.

So why should you bother with such a document?

There are at least several reasons for reviewing patent literature. One motivation for studying patents is to understand the current and prior state of technology. Prior to undertaking a technical investigation or product development, a careful review of patents and other literature can help you to learn what others have already achieved, to avoid repeating work that has already been performed by others. You might also need to know the prior state of the art in order to assess the patentability of an invention, or to assess the validity of a previously issued patent.

Patents and other technical articles complement each other for at least two reasons. In general, papers published in periodicals will become available at an earlier date than patents. In the case of U.S. patent applications, a patent may not issue until 18 months or more after the patent application filing date. Foreign patent applications are generally published 18 months after the filing date of the first-filed counterpart patent application.

On the other hand, while patents and published patent applications are less current than periodicals, patents often describe more complete implementation details and more variations of an idea than do periodicals. Journal articles frequently report only information directly relevant to the specific investigation performed and the specific results obtained. It is assumed that the reader can fill in missing ancillary information.

Another important reason to read patents is to determine whether your patents cover competing products. A competing product may not reach the market until long after a patent issues. At that time, you will need to reassess the scope of your patent coverage.

Conversely, it also is important to read patents to determine whether your products infringe patents owned by others. If you can identify potential patent problems before you begin making and selling a new product, and if an infringing product design is only one of several acceptable choices, you may be able to select an alternative configuration to avoid an infringement claim. On the other hand, if the infringing arrangement is your preferred design, you may be able to negotiate a favorable patent license while noninfringing options remain available, prior to committing yourself to manufacturing an infringing product design.

Patents are merely one source of information available for evaluating the state of the art, patentability, and patent validity. However, they are the sole source of information for determining whether someone owns exclusive rights to make, use, and sell a valuable product or process.

7.2 THE BASIC PARTS OF A PATENT

There are three types of patents available under the laws of the United States: (1) utility patents, (2) plant patents, and (3) design patents. Utility patents are available to cover processes, machines, articles of manufacture, and compositions of matter [1]. Plant patents may cover asexually reproduced plants, other than a tuber propagated plant or a plant found in an uncultivated state [2]. Design patents are available to cover ornamental designs for articles of manufacture [3]. This manuscript will be limited to a discussion of utility patents.

A U.S. patent contains a short title of the invention and a grant to the patentee of the right to exclude others from making, using, and selling the invention throughout the United

States for 17 years (subject to payment of maintenance fees). In addition, a copy of the specification and drawings from the patent application are annexed to the patent and are made a part thereof [4].

Figure 1 shows an example of the formal patent grant with the seal of the U.S. Patent and Trademark Office. Only the original issued U.S. patent contains the formal patent grant. Copies of a patent normally omit this page.

The specification of a U.S. patent contains a written description of the invention and the manner and process of using the invention. The description also must include an account of the best and preferred implementation of the invention of which the patentee is aware at the time the patent application is filed. The specification culminates with one or more claims. The patent claims provide a yardstick for determining the metes and bounds of the subject matter that constitutes infringement of the patent, and for determining the residual subject matter that does not [5].

Not every patent has a drawing, although most do. A drawing is required only when necessary for understanding the subject matter sought to be patented, or when the nature of the subject matter is capable of illustration by a drawing [6]. The drawing of a U.S. patent facilitates an understanding of the invention by showing every feature of the invention specified in the claims [7].

7.3 FIRST PATENT PAGE

All U.S. patents, and most foreign patents and foreign published patent applications, contain a cover page bearing useful information. Figure 2 is an example of a cover page from a U.S. patent.

As shown in Figure 2, the cover page includes such data as the title of the invention, an abstract of the technical disclosure, the names of the inventors, the name of the assignee, and more. Each item of information on the cover page is preceded or followed by a number in brackets. These numbers are called INID codes. (INID is an acronym for Internationally agreed Numbers for the Identification of Data.) The INID codes were developed by an organization of examining patent offices known as ICIREPAT (the Paris Union Committee for International Cooperation in Information Retrieval among Patent Offices) in order to identify bibliographic data appearing on the first page of a patent without knowledge of the language used or the laws applied [8].

Some useful INID codes are listed in Table 1. A complete enumeration of the INID codes can be found in Reference 8.

7.4 THE PATENT SPECIFICATION

The specification is generally organized into the following sections.

- Title
- Abstract

The Commissioner of Patents and Trademarks

Has received an application for a patent for a new and useful invention. The title and description of the invention are enclosed. The requirements of law have been complied with, and it has been determined that a patent on the invention shall be granted under the law.

Therefore, this

United States Patent

Grants to the person or persons having title to this patent the right to exclude others from making, using or selling the invention throughout the United States of America for the term of seventeen years from the date of this patent, subject to the payment of maintenance fees as provided by law.

Acting Commissioner of Patents and Trademarks

Attest

Figure 1   Example of a formal U.S. patent grant

US005233681A

United States Patent [19]

Bahl et al.

[11] Patent Number:	5,233,681
[45] Date of Patent:	Aug. 3, 1993

[54] **CONTEXT-DEPENDENT SPEECH RECOGNIZER USING ESTIMATED NEXT WORD CONTEXT**

[75] Inventors: Lalit R. Bahl, Amawalk; Peter V. De Souza, Mahopac Falls; Ponani S. Gopalakrishnan, Croton-on-Hudson; Michael A. Picheny, White Plains, all of N.Y.

[73] Assignee: International Business Machines Corporation, Armonk, N.Y.

[21] Appl. No.: 874,271

[22] Filed: Apr. 24, 1992

[51] Int. Cl.⁵ G10L 91/00
[52] U.S. Cl. 395/2; 381/43; 381/41
[58] Field of Search 381/41, 43, 51; 395/2

[56] **References Cited**

U.S. PATENT DOCUMENTS

4,748,670	5/1988	Bahl et al.	381/43
4,751,737	6/1988	Gerson et al.	381/43
4,759,068	7/1988	Bahl et al.	381/43
4,783,804	11/1988	Juang et al.	381/43
4,977,599	12/1990	Bahl et al.	381/43
4,980,918	12/1990	Bahl et al.	381/113
5,033,087	7/1991	Bahl et al.	381/43
5,054,074	10/1991	Bakis	381/43
5,072,452	12/1991	Brown et al.	381/43
5,129,001	7/1992	Bahl et al.	381/43
5,131,043	7/1992	Fujii et al.	381/43

OTHER PUBLICATIONS

Bahl, L. R., et al. "Context Dependent Modeling of Phones in Continuous Speech Using Decision Trees", pp. 264–269.
Bahl, L. R., et al. "A Maximum Likelihood Approach to Continuous Speech Recognition", IEEE Transactions On Pattern Analysis and Machine Intelligence, vol. PAMI–5, No. 2 Mar. 1983, V33, N9, Feb. 1991, pp. 179–190.
Bahl, L. R., "Speech Recognition Apparatus Having a Speech Coder Outputting Acoustic Prototype Ranks,"

U.S. Patent Application Ser. No. 781,440, filed Oct. 23, 1992.
Bahl, L. R. et al. "Apparatus and Method of Grouping Utterances of a Phoneme Into Context–Dependent Categories Based on Sound–Similarity for Automatic Speech Recognition," U.S. Pat. Application Ser. No. 468,546, filed Jan. 23, 1990.

Primary Examiner—Michael R. Fleming
Assistant Examiner—Tariq R. Hafie
Attorney, Agent, or Firm—Marc D. Schechter

[57] **ABSTRACT**

A speech recognition apparatus and method estimates the next word context for each current candidate word in a speech hypothesis. An initial model of each speech hypothesis comprises a model of a partial hypothesis of zero or more words followed by a model of a candidate word. An initial hypothesis score for each speech hypothesis comprises an estimate of the closeness of a match between the initial model of the speech hypothesis and a sequence of coded representations of the utterance. The speech hypotheses having the best initial hypothesis scores form an initial subset. For each speech hypothesis in the initial subset, the word which is most likely to follow the speech hypothesis is estimated. A revised model of each speech hypothesis in the initial subset comprises a model of the partial hypothesis followed by a revised model of the candidate word. The revised candidate word model is dependent at least on the word which is estimated to be most likely to follow the speech hypothesis. A revised hypothesis score for each speech hypothesis in the initial subset comprises an estimate of the closeness of a match between the revised model of the speech hypothesis and the sequence of coded representations of the utterance. The speech hypotheses from the initial subset which have the best revised match scores are stored as a reduced subset. At least one word of one or more of the speech hypotheses in the reduced subset is output as a speech recognition result.

31 Claims, 3 Drawing Sheets

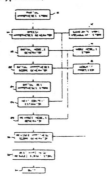

Figure 2   Example of the first page of a United States patent

Table 1 INID Codes

INID CODE	BIBLIOGRAPHIC DATA
11	Number of the Document
19	Identification of the Office publishing the document
21	Domestic application number
22	Date of filing of domestic application
51	International patent classification
52	Domestic or national patent classification
54	Title of the Invention
56	List of prior art documents
57	Abstract or Claim
73	Name of Grantee
75	Names of inventors who are also applicants

- Background
- Summary of the Invention
- Brief Description of the Drawing
- Detailed Description
- Claims

The *title* of the patent appears on the front page of the patent with INID Code 54. The patent title is intended to be a brief description of the invention to which the patent claims are directed. By providing patents with descriptive titles, it is hoped that the titles can aid classifying and searching [9]. In many cases, however, the title is too short and too general to hint at the subject matter that is claimed.

The *abstract* also appears on the front page of the patent. The INID code for the abstract is 57. Like the title, the abstract is intended to provide information useful for searching. The abstract should enable the reader to quickly pinpoint the principal technical disclosure of the patent, making it possible for the reader to decide whether the patent is likely to contain the information being searched for.

In order to induce patent applicants to write an abstract that summarizes the technical disclosure of the patent (as distinguished from summarizing the claimed subject matter), the U.S. Patent and Trademark Office rules provide the assurance that the abstract is not to be used to interpret the scope of the patent claims [10].

The *background* section of the patent starts with a description of the general field of technology to which the invention relates. Thereafter, the background section describes the specific details of the prior state of the art that are most relevant to the patented invention. These details may include references to prior patents and publications and an analysis of the problems encountered in the prior art that are alleviated by the patented invention.

The information provided in the background section of an issued patent is useful for assessing the known prior state of the art. The background section may be relied upon, alone or with other information, to evaluate the patentability of an invention, or to evaluate the validity of another patent.

Importantly, the subject matter described in the background of the invention is often considered by the U.S. Patent and Trademark Office and by the courts to be prior art, which the inventors and the patent owner have admitted as such. Consequently, if the claims in a patent are ambiguous (perish the thought), an understanding of the prior state of the art and the problems of the prior art as described in the background section may provide clues for deducing what subject matter is not within the scope of the patent claims.

The scope of the exclusive rights granted to the owner of a patent are principally determined by the patent claims. However, a synopsis of the patent claims can be found in the summary of the invention section of the patent. The *summary* is intended to succinctly state the nature, operation, and purpose of the invention, to provide the reader with a basis for making an approximate assessment of the patent coverage [11]. The summary also portrays the motivations that led to the invention. These motivations are generally characterized as the "objects" of the invention. The U.S. Patent and Trademark Office rules state that the "objects" should be those of the invention as specified in the patent claims [12].

An individual patent is often a lengthy document addressing a multitude of subissues and subtopics related to the invention. If you do not have either the time or the desire to read the entire patent, you may want to summarily identify the portions of the patent discussing the subtopics of interest to you. Often, it is possible to target these kernels by reading the brief description of the drawing section of a patent. The *brief description* of the drawing may direct you to one or more drawing figures illustrating the feature of concern. If the figure appears to be relevant, the discussion of the figure can be rapidly found in the written description by scanning for the figure number preceded by the abbreviation "FIG.". References to Figures always are printed in boldface type in U.S. patents.

Immediately following the brief description of the drawing, descriptions of specific embodiments or examples of the invention are elaborated in the detailed description section of the patent. The *detailed description* delineates the structure of one or more embodiments of the invention, referring to the drawing to enhance the reader's understanding of the text. The detailed description section also explains how to make and use the invention. The level of particularity provided in the detailed description will be sufficient to enable a person skilled in the technology to make and use the invention. However, it will not be as detailed as a production specification [13].

The detailed description does not directly determine the scope of a patent. A patent's coverage is based primarily on the patent claims. However, the interpretation of a patent claim is dependent, in part, on the detailed description of the invention [14].

For example, the scope of a patent *claim* may be indirectly dependent on the detailed description if one or more claim elements are characterized as a means or step for performing a function.

> [If] an element in a claim is expressed as a means or step for performing a specified function without the recital of structure, material, or acts in support thereof, . . . [then] such

claim shall be construed to cover the corresponding structure, material, or acts described in the specification and equivalents thereof [15].

In addition, the detailed description provides substance to the otherwise abstract terms and phrases often used in patent claims. Each claim element must find clear support or antecedent basis in the *description* [16].

7.5 THE PATENT CLAIMS

A U.S. patent grants the patent owner the right to exclude others from making, using, or selling the patented invention throughout the United States for 17 years (subject to payment of maintenance fees) [17]. The subject matter covered by the patent is precisely defined in the patent claims. If there are several patent claims, they will be numbered consecutively [18].

As a purely legal matter, the interpretation of the claims of a U.S. patent is solely within the power of the U.S. courts [19]. Nevertheless, a business person must understand the meaning of patent claims in order to assess the risk of infringing a patent owned by another, or in order to assess the likelihood that his or her patent is infringed. Since the courts are not available to provide advisory opinions of this type, an attorney should be consulted for an opinion on how a court is likely to interpret patent claims.

In today's competitive worldwide economy, a business person may seek alternatives to hiring expensive attorneys to examine large numbers of patents to decide which are of interest and which are not. As one might expect, in any study of a large number of patents, the probability is high that most of the patents' claims will not be relevant to the product or process being sold or produced. Therefore, it will often be desirable to have a nonlawyer, such as a member of the product design team, perform a preliminary assessment of the patents to decide whether an attorney's opinion should be sought, and if so for which patents. It is for this purpose that the remainder of this paper will provide guidance to the nonlawyer for interpreting patent claims.

7.6 STRUCTURE OF A PATENT CLAIM

Essentially all patent claims contain a preamble, a transition, and a body [20]. Examples I through VII show several sample patent claims and their constituent parts.

EXAMPLE I

preamble	An optical device for continuous control of light transmission
transition	comprising:
body	electro-optical cell means including liquid crystal means having positive dielectric anisotropy disposed between two spaced plates, at least one of which plates is transparent and each plate being electrically conductive at a surface facing said liquid crystal means;

said plates being wall-oriented to cause said liquid crystal means to define a twisted structure in the direction perpendicular to the plates;

polarizing means disposed one before and one behind the liquid crystal means, in the direction of light traveling through the cell means; and

electrical means connected to the plates for controlling the twisted structure of said liquid crystal means [21].

EXAMPLE II

preamble	A pyroelectric target
transition	comprising:
body	a pyroelectric material having a pyroelectric axis, said material being anisotropic dielectrically and having two faces which are substantially planar and which are substantially parallel to each other, said faces being provided with electrodes, characterized in that the angle between the pyroelectric axis and a normal to the planar faces is greater than substantially 0° but less than 90° [22].

EXAMPLE III

preamble	An electroluminescent display system
transition	comprising:
body	a first array of parallel conductors; a second array of parallel conductors forming a grid with said first array of parallel conductors;

an electroluminescent phosphor film interposed between the conductors in said arrays;

a delay line, the conductors in said first array being coupled to said delay line at spaced intervals therealong;

means for sequentially applying lines of information signals to be displayed to one end of said delay line; and

means for sequentially and momentarily energizing the conductors in said second array, said means for sequentially and momentarily energizing the conductors in said second array energizing one of said conductors at a time when a complete line of information signal appears in said delay line between the first and last conductors in said first array coupled therealong, and energizing said one conductor in said second array for only a small fraction of the time required for a signal to travel through said delay line [23].

EXAMPLE IV

preamble	A magnetic domain system
transition	comprising:
body	a magnetic medium in which said domains exist, said medium being an amorphous magnetic material without long range atomic ordering having long range magnetic ordering and a magnetic uniaxial anisotropy which is not due to long range crystalline structure, and means for sensing said domains in said amorphous magnetic medium [24].

EXAMPLE V

preamble	A composite, porous, thermal insulation panel characterized by dimensional stability and structural strength
transition	consisting essentially of
body	expanded perlite particles which are interbonded one to another by interfusion between the surfaces of the perlite particles while in a pyroplastic state to form a porous perlite panel [25].

EXAMPLE VI

preamble	An alloy or intimate mixture
transition	consisting of
body	silver and a measurable amount of indium, with the silver content predominating [26].

EXAMPLE VII

preamble	A method of producing an optical fiber
transition	comprising the steps of
body	providing a glass tube, forming a film or core glass, having an index of refraction different than that of said glass tube, on the inside wall of said glass tube,

heating the composite structure so formed to the drawing temperature of the materials thereof, and

drawing the heated composite structure to reduce the cross-sectional area thereof and collapse said film of core glass to form a fiber having a solid cross-sectional area [27]. |

7.6.1 Preamble

The *preamble* provides the reader with a frame of reference for the elements of the invention. At a minimum, the preamble defines the category of the invention and the field covered by the claim. The categories of patentable inventions are processes, machines, articles of manufacture, and compositions of matter.

Examples I to V illustrate machines and articles of manufacture. Example VI illustrates a composition of matter. Example VII illustrates a patented process.

As further explained below with reference to Example VIII, when the subject matter of an invention is an improvement over a prior combination, the claim preamble may, in addition to defining the category and field of the invention, describe the known elements or steps of the prior combination.

7.6.2 Body of the Claim

In order to understand the significance of the claim transition, it is first necessary to comment on the *body of the claim.* The body of the claim describes the combination of components or elements that form the patented invention. For each element of the invention, the body of the claim describes the features, characteristics, and constituents of that element.

The combination of elements listed in the body of the claim is more than just a catalog or aggregation of distinct parts. Along with each element of the invention, the body of the claim describes the relationships between that component of the claim and the other claim elements.

For a product, process, or composition of matter to be covered by a patent claim, the potentially infringing object must contain each and every element recited in the body of the claim and in the preamble of the claim. Each component of the potentially infringing object that corresponds to an element of the claim must have all of the claimed features and characteristics of that corresponding element. The combination of the components must contain all of the relationships specified in the patent claim.

Thus, every limitation in a claim is material and must be met by an accused product or process to establish patent infringement [28]. Subject to the *doctrine of equivalents*, discussed below, if one claim element is missing, the claimed invention is not infringed; if one claimed feature or characteristic is missing, the claimed invention is not infringed; if a claimed relationship is not present, the claimed invention is not infringed.

7.6.3 Transition

The question may arise, "if the potentially infringing object contains all of the elements, characteristics, features, and relationships of the patent claim, but also contains additional elements, characteristics, features, and relationships, does the claim cover the potentially infringing object?". The answer to this question depends on the words used in the transition of the claim.

As shown in Examples I to VII, the preamble of a claim is usually followed by words such as "comprising", "consisting of", or "consisting essentially of". These *transition terms* inform the reader that the patented invention is a combination of the subject matter that follows in the body of the claim. In U.S. patent practice, these transition terms have assumed special meanings.

7.6.3a "comprising"

The most common transitional word from the preamble to the body of the claim is "comprising". When a claim states that an invention "comprises" a number of elements or components, the claim is interpreted as covering products or processes that contain the recited elements, and that also may contain other constituents or process steps in addition to those recited [29]. The word "comprising" is thus interpreted as meaning "including, but not limited to". A claim using the transitional word comprising is often described as open ended.

Thus, in Example I above, the optical device "comprises" an electro-optical cell, polarizing means, and electrical means. Since the claim is open ended, it also will cover an optical device having an electro-optical cell, polarizing means, and electrical means (with the features and characteristics specified in the claim), and also containing a color filter between the electro-optical cell and the polarizing means.

Similarly, if an element of a claim "comprises" a number of components and features, the claim element is interpreted as including the recited components and features, but not excluding other components and features in addition to those recited.

7.6.3b "consisting of"

On the other hand, when a claim states that an invention "consists of" a number of components, the claim is interpreted as covering products that contain solely and exclusively the recited elements, without other constituents or process steps except for impurities ordinarily associated with the recited elements [30]. A claim using the word "consisting" is described as closed.

In Example VI above, the alloy consists of silver and indium. Since the Claim is closed, it will not cover an alloy of silver, indium, and tin.

7.6.3c "consisting essentially of"

A middle ground between "comprising" and "consisting of" is obtained with the transition "consisting essentially of". (See Example V above.) When a claimed invention or an element of a claimed invention specifies that it "consists essentially of" one or more components, the courts and the U.S. Patent and Trademark Office interpret the claim as including other unspecified constituents that do not "affect the basic and novel characteristics" of the invention defined in the balance of the claim [31].

To determine the nature of these characteristics, one must pay heed to the remainder of the patent specification.

Thus, in the claim of Example V, it was held that the novel characteristic of the invention was that perlite particles were held together without additional material. The claim language "consisting essentially of" excluded the additional materials taught by the prior art for chemically bonding perlite particles together. Therefore, the claim was patentable over the prior art.

7.6.3d "wherein the improvement comprises" (Jepson claims)

When the subject matter of an invention is an improvement over a prior combination, the claim preamble may describe the known elements or steps of the prior combination, and the body may describe those elements, steps, characteristics, and relationships that are new [32]. The transition between the preamble and the body may contain a transitional phrase such as "wherein the improvement comprises", "characterized in that the improvement comprises", or other language describing the relationship between the claim preamble and the claim body. Example VIII illustrates such a claim.

EXAMPLE VIII

preamble   In an electrical system of distribution of the class wherein a variable speed generator charges a storage battery and when the battery becomes sufficiently charged a voltage coil becomes effective to regulate the generator for constant potential,

transition   the combination with said voltage coil of

body   a coil traversed by current flowing to the battery which is acted upon by decreasing battery current to reduce the potential maintained constant by the voltage coil [33].

If the transitional language states or implies that the combination of elements or steps described in the preamble were known in the prior art, then the patentee is irrevocably bound by this admission [34].

7.6.3e "means for"

In the body of a patent claim, each element or component of the product or process of the invention is identified, and its characteristics and relationships to the other elements are described. If an element has a common name, it can be identified by that name. As shown in Example III above, elements of the invention having common names are "conductors", "an electroluminescent phosphor film", and a delay line. Components of the invention that do not have common names can be identified as "means for" performing a described function [35]. In Example III above, elements of the invention that do not have common names are "means for sequentially applying lines of information signals . . .", and "means for sequentially and momentarily energizing. . . .".

A claim element described as a means for performing a described function is deemed to cover the specific embodiments of the element that are explicitly described in the patent application. In addition, the means further covers alternative embodiments that are equivalent to those explicitly described.

[If] an element in a claim is expressed as a means or step for performing a specified function without the recital of structure, material, or acts in support thereof, . . . [then] such claim shall be construed to cover the corresponding structure, material, or acts described in the specification and equivalents thereof. [36]

However, the claim element does not cover all alternatives having the same or equivalent function; the claim only covers structural equivalents [37].

7.6.3f "selected from the group consisting of" (Markush claims)

As described in the previous section, a structural component can be identified by its common name. If the structural component has no common name, it can be identified as a "means for" performing a described function.

If a component of an invention is a composition of matter, it is sometimes the case that one or more materials may be acceptable alternatives for that component of the invention. If the group of alternative materials has a common name, then that name may be used in the claim to identify the group. In Example II above, a class of materials is referred to as pyroelectric materials. In Example III, a class of materials is identified as electroluminescent phosphor. In Example IV, an amorphous magnetic material is recited.

In other instances, however, there is no generic name for a class of materials. In that case, the patentee may define a group of constituents within the claim [38]. Example IX illustrates this technique.

EXAMPLE IX

material selected from the group consisting of aniline, homologues of aniline and halogen substitutes of aniline [39].

In this Example, any one or more of the listed compounds satisfy the claimed material component of the invention.

7.6.3g "multiplicity", "plurality"

When a patent claim comprises, in part, a plurality or a multiplicity of a recited element having specified characteristics, the claim only covers subject matter having two or more of that element having the described characteristics. Thus, in Example X below, an infringing process must utilize two or more conductors arranged substantially parallel to one another (in combination with the other constituents of the claim).

EXAMPLE X

preamble	A process of encapsulating a semiconductor device
transition	comprising:
body	providing electrical connections between electrical terminals of the device and a plurality of conductors arranged substantially parallel to one another, said device and the thusly provided electrical connections thereto being provided on one side of said conductors, disposing the device and portions of the conductors in a mold cavity, and holding the conductors while injecting a fluid insulating material into the mold cavity for subsequently solidifying and embedding said device, the fluid insulating material being injected into a portion of the cavity on the opposite side of said conductors to preclude direct high velocity engagement between the fluid and the device and the electrical connections thereto [40].

In *Texas Instruments v. International Trade Commission* [41], the International Trade Commission (ITC) construed the claim of Example X above as requiring all of the two or more conductors used to be arranged parallel to one another. While the claim alone might be construed as requiring at least two (but not necessarily all) conductors to be arranged parallel to each other, the ITC based its interpretation on not only the language of the claim, but also on the specification, the drawing, and witness testimony.

7.6.3h "substantially"

Precision in language involves an inherent trade off with brevity. The more concise a statement, the less definite its meaning. Conversely, a clearer description of an idea or concept requires a fuller and therefore more prolific composition.

An example of the balance between precision and brevity in patent claims involves the use of the term "substantially". In Example II above, the claim contains the terms "substantially planar", "substantially parallel", and "substantially 0°". In order to determine the meaning of "substantially", it may be necessary to understand the context of the invention as described in the entire specification [42]. Moreover, each occurrence of "substantially" may have a different meaning.

7.7 DEPENDENT CLAIMS

In order to encourage efficiency in both writing and interpreting patent claims, the U.S. patent laws permit both independent and dependent claims [43]. An independent claim stands on its own, without reference to any other claim. All of Examples I to VII above are independent claims.

A dependent claim contains a reference to one or more previous claims. It is construed to incorporate by reference all of the features of the claim to which it refers [44]. Thus, the following dependent claim requires all of the steps of the claim of Example VII, as well as the additional feature of the dependent claim.

EXAMPLE XI

The method of [Example VII] wherein the film of core glass is formed by chemical vapor deposition [45].

A dependent claim which refers to more than one prior claim is called a multiple dependent claim. It may refer to prior claims in the alternative only, as in "A method as claimed in claim 1, 2, or 3 . . ." [46].

A multiple dependent claim is separately construed for each previous claim to which it refers. A single multiple dependent claim which depends from a number N of prior claims is thus a shorthand for writing N separate single-dependent claims each depending individually from only one of the prior claims.

The validity of each claim of a patent is independent of the validity or invalidity of each other claim [47]. Thus, a dependent claim may be valid, even though it depends from an invalid claim. A multiple dependent claim may be valid to the extent it is based on one parent claim, but may be invalid to the extent it depends from another parent claim.

However, since a dependent claim contains all of the features of its parent claim plus additional features recited in the dependent claim, if the dependent claim is invalid, the parent claim is typically invalid too.

7.8 PRODUCT-BY-PROCESS CLAIMS

Ordinarily, a patent claim drawn to a machine, an article of manufacture, or a composition of matter describes the subject matter of the invention by identifying the elements or constituents and their features, characteristics, and relationships to each other. However, sometimes the structure and properties of a product may depend on the process by which it is made. Moreover, it may not be known or feasible to describe the structural differences between the invention and similar products made by other processes. In these cases, the invention may be claimed as a *product-by-process* [48].

Example XII below illustrates a product-by-process claim.

EXAMPLE XII

Shakes manufactured from a shake bolt by the process of making a plurality of cuts into and across the shake bolt to an extent to establish predetermined tip lengths, and splitting the weather end portions of the shakes from the bolt by starting the splits at the inner ends of the cuts and continuing the splits to the end of the bolt [49].

Process limitations in product-by-process claims are required elements of the invention. A similar product made by a process different from the process specified in a product-by-process claim is not covered by the product-by-process claim [50].

7.9 TRAPS FOR THE UNWARY

The U.S. Patent and Trademark Office regulations require that patent applications be written in the English language or be accompanied by a verified English language translation [51]. However, while the written description must be in terms that are "full, clear, concise, and exact" to a "person skilled in the art," there is no requirement that the patent application or the translation be written in "plain English", such as some states have mandated for insurance policies, home and automobile loans, and other consumer contracts [52].

Claims are interpreted in light of the claim language, the specification, and the prosecution history (see below) [53]. Even when the meaning of a claim appears to be clear on its face, the claim may in fact have a different meaning arising out of statements made in the specification, or arising out of actions taken by the applicant during the examination of the patent application.

When the meaning of a term is ambiguous, it may be necessary to look to the remainder of the patent specification and drawing in order to define the term [54]. It also may be necessary to consult sources outside of the patent in the technology to which the invention relates to discover the meaning of a term [55]. Even more burdensome for the reader, if there is a conflict between the definition of a word in a general lay dictionary and either the definition of the word in the technology or a special definition provided in the patent specification, the general dictionary definition yields to the latter [56].

Consequently, when reading a patent claim, one cannot always rely on the expectation that the words used in the claim will have their ordinary meanings.

7.10 DOCTRINE OF EQUIVALENTS

In deciding whether a product or process infringes a patent claim, the initial determination is based on the actual claim language. If the product or process is literally covered by the patent claim, then infringement has generally been established.

On the other hand, if the accused product or process does not fall within the scope of the actual wording of the claim, one cannot automatically conclude that there is no infringement. In this situation, it must be determined whether the accused product or process is equivalent to the claimed invention under the doctrine of equivalents, and therefore constitutes an infringement of the claim under that doctrine.

> . . . courts have also recognized that to permit imitation of a patented invention which does not copy every literal detail would be to convert the protection of the patent grant into a hollow and useless thing. Such a limitation would leave room for—indeed encourage—the unscrupulous copyist to make unimportant and insubstantial changes and substitutions in the patent which, though adding nothing, would be enough to take the copied matter outside the claim, and hence outside the reach of the law. One who seeks to pirate an invention, like one who seeks to pirate a copyrighted book or play, may be expected to introduce minor variations to conceal and shelter the piracy. Outright and forthright duplication is a dull and very rare type of infringement. To prohibit no other would place the inventor at the mercy of verbalism and would be subordinating substance to form. [57].

The doctrine of equivalents provides that an accused product or process is equivalent to a claimed invention, and therefore infringes the patent claim, if the product or process performs substantially the same function in substantially the same way to obtain the same result. These issues of equivalency are to be decided in the context of the patent itself, and the prior state of the art.

In *Graver Tank & Mfg. Co., Inc. v. The Linde Air Products Company* [58], the patent claimed, in essence, an electric welding flux having a combination of alkaline earth metal silicate such as magnesium silicate and calcium fluoride. The accused welding flux substituted manganese silicate (manganese not being an alkaline earth metal) for magnesium silicate, to avoid literal infringement. The court noted that experts testified that manganese and magnesium were similar in many chemical reactions, and that they serve the same purpose in the flux. The expert testimony was corroborated by recognized textbooks on inorganic chemistry. Consequently, the manganese silicate in the accused flux was determined to be equivalent to the claimed alkaline earth metal silicate.

As stated previously, if a product or process is literally covered by a patent claim, then infringement has generally been established. One instance when this general rule is not true involves the reverse application of the doctrine of equivalents. That is, if the principle of operation of an accused product or process differs significantly from the patented invention, so that the accused subject matter performs substantially the same function in a substantially different way, the accused product will not be considered equivalent to the claimed invention. In that case, the patent claim will not be infringed, despite the existence of literal infringement of the claim.

7.11 PROSECUTION HISTORY ESTOPPEL

Before a patent is granted, the U.S. Patent and Trademark Office examines the patent application to ascertain whether it meets all of the requirements under the patent laws. One such requirement is that the invention must be new and nonobvious in view of the state of the art prior to the date the invention was made [59].

During the course of examination, the Patent and Trademark Office examiner may, in part, reject the patent application as being either fully described in the prior art, or as being an obvious variation of the prior art. In response to such a rejection, the applicant may amend the claims and make legal and factual arguments to refute the rejection. These patent application proceedings before the Patent and Trademark Office are called the *prosecution history*. The Patent and Trademark Office's written record of the prosecution history is called a file wrapper. Copies of the file wrappers of unexpired U.S. patents are available to the public [60].

The doctrine of prosecution history estoppel or file wrapper estoppel prevents a patentee from asserting that a patent claim covers an accused product or process if two requirements are met. First, the patentee must have amended the claim or made legal or factual arguments during the prosecution of the patent application which restrict the patent claim from covering the accused product or process. Second, the amendment or remarks must have been made in order to overcome a rejection over the prior art [61]. Prosecution history estoppel may be applied to prevent the patentee from invoking the doctrine of equivalents [62], or as an aid to construing the meanings of terms used in the claim [63].

For example in *Welch v. General Motors*, [64] during prosecution of the patent application, the patentees' attorney argued that the invention could be distinguished from the prior art by the fact that shims, present in the invention, were lacking in the prior art. The court held that the patentees were prevented from asserting that the defendant's device, which has no shims, is infringing under the doctrine of equivalents.

7.12 CONCLUSION

At a minimum, it is hoped that this introduction to reading and understanding patents and interpreting patent claims puts a less intimidating face on patents. Even better, it is hoped that these guidelines will make patents more useful and interesting to the reader.

One final word of caution: know your limits. With your new knowledge comes a responsibility to recognize those instances when you do not have the expertise to understand

and interpret a patent and patent claim. In those situations, you should seek out and obtain competent legal counsel.

NOTES

[1]   Title 35, United States Code, Section 101.

[2]   Title 35, United States Code, Section 161.

[3]   Title 35, United States Code, Section 171.

[4]   Title 35, United States Code, Sections 111 and 154.

[5]   Title 35, United States Code, Section 112, second paragraph.

[6]   Title 35, United States Code, Section 113. Title 37, Code of Federal Regulations, Section 1.81.

[7]   Title 37, Code of Federal Regulations, Section 1.83.

[8]   *Manual of Patent Examining Procedure*, Fifth Edition, Revision 14, November 1992, U.S. Department of Commerce, Patent and Trademark Office, Sections 901.4 and 901.5.

[9]   *Manual of Patent Examining Procedure*, Fifth Edition, Revision 14, November 1992, U.S. Department of Commerce, Patent and Trademark Office, Sections 606 and 606.01.

[10]   Title 37, Code of Federal Regulations, Section 1.72.

[11]   *Manual of Patent Examining Procedure*, Fifth Edition, Revision 14, November 1992, U.S. Department of Commerce, Patent and Trademark Office, Sections 608.01(d).

[12]   Title 37, Code of Federal Regulations, Section 1.73.

[13]   *In re Gay*, 309 F.2d 768, 135 USPQ 311 (CCPA 1962).

[14]   *Intel Corp. v. U.S. International Trade Commission*, 946 F.2d 821, 20 U.S.P.Q.2d 1161 (Fed. Cir. 1991).

[15]   Title 35, United States Code, Section 112, sixth paragraph.

[16]   Title 37, Code of Federal Regulations, Section 1.75(d)(1).

[17]   Title 35, United States Code, Section 154.

[18]   Title 37, Code of Federal Regulations, Section 1.75(f).

[19]   *Bates v. Coe*, 98 U.S. 31, 25 L.Ed. 68 (1878). *Intel Corp. v. U.S. International Trade Commission*, 946 F.2d 821, 20 U.S.P.Q.2d 1161 (Fed. Cir. 1991).

[20]   Landis, John L. *Mechanics of Patent Claim Drafting* (Second Edition). Practising Law Institute, 1974.

[21]   Fergason, James L. *Liquid-Crystal Non-Linear Light Modulators Using Electric and Magnetic Fields*. United States Patent 3,918,796. November 11, 1975.

[22]   Rao, N. Vasanth, *et al. Pyroelectric Targets and Method of Manufacture*. United States Patent 4,495,441. January 22, 1985.

[23]   Rackman, Michael I. *Electroluminescent Television System*. United States Patent 3,513,258. May 19, 1970.

[24]   Chaudhari, Praveen, *et al. Apparatus Using Amorphous Magnetic Compositions*. United States Patent 3,965,463. June 22, 1976.

[25]   *In re Garnero*, 412 F.2d 276, 162 U.S.P.Q. 221 (CCPA 1969).

[26]   *In re Gray, et al*, 53 F.2d 520, 11 U.S.P.Q. 255, 1932 C.D. 85 (CCPA 1931).

[27]   Keck, Donald B., *et al. Method of Producing Optical Waveguide Fibers.* United States Patent 3,711,262. January 16, 1973.

[28]   *Becton Dickinson and Co. v. C.R. Bard Inc.*, 922 F.2d 792, 17 U.S.P.Q.2d 1097, (Fed. Cir. 1990).

[29]   *In re Schaefer*, 171 U.S.P.Q. 110 (Bd. App. 1970). *Ex parte Davis and Tuukkanen*, 80 U.S.P.Q. 448 (Bd. App. 1948).

[30]   *In re Gray et al*, 53 F.2d 520, 11 U.S.P.Q. 255, 1932 C.D. 85 (CCPA 1931). *Ex parte Davis and Tuukkanen*, 80 U.S.P.Q. 448 (Bd. App. 1948).

[31]   *In re Garnero*, 412 F.2d 276, 162 U.S.P.Q. 221 (CCPA 1969). *Ex parte Davis and Tuukkanen*, 80 U.S.P.Q. 44 (Bd. App. 1948).

[32]   Title 37, Code of Federal Regulations, Section 1.75(e). *Ex parte Jepson*, 1917 C.D. 62, 243 O.G. 525 (Comm'r. Pats 1917).

[33]   *Ex parte Jepson*, 1917 C.D. 62, 243 O.G. 525 (Comm'r. Pats 1917).

[34]   *In re Fout, Mishkin, and Roychoudhury*, 675 F.2d 297, 213 U.S.P.Q. 532 (CCPA 1982).

[35]   Title 35, United States Code, Section 112, sixth paragraph.

[36]   Title 35, United States Code, Section 112, sixth paragraph.

[37]   *In re Bond*, 910 F.2d 831, 15 U.S.P.Q.2d 1566 (Fed. Cir. 1990).

[38]   *In re Markush*, 1925 C.D. 126, 340 O.G. 839 (Comm'r. Pats. 1925).

[39]   *In re Markush*, 1925 C.D. 126, 340 O.G. 839 (Comm'r. Pats. 1925).

[40]   *Texas Instruments Inc. v. International Trade Commission*, 988 F.2d 1165, 26 U.S.P.Q.2d 1018 (Fed. Cir. 1993).

[41]   *Texas Instruments Inc. v. International Trade Commission*, 988 F.2d 1165, 26 U.S.P.Q.2d 1018 (Fed. Cir. 1993).

[42]   *In re Mattison and Swanson*, 509 F.2d 563, 184 U.S.P.Q. 484 (CCPA 1975).

[43]   Title 35, United States Code, Section 112, third paragraph.

[44]   Title 35, United States Code, Section 112, fourth paragraph.

[45]   Keck, Donald B., *et al. Method of Producing Optical Waveguide Fibers.* United States Patent 3,711,262. January 16, 1973.

[46]   Title 35, United States Code, Section 112, fifth paragraph.

[47]   Title 35, United States Code, Section 282.

[48]   *In re Hughes*, 496 F.2d 1216, 182 U.S.P.Q. 106 (CCPA 1974). *Manual of Patent Examining Procedure*, Fifth Edition, Revision 14, November 1992, U.S. Department of Commerce, Patent and Trademark Office, Section 706.03(e).

[49]   *In re Hughes*, 496 F.2d 1216, 182 U.S.P.Q. 106 (CCPA 1974).

[50]   *Atlantic Thermoplastics Co. Inc. v. Faytex Corp.*, 970 F.2d 834, 23 U.S.P.Q.2d 1481 (Fed. Cir. 1992), rehearing denied, 974 F.2d 1279, 23 U.S.P.Q.2d 1801, 974 F.2d 1299, 24 U.S.P.Q.2d 1138.

[51]   Title 37, Code of Federal Regulations, Section 1.52(a).

[52]   Title 35, United States Code, Section 112.

[53]   *Intel Corp. v. U.S. International Trade Commission*, 946 F.2d 821, 20 U.S.P.Q.2d 1161 (Fed. Cir. 1991).

[54] *Intel Corp. v. U.S. International Trade Commission*, 946 F.2d 821, 20 U.S.P.Q.2d 1161 (Fed. Cir. 1991).

[55] *Liebscher v. Boothroyd*, 258 F.2d 948, 119 U.S.P.Q. 133 (CCPA 1958).

[56] *In re Salem, Butterworth, and Ryan*, 553 F.2d 676, 193 U.S.P.Q. 513 (CCPA 1977).

[57] *Graver Tank Co. v. Linde Air Products Co.*, 339 U.S. 606, 94 L.Ed. 1097, 70 S.Ct. 854, 85 U.S.P.Q. 328, 330 (1950).

[58] *Graver Tank Co. v. Linde Air Products Co.*, 339 U.S. 606, 94 L.Ed. 1097, 70 S.Ct. 854, 85 U.S.P.Q. 328 (1950).

[59] Title 35, United States Code, Sections 102 and 103.

[60] Title 37, Code of Federal Regulations, Section 1.19(b)(2).

[61] *Townsend Engineering Company v. HiTec Co. Ltd.*, 829 F.2d 1086, 4 U.S.P.Q.2d 1136 (Fed. Cir. 1987).

[62] *Exhibit Supply Co. v. Ace Patents Corporation*, 315 U.S. 126, 86 L.Ed. 736, 62 S.Ct. 513, 52 U.S.P.Q. 275 (1942).

[63] *The Cincinnati Milling Machine Co. v. Turchan*, 208 F.2d 222, 99 U.S.P.Q. 366 (Sixth Cir. 1953).

[64] *Welch et al v. General Motors Corporation*, 330 F.Supp. 80, 170 U.S.P.Q. 22 (E.D. Virginia 1970), aff'd. 170 U.S.P.Q. 1 (Fourth Cir. 1970).

Article

8

HOW A PRODUCT CAN BE BOTH PATENTABLE AND INFRINGE THE PATENTS OF OTHERS

Manny W. Schecter

Manny W. Schecter is Counsel, Intellectual Property Law, at the International Business Machines Corporation Storage Systems Division site in Tucson, Arizona.

Abstract

The patenting of an invention does NOT guarantee one the right to exploit that invention. A patent only provides one the right to prevent others from exploiting an invention. If you are frustrated and confused, read on, you soon will understand!

8.1 IMPROVEMENT PATENTS

The patentability of an invention is determined in view of all known technology at the time an invention is made. There are a number of legal requirements for patentability, most of which are beyond the scope of this article. Perhaps, the most important requirement for patentability is that of nonobviousness. Put simply, for an invention to be patentable it must not be *obvious*. Patented inventions may even be improvements over previously patented inventions, so long as the former is unobvious in view of the latter.

To demonstrate, consider the hypothetical of the windshield wiper. The first windshield wiper was almost certainly the human hand (with or without a rag). The hand was reliable, but hardly convenient. A clever inventor solved the problem with the automatic windshield wiper. Assume for the purposes of this discussion that the first automatic windshield wiper was driven by a single-speed motor, and that later, multispeed motors were developed to allow automobile drivers to adjust the speed of wiper movement to the weather. This still did not allow drivers to conveniently manage light rain conditions, and so intermittent windshield wipers were created. These wipers paused between certain sweeps across the windshield rather than adjust the speed of wiper movement. Finally, variable intermittent windshield wipers allowed the driver to adjust the length of time between wiper sweeps across the windshield.

Also assume each of the four improvements to the windshield wiper were patentable. An automatic windshield wiper could have been unobvious in view of the hand. A multispeed wiper could have been unobvious in view of an original single speed automatic wiper.

An intermittent wiper could have been unobvious in view of a multispeed wiper. A variable intermittent wiper could have been unobvious in view of a simple intermittent wiper. Provided each improvement was judged unobvious in view of the state of the art at the time it was created, individual patents could have issued for each such improvement, and each to a different inventor.

Leave the windshield wiper behind for a moment. Why get a patent at all? The answer is that a patent provides one the right to prevent others from making, using, and/or selling (*i.e.*, exploiting) an invention. A patent owner can maintain a valuable commercial advantage because competitors can be excluded from using the patented invention. Patents can also be licensed in exchange for other items of value, including royalties. A patent license is therefore needed for one to legally market a product that exploits the patented invention of another.

8.2 THE ELEMENTS OF PATENT INFRINGEMENT

Now, consider how one knows whether a product exploits a patented invention of another. For example, referring back to the windshield wiper evolution, does an intermittent wiper exploit a patent relating to a single speed wiper? How about a multispeed wiper? The answer is, "It depends" (what else?), but the answer is not as important as the methodology.

So how does one know whether a product exploits a patented invention of another? Well, a patent is essentially a contract between the public and the patent owner. The public receives a complete description of the invention (one of those other "legal requirements" referred to earlier), thereby eliminating the need for a duplication of research and development. The patent owner receives the exclusive right to prevent others from exploiting the patented invention. Just as any contract contains very specific language describing the agreed-upon obligations of the contracting parties (often annoyingly and/or confusingly so), so does a patent contain very specific language defining the bounds of the exclusive rights of the patent owner.

Every U.S. patent concludes with patent *claims*, the language defining the bounds of the exclusive rights of the patent owner. The claims must recite an invention judged unobvious in view of the state of the art at the time the invention was made. In addition, the claims recite precisely that to which the exclusive rights of the patent owner apply. For example, a simple claim for an automatic windshield wiper might have been:

> An apparatus for automatically wiping a windshield comprising:
>
> an arm having a first end and a second end;
>
> a wiper blade attached to the first end of the arm; and
>
> a motor attached to the second end of the arm for driving the arm and blade in a reciprocating motion.

Infringement of the patent claim is determined by checking whether the product in question includes all of the claimed elements. If so, the product infringes the patent, no matter what other features the product includes. If the product includes less than all of the claimed elements, there is no patent infringement.

Try reading the aforementioned claim upon a multispeed wiper. Does a multispeed wiper infringe the claim? Yes it does. A multispeed wiper includes an arm, a wiper blade, and a motor, all as described in the claim. An intermittent wiper also infringes the claim. It does not matter whether the multispeed or intermittent wipers are themselves patented: if they employ absolutely everything recited in the claim, the claim is infringed. It also does not matter how long the arm is, how many arms are used, what material the blade is manufactured from, or how efficient the motor is in these other wipers—these additional features are all irrelevant because they are not recited in the claim.

A U.S. patent has a 17-year term. So, anyone wishing to make, use, or sell a multispeed or intermittent wiper within the 17-year term of the hypothetical patent for the automatic windshield wiper will require a license from the patent owner. Perhaps you recently read about a real patent for the intermittent wiper. Perhaps you have such an intermittent wiper on your own car, but do not have a license under the patent. The manufacturer of your car is almost certainly licensed, currently negotiating a license under the patent, or challenging the validity of the patent through the legal system. Any license obtained will protect buyers of the car.

Consider another claim, this time for a multispeed windshield wiper:

An apparatus for automatically wiping a windshield comprising:

an arm having a first end and a second end;

a wiper blade attached to the first end of the arm; and

a motor attached to the second end of the arm for driving the arm and blade in a reciprocating motion at a plurality of selectable speeds.

Compare the new claim to the previous claim for an original automatic windshield wiper and note that the last clause relating to the motor has been modified. Does a single-speed wiper infringe the new claim? No, because it does not operate "at a plurality of selectable speeds". This result is expected because our "evolution" tells us the single-speed wiper was invented first, and the claim must distinguish over such. Does an intermittent wiper infringe the claim? It does infringe if it uses a multispeed motor, but it does not infringe if it uses a single-speed motor. The author has never seen a single-speed intermittent wiper, but such a wiper is certainly possible and would not infringe a claim reciting operation "at a plurality of selectable speeds".

Here we have stumbled upon the art of patent claim drafting. The desired goal of the drafter is a claim that recites just enough features to be unobvious in view of the state of the art, yet recites no unnecessary features. Such additional features unduly narrow the claim by allowing developers to avoid infringing patents through the use of alternatives. For example, the multispeed wiper would not infringe the first claim presented to the original automatic windshield wiper had it specifically recited a motor operable at just a "single speed". Here is a claim for an intermittent wiper:

An apparatus for automatically wiping a windshield comprising:

an arm having a first end and a second end;

a wiper blade attached to the first end of the arm; and

a motor attached to the second end of the arm for driving the arm and blade in a reciprocating motion and pausing after certain sweeps of the arm.

As an exercise, the reader should consider how this last claim could be made broader or narrower, whether a variable intermittent wiper would infringe the claim, and how to write a claim for a variable intermittent wiper.

8.3 CONCLUSION

Put together everything you have just learned. You understand that unobvious improvements of a product are patentable, even if earlier products also were patented. You have seen how patent claims define the scope of patent rights and that an improved and patented product may still infringe patent claims relating to earlier products. Viewed together, these principles demonstrate how a patented product can nevertheless infringe the patents of others. Recall again that a patent provides one the right to exclude others from exploiting the patented invention. In short, the patenting of an invention is no guarantee that you have the right to make, use, or sell it—just that you have the exclusive right to prevent others from doing so.

Finally, a few disclaimers are required. You may have read about the recent legal success of a Mr. Robert Kearns in asserting his patents directed to intermittent windshield wipers against various automobile manufacturers. This paper should not be interpreted as an accurate description of the contents of Mr. Kearns' patents or as an opinion upon the validity of Mr. Kearns' legal position. The *evolution* described herein is a hypothetical and logical creation of the author and is used for the sake of simplicity in demonstrating the basic tenets of patent law. You should also know that the teachings herein relate to *utility* patents and do not apply to *design* and *plant* patents.

PREFILING CONSIDERATIONS AND PROCEDURES

This section of the book discusses the reasons for pursuing patent protection, the requisites for patentability, and the circumstances that can prevent a company from successfully obtaining patents on its technology.   MAL

WHY PATENT: A BUSINESS PERSPECTIVE

Roger K. deBry

Roger K. deBry is a Senior Technical Staff Member and manager of Advanced Technology in the Boulder Programming Center of the Pennant Systems Company.

There are a number of reasons for pursuing patent protection.

1. *Unless there is an express or implied contractual obligation to the contrary or some likelihood that the public would be deceived or confused as to the source of a product, anyone can use and copy any unpatented, uncopyrighted aspect of a product that comes into its possession legally. A patent is the only mechanism for protecting against an independent development of an invention by another; actual knowledge of the patent or copying of the invention is not a requirement for patent infringement. Patent protection can also be extremely broad; if properly drafted a patent can sometimes protect the functionality of a product or feature. As a result, a patent may be necessary to adequately protect an investment in research and development.*

2. *One entity's patents can sometimes be used to offset patents held by others through creating a basis for cross-licensing. For example, where there are patents on a basic invention, the only way to obtain a favorable license may be to obtain a patent on an improvement to the basic invention, or some other product feature, that the basic patent owner might want to use.*

3. *A patent is demonstrative evidence of expertise in the technological area of the invention. This can often be a great aid in: obtaining capital from investors; obtaining loans from commercial institutions; in winning competitions for contracts; and, from an individual's perspective, for obtaining employment.*

4. *A patent can also be the source of a substantial royalty income, through institution of a licensing program.*

The following article addresses some of the reasons for obtaining patent protection.   MAL

Abstract

In today's fiercely competitive global marketplace, engineers, scientists, and programmers are under intense pressure from the companies they work for to bring new products to market at an ever increasing pace. In this environment, the urgency of getting a product out the door all too often takes precedence over everything else. Without a proper understanding of the business value of building a strong patent portfolio, technical professionals and managers alike fail to put the proper focus on patenting their work. This failure can have profound effects. This article discusses the importance of a complete patent program to a business and some serious consequences of ignoring or minimizing patent activity. Areas to be focused on include ensuring freedom of action in developing, manufacturing, and marketing products, protecting a company's research and development investment, establishing a source of royalty income, and providing recognition for key technical contributors.

9.1 INTRODUCTION

The environment in which most engineers, programmers, and scientists work today is much different from what it was ten years ago. As competition has become more global and the economics of doing business have become much more challenging, the urgency of putting the next round of competitive products into the marketplace has put intense pressures on technical professionals who work in product R & D. In this environment, product developers and their managers often are measured solely by how quickly a product goes out of the door and whether it meets its cost objectives. Little attention is given to properly protecting the creative and intellectual property upon which the product is built. Product developers, already stretched to make product commitments, find little time to devote to patent activities. Compounding the problem are development managers who frown on their people spending time on patent activities. This occurs because development managers often do not understand the benefit of a strong patent portfolio and working on a patent application takes time away from real product development. At the same time, lack of research funding and the focus on shorter and shorter development schedules has resulted in a significant decrease in exploratory activities that often lead to patents in new areas of technology.

Putting new competitive products out of the door is important, and often being first to market is critical to capturing or keeping market share. For most of us, getting products delivered to our customers pays our salaries as engineers, programmers, and scientists. But, the failure to protect the intellectual property developed while bringing those products to market can have profound effects. The remainder of this article describes the importance of patenting to a business and some serious consequences of ignoring or minimizing the significance of patent activity.

9.2 FREEDOM OF ACTION

Simply stated, *freedom of action* means that a company is free to develop, manufacture, and market its products without being constrained by outside patents. A patent is a right conferred upon the inventor to exclude others from making, using, or selling that which is covered in the patent [1]. Using a simple example, if company ABC develops a new product but needs to use a technology patented by company XYZ, ABC may be constrained from developing and marketing that product because XYZ owns the patent rights to that technology. To obtain the freedom to develop and market its product, ABC must license, or buy, the right to include XYZ's technology in its product. If ABC uses XYZ's patented technology in a product that they market without such an agreement, then ABC is infringing on XYZ's patent. This can be costly. For example, after a federal court ruled that Kodak had infringed on Polaroid's instant-camera patents, Kodak was prohibited from making or selling its instant cameras and films. In addition, Kodak had to pay damages, recall 16 million cameras, close a $200-million plant, and lay off 800 permanent workers [2].

How then does maintaining a strong patent portfolio provide freedom of action? If company ABC has a broad-based patent portfolio with key patents on major technologies in its area of business, company XYZ might be willing to cross-license its patents with company ABC so that it in turn may use some of company ABC's technologies in its own products. That is, for their mutual benefit, companies ABC and XYZ will trade the rights to use inventions on which the other has patents, and both companies enjoy freedom of action with respect to the inventions that they share. This may happen even when the two companies are strong competitors. Two competitors who each own one or more patents that cover some aspect of the other's product have the choice of both licensing the other and staying in business or putting each other out of business. The Kodak example discussed previously may have had a completely different outcome if Kodak had had patents that Polaroid needed. While some companies steadfastly refuse to cross-license with a competitor, cross-licensing agreements can be made when it becomes a matter of necessity.

9.3 INVESTMENT PROTECTION

Bringing a new technology or product to the marketplace is expensive, often requiring millions of dollars worth of research and development. Manufacturing may add millions as new tools and processes are developed and new manufacturing lines or perhaps entire new production facilities are put into place. Having made that kind of investment, no company wants to see a competitive product appearing in the marketplace at significantly less cost because the competitor has not had to bear the cost of the initial research and development required to turn an idea into a product. When this does happen, a company that has protected its investment by patenting the key ideas behind its products can recover damages by suing for patent infringement. U.S. patent law provides that a court shall award damages adequate to compensate the patentee for infringement, but in no event less than a reasonable royalty. Damages may be awarded based on a reasonable royalty, profits made on the infringing products sales, or lost profits the patent owner suffers because of the infringer's product. This amount may be increased threefold [3] where a company willfully violates another's patents. Recently, for example, a federal court ordered Keebler, Nabisco, and Frito-Lay to pay Proctor and Gamble $125 million for infringing its soft cookie patent [4]. This not only provided some measure of compensation for the investment made by Proctor and Gamble in developing its soft cookie idea, but will discourage others from infringing on that particular patent. Imagine how different this example would have been if people at Proctor and Gamble had not taken the time to submit their ideas to the patent process.

9.4 ROYALTIES

Most companies are willing to grant *royalty-bearing licenses* to others as a source of income, although there is nothing in our patent law that makes this mandatory. Granting such a license not only produces income for the patent holder, but because royalty payments become a direct expense to the licensee, there is a doubling effect that helps the holder of the patent be more competitive in the marketplace. Suppose, for example, that company ABC has developed a submersible widget and sells it for $10. Company XYZ also wants to be in the submersible-widget market, but it must license from company ABC the technology required to allow the widget to operate under water. A royalty of $1.00 per submersible widget is negotiated between ABC and XYZ. Now, ABC not only makes $1.00 from every submersible widget that XYZ sells, but, all other things being equal, XYZ's submersible widgets will be more expensive than ABC's because of the $1.00 royalty per widget included in XYZ's costs.

Royalty income can be substantial when a patent is in a critical technology area that is required by anyone else doing business in that area. One excellent example is in the computer industry where Texas Instruments holds some basic technology patents on memory chips. In 1987, Texas Instruments raised its royalties on memory chips. Many companies, including NEC, Matshushita, Fujitsu, and Mitsubishi objected and refused to pay the increased royalties. They were subsequently charged with patent infringement. The result was an acceptance of the royalties and an increased income for Texas Instruments of $281 million over two years. Thus, Texas Instruments not only develops chips and makes money selling them, but because TI owns basic technology patents in the semiconductor field, it makes even more money by selling rights to the technology covered by its patents.

9.5 RECOGNITION

Providing the time for and encouraging inventors to document their work and file for patents when appropriate not only brings great benefit to any company in terms of the ownership of those intellectual assets, but it provides a way for a company to recognize the talents and creativity of those who are contributing those ideas. IBM, for example, actively encourages its employees with a corporate-sponsored invention-disclosure program. IBM inventors are given cash awards for filing their first invention and for achieving various levels of invention activity. In addition, corporate awards are given for the granting of significant patents or for achieving significant levels of patenting activity. Such programs are important because 1) they send a message to employees and their managers that patenting is a desired activity within the company, and 2) they provide special recognition for those employees who are particularly creative and make significant contributions to the technical health and well being of the company.

9.6 SUMMARY

This article has described many reasons why patenting is important. When a company makes significant investments in developing new technologies and new products, it can only be viewed as penny-wise and pound foolish when it does not spend the time and the money required to protect those investments and to ensure its freedom of action. A strong patent portfolio provides freedom of action for a company to develop, manufacture, and market its products with a minimum of patent concern; protects a company's research, development, and manufacturing investment; serves as a basis for determining royalty income; and serves as a means for recognizing key technical contributors. For these reasons patenting ought to be seen as a fundamental part of the job for any engineer, programmer, or scientist. No project ought to be deemed complete until the basic creative work that went into the project has been patented.

NOTES

[1] *Patent Law for the NonLawyer: A Guide for The Engineer, Technologist, and Manager.* Burton A. Amernick, Van Nostrand Reinhold, New York, NY, 1986.

[2] *Protecting Engineering Ideas & Inventions*, Ramond D. Foltz and Thomas A. Penn, Penn Institute, Inc., Cleveland, Ohio, 1987, 1988.

[3] *Patent Law Handbook*, Patricia N. Brantley, Clark Boardman Callahan, 1992–1993 Edition.

[4] *The Perils of Patent Infringement*, Ramond D. Foltz and Thomas A. Penn, Machine Design, pp105–8, April 12, 1990.

SEEKING COST-EFFECTIVE INTELLECTUAL PROPERTY PROTECTION

Thomas G. Field, Jr.

Thomas G. Field, Jr. is a Professor of Law at the Franklin Pierce Law Center in Concord, New Hampshire. Other recent writings include "Access to and Authority to Cite Unpublished Decisions of the PTO," 33 IDEA 153 (1993), "The Science Court is Dead: Long Live the Science Court!" 4 RISK 95 (1993), and "Comment, Review of PTO Intramural Appeals," 33 IDEA 117 (1993).

If a man can . . . make a better mousetrap . . . , though he builds his house in the woods the world will make a beaten path to his door.

Ralph Waldo Emerson

Abstract

Some inventors misconstrue Emerson's dictum and believe that patenting an invention will cause the world to beat a path to their door. Others, who appreciate that it is often easier to patent than to sell an invention, believe that patents increasingly cost more than they're worth. This article will show that reality lies somewhere between these views. Patents do not guarantee market success, but they and other forms of *intellectual property* (IP) can easily be worth more than they cost.

10.1 INTRODUCTION

Cost considerations are more important to some inventors than others. Employed inventors usually need not be concerned; their inventions belong to their employers. Firms large enough to hire professional inventors should have personnel and procedures to weigh IP options and select among alternatives. Inventors not so employed need to do the same thing but often lack the capacity. This discussion should help independent inventors bridge the gap.

IP may be helpful for several purposes such as serving as collateral for business loans or obtaining royalty income. However, in most cases, the value of IP derives from its capacity to prevent others from free riding and that value varies widely depending on many factors. Consider a firm that faces no serious competition and makes a product in sufficient volume that its R&D costs account for less than 1 percent of its selling price. Such a firm might choose to ignore potential IP benefits without serious risk. Yet, a firm where R&D expense is a major part of its selling price would be foolish to ignore IP options. Even if it has no present competitors, success may attract ones that can avoid the R&D markup. Also, small-volume firms facing competition need to appreciate that large-volume competitors are apt to be able not only to sell at lower prices but also to receive higher profits. In such circumstances, IP rights can be the key to survival.

In one sense, IP protection is a lock on the door to the market for specific products. One does not lock up things unlikely to be stolen, much less buy expensive locks. Thus, the first step in seeking cost-effective IP protection is to evaluate the market for the invention.

10.2 EVALUATING POTENTIAL PROFITABILITY

Most critical factors affecting the value of an invention should occur to any thoughtful person who is unencumbered by fantasies of riches and glory. We are all consumers. Inventors must think about how they purchase. What are consumers looking for? Does the product meet their needs? Is the price reasonable in light of any needs it meets? Does it meet only the needs of a select few, or a large number of people? For example, computer users often encounter *shareware* that crashes or has only marginal utility. The prices authors request from users of their shareware are sometimes incredible—unless one considers how easily authors can confuse their time investment with the value of their program.

Purchasers are unconcerned about development cost and effort. Mousetraps that cost twice as much as ones already available but have only 50 percent more value will not sell. This is true even though, in some way(s), a new product might be regarded as many times "better" than ones already on the market.

A set of important factors hinges on potential competitors. Unless one is selling a truly new product to meet a totally new need, competition is likely. The light bulb often epitomizes the great invention. Yet, firms promoting electricity had to face large, well-established utilities and attract enormous resources to displace gas for illumination. Innovators must consider the full range of advantages enjoyed by present and potential competitors, including goodwill, skilled personnel, well-established distribution channels, access to raw materials, and economies of scale.

Such matters have been treated at length by others and are not discussed here. For example, an excellent discussion appears in a 1977 booklet, *Guide to Invention and Innovation Evaluation*. Written by Gerald Udell and colleagues at the University of Oregon, it discusses 33 factors that need to be considered. It also contains a questionnaire for considering each factor with regard to particular products or services.

Confirming what is urged here, the last question is whether the invention may be legally protected. However, that booklet doesn't discuss important relationships between evaluating and protecting an invention.

10.3 BASIC IP BENEFITS AND COSTS

Even the staunchest defenders of market evaluation are unlikely to claim that it is a science. Thus, inventors often have to make IP choices in the face of great uncertainty. Specific strategies for controlling patent costs are discussed below, but first we should consider patents with other potential options. In order of generally increasing effectiveness, they are trade secrets, copyrights, and utility patents. (Utility patents are what most people intend when they refer to patents. Other possibilities such as design and plant patents are not considered here.)

10.3.1 Benefits

Rights in trade secrets protect commercially important information from being used in breach of confidence and from being obtained, for example, by bribing another's employees. However, trade secret law is not effective against another's obtaining the information by reverse engineering (copying a product found in the marketplace) or independent discovery.

For most inventions, copyright offers little potential because it generally will not protect "useful" inventions. It is nevertheless valuable for software and a limited number of other things. Unlike trade secrets, copyrights can be used to stop others from copying products acquired in the market. Still, they suffer serious limitations. First, copyrights are not effective to stop the sale of very similar works independently created. (However, the more widely a work is available, the more difficult for later sellers to establish independent origin.) Second, copyright can be used to prevent others from copying or closely imitating software but cannot be used to prevent them from writing different programs to execute the same functions or achieve the same result. Finally, copyright is of little value in preventing another's copying and use of data—no matter how expensive it may have been to collect.

Utility patent protection is better than copyright in most ways. Although it is doubtful that patents could protect data, they can protect a much wider range of inventions and are effective against works of independent origin. Nevertheless, for inventions such as industrial processes, patents may not be effective. If others can learn to practice an invention from reading a patent, but the patentee cannot easily determine if it is being used, a patent will not be worth much. In such circumstances, trade secrets may be preferred.

10.3.2 Costs

Of the three forms of IP protection, trade secret rights cost virtually nothing to obtain, but maintenance is a different story. Maintenance may require special personnel; employee training; restricted access to plant, equipment, and documents; the need to get agreements from and to educate people with unavoidable access; and the need to monitor disclosures through publications, conferences, and trade shows. The costs of such precautionary measures can be high.

The cost of obtaining and preserving copyright is the lowest. Copyright arises automatically upon creation of proper subject matter. Registration is necessary in the United States only if one needs to bring an infringement suit; it is usually unnecessary elsewhere even for that purpose. However, for both domestic and foreign copyright owners, early U.S. registration confers important remedial advantages. It is also simple and inexpensive. The usual registration fee is $20.00. While simple copyright registration can be done without legal assistance, advice of counsel is desirable for a more complete understanding of copyright rights and limitations in a particular situation.

Finally, patent protection costs thousands of dollars in ever-increasing government fees alone. It is expensive to obtain, maintain, and enforce. Also, unlike copyrights, patents must be obtained in each country where protection is desired, and costs abroad may be even higher than here—particularly if translations are required. This means that few inventions would warrant patent protection in more than a small fraction of possible countries. Still, sophisticated firms clearly regard some foreign patents as worth far more than they cost.

10.4 CONTROLLING PATENT COSTS IN THE FACE OF MARKET UNCERTAINTY

Sometimes, filing a patent application is a waste of money. One should always consider, for example, an invention's expected lifetime in light of the time it may take to obtain protection. Patents issue slowly and confer no benefits until they do. Yet, markets may change quickly because of technology or sometimes fleeting consumer interest. Thus, one should consider whether an invention will be obsolete before a patent might issue.

Assuming that patent protection is not rejected almost immediately, inventors often face the challenge of trying to evaluate the possible advantages of protection when the profit potential of the invention is very much in doubt. Potential free riders on an inventor's efforts face far less uncertainty. They will weigh their options after market demand is shown.

Otherwise sophisticated people often fail to appreciate that patents vary enormously in their ability to forestall competition. Generally, inventors get what they choose or, more likely, can afford to pay for. If their patent protection proves to cover too little technological territory, or to be in the wrong geographic or market location, a patent cannot help. For example, an inventor without European patents cannot prevent others from sharing, or even taking over, European markets when his or her invention proves to have great consumer demand in those countries. Conversely, patents covering empty markets are a waste.

Because inventors often lack important information when cost-critical choices have to be made, it may be useful also to think of IP protection as insurance. How can one purchase adequate insurance at the least cost? Where can corners be cut, at what risk? One way to cope is to do as much as possible yourself.

10.4.1 Prior Art Searches

The first step in determining whether an invention is patentable is a *prior art search*. If it is old or obvious to those familiar with the technology, it cannot be patented. Inventors should not omit the prior art search before filing applications. Patent examiners do searches, but it is not dollar wise to have examiners tell you what can be learned more cheaply. Given the difficulty of marketing new products, an inventor must not assume, because a product is unavailable, that it is novel. For example, two inventors called me, many years apart, about the same life-saving invention (a signal balloon for use where someone lost at sea or in rugged terrain might otherwise use a flare). I do not know if the product was ever marketed, but a search will find at least four expired patents covering the basic idea. (Yet, the second inventor was trying to locate a source of thousands of dollars being requested by an invention promotion firm.)

Also, prior art searches may reveal unexpired patents that could block sale of patentable improvements. A patent does not permit one to sell—only to prevent others from selling an invention. Thus, one must consider, for example, the time left for any blocking patent and whether licenses are available.

If inventors search as much literature as possible, including patents, initial attorney consultations will accomplish more—and, if further searches prove necessary, they will cost less.

10.4.2 Preparing Applications, Seeking Assignees

Inventors should not try to save money by stinting on application preparation fees. The challenge of preparing an application is greater than that of provisioning a boat for a long voyage. Once it has been filed with the U.S. Patent and Trademark Office (PTO), afterthoughts are expensive. Supplemental applications, called continuations-in-part, are possible but expensive. Also, claims to the added matter do not get the benefit of the original filing date.

Better applications can be filed more cheaply when inventors study the prior art and can explain how their inventions differ from what has gone before, focusing on unexpected advantages. Inventors are usually most familiar with their technology, and, the more they do, the less attorneys have to charge.

Once an application is filed in the United States, test marketing is possible without forfeiting rights. Also, inventors have approximately a year to decide whether to file foreign patent applications.

It may take a year or more before the first response is received from the PTO. This window of opportunity should not be wasted. Once an application is filed in the U.S., inventors can approach prospective manufacturers with less concern about having inventions stolen. In fact, many manufacturers will not consider outside submissions until a patent application has been filed. If the market and prior art prognoses are good, and applications are well prepared, this will increase a manufacturer's interest. If a pending application can be assigned, an inventor can avoid further patent expenses. Also, a manufacturer will have a better idea of whether foreign protection is warranted, and, if so, where. Still, keep in mind that prospective assignees will be concerned about their own costs and risks: The higher the likely costs, and the lower the chances for profit, the lower licensing royalties are apt to be.

10.4.3 Prosecuting, Maintaining, and Enforcing Patents

Before a patent issues, a dispute with the PTO is likely to occur. Contrary to what some believe, initial PTO action allowing all claims is not good news. This situation is akin to offering a house for sale and having the offer immediately accepted by the first person to look at it. That would suggest that the house was priced too low. Similarly, allowance of all claims in the first Office action suggests that the patent claims sought too little.

The downside of one or more claims being denied, of course, is the expense of responding, filing multi-tiered appeals or taking measures to show unexpected advantages of the invention. How far should an applicant go? An answer is impossible without at least a good guess about the value of contested territory that the patent could cover.

If an invention's value proves to be comparatively low, or allowable patent claims prove inadequate to protect potential markets, an application can be abandoned. This avoids further prosecution costs, an issue fee that is higher than the filing fee and maintenance fees. Also, because the PTO does not disclose the contents of pending applications, trade secrets still may remain as an option.

Even after patents are granted, three escalating maintenance fees, and possibly enforcement costs, must be faced. Whether such expenses are warranted, again, can be determined only by the value of what is being protected.

10.5 SUMMARY

The cost and availability of IP options vary considerably depending on the nature and subject matter of inventions. It is often more difficult to sell than to patent an invention, and it is unwise to spend money to prevent others from copying something that will not sell. Yet, it seems foolish to give away something of great commercial value. Those who have an invention that is worth much more than the cost of protection should not be scared away by skyrocketing PTO fees.

As soon as an invention's income potential appears to justify it, IP options should be explored with experienced counsel. In doing so, inventors need to appreciate, first, that patents do not always offer the only or even the best protection; second, that other IP options may be adequate and much cheaper; and, finally, that patent costs can be controlled.

Just as title to real estate may cover a square inch of Arctic tundra or a square mile of Manhattan, patent claims may be broad or narrow and cover various kinds of products or processes. Once this is understood, it becomes clear that, if patents continue to be worth pursuing, the need to consider protection in light of an invention's value stops only when the market proves to be worth any price its owner could conceivably have to pay.

The costs of filing and prosecuting patent applications and of maintaining and enforcing patents, when warranted, represent money well spent. If an invention quickly proves less valuable than hoped, the bulk of potential costs can be avoided. If it proves ultimately very valuable, others can be prevented from being unfairly rewarded. Finally, entrepreneurs in particular should consider how, when properly used, patents and other mechanisms for protecting intellectual property can be critical to their survival.

ASSESSING PATENTABILITY OF AN INVENTION

I.D. Zitkovsky and G.A. Walpert

Ivan D. Zitkovsky is a registered patent agent with the law firm of Fish & Richardson in Boston, Massachusetts, and is involved in patent prosecution.

Gary Walpert is a partner at Fish & Richardson, in its Boston office. His practice concentrates on patent, trademark, copyright, and other intellectual property matters and, in particular, on electrical high technology matters, including software protection.

Not every invention is patentable. To be patentable the invention must be:

- *A "new and useful process, machine, manufacture, or composition of matter, or any new or useful improvements thereof;"*
- *Novel; and*
- *When viewed as a whole, "unobvious" to a person of "ordinary skill in the art."*

The patent statute defines novelty *by expressly precluding a patent under certain circumstances, referred to as statutory bars, where the invention is considered either to have already passed into the public domain, i.e., become public property, or to have already become the property of another.*
A patent is precluded if, for example:

- *The invention is publicly known before the inventor conceives it;*
- *The invention is disclosed, commercially exploited, or used in public too far in advance of filing the application;*
- *The inventor subjectively intends to abandon the invention;*
- *A corresponding foreign patent application is improvidently filed; or*
- *Someone else* made *the invention in the United States first and did not abandon, conceal, or suppress the invention.*

The more difficult issue is whether the invention is "unobvious". This determination objective is based upon a number of factors:

(1) the scope and content of prior patents and publications;

(2) the "level of ordinary skill in the art" (typical education level in the pertinent area of technology);

(3) the differences between the invention as claimed and the prior art; and

(4) whether the invention provides unexpected results, fulfills a long-felt need, and/or is commercially significant.

The nonobviousness of the differences is then measured, not against what was subjectively obvious to the inventor, but rather against the general knowledge of practitioners in the pertinent area of technology at the time of the invention. It must be recalled that invention is often a gradual process. Things that an inventor deems obvious are often not at all obvious in a patent sense.

The invention also must be considered in total context and without hindsight. For example, the solution to a problem may be patentable even though the solution, with the benefit of hindsight, is very simple; the identification of the problem can constitute a patentable invention.

As a practical matter, if one or more elements of an invention as claimed are not disclosed in prior patents or publications, or if the invention as claimed combines known elements, but no prior patent or publication expressly or impliedly suggests combining those specific elements, the invention is probably nonobvious.

Some of the more aggressive companies ignore the issue altogether; applications are filed on every novel invention of commercial significance and the determination of unobviousness is left for the examination process.

The following articles address assessing the patentability of inventions, and the statutory bars.   MAL

Abstract

In a patent, an inventor fully discloses his invention to the public and the government gives him, in return, a 17-year monopoly to the invention defined in the patent claims. The U.S. Patent and Trademark Office will grant the patent only if the claims are directed to patentable subject matter, comply with formal requirements, and are novel in view of "prior art" that includes information in the public's possession before the invention. This article discusses what is included in the term "prior art" and how an inventor can assess novelty of his invention.

11.1 INTRODUCTION

An inventor has a right to obtain a U.S. Letters Patent for a "new and useful process, machine, manufacture, or composition of matter, or any new or useful improvements thereof" (35 U.S.C. §101). The patent statute (Title 35 of the United States Code) and the corresponding case law legally define what constitutes a patent, the examination underlying the award or grant of a patent, and the duration and enforceability of a patent. A patent is a form of contract between the government and an inventor. The inventor fully discloses his invention to the public and, in return, the government grants the inventor the "exclusive right" to the invention for up to 17 years.

The patent document has essentially two parts. The first part (the specification) describes the invention in sufficient detail so that a person of ordinary skill in the particular art can practice (make and use) the invention. This part also identifies one or more preferred embodiments of the best mode for implementing the invention. The second part of the patent document consists of one or more claims (the numbered paragraphs at the end of the patent) that legally define the scope of the invention. Based on the scope of the claims, a patent owner can exclude others from making, selling, or using the invention. The language of the claims is crucial for determining the scope and patentability of the claimed invention.

Thus, one should consider how the invention can be broadly defined in the claims (the scope of possible applications) and then consider and adjust the scope of the claims (the invention) in view of the previously known information that may be relevant to the invention. In what follows, we shall first discuss briefly the claims and then describe how to assess the patentability of the claims in view of the relevant information in the public domain, and the activities of the inventor and others.

11.2 CLAIMS

The patent claims precisely define what the inventor regards to be his or her invention. Even though formulating patent claims requires at least some experience and knowledge of patent law, an inexperienced inventor can summarize his or her invention in a short description consisting of a set of elements that form the invention. The elements should explicitly describe the invention and should be linked to each other using structural or functional language. Such a summary can form the basis for one or more claims.

In general, many claims of varying scope are necessary to protect various aspects of an invention. A broad claim has the smallest number of elements that still define the invention. A narrower claim includes additional elements that further limit the scope of the invention. In a simple example, we assume that the invention is an incandescent light bulb. The inventor can define broadly the invention as follows: A device for generating light that includes (a) two electrical contacts connectable to a source of electricity; (b) a filament of relatively high electric resistance connected conductively to the contacts; and (c) a light-transparent, heat-resistant shell adapted to encapsulate the filament in (d) vacuum. A narrower claim would define (e) the shell as made from glass, and another claim could specify (f) the filament as made from tungsten. Additional claims can describe (g) a support wire for supporting the filament inside the shell or (i) additional specific features for creating a vacuum seal around the contacts located outside the shell.

Distinctive claims are used to claim an apparatus, a process, a machine, or a product created by the same conceptual invention. The requirements for the form of the claims and the specification needed to support the claims are described in one of the sections of the patent statute, 35 U.S.C. §112.

11.3 PATENTABILITY OF AN INVENTION

11.3.1 Prior Art

An inventor is entitled to a patent, based on a properly drafted patent application, if the claimed invention describes patentable subject matter and if the claims meet the legal requirements for patentability. Categories of patentable subject matter are defined in 35 U.S.C. §101, and the corresponding case law. In general, most inventions belong to patentable categories. Unpatentable categories include printed matter, pictures, abstract ideas, and mathematical algorithms. Software based inventions, discussed in another section of this publication, are frequently patentable.

Conditions that exclude patentability of a claim (prohibit granting of a patent on the claim) are described in 35 U.S.C. §§102 and 103 reproduced in Appendices A and B. The interpretation of these two sections is defined by a constantly evolving body of voluminous case law. The exclusion conditions are intended to both assure that a patented invention is novel in respect to the existing knowledge that is already in the public's possession (called *prior art*), and to encourage diligent pursuit and prompt filing of a patent application. These exclusions are briefly described in the following paragraphs.

A first class of prior art is matter "known or used by others *in this country* or patented or described in a printed publication *anywhere in the world* before the invention by the applicant for patent". (35 U.S.C. §102(a)) (emphasis added). This section of the statute thus concentrates upon when the invention was first made. (There are special rules for determining this date.) A tangible form of this class of prior art includes publications such as patents, books, journal articles, abstracts, advertisements, promotional literature, and even papers of fairly limited distribution, for example, handouts at meetings held anywhere in the world prior to the date of the invention. This class of prior art also includes all subject matter either known or used in the United States by others than the inventor.

35 U.S.C. §102(e) defines another class of prior art held in the Patent Office. This prior art involves inventions "described in a patent granted on an application for patent by another filed in the United States before the invention thereof by the applicant for patent". In effect, the statute recognizes the filing of a patent application as proof of what others knew—"the state of the art" at the time the prior art patent was filed. Accordingly, it is appropriate to measure the patentability of a claimed invention against patents that were filed before the claimed invention was made.

The statute also includes provisions to assure that two separate inventors will not receive a patent for the same claimed invention. In such a case, who gets the patent is resolved in accordance with paragraph (g) of 35 U.S.C. §102. The law according to this paragraph gives the patent to a person who not only first conceived the claimed invention but also diligently pursued the invention to either an actual reduction to practice or to filing the patent application.

Another class of prior art is created to assure timely filing of U.S. patent applications by setting a statutory one year time period before the end of which, a filing must take place. According to paragraph (b) of 35 U.S.C. §102, an inventor is barred from obtaining a valid patent if "the invention was patented or described in a printed publication in this or a foreign country or in public use or on sale in this country, more than one year prior to the date of the application". This class includes activity by the inventor or any person acting on behalf of the inventor in the United States and includes, for example, sales, offers for sale, oral presentations, exhibits, public uses, or printed publications. This class also includes activities by others, which are described in the first class noted above. Thus, even if the claimed invention was made before the pertinent prior art came into existence, the inventor cannot obtain a valid patent if the invalidating prior art is more than one year old at the time of filing the patent application. Therefore, it is useful to file routinely a patent application within one year of the invention date to preempt such invalidating prior art created by others, frequently beyond the inventor's control, after the invention date.

The one-year grace period for an applicant's own activity applies also to applications first filed outside of the United States in certain circumstances, as recited in paragraph (d) of 35 U.S.C. §102.

11.3.2 Examining Claims for Novelty

After a patent application is filed in the Patent Office, a patent examiner compares the claims with the above-described *prior art*. An inventor can assess patentability of his or her invention prior to completing and filing the patent application by using the same analysis. First, the inventor should search for the closest prior art defined above. Practically speaking, prior art is frequently within the inventor's knowledge, or in his or her files if the inventor had worked in the field and followed scientific or trade journals. The inventor may also decide to use a person experienced in patentability searches to uncover prior art. Next, the inventor needs to determine whether any of his or her claims are anticipated, that is, fully disclosed by a single prior art reference. In this anticipation analysis, the inventor should take the claim as a whole and determine whether each element of the claim is disclosed by the reference. The inventor should not ignore structural or functional differences between the claimed invention and the prior art reference since these may justify patentability of the claim.

For example, assume that before the invention of the incandescent light bulb summarized above, a prior art reference described a simple electric cigarette lighter similar to a car cigarette lighter. The cigarette lighter has a partially encased resistive filament connected conductively to two electric contacts. The contacts are connectable to an electric source. The casing allows access to the filament and is connected to a handle for easy use. Would this prior art anticipate the claimed invention? No. The prior art discloses two electric contacts connected to a resistive filament, that is, elements (a) and (b) of the invention, but it does not disclose the light-transparent, heat-resistant shell adapted to encapsulate the filament in vacuum, that is, elements (c) and (d).

If no single reference anticipates the claimed invention under 35 U.S.C. §102, the claim passes the anticipation test. In the following section, we assess whether any claim would be obvious in view of one, or a combination of a several, prior art references.

11.3.3 Examining Claims for Obviousness

35 U.S.C. §103 excludes patentability

> if the differences between the subject matter sought to be patented and the prior art are such that the subject matter *as a whole* would have been obvious at the time the invention was made to *a person having ordinary skill in the art* to which said subject matter pertains. Patentability shall not be negatived by the manner in which the invention was made. (emphasis added)

In other words, a claimed invention, taken as a whole, is not patentable if the invention would have been obvious in view of several combined references to a hypothetical person at the time the invention was made. This "standard" person, who is not an inventor, is defined as having ordinary skill in the relevant art. Theoretically, there is no limit on the number of prior art references that can be cited against a claim. There is a body of case law that deals with the question of what references can be properly combined against a claim. Typically, all the references must be at least from related fields of art so that the hypothetical person, faced with the particular problem, would have looked to the references for solution. Further, the references may need to show, or at least suggest, the desirability of combining elements of the examined claim separately disclosed in the prior art references. Of course, the fact that the inventor did not know before the invention date about a particular reference is irrelevant.

In our example, assume that prior to the invention date, there is an advertisement for a portable oil lamp. The advertisement describes the lamp as having an easily removable glass cover that enables convenient access to the wick. The advertisement also mentions that a user of the lamp can ignite the wick using an electric cigarette lighter, and can also do this in the dark just by the glow generated by the electric lighter. Would the claimed invention be obvious over the electric lighter reference in view of this advertisement? No. Even though the two references may be properly combined, they not only do not disclose all elements of the claimed invention, specifically there is no mentioning of vacuum around the filament of the lighter, but also they do not render the invention as a whole obvious. Would an additional reference disclosing some unrelated use of vacuum render the invention obvious? Certainly not, since these prior art references still would not provide the motivation for encapsulating the filament of the light bulb in vacuum. However, now assume there is an additional conference paper, distributed by a cigarette lighter manufacturer, which describes durability tests of different resistive filaments in different media. This paper also discloses that "in vacuum, which is not practically usable for cigarette lighters, particular filaments seem to last much longer and also generate a much brighter glow." Would this reference in combination with the other prior art references render the invention obvious? Now the answer is not so clear. Arguments for both supporting and rejecting obviousness can be made.

Clearly, judging obviousness involves more experience than judging anticipation since frequently, despite a very small difference, the subject matter as a whole would not have been obvious, at the time of the invention, in view of the prior art. This test is subjective and involves hindsight. The standard of obviousness can also vary in different fields of art. If the claimed invention exhibits, for example, a new and different function or a new, different, unexpected, or even surprising result, the claimed invention is usually not obvious.

Sometimes, the inventive contribution resides in discovering the essence of a problem that people in the art struggled with for a long time. Once this is discovered, the actual solution may be obvious to the person having ordinary skill in the art. Nonobviousness is strongly suggested, even when the invention is a combination of known elements, if there are new, unexpected or different results, or there is disbelief by others, skilled in the art, that the invention works. Furthermore, evidence that an invention was needed for a long time, enjoys success on the market, and is widely used, praised, or copied by people skilled in the art also points toward nonobviousness. Accordingly, when faced with close prior art references, patentability under the §103 obviousness test is often difficult to judge even for an experienced practitioner.

If the invention passes the §§101, 102, and 103 tests, then the invention is likely to be patentable.

APPENDIX A
35 U.S.C. §102 CONDITIONS FOR PATENTABILITY;
NOVELTY AND LOSS OF RIGHT TO PATENT

A person shall be entitled to a patent unless:

(a) the invention was known or used by others in this country, or patented or described in a printed publication in this or a foreign country, before the invention thereof by the applicant for patent, or

(b) the invention was patented or described in a printed publication in this or a foreign country or in public use or on sale in this country, more than one year prior to the date of the application for patent in the United States, or

(c) he has abandoned the invention, or

(d) the invention was first patented or caused to be patented, or was the subject of an inventor's certificate, by the applicant or his legal representatives or assigns in a foreign country prior to the date of the application for patent in this country on an application for patent or inventor's certificate filed more than twelve months before the filing of the application in the United States, or

(e) the invention was described in a patent granted on an application for patent by another filed in the United States before the invention thereof by the applicant for

patent, or on an international application by another who has fulfilled the requirements of paragraphs (1), (2), and (4) of section 371(c) of this title before the
invention thereof by applicant for patent, or

(f) he did not himself invent the subject matter sought to be patented, or

(g) before the applicant's invention thereof the invention was made in this country by
another who had not abandoned, suppressed, or concealed it. In determining priority of invention there shall be considered not only the respective dates of conception and reduction to practice of the invention, but also the reasonable
diligence of one who was first to conceive and last to reduce to practice, from a
time prior to conception by the other.

APPENDIX B
35 U.S.C. §103 CONDITIONS FOR PATENTABILITY;
NONOBVIOUS SUBJECT MATTER

A patent may not be obtained though the invention is not identically disclosed or described as set fourth in section 102 of this title, if the differences between the subject matter sought to be patented and the prior art are such that the subject matter as a whole would
have been obvious at the time the invention was made to a person having ordinary skill in
the art to which said subject matter pertains. Patentability shall not be negatived by the manner in which the invention was made.

Subject matter developed by another person, which qualifies as prior art only under
subsection (f) or (g) of section 102 of this title, shall not preclude patentability under this
section where the subject matter and the claimed invention were, at the time the invention
was made, owned by the same person or subject to an obligation of assignment to the same
person.

AVOIDING THE LOSS
OF PATENT RIGHTS

Michael K. Kelly

Michael K. Kelly is an attorney with the firm of Snell & Wilmer in Phoenix, Arizona, with a practice concentrated in intellectual property.

The previous article reviewed the statutory bars, circumstances where the invention is considered either to be public property, or the property of another, from the after-the-fact perspective of assessing patentability. From a prospective standpoint, the statutory bars can be pitfalls that often trip up the unwary. Rights can be inadvertently lost. The statutory bars are not intuitive, and most countries have requirements even more stringent than the United States. The next article provides some insight into these potential pitfalls and how to avoid inadvertently creating a statutory bar. MAL

Abstract

Under the U.S. patent laws, an invention is eligible for patent protection if it satisfies the various statutory requirements for patentability. Some of these statutory requirements address whether the invention is sufficiently new to warrant patentability, whereas other aspects of the U.S. patent laws focus on the loss of patent rights. In particular, an invention that is otherwise patentable may be rendered ineligible for patent protection in the United States because of certain acts or omissions undertaken by the inventor or his company. This article addresses conduct relevant to avoiding the loss of patent rights.

12.1 INTRODUCTION

The patent laws of the United States and the other industrial nations of the world are designed to encourage and reward the development of new and useful technologies. Every patent granted by the U.S. Patent and Trademark Office bestows upon the inventors the honor and recognition associated with having satisfied the rigorous criteria for patentability established by the Congress of the United States.

Perhaps more important, however, each patent carries the privilege of a limited statutory monopoly and, with it, the promise of considerable economic gain. It is indeed tragic, then, that many inventors unwittingly lose their right to patent otherwise patentable inventions simply because a patent application is not filed in a timely manner.

This article examines particular provisions in the U.S. patent laws, known as the *statutory bars*, which require a patent application to be filed within one year from the happening of certain triggering events. The impact of these triggering events on foreign patent applications also will be discussed.

12.2 THE U.S. PATENT LAWS

The U.S. patent laws are set forth in Title 35 of the United States Code (35 U.S.C.). 35 U.S.C. §103 and certain subsections of 35 U.S.C. §102 generally define the standards for patentability, whether an invention is patentable over the prior art. Other subsections of §102 function to bar a patent if certain circumstances exist.

For example, under §102(c) the work of others occurring after an invention is made that would not otherwise preclude patentability may bar a patent if the applicant previously abandoned, suppressed, or concealed the invention. Section 102(d) bars a patent if a U.S. application is not filed in a timely manner following the filing of a foreign application for the same invention.

This article focuses primarily on the statutory bar provisions of §102(b), which states that a person shall be entitled to a patent unless:

> . . . the invention was patented or described in a printed publication in this or a foreign country or [was] in public use or on sale in this country, more than one year prior to the date of the application for patent in the United States.

The foregoing provision embodies four distinct *triggering events*, which start the one-year clock during which a patent application must be filed in the United States. These events are described in more detail below.

12.3 PATENTS AND PRINTED PUBLICATIONS

Issues regarding the first two triggering events, namely, whether an invention was "patented or described in a printed publication in this or a foreign country," are generally straight forward; hence, they typically are resolved with relative ease. Indeed, this language is virtually identical to the language of §102(a) regarding the impact of third party patents and publications on the patentability of inventions.

In this regard, a number of cases have considered the definition of a "printed publication" as used in §102(b) and, although the law is not entirely clear, several concepts have emerged. For example, as a general rule, the distribution of literature setting forth the invention generally constitutes a printed publication under the statute. Indeed, an academic or scholarly paper is deemed a "printed publication" once it is indexed or catalogued in a library or other retrieval system, or is otherwise generally accessible [1]. While the law regarding printed publications will certainly continue to evolve in view of advances in technology (*e.g.*, electronic journals and bulletin boards), for purposes of this discussion it is sufficient to note that a U.S. application must be filed within one year following the date on which the subject matter of an invention is first published anywhere in the world.

12.4 THE ANALYTICAL FRAMEWORK FOR EVALUATING *ON SALE* AND *PUBLIC USE* BARS

The third and fourth events that trigger the one-year clock are known as the *on sale* and *public use* bars, respectively.

Factual situations involving public use and on sale activity, when viewed in terms of the policies underlying §102(b), "present an infinite variety of legal problems wholly unsuited to mechanically-applied, technical rules" [2]. Consequently, rigid standards are not well suited to the on-sale and public use elements of §102(b), where "the policies which underlie the public use or on sale bar, in effect, define the terms of the statute" [3]. Principal among these policies are:

(1) "discouraging removal of inventions from the public domain which the public justifiably comes to believe are freely available" [4];

(2) "encouraging prompt disclosure of new and useful information" [5];

(3) "discouraging attempts to extend the length of the period of protection by not allowing the inventor to reap the benefits for more than one year prior to the filing of the application" [6]; and

(4) "giving the inventor a reasonable amount of time (one year, by statute) to determine whether a patent is worthwhile," [7] *i.e.*, "allowing an inventor time to perfect his invention, by public testing, if desired, and prepare a patent application" [8].

In contrast to the apparent flexibility suggested by the foregoing policies, the *critical date, i.e.*, exactly one year prior to the effective U.S. filing date, is immutable. Moreover, the date must be determined retrospectively. In view of the substantial property rights that turn on a patentee's ability to determine with precision when a bar comes into being, it is imperative that inventors be able to recognize an event that triggers the one-year clock.

12.5 THE ON SALE BAR

As a general proposition, an applicant is barred from seeking a patent if a product embodying the claimed invention was sold or offered for sale to the public (or to any interested prospective buyers) in the United States before the critical date. Stated another way, a U.S. application must be filed within one year of the date on which a product embodying the claimed invention was first sold or offered for sale in the United States. This is so regardless of whether an offer is ever accepted or rejected, and regardless of whether the thing sold is ever delivered.

A product or method may, under certain circumstances, be sold on a confidential basis without triggering §102(b). For example, a consultant or contractor who develops an invention and "sells" it under his consulting agreement to his employer may not trigger §102(b).

The sale or offering for sale of a product embodying the "invention", however, must be distinguished from the sale of potential patent rights associated with the invention, or obtaining financing for a company that will exploit the invention, neither of which are prohibited by §102(b) [9].

In applying the on sale bar to a particular fact pattern, it is important to keep in mind that the thing that is sold or offered for sale need not embody every element of the claimed invention; it is only necessary that the claimed invention would be obvious in view of the thing sold.

An on sale analysis also should address the relationship between the entity offering the thing for sale and the entity to whom the sale is proposed. In this regard, the law is well settled that a sale or offer between related entities, for example two companies wholly owned and/or controlled by the same entity, will not give rise to an on sale bar. Similarly, a sales transaction that takes place outside the United States is generally beyond the scope of the on sale bar.

Nor will the on sale bar apply if a product embodying the claimed invention is sold or offered for sale prior to the critical date as part of a sale or reorganization of a business activity [10]. This is consistent with the policies underlying §102(b), since a sale pursuant to the reorganization of a business entity does not effectively extend the period of the inventor's monopoly.

Finally, the question often has arisen as to the effect of an offer to sell an invention that is not yet complete. This is especially important for companies that supply goods to the government, for example when the government floats a *request for proposal* (RFP) within an industry. As part of a company's response to an RFP, it often offers to sell the government something that does not yet exist.

The issue of when an invention is sufficiently complete for purposes of the on sale bar also arises in the context of a public use bar. The factors that bear on when an invention is "complete" under §102(b) are discussed below in connection with the experimental use doctrine.

12.6 THE PUBLIC USE BAR

The fourth triggering event under §102(b) is known as the public use statutory bar. Briefly, a patent may not be obtained if the invention is publicly used in the United States before the critical date. In other words, a U.S. application must be filed within one year from the date on which the invention was first in public use in the United States.

Public use of a claimed invention under §102(b) has been defined as "any use of that invention by a person other than the inventor who is under no limitation, restriction or obligation of secrecy to the inventor" [11]. This is in contrast to the on sale bar, which is un-affected by the "secret" nature of a sale.

As with the on sale bar, the public use bar applies even though only a single instance of true public use may have occurred.

The question of whether a particular activity constitutes "public" use under the statute recently arose in the context of an appliance for positioning teeth, wherein the evidence clearly established that the inventor used the device in at least three patients more than one year prior to the filing date of the patent application [12]. The patients were under no lim-itation, restriction, or obligation of secrecy to the inventor.

In reviewing the lower court's decision, the Appeals Court [13] stressed that a deci-sion regarding a public use can only be made upon a consideration of the entirety of the sur-rounding circumstances. The court concluded that the nonsecret use of the dental appliance prior to the critical date was not dispositive of the public use issue, finding that the dentist's use of the appliance fell within the purview of the experimental use doctrine and, as such, did not constitute a "public use" under the law.

If an inventor is making commercial use of the invention, such use may be deemed "public use" under §102(b) regardless of whether the use is made under circumstances that preserve its secrecy. Judge Learned Hand, often quoted for his insightful opinions on patent-related topics, referred to this type of public use as use that simply "does not inform the art" [14], even though such commercial use may nonetheless pose a public use bar.

The preclusive effect of the public use and on sale bars must be balanced against the countervailing policy of allowing an inventor to complete his invention before requiring the application to be filed. Out of these competing objectives has emerged the experimental use doctrine.

12.7 THE EXPERIMENTAL USE DOCTRINE

Succinctly, the *experimental use doctrine* holds that a reasonable amount of experi-mental/developmental activity is permissible, *i.e.*, is outside the gambit of §102(b), notwith-standing the existence of commercial indicia surrounding the activity.

Although the on sale bar is distinct from the public use bar, they both nonetheless are avoided if the primary purpose of the activity is experimental, regardless of whether it also implicates the "sale" or "use" provisions of the statute [15].

One of the earliest cases involving experimental use is *City of Elizabeth v. American Nicholson Pavement Co.*, 97 U.S. 126 (1877). There, a section of a toll road, built accord-ing to the patent in the suit, was constructed by the inventor six years before he filed his patent application. The section of road consisted of approximately 70 feet of wooden pave-ment, which the inventor sought to test by subjecting the road to daily use by the general public for the six year period.

According to the Court, there was no question that the use of the pavement was, in one sense, public. The focus, however, was whether such use constituted impermissible public use within the meaning of the statute. The Court placed primary reliance on the fact that the nature of a street pavement is "such that it cannot be experimented upon satisfactorily except on a highway, which is always public" [16]. Thus, even though "[t]he public had the incidental use of the pavement", such use did not constitute "public use" under the statute. 123 U.S. at 136.

The Federal Circuit continues to place primary reliance upon the rationale enunciated in *Elizabeth*. For example, in *Grain Processing Corp. v. American Maize Prods. Co.* [17], the Federal Circuit reiterated: "The use of an invention by the inventor himself, or of any other person under his direction, by way of experiment, and in order to bring the invention to perfection, has never been regarded as . . . a [public] use".

In the *Smith & McLaughlin* case, the Federal Circuit drew a bright line between permissible experimentation and impermissible commercial exploitation [18]. In *Smith*, the precritical date activity involved the testing by seventy-six consumers of a vacuumable, powdered carpet composition used as a room deodorizer. The consumers were provided with two versions of the product and were instructed to use the product in their homes for two weeks and thereafter answer questions regarding their preference. The patent applicants contended that the test was necessary to obtain scientific data on the operation and usefulness of their invention and, as such, it fell under the experimental use exception.

The Federal Circuit emphatically asserted that the experimental use exception "does not include market testing where the inventor is attempting to gauge consumer demand for his claimed invention" [19]. The court viewed the dominant purpose of the tests as an attempt to determine whether potential consumers would buy the product and how much they would pay for it, the tests being only incidentally geared toward technological improvement. This was so despite the sworn affidavit testimony of the applicants that they did not consider the tests to be commercial [20].

Thus, the line between commercial exploitation and experimental use was clearly drawn, although other important factors in the experimental use equation were yet to evolve.

In the tooth positioning case discussed above, the Appeals Court stressed that a public use is avoided so long as the inventor is engaged, in good faith, in testing the operation of the device ". . . and no one would say that such a use, pursued with a bona fide intent of testing the qualities of the machine, would be a public use, within the meaning of the statute" [21]. The court took a sympathetic view toward an inventor's good faith attempt to perfect his invention, stating that "the public interest is also deemed to be served by allowing an inventor time to perfect his invention, by public testing, if desired, and prepare a patent application" [22].

12.8 THE CURRENT ANALYTICAL FRAMEWORK

The absence of rigid rules in a §102(b) analysis is consistent with the mandate that all the facts and circumstances of each particular case be considered; no one factor is universally controlling. It is clear, however, that commercial exploitation is the linchpin of a

§102(b) bar and that experimental use precludes application of a §102(b) bar. This is equally true in an on sale or a public use contest: ". . . [A] use or sale is experimental for purposes of Section 102(b) if it represents a bona fide effort to perfect the invention or to ascertain whether it will answer its intended purpose" [23]. Stated another way, a certain amount of commercial exploitation is acceptable if it is "merely incidental to the primary purpose of experimentation to perfect that invention" [24].

Clearly, activity that can be demonstrated to be experimental falls outside the purview of the sale and use provisions of §102(b). Although no easy test has been articulated for determining whether a particular activity constitutes experimental use, a review of the court decisions can provide guidance that will help inventors and companies tailor developmental activity to ensure that it is treated as experimental (rather than commercial) use, as described below.

12.9 INDICIA OF EXPERIMENTAL USE

In determining the purpose of alleged experimental activity, objective evidence is preferred over an inventor's subjective intent [25]. Such objective evidence may involve proof of whether the inventor inspected the invention regularly during the experimental period; whether the inventor retained control over the invention; and whether any commercial exploitation was merely incidental to the primary purpose of the experimentation. In the carpet cleaner case, side-by-side testing of two versions of the carpet deodorizer worked against a finding of experimentation inasmuch as the test was designed to gauge consumer preference for optimum pellet size. Moreover, it is settled law that the experiments performed with respect to unclaimed features of the invention (*e.g.*, pellet size) will not save the activity from a §102(b) bar [26].

Other factors include whether or not restrictions were placed on the participants in the experiments; whether confidentiality was imposed; whether the samples were required to be returned; whether the experiment was (or could have been) conducted at the inventor's facilities; and whether the real purpose in the activity was "to improve and perfect the invention", rather than being merely incidental and subsidiary to a commercial motivation [27].

Other facts relevant but not dispositive to experimental use include the length of the test period; whether or not payment is made for the device; whether records are kept of the progress of the experiment; whether persons other than the inventor conducted the experiment; how many tests were conducted; and how long the testing period was in relationship to tests of similar devices.

Although it is difficult to extract working rules of law from these decisions, courts are not likely to impose a bar where genuine technological development was being conducted in the presence of incidental commercial activity. In cases in which a §102(b) bar was imposed despite the patentee's protestations of experimental use, it appears that the patentee attempted to retrospectively recast ordinary sale and public use activity as "experimental use" simply because they waited too long to file the patent application.

12.10 EFFECT OF PUBLICATION OR PUBLIC USE ON FOREIGN PATENTING

The one-year grace period set forth in §102(b) is essentially unique to U.S. law. That is, a publication or public use of the invention at any time prior to placing an application on file generally precludes patenting in other industrialized countries (although at sale or offer for sale does not in itself preclude foreign filing). Accordingly, for those inventions in which foreign protection may be sought, it is necessary to place an application on file before any such use takes place.

Under an international treaty recognized by most industrialized countries, if a foreign patent application is filed within one year of the filing of a U.S. patent application, the foreign application is treated as if it had been filed on the same day as the U.S. application (Taiwan being a notable exception). Thus, it may be most efficient to prepare and file in the U.S. before publication or public use takes place, and thereafter file corresponding applications in desired foreign countries during the ensuing year, claiming priority on the prior filed U.S. application. Filing in the U.S. first is further recommended in view of the rigorous formal requirements of U.S. law; if the text of a patent application meets the rigorous statutory requirements of U.S. practice, it will certainly survive formal scrutiny by most foreign patent offices. The converse, however, may not be true. Thus, one should proceed cautiously when filing an application in the U.S. Patent and Trademark Office that was prepared by a non-U.S. patent attorney for filing in a foreign patent office.

12.11 CONCLUSION

Substantial patent rights may be irretrievably lost in the United States and abroad as a result of the untimely disclosure of an invention. If foreign patents are of concern, an application should be filed in the United States before any public disclosure or use of the invention.

Even when foreign patent rights are not in issue, inventors are well advised to carefully monitor sale and use activity to avoid inadvertent loss of rights. Given the complexity and ever changing nature of the law surrounding §102(b), any questions regarding the applicability of the statutory bars should be resolved through consultation with patent counsel.

NOTES

[1] See *Massachusetts Institute of Technology v. A.B. Fortia*, 227 U.S.P.Q. 428 (Fed. Cir. 1985); *In re Hall*, 228 U.S.P.Q. 453 (Fed. Cir. 1986).

[2] *Western Marine Elecs. v. Furuno Elec. Co.*, 226 USPQ 334, 337 (Fed. Cir. 1985).

[3] Barmag, 221 USPQ at 565.

[4] *King Instrument Corp. v. Otari Corp.*, 226 USPQ 402, 406 (Fed. Cir. 1985).

[5] *T.P. Labs., Inc. v. Professional Positioners, Inc.*, 220 USPQ 577, 580 (Fed. Cir. 1984).

[6] *Id.*

[7] *Western Marine Elecs. v. Furuno Elec. Co.*, 226 USPQ 334, 337 (Fed. Cir. 1985).

[8] T.P. Labs., 220 USPQ at 580.

[9] *Molecular Research Corp. v. CBS, Inc.*, See pg 6–54 of Chisolm.

[10] *Micro-Magnetic Indus., Inc. v. Advance Automatic Sales Co.*, 180 USPQ 118 (9th Cir. 1973).

[11] *In re Smith & McLaughlin*, 218 USPQ 976, 983 (Fed. Cir. 1983) (citing *Egbert v. Lippmann*, 104 U.S. 333, 336 (1881)).

[12] *T.P. Labs., Inc. v. Professional Positioners, Inc.*, 220 USPQ 577, 580 (Fed. Cir. 1984).

[13] The Court of Appeals for the Federal Circuit has exclusive appellate jurisdiction over all matters arising under the patent laws.

[14] *Gillman v. Stern*, 46 USPQ 430, 434 (2d Cir. 1940).

[15] Baker Oil Tools, *supra*, 4 USPQ2d at 1213.

[16] *Id.*

[17] 5 USPQ 2d 1788, 1792 (Fed. Cir. 1988).

[18] 218 USPQ at 983.

[19] 218 USPQ at 983.

[20] *Id.* at 979–80.

[21] *Id.* at 581 (quoting City of Elizabeth, 97 U.S. at 134–35).

[22] 220 USPQ at 580.

[23] *Pennwalt Corp. v. Arizona, Inc.*, 222 USPQ 833, 838 (Fed. Cir. 1984).

[24] Barmag, 221 USPQ at 567; *Pennwalt Corp. v. Akzona, Inc.*, 222 USPQ 833, 838 (Fed. Cir. 1984).

[25] *In re Smith*, 218 USPQ at 982.

[26] *Id.* at 984.

[27] *Id.* at 983–84.

Article

13

PATENTING SOFTWARE INVOLVING MATHEMATICAL ALGORITHMS

Joseph A. Biela

Joseph A. Biela is an Intellectual Property Attorney and Assistant Counsel for the International Business Machines Corporation.

Perhaps the most hotly contested issues of intellectual property law in the last few decades have related to the protection of software products under the patent and copyright laws.

Historically, there has been a great deal of controversy in the courts as to whether software and firmware developments come within any of the categories of patentable subject matter specified by the patent statute. It is now clear that, as a practical matter with the exception of abstract implementations of mathematical algorithms, patent protection is available for software inventions. It is only necessary that the patent claims be competently drafted.

There is also much controversy as to whether various nonliteral aspects of software are more properly categorized as expression *and thus copyrightable, or as an* idea *or dictated by function and thus uncopyrightable. The law on point is very much in flux; the breadth of copyright protection as applied to nonliteral aspects of software varies from court to court.*

The following articles discuss the patentability of software inventions and the present state of the law with respect to software protection. MAL

Abstract

Whether *software* inventions should fall within that class of inventions that are patentable has been discussed and debated for more than 30 years. In the early 1960s, software houses supported the patentability of computer programs. The software houses wanted a variety of forms of legal protection for programs in view of their commercial value. However, hardware manufacturers were generally against the patenting of software because of the perceived negative impact that patented software would have on the sale of computer hardware. Universities were opposed to the patenting of software, as was the U.S. Patent and Trademark Office (PTO). The PTO was opposed for several reasons, one being the lack of experience, at that time, of most PTO Examiners in software technology. Nevertheless, in the late 1960s, the PTO began accepting patent applications having claims directed to software inventions. One of the first software patents to be allowed by the PTO was issued in 1968 and claimed a method of sorting. Since the 1960s, many software inventions have been patented, but only after the claimed inventions were found to have satisfied a number of requirements. A threshold requirement, which is the focus of this article, is that a claimed software invention must fall within a category of subject matter that is amenable to patent protection. (The statutory categories are enumerated in §101 of the 1952 Patents Act, Title 35.) Whether a claim directed to a software invention constitutes statutory or patentable subject matter has not been entirely resolved despite years of controversy and judicial interpretation of §101. However, in view of the many judicial pronouncements on the patentability of software, several issues appear to have been settled. These well-settled issues have established the opposite ends of a *patentability spectrum* for software inventions that involve mathematical algorithms [1].

13.1 NONSTATUTORY (UNPATENTABLE) SUBJECT MATTER

It appears to be clear that, at one end of the spectrum, a software invention won't fall within a statutory category, *i.e.*, won't be regarded as patentable subject matter, if it merely presents and solves a mathematical problem or algorithm. That is, if the claim recites, either directly or indirectly, the steps for solving a mathematical equation (resulting in the generation of an abstract numerical solution), then the claim will not be patentable. As an example, consider the "well-known" mathematical expression

$$\int H \bullet d\ell = \int_s (J_{cond} + J_{disp}) \bullet ds$$

which says that the line integral of the H field, as measured by amperes per meter, around a closed contour is equal to all conduction and displacement currents enclosed. (The equation should be recognizable as one of Maxwell's equations derived from Ampere's Law.) A claim directed to this or any similar expression would not pass the threshold requirement of patentability. That is, a claim presenting and solving an equation would not be considered patentable subject matter. Such a claim, if allowed, might arguably preempt all uses of the mathematical expression. Electronic circuits having physical elements such as resistors through which a conduction current

$$(J_{cond})$$

passes and capacitors through which a displacement current

$$(J_{disp})$$

passes would constitute patentable subject matter because capacitors, resistors, and circuits that comprise those as well as other electrical apparatus clearly fall within the statutory *machine* category. The operation of patentable electronic circuits and circuit elements can be explained by equations such as Maxwell's equations, but such equations, in and of themselves, would not be patentable, *i.e.*, would not be regarded as falling within that category of subject matter that is amenable to patent protection.

13.2 STATUTORY (PATENTABLE) SUBJECT MATTER

At the opposite end of the spectrum, it appears to be clear that an invention *involving software* will fall within a statutory category, *i.e.*, can be regarded as patentable subject matter, if an arithmetic expression is implemented in a specific manner to define structural relationships between physical (hardware) elements of a claim or to refine or limit process steps. An example of a statutory invention involving software is the process of operating a rubber mold (press) using a computer program that repetitively calculates an equation—the Arrhenius equation—at frequent intervals while the rubber that is being molded is curing [2]. The mold or press is opened at the moment when the elapsed curing time is determined to be equivalent to the required curing time, which is periodically calculated using the Arrhenius equation. The curing time is a function of the temperature, which is being constantly monitored at a location closely adjacent to the mold cavity in the press and provided as data to the equation each time the required curing time is calculated. The invention is understood to be a process for molding rubber and not a mathematical formula. The invention would not preempt all uses of a mathematical formula . . . the Arrhenius equation. Implementation of the Arrhenius equation refines or limits the steps of the molding process.

13.3 OTHER SUBJECT MATTER

Somewhere in between the fairly clearly defined ends of the spectrum are software inventions that are not clearly patentable (statutory) nor clearly unpatentable (nonstatutory). Deciding whether such inventions are patentable or unpatentable can raise questions having to do with each invention's connection to hardware or to a process the answers to which can be fairly subjective. These inventions often involve mathematical expressions that are applied in some manner to physical elements or process steps. Whether these inventions are patentable (meet the statutory subject matter requirement) will depend on whether or not the application of the expression—the algorithm—can be circumscribed by more than a field of use limitation or nonessential post solution activity. *Nonessential post solution activity* could be the mere generation of a numerical result that is stored in a memory location or the use of that stored numerical result to ring a bell. An example of an invention that falls between the two ends of the spectrum is the one described and claimed in U.S. Patent 4,744,028. The invention is directed to an improved numerical dynamic programming (optimization) algorithm called the "simplex method". (*Note* that since the invention was patented, the inventor was able to successfully demonstrate that the application of the algorithm was circumscribed by more than a field of use limitation or nonessential post solution activity in order to pass the threshold requirement of patentable subject matter. However, in my opinion it could have been successfully argued that the invention was not patentable because it did not fall within that category of subject matter that is amenable to patent protection.)

It is known that by using the simplex method, one can determine how best to allocate limited resources among competing activities, *i.e.*, by optimizing an objective function that includes variables that represent all competing activities. One can arrive at the optimal solution by interactively *moving* from one feasible solution (allocation) to another until no better solution (allocation) exists. This method does not require that all possible solutions be considered.

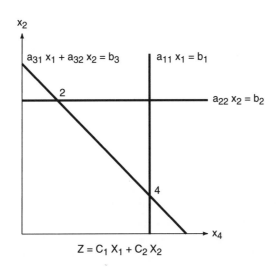

Referring to the above graph, the objective function to optimize is provided as

$$Z = C_1 X_1 + C_2 X_2$$

where each

$$X_j$$

represents the level of a competing activity

$$j$$

and each

$$C_i$$

represents an increase in Z, *e.g.* cost, that results from each unit increase in

$$X_j$$

The constraints placed on the objective function are

$$b_i \text{ ge } a_{11} X_1, \quad b_2 \text{ ge } a_{22} X_2$$

and

$$b_3 \text{ ge } a_{31} X_1 + a_{32} X_2$$

where

$$b_i$$

represents the amount of resource

$$i$$

available for allocation and

$$a_{ij}$$

represents the amount of resource

$$i$$

consumed by each unit of activity

$$j$$

All

$$X_j$$

are greater than or equal to zero. The constraints are illustrated graphically in Figure 1.

The simplex method begins at a corner-point feasible solution (corner-point 1) and then iteratively *moves* to a better adjacent corner-point feasible solution (corner-point 2) until no better adjacent corner-point feasible solution exists that also satisfies the constraints placed upon the objective function. The optimal solution is provided by the values of the variables

$$X_1$$

and

$$X_2$$

which will optimize Z and still satisfy the constraints.

The inventor realized that this mathematical method for finding an optimal solution was not sufficiently fast to be implementable in a real-time control environment. The *old* simplex method was too slow to be used to control, dynamically, an on-going process, *e.g.*, a telephone routing process. The inventor found that he could speed up the method by obtaining the optimal values of the variables after fewer iterations. He accomplished this by normalizing the variables with respect to the constraints placed upon the objective function before evaluating each feasible solution in order to progress more quickly to the optimal solution, *i.e.*, to the optimal allocation of resources.

The claim shown in Figure 2 is one of several independent claims that issued in the patent. The claim presents and solves a mathematical algorithm—an improved simplex

USP 4,744,028–CLAIM

A METHOD FOR ALLOCATING PHYSICAL RESOURCES USING A LINEAR PROGRAMMING MODEL INCLUDING THE STEPS OF:

PRESCRIBING A LINEAR PROGRAMMING MODEL WITH AN OBJECTIVE FUNCTION AND A PLURALITY OF CONSTRAINTS WHICH ADEQUATELY DESCRIBES FEASIBLE ALLOCATIONS OF SAID PHYSICAL RESOURCES,

IDENTIFYING A TENTATIVE PHYSICAL RESOURCE ALLOCATION WHICH IS STRICTLY FEASIBLE,

ITERATIVELY IMPROVING SAID TENTATIVE RESOURCE ALLOCATION BY *NORMALIZING* SAID TENTATIVE RESOURCE ALLOCATION WITH RESPECT TO SAID CONSTRAINTS AND ALTERING SAID TENTATIVE RESOURCE ALLOCATIONS IN THE DIRECTION SPECIFIED BY SAID OBJECTIVE FUNCTION, AND

ALLOCATING SAID RESOURCES IN ACCORDANCE WITH THE MOST IMPROVED TENTATIVE RESOURCE ALLOCATION.

Figure 2   An example of an independent claim, issued in a patent

method—which is, to some degree, applied to physical elements, *i.e.*, the allocation of physical resources. The claim doesn't clearly fall at either end of the *patentability spectrum.* However, it apparently has been demonstrated to the satisfaction of the PTO that the mathematical algorithm has been sufficiently applied to physical elements so that the claimed invention arguably falls nearer to the statutory (patentable) subject matter end of the spectrum. Prior to submitting a claim to the PTO for examination for inventions of this type, it will be difficult to determine with any degree of certainty if it will or will not pass the threshold statutory subject matter requirement.

An approach that an inventor could take would be to initially draft a claim that applies the algorithm to physical elements or process steps. Merely stating in the claim an environment in which the algorithm could be used or an insignificant use of the solution without demonstrating how the algorithm is applied to physical elements or process steps will likely not be sufficient. Once the claim is drafted, the inventor should then decide how important the claim would be to others if allowed. If it would be important, it may be worth pursuing despite the uncertainty as to its patentability [3].

13.4 REFERENCE BIBLIOGRAPHY

Pollack, "The Gordian algorithm: an attempt to untangle the international dilemma over the protection of computer software", 22 Law and Policy in International Business 815 (1991).

Whitmeyer, "A Plea for Due Process: Defining the Proper Scope of Patent Protection for Computer Software", 85 Nw. U.L. Rev. 1103 (1990).

Chisum, "The Future of Software Protection: The patentability of algorithms", 47 U. Pitt. L. Rev. 959 (1986).

Simenauer, "Patentability of Computer-Related Inventions: A criticism of the PTO's view on algorithms", 54 Geo. Wash. L. Rev. 871 (1986).

Hanneman, Dr. H. W., *The Patentability of Computer Software*, (Kluwer Law and Taxation Publishers, 1985).

NOTES

[1] There are software inventions that do not involve mathematical algorithms. Very often such inventions involve program structure such as control blocks, tables, fields in tables, pointers to those fields, etc. It is beyond the scope of this paper to attempt to define what a software invention is and to discuss the differences.

[2] *In re* Diehr and Lutton, 203 USPQ 44 (CCPA 1979), *Diamond v. Diehr and Lutton*, 209 USPQ1 (US Supreme Court 1981).

[3] If the claim passed the threshold test, it would still have to satisfy the legal requirements of novelty, unobviousness, and utility.

THE STATE OF INTELLECTUAL PROPERTY LAW GOVERNING PROTECTION OF COMPUTER PROGRAMS*

David Bender

David Bender is Of Counsel to White & Case in New York City, where his practice involves litigation, counseling, and transactional matters relating to computer law and intellectual property law. He is the author of *Computer Law: Software Protection and Litigation*, a three-volume treatise published by Matthew Bender & Co.

Abstract

This article addresses the panoply of mechanisms available to the proprietor of intellectual property rights in computer programs [1] for protecting those rights [2]. The proprietor must appreciate the scope and nature of its rights in order to appreciate how to preserve and protect them, so as to optimize its exploitation of the software. Moreover, an adverse party must comprehend the scope of the proprietor's rights so as to recognize the bounds of its own legitimate conduct, and to assist it in acquiring from the proprietor rights under the software.

The underlying premises are (1) that the proprietor has invested much time, effort and expense in developing and marketing its software, and (2) that the law and circumstances may afford protection to certain aspects embodied in software. The *trick* for the proprietor is to find a way of applying the law and circumstances so as to protect those aspects whose protection significantly advances its interests.

14.1 THE GOAL OF SOFTWARE PROTECTION: THE TWO IMPORTANT QUESTIONS

The proprietor's goal in protecting its software is to optimize the exploitation of it. The goal is not to protect every aspect of the software to the full extent possible. Rather, it is to identify and implement a plan for protecting those aspects of the software that commercially merit protection, so as to promote the proprietor's commercial interests.

In pursuing this goal, the proprietor must answer two important questions: (1) What are the commercially important aspects of the software? [3] (2) What is the technical and commercial environment in which the software must function? It is only after answering these questions that the proprietor can meaningfully address the protections that may be available and fashion a plan for achieving its goal.

The answer to the first question requires the proprietor to focus on the subject matter worth protecting (many aspects of the software, while eminently protectable, will not be worth protecting). The answer to the second question affords valuable information on the realities of which types of protection will *work* for the software in question.

14.2 THE NATURE OF SOFTWARE (AND WHY IT IS DIFFICULT TO APPLY TRADITIONAL IP LAW)

14.2.1 The Software Development Process

The process of creating a program can conveniently be broken into five phases: problem definition, flow charting, coding, debugging, and documentation. Problem definition defines what the computer will be asked to do. Programmer and user discuss the function of the program, and develop specifications setting forth a precise statement of the problem, the data to be input, the data to be output, and other matters such as programming language to be used, hardware on which the program must function, and compatibility requirements.

In the flow charting phase, the program takes on shape and intermediate detail by means of pictorial representation. The flow chart is a graphical link between the somewhat general problem definition and the detailed coding. The program is divided into interdependent parts (*modules*) whose interrelationship (the *architecture*) is defined. The flow chart sets forth the sequence of steps describing the computing process and is comprehensible to programmers. In understanding the functioning of the program, the flow chart is invaluable [4]. The flow chart is the *blue print* of the program.

In this phase the general algorithms are determined [5]. An algorithm embodies the particular method to be used in solving the problem.

The coding phase involves the actual writing of the instructions comprising the program, in the appropriate programming language. Each instruction consists of one or more words or symbols with predetermined precise meanings. Most coding today is done in *source code*, which utilizes instructions, often vaguely resembling English, which are comprehensible to programmers [6].

Debugging is a most frustrating phase of the programming process, and consists of ascertaining that the program functions as desired. The difficulty of debugging increases with program size. For a sizeable program, at least half the total effort in the programming process may be devoted to debugging.

The most thankless phase of the program process is documentation. After debugging (if not before), two types of instructional manuals must be created. User documentation informs the user how to operate the software; system documentation instructs programmers responsible for maintaining and modifying the software as to how it functions. A person armed only with user documentation has sufficient information to use the program, but not to modify it or rectify errors that crop up [7]. A knowledgeable person armed with system documentation is able to modify the program and rectify errors in it. Many licensors transmit to their licensees only object code and user documentation. This permits the licensee to use the program, but not to modify or *fix* it.

14.2.2 Types of Programs

For purposes of determining how best to protect programs, there are a number of characteristics that may be used as a basis for dividing up the universe of programs. One useful characteristic is the size of the computer on which the program is designed to run. *Mainframe* computers are the large gray or blue boxes that stand on the floor of corporate data processing centers; a mainframe may cost $80,000–$12,000,000 [8]. Because software for mainframes is generally expensive and used in a corporate (or government) environment, it is generally possible to have an executed written agreement when rights in such software are conveyed.

At the other extreme in size stands the microcomputer or personal computer (PC), occupying space on a desk and costing from a few hundred dollars to perhaps $40,000 [9]. Many PC's are owned by individuals, and a PC software package typically is marketed for $50–$600. The number of PC's in use is many times the number of mainframes, and a popular PC software package may be marketed to the extent of several hundred-thousand copies. In contradistinction, a popular mainframe package may be marketed to a thousand users. Because PC software is marketed *over the counter* and for a relatively small sum of money, a conveyance of rights in PC software is rarely accompanied by an executed written agreement.

Another way of breaking down the universe of programs is by function. Programs that are inherently involved in the functioning of the computer, regardless of the specific task undertaken are *system programs.* For example, system programs ascertain that the various parts of the computer function together, they load other programs into the computer, they interrupt processing when necessary, they allocate storage space, and they determine what action to take when an error is detected. On the other hand, programs directed to the particular result desired by the user (such as calculating and printing the payroll) are *application programs.* In most instances the system programs in use emanate from the hardware manufacturer, whereas the vast majority of application programs come from other vendors.

14.2.3 Unusual Aspects of Computer Programs

In certain of its characteristics, the program is unusual if not unique, and this often causes confusion when the traditional rules of intellectual property (IP) law are applied in the program scenario. Technically, the program is unusual in that it assumes a number of different manifestations, *e.g.*, source code, object code, print-out, embodied on a silicon chip, embedded in a floppy disc, represented by electronic pulses internal to the computer. Commercially, programs are unusual in their ubiquity. Long ago, they spilled over the transom of the computer from and into all areas of our lives. They control our industrial processes and even operate within the engines of our cars. It is difficult to get away from them. As a result, in many transactions that previously would have involved, for example, only chemical technology, we must today be aware of important software issues.

The program is unusual also in that there (still) are many in positions of corporate power who do not recognize the importance and expense associated with software [10]. Software and biotechnology are the two fastest growing areas of technology (by far). Another way that programs are unusual is that the field is subject to more than its share of nomenclature problems. Legally, programs are unusual because attached to them is more than the normal degree of uncertainty regarding legal protection. The program has a number of different aspects, and each of these has protectability considerations. Some appear to conflict with others, and there is no general agreement about how best to protect interests in programs.

Underlying much of the confusion is the fact that programs are the only form of technology where a written expression interacts directly with a machine and causes it to perform a process. In this way, something that may be characterized as a writing becomes part of a machine and controls a process. This raises issues regarding the boundary of the domain of protection that traditionally has been directed to writings, and the domain of protection traditionally directed to processes.

14.2.4 Software Aspects You Might Want to Protect

Each proprietor must give thought to those aspects which, if protected, would give it a significant edge in the marketplace. Some aspects for which many proprietors have sought protection are: source code; object code; architecture; input screens; use of particular keyboard keys for specific functions; algorithms; documentation; and input format.

The key to effecting meaningful protection is to identify one or more commercially valuable aspects of the program in question that can effectively be protected by one or more available mechanisms.

14.3 COPYRIGHT PROTECTION OF SOFTWARE

14.3.1 Summary

Copyright is available to exclude unauthorized third parties from copying or distributing reproductions of the protected work and, in particular, is directed to precluding the reproduction of expression, as opposed to idea. Although the U.S. Supreme Court has yet to rule on these issues, the strong consensus of lower court opinions is that the content and structure of program code are protectable by copyright, and the majority of courts opining on the issue have held that the *look and feel* of input screens are likewise protectable under copyright.

Copyright protects against copying, but not against independent development. Moreover, copyright has a duration that, in the program environment, may be equivalent to eternity—the author's life plus 50 years, or for *works made for hire*, 75 years. Remedies for infringement include preliminary and permanent injunction, impoundment and destruction, damages and profits, and a discretionary attorney's fee. And willful infringement for profit constitutes a crime.

14.3.2 Statutes

The Copyright Act makes only scant specific reference to programs. Section 101 of the Act defines the term *computer program*, and Section 117 provides in part: ". . . it is not an infringement for an owner of a copy of a computer program to make . . . another copy or adaptation . . . provided . . . such a new copy or adaptation is created as an essential step in the utilization of the computer program in conjunction with a machine and that it is used in no other manner". That section also authorizes the reproduction of a copy for archival purposes.

Section 101 defines a copy as a material object "in which a work is fixed by any method now known or later developed, and from which the work can be perceived, reproduced, or otherwise communicated, either directly or with the aid of a machine or device".

Section 102 provides that copyright subsists "in original works of authorship fixed in any tangible medium of expression now known or later developed, from which they can be perceived, reproduced, or otherwise communicated, either directly or with the aid of a machine or device. . . ." Section 102(b) excludes from copyright "any idea, procedure, process, system, method of operation, concept, principle, or discovery, regardless of the form in which it is described, explained, illustrated, or embodied in such work".

14.3.3 Cases

Although the propriety and bounds of copyright protection for programs have attracted interest since the early 1960s, there were no cases of great import before 1978. By 1981, however, the cases were cascading down. What we have had since then is what I characterize as three *waves* of cases. First wave cases treated various issues of copyright protection for the content of program instructions. Second wave cases dealt with protectability of the structure, sequence, and organization of program instructions. Third wave cases spoke to protectability of various aspects for the user program interface—the so-called *look and feel* of a program and its use.

The First Wave—A barrage of first wave cases have come down dealing with copyrightability for source code and of object code, with whether a ROM and a diskette were copies, and with whether system programs (as well as application programs) are copyrightable [11].

Accordingly, after the first wave of computer program copyright cases, the decisions were unanimous in holding that: source code and object code are copyrightable; both application programs and system programs are copyrightable; and ROMS and diskettes embodying programs are copies. It was left to the next wave of cases to determine (at least in part) just what about a program is protectable by copyright.

The Second Wave—The most frequently cited second wave cases are *Computer Associates Int'l, Inc. v. Altai,* 982 F.2d 693 (2d Cir. 1992) and *Whelan Associates, Inc. v. Jaslow Dental Lab., Inc.,* 797 F.2d 1222, 230 U.S.P.Q. 481 (3d Cir 1986), cert. denied, 479 U.S. 1031 (1987). *Whelan*'s major contribution lies in the methodology adopted to distinguish idea from expression. Defendant had access to plaintiff's source code and then created a functionally similar program in a different programming language.

Whelan adopted a useful tool for making the idea/expression distinction: to set forth the steps involved in program development, from problem identification through coding and beyond [12]. This progression, with each step embodying more detail than the preceding one, was critical to development of a basis for drawing the line between idea and expression.

The steps identified were: problem identification; problem definition; flow charting; formulation of architecture; determination of input; arrangement of data files: coding; and certain steps beyond coding. Presumably all would agree that the first step (problem identification) is not in and of itself protectable by copyright. Similarly, all would likely agree that the cases overwhelmingly hold and suggest that code is so protectable. These are the two end points of the idea/expression spectrum in the computer program milieu. The court decided the subject matter before it was expression and therefore protectable.

This methodology brought the copyright computer program cases into line with traditional copyright doctrine, as expressed at least as long ago as 1930, in *Nichols v. Universal Pictures Corp.* [13]. Although that case dealt with a play, Learned Hand's words are equally applicable to a program:

> [Copyright] cannot be limited literally to the text, else a plagiarist would escape by immaterial variations. . . Upon any work . . a great number of patterns of increasing generality will fit equally well, as more and more of the incident is left out. The last may perhaps be no more than the most general statement of what the play is about, and at times might consist only of its title; but there is a point in the series of abstractions where they are no longer protected, since otherwise the playwright could prevent the use of his ideas to which, apart form the expression, his property is never extended . . nobody has ever been able to fix that boundary, and nobody ever can. In some cases the question has been treated as though it was analogous to lifting a portion out of the copyrighted work . . . ; but the analogy is not a good one, because, though the skeleton is a part of the body, it pervades and supports the whole.

Although not citing *Nichols, Whelan* held that copying the structure, sequence, and organization of a program constitutes infringement. However, in determining where to draw the idea/expression line, the *Whelan* court held that the purpose of a program is the idea, and anything more detailed than that is expression, surely a surprising result.

It was left to *Altai* to rectify this deficiency by applying a three-step test (abstraction, filtration, comparison). First, plaintiff's work is broken into its different levels of abstraction. Next, on each level a filtration is performed to excise material not protectable by copyright. Thus, for example, ideas and processes are cast out because they are not expression. And expression merged with idea or considered a stock device or dictated by functional considerations is also cast out as being not within the realm of copyright. Finally, that which remains is compared with defendant's work. If there is substantial similarity, there is infringement.

The Third Wave: Look and Feel—The third wave of cases goes beyond the program itself and seeks to protect the *interface* between the user and the program. Generally, this interface relates either to the display screens projected on the CRT by the program (permitting the user to select various options and/or to input data in prescribed format), or to the use of particular keys, on the various standard keyboards, to perform particular functions. The third wave of cases represent a bold attempt by software developers to focus on those aspects of the use of their software that they view as commercially important. Having identified those aspects, they have sought, by use of copyright, to exclude others from using them. Third wave cases seem generally to be proceeding more slowly and tentatively than did the first and second wave genre.

The two most famous third wave cases are *Lotus Dev. Corp. v. Paperback Software Int'l* [14], and *Apple v. Microsoft* [15]. Plaintiff in *Lotus* sought to preclude copying of the *look and feel* of the user interface [16] for its popular spreadsheet program. The court promulgated a three-part test for determining whether a work constituted copyrightable subject matter [17]. Applying its test, the court found the user interface to constitute copyrightable subject matter, and further found that substantial portions were infringed.

In *Microsoft,* Apple sued Microsoft [18] and Hewlett-Packard [19] for infringement of audiovisual copyrights in the graphical user interface (GUI) [20] for Apple's Macintosh computer. Microsoft had developed the DOS operating system used in IBM-compatible PC's; DOS had a character-based user interface. The Mac GUI was more *user friendly* than the character-based interface [21]. In 1985, Microsoft released Windows 1.0, which operated *on top of* DOS to extend its graphical capabilities. Each new version of Windows seemed to resemble the Mac GUI more closely. The court had previously determined that a license agreement authorized Microsoft to use features in Windows 1.0; the court was now called upon to determine which (if any) protectable elements of Windows 2.3 and 3.0 defendants were not authorized to copy [22].

The court enumerated aspects of a work that are not protectable. Where idea and expression cannot be separated, only identical copying may be barred. If technical or conceptual constraints limit the ways to express an idea (*indispensable expression*), only *virtually identical* copying is prohibited. Stock features and stereotyped expression are *scenes a faire* and not protectable. Functionality may deprive a feature of protectability. Lack of originality renders a feature nonprotectable. Based on its analysis of the many details alleged to be protected by copyright, the court held that almost all of them fell under one or another of these rubrics, so that very little about the GUI was protected by copyright.

Thus, software copyright plaintiffs, who sailed through the first wave unscathed and who won the majority of their battles also in the second wave, have run into somewhat tougher sledding in the *look and feel* third wave. Implicitly this may be the result of trying to ride the copyright horse too hard. There is growing concern that the scope of protection afforded to software by the first, and especially the second, waves, may be contorting the fabric of copyright. Hence, there is a tendency to *go slow* in the third wave.

14.3.4 Criminal Copyright Law

Section 506 of the Copyright Act provides that willful infringement for profit constitutes a crime; a violation is punishable by imprisonment for up to five years and a fine of up to $250,000. Possible advantages to criminal proceedings are court calendar precedence, reduced expense, rapid determination of critical facts, and possibly a diminished possibility of a counterclaim. Disadvantages include a loss of control over the proceedings and possible adverse effect on the proprietor's employees.

14.4 PATENT PROTECTION OF PROGRAM-RELATED INVENTIONS

14.4.1 Summary

The two most prominent questions in the area of *software patents* are what constitutes appropriate subject matter for a patent and how much must be disclosed in a patent application. Regarding subject matter, a bare *mathematical algorithm* is not proper, but an application of it may be proper. Regarding disclosure, the critical issue is whether the source code must be disclosed and the answer seems to depend on precisely what the claimed invention is. As a practical matter, since 1985, the flow of *software patents* has been steadily increasing, and there are today many thousands of them.

14.4.2 Thumbnail Sketch of Patent Law

To be the subject of a valid patent, a development must (among other things) meet three requirements: it must be new [23]; it must be nonobvious [24]; and its subject matter must be appropriate for patents [25].

The requirement of newness (*novelty,* in patent terminology) poses a significant impediment to program-related inventions, as it does in all other fields. This is as it should be. Patents are not meant to be available for reinventing the wheel. Moreover, even a novel development will not qualify for a valid patent if it would have been obvious at the time made to one of ordinary skill in the pertinent technology.

In obtaining a patent, the patentee effectively cuts a deal with the government: in return for disclosing the invention [26], the patentee obtains a 17 year exclusive right [27]. That exclusive right is not to be granted for something already known, or something obvious in light of what is already known. The copyright standard is originality, which basically means simply that the work was not copied. That is a subjective standard. But the patent novelty and nonobviousness standards are objective; the invention must really be new and not obvious to ordinary practitioners. Many program-related developments will fail that standard. Nevertheless, the more meaningful point is that many program-related inventions of significance will meet it.

But despite the foregoing, most software patent litigation has dealt with neither novelty nor nonobviousness. Rather, it has focused on whether the subject matter of the development was *statutory, i.e.,* within the classes of patentable subject matter set forth in the Patent Act [28]. For present purposes, the Patent Act recognizes two types of subject matter as appropriate for patents: machines and processes [29]. If a program-related development fits within neither of these rubrics, it cannot be the subject of a valid patent, even if novel and nonobvious.

To be sure, statutory subject matter includes everything under the sun made by a human, subject to judge-made exclusions for laws of nature, physical phenomena and abstract ideas [30]. But the mere inclusion of a law of nature, mathematical algorithm, formula, or computer program in a patent claim does not make it nonstatutory [31]. In particular, where the claim recites a mathematical algorithm, a long string of appellate cases now teach that a distinction must be made. If it recites the algorithm and nothing more, the claim is nonstatutory. But if it implements or applies that algorithm in a structure or process that, when considered as a whole, performs a function the patent laws were designed to protect, it is statutory [32].

14.4.3 Contemporary Software Patents [33]

The earliest software patents issued as the result of a *business as usual* attitude on the part of many patent attorneys. As mentioned above, process control equipment was traditionally the subject of patent. While it was gradually converted to software control, it remained the subject of efforts to patent it. The U.S. Patent and Trademark Office (the PTO) received many artfully drafted applications, in which it often was not apparent that software control was contemplated. Even though the PTO for many years had a negative attitude toward software patents, thousands of them issued in the process control area, and they continue to issue at a considerable rate [34].

But they are no longer alone. In 1981, the U.S. Supreme Court decided an important case on the issue of what constituted statutory subject matter in the program field [35]. The Court made it clear that certain program-related inventions qualified for patent. Some 3,000 patent applications had been held up in the PTO awaiting disposition of that case. Since then, many thousands more have been filed and been passed to issue.

These patents tend to claim inventions in two areas besides process control: computer-implemented business methods [36], and the user/computer interface [37]. An example in the first of these areas is presented by a Merrill Lynch patent [38] that is interesting for a number of reasons. First, it represents a departure from the norm whereunder financial institutions have shown little interest in patents, especially as to their internal operations.

Also, it is interesting because it claims a method of doing business. The conventional wisdom has long been that a patent will not issue on a method of doing business [39]. Finally, the patent is interesting because it was the subject of litigation.

Specifically, that patent states that the "invention relates to financial business systems and . . . to data processing methodology and apparatus for effecting an improved securities brokerage and cash management system. It is an object of the present invention to provide an improved . . . data processing implementation for a brokerage-cash management financial system which provides for automatic investment of free credit cash balances in . . . money market funds; a full range of security brokerage transaction functions, . . . and ('charge') card and check charges. . . ." The figures depicted in the patent are flow charts and block diagrams.

Over in the market place, Merrill Lynch offered its Cash Management Account, and other brokerage houses offered competitive services. Paine Webber and Dean Witter sought a declaratory judgment of patent invalidity and moved for summary judgment, alleging that the patent claimed nonstatutory subject matter. But the U.S. District Court for the District of Delaware held that the claims were statutory because they recited a method of operation on a computer to effectuate a business activity [40]. The suit was thereafter settled.

Beyond process control and computer-implemented business methods, patents are issuing on various aspects of the user/computer interface. An example here is provided by a patent that issued to IBM [41], and that states that the invention comprises a "document preparation program for use in connection with a [word processor] and includes a succinct identification and listing of designated parts of a . . . document, each unique part having access to an associated file which contains the basic text and formatting controls for the particular part. The user . . . may readily assemble a document from the parts inventory displayed on a . . . screen by . . . cursor references or by keying the name of designated parts and have the newly created document displayed, or printed. . . ." The figures shown in the patent comprise flowcharts and a master menu.

Many patents have issued in the past three years or so in both of these areas (computer-implemented business methods and user/computer interface). Moreover, the list of patentees reads in part [42] like a *Who's Who* of corporate America (and beyond), and especially (but not exclusively) of high-tech companies. Names such as IBM, AT&T, Texas Instruments, General Electric, Hewlett Packard, Wang, Hitachi, and Siemens appear repeatedly. None of these corporate giants is known for taking extreme positions. If it does nothing else, the acquisition of many software patents by such corporations gives legitimacy to the notion of software patents.

14.4.4 The New Patent Landscape

Now let's step back from software patents specifically, to take a broader view of what's happened to patent law generally. To be sure, in the past eight years, the world of software patents has seen marked change. But the environment surrounding U.S. patents generally also has witnessed kaleidoscopic changes. The most important aspect of this transformation occurred in 1982 with the creation of the U.S. Court of Appeals for the Federal Circuit, which now has appellate jurisdiction over all patent infringement cases. The result has been nothing short of an enhanced viability for the entire U.S. patent system.

Historically, courts were rather receptive to patents, which they regarded as property. But beginning in the 1930s, courts increasingly viewed patents as evil monopolies that, wherever possible, should not be enforced. This attitude reached its zenith in the 1970s. The late Justice Abe Fortas once observed that a typical federal judge regards patents in much the way a city boy regards a handful of snakes. The rationales offered by various observers to support this hostility include the ascendancy of antitrust law and the discomfiture of a judiciary, untrained in technology, with these increasingly technical creatures. But this hostility began to dissipate with the creation in 1982 of the Federal Circuit, several of whose judges are patent attorneys, and none of whose judges appear hostile to patents.

As a result of this Court, the substantive patent law is now more consistent and more pro-patent. Forum shopping (raised to the level of a high art by the patent bar) is sharply down. It has become clear that prevailing patentees are entitled to a permanent injunction. Even the conventional wisdom that unadjudicated patents will not be the subject of preliminary injunctions is being challenged. Further, compensatory damages are more generous and treble damages (for willful infringement) more frequent.

Coupled with this, there have been two important procedural developments over the past decade. Increased docket control is evident in the federal courts (where all patent infringement suits must be brought). And federal litigation (including patent suits) simply doesn't take as long as it used to. Meanwhile, over in the PTO, processing times have steadily decreased for patent applications. Twenty-five years ago average time from filing to issue of the patent (where one issued) was three-and-a-half years. Today it is about 18 months. (Software patents probably take an average of 2 years.)

So what we have is an item of intellectual property—the patent—that has teeth, coupled with a system that can produce it in a viable time frame. It can be argued that a decade ago we had neither. Patentees no longer consider themselves an endangered species. And a U.S. patent is worth having again.

14.5 TRADE SECRET PROTECTION OF SOFTWARE

14.5.1 Summary

Trade secret law proscribes misappropriation of another's trade secret. A trade secret is information (a) that is generally not known in the industry; (b) as to which its proprietor uses reasonable measures to maintain it in secrecy; and (c) which gives its proprietor an opportunity to secure competitive advantage. Misappropriation comprises unauthorized disclosure or use of, or access to, a trade secret. In the early days of computing, most programs were created in-house and protected, if at all, by trade secret law. Industry reliance on this protective mechanism continues to this day.

14.5.2 Statutes

Prior to 1981, almost all trade secret civil law was common law. However, since that year, more than 30 states [43] have enacted the Uniform Trade Secret Act [44]. Nevertheless, the vast majority of existing opinions were decided under common law doctrines, largely under the 1939 version of the Restatement of Torts.

14.5.3 Cases

There are hundreds of cases affording trade secret treatment to programs, including many cases holding specifically that programs are appropriate subject matter for such protection [45]. The cases testify to the all-encompassing nature of trade secret protection. Unlike its copyright and patent cousins, trade secret protection functions as a blanket, protecting everything beneath it that meets the three criteria noted above. This is a doctrine that protects both idea and expression, and will apply to algorithms as easily as to documentation. While trade secret protection arises by operation of law in a number of situations (*e.g.*, the employer/employee relationship), most commentators recommend a well-drafted contract to protect the proprietor's rights, even in these situations.

14.5.4 Criminal Trade Secret Law

Until the mid-1960s there was no specific trades secret criminal law, although some states had interpreted their general theft statutes to apply to trade secrets. However, beginning in 1964, states began enacting statutes that specifically proscribed theft of trade secrets, and about half the states presently have such statutes [46]. An example of an application of such a statute is found in *Ward v. Superior Court of California* [47], where a service bureau employee was convicted of theft of a program from a competitor's computer through unlawful access over phone lines.

The advantages and disadvantages of a trade secret criminal (vis-a-vis civil) action are similar to those described above (Section 4 (d)) in connection with copyright. But in addition, the trade secret environment has the disadvantage of increasing the possibility that the trade secret will be disclosed in the litigation (because the proprietor has a more limited role in the litigation).

14.5.5 Possibility of Preemption

Section 301(a) of the Copyright Act provides that ". . . all legal or equitable rights . . . equivalent to any to the exclusive rights within the general scope of copyright . . . in works of authorship within the subject matter of copyright . . . are governed exclusively by this title . . . no person is entitled to any such right or equivalent right in any such work under the common law or statutes of any state." Accordingly, the question has been posed whether this provision preempts the state law of trade secrets.

While there have been many cases involving preemption under this provision, in only a few was trade secret law the focal point. In *Balboa Ins. Co. v. Trans Global Equities* [48] and *Warrington Assocs., Inc. v. Real-Time Engrg. Systs., Inc.* [49] the court squarely held that §301 did not preempt trade secret law, concluding that trade secret rights were not *equivalent* to copyright. And in two cases decided shortly before the present Copyright Act came into effect, the courts noted that the new Act would not preempt trade secret law [50].

However, in *Videotronics, Inc. v. Bend Electronics* [51], the court flatly stated (in what may be an alternative holding), without espousing any rationale, that trade secret law was preempted. And *Avco Corp. v. Precision Air Parts, Inc.* [52] can be read to state or even hold that such a preemption has taken place. Finally, in two cases, *Computer Assocs. Int'l, Inc. v. Altai* and *Foresight Resources Corp. v. Pfortmiller* [53] each court stated that trade secret law was not necessarily preempted, but the trade secret claim before it was, because it was based on the same facts as the copyright claim.

Of interest is that almost every case treating possible preemption of trade secret law by copyright law involved software.

14.6 CONTRACT & QUASI-CONTRACT

14.6.1 Contract

Contractual protection is generally used as an adjunct to trade secret or copyright protection. A contract can give (and prove) notice and add to the obligations imposed by substantive law. In the trade secret environment, one major function of the contract is to recite the confidential relationship, and set out steps that should be taken, and prohibitions that should be maintained, pursuant to that relationship. Generally, such an agreement will set forth specific restrictions, such as limitation of use to a single facility or even single computer; description of the materials to be delivered to the user; acknowledgement of the vendor's IP rights; limitations on for whose benefit the program may be used (can it be used to process a third party's data?); type of system in which use is permitted (is network use allowed?); restrictions copying (and proprietary marking of copies); and disposition of materials on termination of agreement.

14.6.2 Source Code Escrow

Typically, the vendor is not required to, and does not, deliver source code to the user. Absent source code, the user is unable itself to *fix* bugs in the program, or to modify it. This may be of no import so long as the user has contracted with a stable vendor or some capable and stable third party to maintain the software. However, there is always a possibility that at some point the party obligated to maintain the software will be unwilling or unable to do so. In such event, if the software is important to the user's operation, it is paramount that the user have access to the source code.

One mechanism that has evolved to deal with this situation is the *source code escrow,* wherein source code escrow, source code along with user and system documentation are deposited in an escrow maintained by a neutral third party. By agreement among vendor, user, and third party, the vendor is required to update the deposit either periodically or as new versions are issued. The escrow arrangement prescribes a procedure for releasing the escrow deposit to the user in the event that one of a number of specifically described conditions transpires. One common condition is the service company's failure to maintain the software.

There are different types of escrow arrangements, from the passive to a rather active one wherein the escrow determines that each deposit is what it should be. One of the most critical items in this type of arrangement is the set of conditions under which release will take place, as well as the procedure for invoking a release condition. The user wants broad conditions and a procedure not easily thwarted by a recalcitrant vendor. The vendor wants a set of conditions and a procedure that will not make it easy for the user to acquire possession.

14.6.3 *Shrink-Wrap Agreements*

The *shrink-wrap agreement* (also called a *tear-open, blister,* or *box-top* agreement) is a device used by mass-market software proprietors who: (1) rely on copyright, but want more than it may offer; (2) seek the benefits of trade secret protection but lack the relationship or opportunity for a written executed agreement that would clearly give rise to it; and (3) have a per package fee too low to justify execution of a written executed agreement. The legal effect of this device is presently unclear.

The software is marketed inside a transparent, heat-sealed wrapper. Visible through the wrapper is a notice with a clearly marked admonition that anyone tearing open the wrapper thereby agrees to the conditions listed on the wrapper. Alternatively, the event purportedly triggering acquiescence may be the completion (and perhaps execution) and return of a warranty card. The conditions typically include imposition of a licensor/licensee relationship; restriction of vendee's right to rent, duplicate, reverse engineer, and modify the software; imposition of a confidential relationship; and restriction to use on a single computer.

Some of the legal issues attendant to whether such an arrangement gives rise to an enforceable contract are: whether tearing the wrapper constitutes informed consensual *acceptance*; whether there was adequate notice; whether (when the warranty is the purported trigger) there was consideration (*i.e.,* did the warranty go beyond what was required by operation of law in the absence of an express warranty); if there is indeed an agreement, is it unenforceable as an adhesion contract in violation of public policy. Two states enacted statutes providing for the validity and enforceability of shrink-wrap agreements that met certain minimum criteria. However, the Illinois statute was later repealed, and a portion of the Louisiana statute was held preempted by the copyright law. Given the extent to which shrink-wraps have been used, it is surprising how little litigation there is regarding their validity and enforceability.

In *Vault Corp. v. Quaid Software Ltd.* [54], the vendor sought to enforce the shrink-wrap pursuant to the Louisiana statute. The court held that the part of the statute was preempted and therefore unenforceable. The statute permitted total prohibition of copying, whereas the federal copyright law permitted copying that was essential for use and for archival purposes. Further, the state statute authorized a perpetual bar, whereas the copyright law limits the right to 50 years after the author's death. Also, the statute places no limitation on programs that are protected, whereas copyright requires an original work of authorship. Finally, §117 of the copyright law permits the owner of copy to make an adaptation if essential for use or preparation of an archival copy, but the statute prohibits that.

More recently, in *Step-Saver Data Systems, Inc. v. Wyse* [55] a shrink-wrap was held unenforceable, but the transaction in question was one between vendor and its value added reseller (VAR) (rather than the typical vendor/user situation). Such factors as predelivery oral communications, exchange of written purchase orders and invoices, prior course of dealing, and the fact that the vendee was not a consumer differentiate this situation from the typical one. Further, the result turned on a test for determining whether a counter-offer had been made. There are three rules used by the various states to make this determination. The result of the instant fact situation may be different in a jurisdiction adhering to one of the other two rules.

14.7 EXTRA-LEGAL PROTECTION OF SOFTWARE

Legal protective mechanisms do not constitute the universe of devices available to the proprietor for protecting its software. A knowledgeable proprietor may be able to secure a significant degree of protection by using extra-legal devices either in lieu of or (more frequently) in addition to, legal methods of protection.

14.7.1 Commercial

The proprietor is sometimes able to structure the commercial environment so as to reduce the incentive to misappropriate. One such step that licensors often take is to provide program support in the form of maintenance (*i.e.*, fixing the program when it malfunctions) and enhancements (*i.e.*, adding features to the program over time). This support is often necessary for the user to make commercial use of the program, and in such a case a copy of a program that is maintained is worth much more than a copy not maintained. In order to receive maintenance, a user must be a legitimate licensee. Accordingly, offering maintenance to legitimate licensees makes a legitimate copy of the program worth more than a pirated copy.

14.7.2 Technological

The proprietor is sometimes able to use technology to make piracy more difficult. One way is to alter each copy of the software so that it will function with only a single computer whose identity is incorporated into that copy. Another such device is to use firmware in connection with the program, such that the firmware verifies authenticity of the user. A further mechanism is to *scramble* the software in accordance with a cryptographic algorithm, and to embed in the hardware a microprocessor chip that will decode the scrambled software. None of these methods is *fool-proof*, but each increases the level of difficulty that a pirate must undertake.

14.8 INTERNATIONAL PROTECTION OF SOFTWARE [56]

Software protection at the moment has received more attention in the United States than in any other nation. Nevertheless, a number of other countries have well developed bodies of law that treat the subject, and some—including France, Canada, Germany and the U.K.—have a number of cases interpreting their law. Further, in the past decade many nations, developed and developing, have enacted new laws to cope with the software invasion.

Most countries are placing their primary emphasis on copyright. Under the Berne Convention, each member accords to nationals of other countries the same rights it accords to its own nationals. Moreover, it seems clear that copyright will apply to programs in each member nation. However, the nature of copyright protection will differ from nation to nation. For example, at this moment German copyright law requires a standard of creativity above the *originality* level adequate under the law of the United States and most other concerned nations [57]. Also, it is far from certain that other nations will expand copyright protection into the *structure, sequence, and organization* and *look and feel* areas, as U.S. courts have done.

In many other nations, patent protection is available for certain program-related inventions, despite broad proscriptions against patent protection for programs themselves. Further, many nations afford trade secret protection to programs. And finally, contractual protection is recognized in virtually all nations.

14.9 SUMMARY OF ADVANTAGES AND DISADVANTAGES OF LEGAL METHODS OF PROTECTION

COPYRIGHT

Advantages

- Feasibility of securing preliminary relief
- Suitability for a well-proliferated work
- Great duration
- Ease of availability and maintenance
- Inducement to create compatible programs
- Availability of relatively uniform international protection

Disadvantages
- Difficulty of protecting algorithms
- Uncertainty as to scope of protection
- Inability to exclude independent development
- Uncertainty regarding reverse compilation
- Difficulty of policing

PATENT

Advantages

- Algorithm Protection
- Breadth of Protection
- Protection Against Independent Creation
- Unnecessary to Show Copying
- Ease of Licensing and Maintenance
- Facilitates Commercial Disclosure
- Suited to Proliferation
- Long Term

Disadvantages

- High Standard
- Subject Matter Uncertainty
- Databases and Documentation
- The Time Factor
- Preliminary Relief
- High Cost
- Restrictions on Exploitation

TRADE SECRET

Advantages
- Possibility of Preliminary Injunction
- Clear Applicability
- Wide Range of Subject Matter
- Broad Scope of Protection
- Lack of Proliferation Limits Opportunity for Misuse
- No Waiting Period to Secure Protection
- Duration May be Lengthy

Disadvantages
- "Cesspool of Secrecy"
- Possible Loss of Protection

- Difficulty of Maintenance
- Not Well-Suited to Wide Proliferation
- Preemption Possibility

NOTES

[1] The treatment in this paper is obviously not meant to be exhaustive. For a detailed treatment of the topic of software protection, see the three-volume treatise D. Bender, *Computer Law: Software Protection and Litigation* (Matthew Bender 1991). For a more summary treatment, see D. Bender, "Software Protection," printed as Chapter 11 of Horwitz & Horwitz, *Intellectual Property Counseling and Litigation* (Matthew Bender 1991).

[2] This paper does not set forth in detail the underlying substantive law regarding the various doctrines of intellectual property, but rather discusses only those elements necessary to understand the problems of software protection.

[3] *I.e.,* what are the aspects whose protection would significantly foster the proprietor's commercial interest?

[4] Program developers today often use *pseudo-code* instead of a flow chart. Pseudo-code is a textual representation of the program which effectively summarizes its functioning.

[5] An algorithm is a rigidly defined step-by-step procedure for solving a particular problem under all circumstances in a finite number of steps.

[6] Before directly executing the program, the computer must translate the source code into a string of zeros and ones, known as *object code.*

[7] In fact, the inability to rectify errors may as a practical matter mean that the user is unable to use the software.

[8] For convenience, here we lump into the mainframe category those computers known as *minicomputers.*

[9] We lump into this category the work station.

[10] In the early days of the computer industry, it was common for many valuable programs to be given away free. Although this is no longer the case, there still are many managers who do not fully appreciate the cost or value of software.

[11] See *inter alia: Williams Electronics, Inc. v. Arctic International, Inc.,* 685 F.2d 870, 215 U.S.P.Q. 405 (3d Cir. 1982) (program embodied in ROM is copyrightable); *Apple Computer, Inc. v. Franklin Computer,* 714 F.2d 1240, 219 U.S.P.Q. 113 (3d Cir. 1983), pet. dism., 464 U.S. 1043 (1984) (object code copyrightable; program in ROM copyrightable; system program copyrightable); *Apple Computer Inc. v. Formula International Inc.,* 725 F.2d 521, 221 U.S.P.Q. 762 (9th Cir. 1984) (system programs copyrightable); *Tandy Corp. v. Personal Microcomputers, Inc.,* 524 F.Supp. 171, 214 U.S.P.Q. 178 (N.D. Cal. 1981) (program is subject to copyright; ROM containing program constitutes copy); *Hubco Data Products Corp. v. Management Assistance, Inc.,* 219 U.S.P.Q. 450 (N.D. Idaho 1983) (object code copyrightable; system program copyrightable); *Midway Manufacturing Co. v. Strohon,* 564 F.Supp. 741, 219 U.S.P.Q. 42 (N.D. ILL. 1983) (ROM constitutes copy; object code copyrightable).

[12] The steps identified by the court are similar to those set forth in §2.06 of 1 D. Bender, *Computer Law: Software Protection and Litigation.*

[13] 45 F.2d 119 (2d Cir. 1930), cert. denied, 282 U.S. 902 (1931).

[14]   740 F.Supp. 37, 15 USPQ2d 1577 (D. Mass. 1990).

[15]   *Apple Computer Inc. v. Microsoft Corp.,* 799 F.Supp. 1006, 24 USPQ2d 1081 (N.D.Cal. 1992). For a description of the features discussed (but not described in much detail) in this opinion, see *Apple Computer Inc. v. Microsoft Corp.,* 709 F.Supp. 925, 10 USPQ2d 1677 (N.D.Cal. 1989); *Apple Computer Inc. v. Microsoft Corp.,* 717 F.Supp. 1428, 11 USPQ2d 1618 (N.D.Cal. 1989); and *Apple Computer Inc. v. Microsoft Corp.,* 759 F.Supp. 1444, 18 USPQ2d 1097 (N.D.Cal. 1991).

[16]   Plaintiff defined the user interface as "the menus (and their structure and organization), the long prompts, the screens on which they appear, the function key assignments, [and] the macrocommands and language".

[17]   The elements are: (l) focus on a spectrum of representations that all fit the work, but which differ in their degree of particularization, so as to identify the *idea*; (2) determine whether plaintiff's expression contains elements not necessary to the idea; (3) ascertain whether the nonessential elements are a substantial part of plaintiff's work.

[18]   The Microsoft products alleged to infringe were certain versions of its *Windows* software.

[19]   The Hewlett-Packard product alleged to infringe was its *New Wave* software.

[20]   A user interface comprises the screen display and the keys available on the keyboard for input.

[21]   The court explained that on the Macintosh, "the screen displays include icons or symbols to represent programs or information, pull down menus or lists of commands or information, use of windows to display information and the ability to move, re-size, open or close those windows to retrieve, put away or modify information, and a display of text by a proportionally spaced font in all menu items, title bars, icon names and text directories for a consistent and distinctive appearance." 24 USPQ2d at 1084.

[22]   Apple's posture was somewhat hampered in that the court, in deciding a number of motions, had already determined these issues adversely to Apple. In litigating those motions, Apple had declined to submit any detailed position on these issues. The instant opinion was written in response to Apple's motion for reconsideration, supported for the first time by a detailed position.

[23]   35 U.S.C. §102.

[24]   35 U.S.C. §103.

[25]   35 U.S.C. §101.

[26]   The patent document must include a description of the invention, and the manner of making it, sufficient to enable one of ordinary skill in the appropriate technology to make and use the invention. Moreover, it must set forth the *best mode* contemplated by the inventor. And it must particularly point out and distinctly claim the subject matter that the patentee regards as his or her invention. 35 U.S.C. §112.

[27]   35 U.S.C. §154.

[28]   For a detailed discussion of the present status of statutory subject matter as applied to program-related inventions, see 1 Bender, *Computer Law: Software Protection and Litigation,* Sec. 3A. 03 (Matthew Bender & Co. 1991).

[29]   35 U.S.C. §101 provides that the inventor of "any new and useful process, machine, manufacture or composition of matter, or any new and useful improvement thereof, may obtain a patent therefor. . . ."

[30]   *Diamond v. Diehr*, 450 U.S. 175, 101 S.Ct. 1048, 67 L.Ed.2d 155, 209 U.S.P.Q. 1 (1981).

[31] *Id.*

[32] *In re Walter,* 618 F.758, 205 U.S.P.Q. 397 (CCPA 1980); *In re Freeman,* 573 F.2d 1237, 197 U.S.P.Q. 464 (1978).

[33] For an extensive presentation as to the current status of "software patents," see 1 D. Bender, *Computer Law: Software Protection and Litigation* Sec. 3A. 07 (Matthew Bender 1991).

[34] See, *e.g.,* U.S. Patent No. 4,734,866, "Computer Controller for an Industrial Multiaxis Robot," issued 29 Mar. 1988, named inventors Bartelt and Meier, assignee Siemens Aktiengesellschaft; U.S. Patent No. 4,729,105, "Continuous Processing System With Accumulator Model for Product Flow Control"; issued 1 Mar. 1988, named inventors Thompson and Gold, assignee Adolph Coors Co.; U.S. Patent No. 4, 724, 524, "Vibration-Sensing Tool Break and Touch Detector Optimized for Machining Conditions", issued 9 Feb. 1988, named inventors Thomas, Lee, Bedard, Hayashi, and Harris, assignee General Electric Co; U.S. Patent No. 4, 718, 014, issued 5 Jan. 1988, "Apparatus for Controlling Ignition Timing in an Internal Combustion Engine," named inventors Hattori and Norota, assignee Toyota.

[35] Diehr, N. 28 *supra.*

[36] See, *e.g.,* U.S. Patent No. 4,674,044, issued 16 June 1987, "Automated Securities Trading System," named inventors Kalmus, Trojan, Mott and Strampfer, assignee Merrill Lynch Pierce Fenner & Smith, Inc.; U.S. Patent No. 4, 694, 397, issued 15 Sept. 1987, "Banking/Brokerage Computer Interface System," named inventors Grant and Vignola, assignee The Advest Group. 36.

[37] See, *e.g.,* U.S. Patent No. 4,730,252, issued 8 Mar. 1988, "Document Composition from Parts Inventory," named inventor Bradshaw, assignee International Business Machines Corp.; U.S. Patent No. 4,674,065, issued 16 June 1987, named inventors Lange and Rosenbaum, assignee International Business Machines Corp.

[38] U.S. Patent No. 4,346,442, "Securities Brokerage-Cash Management System," issued 24 Aug. 1982, named inventor Musmanno, assignee Merrill Lynch Pierce Fenner & Smith, Inc.

[39] See, *e.g., In re Patton,* 127 F.2d 324, 53 U.S.P.Q. 376 (CCPA 1942); *Berardini v. Tocci,* 190 F. 329 (SDNY 1911), aff'd, 200 Fed. 1021 (2d Cir. 1912).

[40] *Paine Webber, Jackson & Curtis, Inc. v. Merrill Lynch, Pierce, Fenner & Smith, Inc.,* 564 F. Supp. 1358, 218 U.S.P.Q. 212 (D. Del. 1983).

[41] U. S. Patent No. 4,730,252, "Document Composition From Parts Inventory," issued 8 Mar. 1988, named inventor Kenneth A. Bradshaw, assigned to International Business Machines Corp.

[42] Not to be outdone, a large number of small companies engaged in development, in the vigorous markets for software and computer services, have also obtained many patents of this type. Although sometimes criticized as a *tool* of large corporations, the patent system on the whole is probably of more value to small companies seeking to carve a niche for themselves with a new product or service they pioneered.

[43] See, *e.g.,* West's Ann. Cal. Civ. Code Secs. 3426–3426.10.

[44] For a discussion of that Act, see D. Bender, "Standards of Protectable Trade Secrets," printed as Chapter 5 of Horwitz & Horwitz, *Intellectual Property Counseling and Litigation* (Matthew Bender & Co. 1991).

[45] See, *e.g., Amoco Production Co. v. Lindley,* 609 P.2d 733, 208 USPQ 513 (Okla. 1980); *Cybertek Computer Prods., Inc. v. Whitfield,* 203 USPQ 1020 (Cal. Super. L.A. Co. 1977); *Telex*

Corp. v. IBM Corp., 510 F.2d 894, 184 USPQ 521 (10th Cir. 1975), cert. dism., 423 U.S. 802. But see *Integral Systems. Inc. v. PeopleSoft Inc.,* F.2d (N.D. Cal. 1991) which, although paying lip service to the notion that programs are protectable by trade secret law, strikes a disconsonant note in its treatment of plaintiff's alleged trade secret program.

[46] These statutes are separate and distinct from the *computer abuse* criminal statutes more recently enacted by virtually every state. Some of the computer abuse statutes may apply to software misappropriation.

[47] 3 Computer L. Serv. Repr. 206 (Cal. Super. 1972).

[48] 218 Cal.App.3d 1327, 267 Cal.Rptr. 787 (3d Dist. 1990).

[49] 522 F.Supp. 367 (N.D. Ill. 1981).

[50] *M. Bryce & Assocs., Inc. v. Gladstone,* 107 Wis.2d 241 319 W.W.2d 907 (Wis. App.), cert. denied, 459 U.S. 944(1982); *Management Science America, Inc. v. Cyborg Systs., Inc.,* 1977-1 CCH Tr. Cas. par. 61,472 (N.D. Ill.). And in a third case preceding the effective date of the Act, the court (without reference to the soon-to-be-effective law) saw no inherent conflict between copyright and trade secret law. *Technicon Medical Info. Systs. Corp. v. Green Bay Packaging, Inc.,* 687 F.2d 1032 (7th Cir. 1982), cert. denied, 459 U.S. 1106 (1983).

[51] 564 F.Supp. 1471 (D. Nev. 1983).

[52] 210 USPQ 894 (M.D. Ala.), aff'd on other grounds, 676 F.2d 494 (11th Cir.), cert. denied, 459 U.S. 1037 (1982).

[53] Respectively, 1991 CCH Copyr. L. Rep. par.26,783 (E.D. 1991); and 719 F.Supp. 1006 (D.Kan. 1989).

[54] 775 F.2d 638 (5th Cir. 1986).

[55] 939 F.2d 91 (3d Cir. 1991).

[56] For a more or less detailed, and frequently updated, description of the status of software protection in some 40 foreign nations, see 2 D. Bender, *Computer Law: Software Protection and Litigation*, Chapter 4B (Matthew Bender & Co. 1991).

[57] This German standard may have to change to bring German law into conformity with the EEC's 1991 Software Directive.

KEEPING RESEARCH RECORDS

Patrick D. Kelly

Patrick D. Kelly serves as "Of Counsel" for Haverstock, Garrett & Roberts in St. Louis, specializing in medical technology, including the use of computers in medicine. He also is an inventor and the President of JFKM Research, LLC, which is studying anti-viral topical lubricants that may be able to slow the spread of AIDS and other sexually transmitted diseases.

Keeping up lab notebooks and documenting R&D efforts can be a colossal pain. There is no question about it. However, there is also no question that it is a necessary insurance. There are a number of instances when it becomes necessary to prove the date and nature of technical activities and the project with which the activities are associated. For example, the ability to prove the date and nature activities often are determinative in:

- *Disputes regarding ownership of technology—whether certain technology was first made under a particular development contract or Government contract;*
- *Disputes regarding whether particular technology is covered by a particular license agreement;*
- *Disputes regarding whether certain technology is subject to a confidentiality or nonuse agreement;*
- *Defending a charge of trade secret, copyright, or maskwork infringement based upon independent development of the technology or software at issue;*
- *Defending a charge of patent infringement on the basis that the invention was previously developed, not abandoned, suppressed, or concealed (under 35 U.S.C. §102(g)); and*
- *Interference proceedings before the Patent and Trademark Office—contests to determine priority of invention when more than one entity applies for a patent on the same invention.*

As discussed in various of the articles, the U.S. patent law, in contradistinction to the rest of the world, provides that the first to have "made" an otherwise patentable invention in the United States, who did not abandon, suppress, or conceal the invention, is the person entitled to the patent. This may or may not be the first person to file an application on the invention. Where two inventors both file applications relating to the same invention, an interference proceeding is conducted by the PTO to determine relative priority of the inventors (who made the invention first).

Under U.S. law, "making" an invention is a two-step process. The first step is conceiving *the invention. This is basically the mental portion of the inventive act. The second step is referred to as* reducing the invention to practice. *In basic terms,* reducing to practice *is building the invention and proving that it works for its intended purpose. The filing of a patent application is considered to be a* constructive reduction to practice.

The diligence *of the inventor in reducing the invention to practice also can be a factor in the interference. As a general proposition, an inventor who is first to both conceive and reduce the invention to practice will win the interference. Diligence becomes a factor where one inventer conceives the invention first, but the other inventor is the first to complete reducing the invention to practice. The inventor who was the first to conceive the invention will win the interference only if he or she can prove diligence in pursuing the reduction to practice from a time period prior to the conception of the invention by the other inventor. If the inventor who was the first to conceive the invention cannot prove reasonable diligence, the inventor who was first to reduce the invention to practice will win the interference and be awarded the patent.*

Again, each element of making the invention: conception; reduction to practice; and diligence must be proven. The sufficiency of the proof of R&D activities is an evidentiary issue, a direct function of the trustworthiness and persuasiveness of the proof.

As a general proposition, the word of an inventor *(or even co-inventors) as to when and where an invention was conceived or reduced to practice is essentially worthless without some form of* corroboration. *Corroboration can be in the form of dated documents, drawings, time records, and oral testimony by* noninventors.

In a nutshell, a corroborated documentary record should be maintained capable of establishing: the dates and activities comprising each of the elements of "making" an invention; the identification of individuals involved in the work who can provide testimonial proof; and identification of the particular project with which technical work is associated. The records pertaining to "making" an invention should include all development and testing efforts (both successes and failures), from the time the invention was conceived until it was reduced to practice.

The following article discusses the necessity of keeping good records of development in the event of an interference proceeding in the PTO and provides examples of corporate guidelines for keeping records. MAL

Abstract

This article relates to keeping research records and provides examples of "Guidelines for Keeping Research Records", for conventional recordkeeping (*e.g.*, lab notebooks with machine-numbered pages) and for research records kept on computers. These guidelines may be adopted by any company that wishes to use them. The background information contained in this article focuses mainly on (1) the requirement for *corroboration* of any evidence submitted by would-be inventors, and (2) a discussion of several approaches that can increase the evidentiary value of research records kept on computers.

15.1 INTRODUCTION

Nearly any researcher who follows sophisticated company guidelines for maintaining a lab notebook or documentation of R&D will at some time wonder, "Why do these procedures have to be so complicated? Why can't they just tell us to keep good, readable, reliable records?" This article attempts to answer those questions and provide the rationale and explanation for both sets of guidelines for some of the more complicated record keeping procedures.

15.2 INTERFERENCES: THE U.S. SYSTEM

A patent *interference* is a proceeding within the U.S. Patent and Trademark Office (PTO) to determine who was the first person to make an invention. It occurs when two or more competing inventors or companies file patent applications with equal or overlapping claims, within (roughly) a year of each other. Each application is kept secret by the PTO unless and until it issues; however, the PTO has internal procedures to determine when two or more applicants are trying to patent the same invention. In some situations, an interference can be declared before either of the patent applications is issued as a patent; however, the recent practice of the PTO has been to issue a patent based on the first-filed (senior) application, and then reject any later-filed applications while citing the newly issued patent as prior art against the later application. If a rejected applicant thinks he (or she) can beat the senior applicant, an interference can be requested (37 CFR 1.611).

Interferences are peculiar to U.S. law; every other nation in the world has adopted a first-to-file system instead, where the first party to file a complete application on an otherwise patentable invention will be awarded the patent. But that's not to say that they must be right and we're wrong; the United States is the most creative and innovative nation in the world, and part of the stimulus that drives our creativity may well come from the rules of competition fostered by our system.

Interferences are complex, expensive, and highly adversarial. The procedure is analogous to a lawsuit, except the arguments are made to a panel of senior patent examiners, rather than a judge. Each side is represented by one or more attorneys. Both sides must go through discovery (*i.e.*, demanding evidence from the other side through written interrogatories, demanding documents, deposing witnesses, etc.), and each side's attorneys can attack any evidence offered by the other side. Careers, reputations, money, and job security are often at stake. A typical interference takes two years or more, and the costs are often well over $100,000 for each side.

Each side is required to PROVE when they made the invention at issue, and the sufficiency of your research records as evidence under the scrutiny of your adversary's attorneys can determine who wins or loses. If there are any gaps or other problems in your research records, they won't be analyzed with detached objectivity. Instead, the problems (and you, since you created them) will be attacked by a highly motivated, determined opponent. Any hint of trouble will be probed, prodded, and pried open, and by then, it will be too late to try to fix anything that wasn't done properly.

To drive this point home, let me offer yet another warning. If you're a researcher working for a corporation, and you haven't kept your research records properly, and those records suddenly become important in an interference, you're likely to suddenly find yourself under severe and possibly even hostile scrutiny from your own company.

The primary question decided in an interference is: which person or team "made" an invention first? The crucial factor in every single item of evidence will be time. Every item of evidence or testimony submitted by either side is weighed under a single standard: does it help to prove when that person did his or her work? An elegant piece of logic, a brilliant insight, a remarkable experiment, and a stunning observation are all worthless unless they were reliably dated (either when they were first created, or shortly afterward). In this context, *reliably* means "able to withstand an attack by a determined opponent".

Who wins the battle? In abbreviated form, the patent law says this: whoever completed the conception (*i.e.*, the complete mental embodiment, where the creative mental work was complete and all that was left was to actually build the device or synthesize the compound) first will win—but only if he or she also reduced it to practice first, or can prove that he or she worked diligently to reduce it to practice or file a patent application.

Therefore, each claimant in an interference needs to prove a number of different things: (1) an early date of conception; (2) an early date of reduction to practice; and, perhaps, (3) diligent efforts to reduce the invention to practice (or file a patent application) from a point in time before the adversary conceived the invention. As a practical matter, an effort is made to prove diligence from the initial conception until reduction to practice or until the patent application was filed.

15.3 THE CORROBORATION REQUIREMENT

Any evidence submitted during an interference is labelled as *self-serving* if it was created by someone claiming to be an inventor. Such evidence must be corroborated by independent evidence. This means it must be supported and confirmed by evidence originating with someone who does not claim to be an inventor. It would be too easy, and too tempting, for one person acting alone to create a document after a dispute arises, and then swear that the document had been created earlier. By requiring corroboration from other people who have no incentive to commit fraud, the likelihood of an attempted fraud (and the temptation people would feel to commit frauds) are greatly reduced.

Corroborating evidence does not need to be completely independent or neutral. For example, it can be created by a co-worker at the same company where the claimant works. The co-worker presumably will be biased, since he wants his company to win. That's a compromise that is necessary in the real world, since co-workers are often the only people who were aware of what an inventor was working on, especially during the early stages. The only requirement is that the co-worker cannot be listed on the patent application as a co-inventor.

In some cases, testimony from an independent third party witness might provide adequate corroboration. However, testimony alone should never be used as the sole support unless absolutely necessary, and some court decisions explicitly state that corroboration requires "a cohesive web of tangible evidence". *Tangible* refers to evidence that is in physical form. A relevant piece of paper (such as an invoice, or a page from a lab notebook), a photograph, a videotape, a floppy disk that holds a relevant file, or a sample of a compound are all tangible. By contrast, testimony is not tangible; neither is a memory.

How much corroboration is required? There is no fixed amount. The Court of Appeals for the Federal Circuit (CAFC) has adopted a *rule of reason*, which says that no specific type or amount of corroboration is required, so long as the evidence submitted forms "a cohesive web of tangible evidence."

The requirement of *a cohesive web* means that the evidence must amount to more than an isolated item, with no support and no context. Enough evidence must be submitted to establish a pattern that appears to be consistent. A single piece of paper (such as a dated invoice listing highly specialized reagents or custom-machined components) might be enough, but only if it is supported by sworn testimony that describes exactly when and how that piece of paper came to exist (any such testimony must withstand hostile questioning by the opponent's attorney).

The *rule of reason* is based on at least two factors. First, no single type of corroboration can fairly be expected from all inventors. A lone individual working in his basement cannot be expected to keep records as thorough as the records kept by a team of scientists in a large company. Second, any corroboration requirement needs to be flexible, to cope with human error. If a researcher forgets to have a page in his lab notebook witnessed, he should at least have a chance to provide other documents (such as project reports, purchase orders, sworn affidavits by co-workers, etc.). The PTO considers any evidence that is submitted and decides each case based on the facts of that particular case.

Although corroboration of a paper document (such as a page in a lab notebook, or a strip chart from a lab device, *i.e.*, a chromatograph) can be provided in a variety of ways, the safest, simplest, least expensive way involves witnessing. Someone who is not working on that project (and therefore is not likely to become a co-inventor) signs and dates the piece of paper. If necessary, he or she can testify several years later, "I believe I signed that page on the date indicated, because I never back-dated my signatures. Although I don't recall what that specific page said when I signed it, I believe it looked proper when I signed it, because I never witnessed any pages unless they looked proper. I also believe that page was filled when I signed it, because I always make a big X in any large blank areas if the page isn't filled."

The signature, dated several years earlier, is the tangible evidence. The witness's testimony, even though it is not created until after the interference arises, helps provide a cohesive web.

The PTO and the courts recognize that documents on paper, even if they have been witnessed, are not tamperproof. A witness's signature cannot prove that the author of a notebook page did not add more data to the page after the witness signed it. Nevertheless, witnessing is a reasonable and therefore widely accepted method of corroboration. Any company can use it safely, because it has become a standard practice that is respected by the PTO and the courts.

Some court decisions imply that evidence submitted by a first inventor can be corroborated by evidence submitted by a second inventor. According to those decisions, all that is needed is simply corroboration of an inventor's evidence, by means of tangible evidence generated by someone else—presumably, anyone else. Some commentators also suggest that the best witness for lab records is a group leader or project leader, since he or she will be more likely to know what is going on in some detail, and would therefore make a better witness. However, there is a risk in that approach, since an opponent will argue strenuously that the project leader has as much motivation to be self-serving and biased as the inventor(s). Therefore, in this author's opinion, witnessing by someone from a different area or project is preferable; this will allow both the outside witness and the project leader to testify, and two people testifying consistently have a better chance to create a "cohesive web" than either one testifying alone.

15.4 COMPUTERIZED RESEARCH RECORDS

Research records kept on computers can be used as evidence in interference proceedings. However, since most files kept on computers can be easily modified without leaving any trace of the modification, computer files tend to be viewed with much more skepticism by judges trying to decide whether the files reliably corroborate the date of an event. Therefore, they will require substantially more extensive testimony to establish and defend their creation and custody.

To the best of the author's knowledge, no interference decisions have been published to date that relate directly to corroboration by research records that were gathered by or stored on computers. Usually, computerized records are only part of the evidence in any important research project, and the PTO may try to avoid or minimize the issue for as long as possible (by acting as though computer records are just one more type of evidence).

But as any researcher knows, more and more data are gathered by computerized devices, processed by computers, and stored in computer memories. Scientists are abandoning pen and paper in favor of terminals, and even memos and letters are being generated, transmitted, and stored on computers or other electronic devices as the preferred format, with paper printouts becoming optional or even discouraged in many situations. The issue of the sufficiency of computerized records will unquestionably arise.

The question therefore becomes: which types of computer records are reliable enough to deserve deference? Obviously, not all computer records are sufficiently reliable. However, under a fair application of the "rule of reason" standard, which has already been adopted by the PTO and the courts, if a company can show that it has taken carefully planned and carefully guarded steps to ensure the reliability of a set of computerized files, then there is no reason why those computer files cannot provide enough corroboration to win an interference.

15.5 THE *SECURE FILE* APPROACH

Suppose a chemist operates a stand-alone microcomputer connected to an instrument or analytical device such as a spectrophotometer. He synthesizes his own compounds and then runs them through the spectrophotometer. His job is to create compounds, which will be sent to other researchers, who will screen those compounds for new and useful effects. The data from each run are analyzed by the instrument, transferred directly to the micro-computer, and stored on floppy disks.

The following procedures can be used by the scientist to generate evidence that can be offered in case a patent interference arises. They are listed in increasing order of security.

15.5.1 Level 1: Very Little Security

The researcher controls all of his disks, with all of his original and backup files. If he wishes, he can use his computer to edit any file without assistance from anyone else.

In this situation, an opponent in a patent interference could easily cast doubt upon the reliability of any date in any of his files. Corroboration probably would need to be based upon other documents.

15.5.2 Level 2: Better, But Not Much

Every week, the researcher makes a backup copy of any active disk, just in case his computer crashes and wipes out a disk. He gives the backup disk to a librarian, a secretary, or a co-worker, who dates and stores it. The dating and storage of the disk by the neutral per-son serves, in effect, as a witnessing of the disk, but not of the files on the disk. Assuming the disk was secured, *i.e.*, access precluded, *chain of custody* testimony from the librarian can establish that the disk was not tampered with, and is the same as when it was stored.

However, the custody of the disk must be maintained. If a disk can store several months worth of data, and the researcher trades disks every time the backup is updated, rather than supplying a new backup disk each week, the date of "corroboration" (if it can be called that) will be the last date on which a backup disk was given to the neutral person. Any earlier dates will be rendered totally unreliable, by the fact that earlier backup disks containing those data were modified by the researcher.

15.5.3 Level 3: Even Better, But a Question Remains

Every week, the researcher backs up his data by sending a copy of any file with a re-cent date to a mainframe computer that is operated by independent programmers in the com-pany's MIS (Management Information Systems) group. The mainframe unit records the date that the file is transferred to it and each revision date. Although it may be possible for an MIS operator to create a program that would falsify a date, no researcher working in the labs could do so without the cooperation of an MIS employee, since only MIS employees have access to MIS files or passwords.

If a patent interference arises, an MIS employee can testify to the effect that, "I examined a directory of this file, which indicated that the file has not been revised since such-and-such a date".

This procedure suffers from a key limitation: what happens if the researcher revised the file? The directory will probably indicate the date but not the content of the revision. Even if the revision was minor and was completely unrelated to the issue being contested in a patent interference, a recent revision date casts serious doubt on any efforts to establish a date for anything in the file.

15.5.4 Level 4: Better Yet

Data is transferred from the researcher's microcomputer to a mainframe in the MIS group, which puts the data in a *secure file*. The researcher can access and copy the file on a read-only basis, but he cannot revise it without a password that is known only to the MIS staff. If a revision must be made to a secure file, it is done by one of the following methods: (1) the original secure file is maintained, and a second secure file is created with the revised data; or, (2) the researcher sends the MIS staff a memo or a file, listing the superseded data and the revised data.

In the author's opinion, this procedure is practical and reasonable, and it should satisfy the PTO or a court. In addition, it would require only minor modifications in the procedures already being used by many corporate MIS groups, which is a major point in its favor.

15.6 COMPILATION FILES

There are other options in addition to the *secure file* approach, which involve the concept of *compilation files*. These approaches may offer a good way to balance the needs of patent lawyers and researchers.

Suppose a researcher operates an instrument that is coupled to a computer. Using this equipment, the researcher runs numerous samples each day, and each run generates its own file and/or printout.

Rather than having to sign and date every printout, and then getting a witness to sign and date each one as well, the researcher can use a specialized program that will (1) sample several bytes from each file and save those bytes in a separate memory file without altering the data file; (2) calculate at least two computerized values (such as the *checksum* and *CRC* values) that will depend upon all the bytes in the file, and (3) generate a compilation report that contains the directory information for the file (the filename and the date and time it was most recently revised), the sampled bytes, and the checksum and CRC values. The researcher can then either (1) print the compilation file, sign it, get it witnessed, and send it to the company technical library for storage, or (2) transfer the electronic compilation file to the MIS group for storage as a secure file.

Checksum and CRC values are widely used in sending files via modem, to ensure accuracy. If a single byte is changed in a file, the CRC and the checksum value will both change—and they will change in different ways. Therefore, it would be extraordinarily difficult for anyone to alter any data points in a computer file and then somehow restore both the checksum value and the CRC value to their original values.

This is just one possible approach; still other approaches have been developed to *digitally time-stamp* computer files, using math procedures with names such as "one-way hash functions" (see, *e.g., Science* 261: 162, 9 July 1993).

Still other approaches are suggested by "compression" utilities, which are widely used to reduce the size of electronic files being stored or transmitted. These programs condense files by methods such as replacing long strings of bytes with shorter strings that correspond to the longer strings on a one-to-one basis. The key point is this: good compression utilities generate confirmation files, which allow users to determine whether a compressed file was corrupted. These confirmation utilities may offer some useful ways to generate corroboration files that can be printed, signed, and stored just like lab notebook pages. These routines, which can be programmed to be done entirely by the computer on a weekly basis, might be able to eliminate the chore of signing dozens or hundreds of small printouts each week. People specializing in computer security and cryptography have developed any number of ways to boost, protect, or confirm the security of computer files. It is possible, using computers, to corroborate electronic files with more reliability than can be provided by witnesses testifying about something that happened years earlier. Based on "the rule of reason", any computer file that has in fact been protected and confirmed in a reasonable manner should be acceptable in an interference.

15.7 EXAMPLE ONE

THE ABC COMPANY
GUIDELINES FOR KEEPING RESEARCH RECORDS

I. Introduction
    A. Policy
    B. Applicability and Modifications
    C. Responsibilities of Researchers and Supervisors
    D. Categories of Research Records
    E. Related Procedures
II. Notebook Entries
    A. General Comments
    B. Conceptions of Ideas; Plans for Work

I. Introduction

A. Policy

All research records created by ABC personnel must:

1. be sufficiently clear and complete to allow others to repeat the work and to plan and conduct further work;
2. provide acceptable legal evidence to establish what was done, when it was done, and who did it;
3. be properly indexed and stored.

Your knowledge and skill are extremely valuable. But knowledge, skill, thoughts, and observations are merely potentials; they can be converted into products, recognition, and rewards only by a complex process. The key step in that process occurs when you record what you think or recognize, in a way that other people can understand and use. The era is long dead when an explorer could claim territory merely by raising a flag. If you create an invention, you must do more than announce it and explain it; you must create records to defend it against competitors. If a patent interference arises to determine who first invented something, your records will be challenged and criticized by competitors in every way possible. You won't have a chance to explain any oversights or omissions; the records will be taken away from you, scrutinized closely, and criticized while you can only watch. The proper time to protect your ideas and efforts is before a dispute arises, by carefully following these guidelines.

B. Applicability and Modifications

These guidelines apply to all research activities throughout The ABC Company. As used herein, *research* includes any activity that generates data or records that may be useful to support patents. This includes all laboratory work, as well as research involving (for example) better manufacturing processes. Consult a research supervisor or the ABC Patent Department if questions arise.

Any division or research group may supplement these guidelines to adapt them to specific situations. Such supplements must be described in writing, and must be approved by the Research Director and the patent attorney for that unit.

C. Responsibilities of Researchers and Supervisors

1. All personnel who generate or record research data must comply with these guidelines.

2. A researcher who believes these guidelines do not apply adequately to a particular situation must inform his/her supervisor of the problem rather than ignoring these guidelines. As noted above, modifications may be adopted to accommodate specific needs.

3. Researchers (especially new employees and people who transfer into new units) should take the initiative to find out whether these company-wide guidelines have been modified by their divisions. In particular, researchers should ask (1) whether job numbers must be noted on each notebook page; (2) whether certain company-assigned numbers must be used to refer to certain compounds; and, (3) whether special government-related guidelines apply in their division.

4. Every research supervisor has a responsibility to supervise research recordkeeping. All supervisors must ensure that (1) their subordinates are properly trained to use these guidelines; (2) notebook entries and computer reports are properly witnessed (see Section V); and (3) notebooks are returned to the library when appropriate (see Section VI). Supervisors also must decide whether any researcher (a summer researcher, contract employee, etc.) is not required to keep a bound notebook, and must implement alternate guidelines for researchers who do not keep bound notebooks (see Section III).

5. Final responsibility for research recordkeeping rests with each unit's Research Director.

D. Categories of Research Records

Several methods have been developed for recording research ideas and results. These methods are grouped into three categories:

1. *Notebooks.* These are hard-bound notebooks with numbered pages, issued to scientific and technical employees by the Technical Library.
2. *Supplementary records.* This category includes items that are not affixed to notebook pages such as (1) documents generated by computers, instruments, or other devices (strip charts, chromatographs, etc.) and (2) forms (often called "worksheets") that are used to collect data as an experiment is being performed. Supplementary records are discussed in Section III.
3. Computer-generated test reports, referred to herein as *computer reports*. Computer reports are a special type of supplementary record. These are discussed in a separate document; see Section IV.

E. Related Guidelines

Researchers should be aware of:

(1) *Good Laboratory Practice* (GLP) and *Good Manufacturing Practice* (GMP) guidelines, which are issued by the Food and Drug Administration and the Environmental Protection Agency; and

(2) the ABC repository for chemical and biological samples.

II. Notebook Entries

A. General Comments

1. There are important reasons for using bound notebooks with numbered pages, including the following:

a. If pages are removed or inserted, there will be some indication of tampering.

b. Bound notebooks prevent pages from becoming lost, scattered, or rearranged out of sequence.

c. Notebooks can be indexed, handled, and retrieved more easily than loose pages.

Loose pages do not have these advantages, and they are less useful as evidence if a patent or other dispute arises. Therefore, data must be kept in bound notebooks rather than on loose paper unless a supervisor approves a different procedure. For example, if a photocopied worksheet helps a researcher record all relevant data while the experiment is in progress, then a worksheet may be used; it must be handled properly (see Section III). The general excuse, "I prefer loose papers because they're more convenient than bound notebooks" is not a sufficient reason for using looseleaf paper rather than a notebook.

2. Unless a specific situation requires it, researchers should not take notes onto scratch paper and later copy the notes into a notebook. Instead, entries should be made directly into the notebook as work is being done. This saves time for the researcher, it eliminates transcription errors, and it ensures that a permanent record is made without delay.

3. In these guidelines, the person to whom a notebook is assigned is called *the holder*. The notebook belongs to ABC; the holder is responsible for its proper use. Notebooks should not be removed from ABC premises.

4. Ordinarily, only the holder should make entries in a notebook. Whenever any other person makes an entry in a notebook, that person should sign and date the entry. A notebook relating to a single project or machine may be shared by two or more researchers. In this case, a statement identifying the machine and the people involved must be placed in the front of the notebook.

5. Entries should be made in black ink, which is reproduced more legibly than other colors. Use black ink which is permanent, waterproof, and not erasable.

6. Incorrect entries should not be erased, deleted, or covered; instead, they should be lined through so the incorrect entry is still readable. If a correction is substantive, it should be accompanied by a dated explanatory note. If the correction is made after the notebook page has been witnessed, the correction should also be witnessed and dated (however, cross-references may be added without witnessing; see Section II-F). Entries cannot be changed or added after a notebook has been returned to the Technical Library; see Section VI-2.

7. All entries on a page should relate to a single project. Information about different projects should be written on separate pages.

8. If a page is dated at the top, it is presumed that all entries were made on that day. The holder should individually date any entry that is recorded on a different day.

9. If a substantial space (more than about three lines) is left blank on a page, the holder should mark through the blank space (for example, with a large X) before signing the page, unless it is specifically anticipated that certain data will be added to that page later. For example, if an entry on the top of a page describes how an experiment is conducted, the bottom of the page may be left blank to insert (and date) the experimental results when they become available.

10. All entries must be legible; if something cannot be read, it is worthless to you and to ABC.

11. The back (unnumbered) side of a page should not be used, and items should not be affixed to it.

12. Freehand drawings, flow charts, and other figures are strongly encouraged. In addition to helping other people understand your data and ideas, they often contain implicit suggestions that would be overlooked in a written description.

B. Conceptions of Ideas; Plans for Work

1. In addition to recording experimental data, bound notebooks are ideally suited for recording:

    a. the conception of an idea, a principle, an application, etc., which may precede experimental work;

    b. plans for implementing a research program;

    c. ideas for additional work arising as research efforts continue, and

    d. discussions with other people concerning research.

Such information is reliably recorded when entered, dated, and witnessed in a notebook. In addition, unlike most memos and reports, such information is stored permanently.

2. When describing a conception, plan, etc., use enough detail so that it could be understood by others who do similar work. Describe the goal of your idea, and include (1) a brief description of related earlier work, (2) citations to articles, and (3) an indication of how your idea differs from the earlier work.

3. It may be useful to send a photocopy of a notebook entry describing a new idea to your patent attorney, who may suggest an additional notebook entry or an invention disclosure to explain your idea more fully. This procedure is quick and informal, and it can greatly improve the quality of the earliest records.

4. A good method for corroborating an idea is to discuss the idea, and the notebook entry, as soon as possible with a co-worker, who should sign and date the entry.

5. Always enter a phrase describing your idea or plan in the index of your notebook (see Section II-F-3).

C. Records of Experiments or Other Work

1. Notebook records of experimental work must be able to stand alone; a skilled researcher should be able to repeat the work based solely on the records, without needing clarification or further explanation by the notebook holder. For example, identify chemical concentrations and purities, reaction parameters, cell or animal or plant strains, etc. For special reagents, relevant details such as the name of the manufacturer or chemist, the concentration, the lot number, date of synthesis, and any analytical results should be noted or cross-referenced. Indicate baseline or calibration values if appropriate. If a computer program (whether developed by ABC or an outside source) is used in an experiment, the program should be identified. Substances identified by trademark or commercial name, unless they are common and widely used, should also be identified by scientific nomenclature, structural formula, or analytical results.

2. A record of an experiment or other work should explain the purpose of the work and/or provide a cross-reference indicating its relationship to prior work or to a previously recorded idea or plan.

3. For any calculation, indicate how each starting value was obtained (measured, estimated, calculated, etc). Unless obvious, indicate any mathematical formulas used, and include a sample calculation if appropriate.

4. Identify the people (other than yourself) who conducted the experimental work, and describe or cross-reference any special instructions given to them. Cross-reference any supplementary records.

5. Describe experimental results or other work in specific factual terms rather than absolute or conclusory terms or opinions. Some examples:

Poor language: "These two chemicals don't react."

Better: "No reaction was observed."

Poor language: "This material has low/poor/lousy impact strength."

Better: "This material has an impact strength of 2 ft-lb/inch."

6. In particular, describe negative results in specific factual details rather than as conclusions or opinions. If known, indicate any conditions that contributed to the negative result (equipment upset, problems with control samples, etc). Indicate in detail when and how

a substance performed with regard to specific criteria, without calling it a failure. In a specific experiment, terms such as "Inactive" or "No result" (NR) may be used, if it is clear that those terms are based on a specific test.

The PTO has held that a notebook entry saying, "This approach won't work" can constitute an abandonment of efforts to reduce an invention to practice. If a similar effort is started up again later, the date of the earlier work may be lost for patent purposes. A new conception occurs when researchers decide to take another look at the idea that was previously labelled as a failure. The new conception usually occurs much later than the first conception; this should be avoided.

Therefore, do not label samples or methods as "Failed" or "No Good". Even if it is clear to the researcher that such phrases refer to the results of a specific test, other people might take that phrase out of context and regard it as a general conclusion.

D. Abbreviations and Symbols

1. Abbreviations and symbols that are recognized as standard within the scientific literature may be used. The following are recommended as good sources of abbreviations and symbols:

"Standard Abbreviations, Acronyms, Special Characters and Symbols in CAS Computer-Readable Files and Publications," by Chemical Abstracts Service, 1982.

J. Rigandy and S. P. Clesney, *Nomenclature of Organic Chemistry,* IUPAC (Pergamon Press, 1979).

The Journal of Biological Chemistry (the first issue of each year).

2. Researchers may use any other abbreviations or symbols for their own convenience if either of the following guidelines is followed:

a. A researcher may use any abbreviations or symbols that are listed and explained in the front of his/her notebook. It is not sufficient to note the abbreviation or symbol on the page where it is first used, since that notation may be difficult to locate.

b. A division within ABC may adopt a list of additional abbreviations or symbols for the convenience of its researchers.

   The list must be filed with the Patent Department and the library. This procedure is well-suited for listing commonly-used items such as buffers and reagents.

E. Items Affixed to Notebook Pages

1. An item (such as a graph, photograph, or small strip chart) that is affixed to a notebook page becomes a notebook entry. An item that is not affixed in a notebook page is classified as a supplementary record, described in Section III.

2. Items should be permanently affixed to notebook pages by tape, glue, or staples. They must not be merely inserted between pages, since they might fall out. Where appropriate, at least two edges of the item should be stapled or taped to ensure that the item will lie flat on the page.

3. An affixed item should not cover up a notebook entry, page heading, or signature. Even if a note is added to the page mentioning that an entry is beneath the affixed item, that note might be missed during microfilming by the camera operator.

4. See Section III-5 regarding hand written notes on instrument-generated items.

F. Job Numbers, Cross-References, and Indexes

1. Project numbers are very useful in locating data and correlating notebook entries to project reports and other records. Whenever a project number applies to an entry, the number should be indicated on each notebook page, or at the start of a notebook if the entire notebook is devoted to a single project.

2. Cross-references in notebooks are strongly encouraged and should be used freely to correlate different entries within a notebook or in different notebooks. They also should be used to correlate notebook entries with supplementary data, computer reports, project reports, and other documents not contained in notebooks. A cross-reference should be signed and dated, but it does not need to be witnessed, regardless of when it is added to a page.

3. A complete index is essential to subsequent use of a notebook. The notebook holder should start an index of anticipated work as soon as he or she receives the notebook. The index should be supplemented continually while the notebook is being used and must be completed before the notebook is sent to the library for microfilming.

III. Supplementary Records

1. The term *supplementary record* is used to describe any document that is not affixed to a notebook page. Supplementary records can include the following:

a. computer programs and reports (see Section IV);
b. documents generated by instruments or other devices such as strip charts or chromatographs;
c. forms (often called *worksheets*) that were used to collect data as experiments were being performed.
d. engineering drawings and circuit diagrams;
e. plant or pilot plant logs; and
f. test protocols, screening procedures, etc.

2. A supplementary record should always be signed and dated by its originator. In addition, the originator must place a cross-reference on the supplementary record, referring to a related notebook entry or other document, which is uniquely identified.

3. Supplementary records should be witnessed and dated, unless

a. the cross-referenced notebook entry summarizes key data points, such as the location of two or more peaks on a chromatograph; or,

b. the cross-referenced notebook entry refers to a unique number or heading that is printed on the supplementary record; or,

c. section III-4 applies.

Any other substitute for witnessing supplementary records must be approved by the ABC Patent Department.

4. If an instrument, microprocessor, or other device is used to create numerous small reports or other outputs, it is not necessary to sign and witness each individual report if a compilation is periodically created, signed, and witnessed. For example, if a chromatograph hooked up to a microprocessor is used for ten runs each day, the microprocessor might be programmed to compile several data points from each run and to print a report of all runs once each week. If the compiled weekly report is properly signed and witnessed, the individual reports do not require signing and witnessing. The maximum time between compilations is two weeks, and the individual reports must be stored as permanent records unless Patent Department approval to discard them is obtained.

5. Supplementary records are permanent records. They must not be discarded, even if all the information in them is subsequently printed in a computer report or other compilation. They must be submitted to the library for microfilming and storage along with the related notebooks or computer reports.

6. Handwritten notes may be added to a supplementary record or item affixed to a notebook page, if it is clear that the notes are intended to help others interpret the data. Such comments must not alter the data. For example, on a chromatograph, notes and arrows may be used to indicate which peaks are calibration substances and which peak is the substance being analyzed. As another example, if two different values printed in a table are multiplied to give a third value printed in the same or a different table, a sample calculation can be shown in the margin. Any such handwritten note should be initialed or signed, and dated.

IV. Computer Reports

A separate document entitled *Guidelines for Keeping Research Records Using Computers* discusses procedures for creating and documenting research records using computers.

V. Witnessing

1. Every research supervisor is responsible for ensuring compliance with the following guidelines. Witnessing is the best way to satisfy a doctrine of patent law that requires that self-serving data submitted by an inventor must be *corroborated* by someone who is not a co-inventor.

2. It is mandatory that every notebook entry and computer report be signed and dated by a witness within two weeks after creation. In addition, supplementary records also must be witnessed unless certain criteria are met (see Section III-3).

3. Anyone who might be a potential co-inventor, if an invention arises from the work, should not be used as a witness. In addition, do not use temporary employees such as post-doctorals, interns, or summer students as witnesses.

4. The witness asserts that he or she has "read and understood" the entry. It is not necessary for the witness to master the entry before witnessing it; however, the witness must read the entry and have a basic grasp of what it means. If any errors, omissions, or questions arise, the witness should bring these to the attention of the notebook holder; the holder should make corrections as necessary before the entry is witnessed. If words are illegible, the witness should ask the holder to clearly print the word next to the illegible word. The witness should ensure that the holder signed and dated the pages and crossed out any large blank spaces.

5. Any information (other than a cross-reference) that is added to a page after the page has been witnessed should be added in the presence of a witness (preferably the original witness). Such additions should be signed and dated by the notebook holder and the witness as soon as they are entered. Such additions should be enclosed within a hand-drawn box that includes a heading such as "The following information was added on (date) by (name)". A statement may be inserted explaining why the information was added, such as a reference to a later entry involving research that casts new light on the entry.

6. Stamped signatures or dates are not reliable, and should not be used.

VI. Microfilming, Storage, and Security

1. Each notebook and all related supplementary records must be returned to the Technical Library for microfilming as soon as the notebook has been completed, but no later than one year after it is issued to the researcher. If an extension of time is necessary, contact the library.

2. The library produces two microfilm copies of each notebook. The original notebook and one copy are kept by the library, and are available to researchers. The second microfilm copy is stored elsewhere, and is not available.

3. After a notebook or supplementary record has been microfilmed, it may be returned to the author if requested. However, this is discouraged, and notebooks not in active use should remain in the library. Additions, corrections, or other changes should not be made after microfilming.

VII. Closing Comments

It is official ABC policy that all research records must be kept according to these guidelines, or according to modifications approved by the Patent Department. ABC recognizes that these formalities can be time-consuming and inconvenient. Nevertheless, they are essential to ABC's business. It is useless and counterproductive to speed up research if the resulting records suffer and become invalid as evidence. A researcher must have enough time to conduct his or her research and keep valid records. If not, a serious problem exists. The researcher must notify his or her supervisor of the problem, rather than neglect to keep proper records.

15.8 EXAMPLE TWO

These guidelines have been written in the name of a hypothetical "ABC Company". They are designed for modification and adoption by companies that use computers in scientific research.

THE ABC COMPANY
GUIDELINES FOR KEEPING
RESEARCH RECORDS USING COMPUTERS

These guidelines are intended for distribution to researchers who actively use computers in research. They accompany a second set of conventional guidelines that cover hard-bound notebooks and other standard methods that should be used by all researchers regardless of whether they use computers.

CONTENTS

I. Introduction

A. Purpose and Applicability

1. These guidelines supplement the ABC Company *Guidelines for Keeping Research Records*. All researchers and their supervisors are responsible for complying with those guidelines and ensuring that all research records that might be needed to support patentable

inventions are *corroborated* (supported by tangible evidence that was not generated solely by an inventor). When paper documents are involved, corroboration is usually provided by having an independent witness sign and date the documents within two weeks after the documents are created.

These supplementary guidelines, which follow, provide additional information on how to satisfy the special needs that arise when research records are gathered by, or stored on, computers or computerized instruments. Any researcher who uses computers in gathering or processing patent-related research data must understand and comply with these special requirements.

2. Computerized data may be corroborated in either of two ways:

a. A printout may be signed and dated by the creator(s) and by a witness; or,

b. If the research is done in a unit of ABC that has an approved procedure, the researcher may transmit the data electronically to a separate computer operations group, which will store a dated copy of the data and control any subsequent access to the data. Procedures to allow this method of corroboration are developed by the computer operations group for that unit of ABC, in cooperation with the Patent Department. Researchers who wish to use such a procedure should contact their computer operations group.

3. These guidelines can be modified to accommodate specific situations. Any modification must be approved by research management and the Patent Department.

B. Types of Computer-Related Records

There are four types of computer-related records:

1. test procedures describe how experiments were performed and how data were gathered.

2. computer programs contain the software used to process raw data and generate legible results.

3. printouts are paper documents that contain the results of a specific experiment or a related series of experiments. Some printouts contain all processed data, while others contain only extracted data. Any printout that might become important for patent purposes normally must be signed by the creator, witnessed, and filed with the Technical Library, unless an alternate procedure has been approved. Regardless of how the data are subsequently used or modified, the witnessed printout will remain on file as a permanent record, as proof that the data were gathered before the date of the witness's signature.

4. secured electronic files are maintained by a Management Information Systems (MIS) group after the data is transmitted to MIS. The MIS group will control all access to secured files and will maintain dated records of any alterations.

C. Relationship with Bound Notebooks

In most circumstances, bound notebooks and computerized recordkeeping should be used together, as follows:

1. A researcher will decide to test a process or substance. If this decision involves a new idea with potentially patentable value, it should be described by the researcher in his or her bound notebook, in narrative form (see Section II-B of the *Guidelines for Keeping Research Records*).

2. A test procedure should be prepared and documented (as described in Section II below) to describe how each step in the test is performed.

3. The researcher and/or assistants will conduct the experiment(s), following the test procedure. The resulting data are collected by a computerized instrument or other device, or otherwise entered into a computer. If the procedures described below are followed, such data do not need to also be entered by hand into a bound notebook; however, the notebook should indicate where the data are contained (such as the name of the electronic file, and the label on the disk where it is stored).

4. After the raw data are collected, they are processed and printed by the computer and either:

    a. printed on paper and treated as described in Section III below, or

    b. transmitted to MIS to be kept as a secured electronic file (see Section IV).

In either case, records of the test procedure and computer program should be kept by the researcher.

5. If a researcher observes a potentially useful correlation in the experimental results or in the computer report, he or she should describe the correlation in his or her bound notebook and have that entry witnessed (*i.e.*, signed and dated by someone who is not a potential co-inventor).

II. Test Procedures and Computer Programs

1. A test procedure should describe each step in an experiment, in enough detail so the test can be repeated by any researcher familiar with that type of work. Each test procedure should describe all aspects of the materials and processes used in the experiment, including quantitative data (volumes, concentrations, times, temperatures, etc.) and, if appropriate, a narrative description of what information is being gathered and why it is significant. It can refer to a published procedure, such as "see ASTM Test Method 123" or "see the method of Smith *et al*, Science 200: 123 (1990)." If appropriate, the test procedure should refer to any computer programs used to process the data.

2. The procedure should be written down as soon as possible after the steps have been finalized. The final written version must be approved by a supervisor, and a copy must be sent to the Technical Library for storage as a permanent record. For identification and

search purposes, each test procedure should be assigned a unique number. If the procedure is in a bound notebook or project report, a notebook page or report number should be used. Otherwise, the Library will assign a number to the procedure. This number subsequently must be cited in any related printout. The phrase "ABC Company Confidential" must appear on every test procedure that is not in a bound notebook.

3. When a test procedure is sent to the Technical Library, it should be accompanied by a memo that cites any relevant documents, such as the earliest proposal or description in a bound notebook, earlier versions of the test procedure, and notebook entries describing experiments used to develop the procedure.

4. During actual tests, any deviations from the written procedure should be noted, either in a lab notebook or as a written note on a printout, with a brief description of why the deviation was necessary.

5. If a test procedure is revised, the revised version must be sent to the Technical Library along with a memo that briefly summarizes what is different and why. The original and revised versions will both be stored by the Library. Experimental data collected during the development of the test procedure should be stored as a permanent record.

6. If a printed or photocopied form (often called a *worksheet*) is used to collect data, a copy of the form should be included as part of the test procedure. When data are entered onto such a form, the form becomes a *supplementary record* as described in Section III of the *Guidelines for Keeping Research Records*. Unless otherwise approved by the Patent Department, completed forms containing test data should be stored as permanent records, even if all the data in them is subsequently printed in a printout.

7. Usually, a printout or secured file contains numerical results without a supporting explanation of how the raw data were processed. For internal purposes as well as legal use, the researcher should ensure that the computer programs that process the data are either (a) commercially available or (b) stored appropriately. If a computer program relates solely to printout format, searching, etc., historical records may not be required. However, if a program relates to calculations or other data conversion, it may be of interest. Records of such programs should be filed with the Technical Library unless the Director of Research and the Patent Department approve a different procedure. If a program is purchased from a commercial supplier or obtained under a license agreement with a confidentiality obligation, the program should be mentioned in the test procedure, or a memo indicating the relevant facts should be stored instead of the computer program.

III. Computer Printouts

A. General

1. The standard way to corroborate research data kept on a computer is to (a) create a printout of the data (or of selected data points), and (b) have the printout signed and dated by the creator, and by a witness who is not likely to become a co-inventor. This method should be used unless an alternate procedure has been approved for a specific researcher or instrument by a research manager.

2. When an experiment generates computerized data that is recognized to be significant to a patentable invention, the most directly relevant data will usually be summarized in a research or project report that will be circulated among research management. Following normal company procedures, a copy of any such research or project report is sent to the Technical Library, which date-stamps the report, catalogs it, and stores it as a permanent record. That filed report will normally serve as corroboration of any data summarized or contained therein. Under many circumstances, no further action will be required of the researchers.

3. If research management, in consultation with the Patent Department, decides that a witnessed printout containing all the data in a particular computer file or database might be useful in a patent interference or lawsuit (above and beyond the normal corroboration provided by a research or progress report), then a full printout should be generated, signed and dated by the creator, and signed and dated by a witness. The witnessed printout must be filed with the Technical Library.

4. If a researcher wishes to alter an existing electronic file (such as by adding more data that were gathered after the first corroboration) instead of generating a new file, research management will be responsible for deciding whether the electronic file may be directly altered, or whether a copy of the file must be kept in unaltered form while a second copy is created and then modified as desired. If a complete printout of a file or database has been witnessed and filed with the Technical Library, there is no need, from the viewpoint of patentability, to maintain the data in unaltered form in an electronic file; the stored printout will be sufficient. However, in most circumstances, researchers will recognize the prudence of maintaining backup files in a separate location whenever work is done involving computers, as a standard precaution against fire, theft, or disk failure. Accordingly, the standard and preferred practice will be to store an unaltered copy of any electronic file that is sufficiently important to be worth corroboration. Such files preferably should be transmitted by the researcher to an MIS group, for storage as secured files.

5. If any changes having patent-related significance are made to a file or database, the researcher doing the work should consider creating and filing another witnessed printout, to prove that the changes were made before the date of the second printout.

6. An example of a printout with proper heading, signature, and witnessing format is available from the Patent Department. Any substantial deviations should be reviewed with the Patent Department.

B. Data-Sampled Compilation Reports

1. If an instrument, microprocessor, or other device is used to create numerous small computerized files (for example, if a chromatograph is used to analyze chemical samples, and if the data from each sample are stored in a file with a unique file name), it is not necessary to print, sign, and witness each individual file, if a compilation report containing sampled data is created as described in this section. For example, the computer that con-

trols the instrument can be programmed to (1) sample several data points from each data file; (2) calculate the "checksum" and cycle redundancy check (CRC) values for each file, or generate a *hash value* for the file; and (3) generate a compilation report containing the name, directory data, sampled data points, and checksum/CRC or hash values for each sampled file.

2. If this approach is used, a compilation report must be generated every two weeks. It must cover all files that were created or revised since the last compilation was run. If properly sampled and corroborated in this manner, the electronic files can be maintained by the researcher in his or her office or lab, on a floppy disk or other electronic media. The researcher is responsible for safe storage of the floppy disks or other media. *Important*: the researcher who keeps the electronic files should not revise a file that has already been sampled and corroborated. Since compilation reports normally will be used to sample data that has already been gathered, it usually will not be necessary or advisable for a researcher to subsequently modify the data. If any revisions to an already-sampled file become necessary for any reason, a copy should be made and given a new and unique name. The copy (rather than the original) can be altered, and afterwards, it must be sampled and corroborated using the normal compilation procedures.

3. Researchers should be aware that if a single byte is altered in an electronic file, it will alter the checksum/CRC or hash values in totally different ways that are nearly impossible to reconcile with each other. For unaltered files, sampling and checksum/CRC values therefore provide a reasonable level of assurance that the file has not been altered. However, if an electronic file is revised in any way, even if the directory date and file size are kept the same, the changes in the checksum and CRC values will invalidate any compilation report created prior to the alteration.

4. Compilation reports can be corroborated in either of two ways: (a) the compilation report can be printed on paper, and the printout can be signed by the creator, witnessed by someone who will not be a co-inventor, and delivered to the Technical Library for permanent storage; or, (b) the compilation file can be transmitted to the MIS group, for storage as a secured electronic file.

C. Titles and Identifying Numbers

1. Every witnessed printout or secured file must indicate which group created the printout or which project it involved. It must also contain a title that is reasonably descriptive of the test that was done. Any title changes should be documented in the test procedure.

2. For indexing and search purposes, every printout or secured file should contain a unique number that should either:

    a. correspond to a page number in a bound notebook, or

    b. contain information such as the operator's initials, the machine number, and the run number.

D. Confidentiality Statement

1. If possible, a statement such as the following should be printed on the first page of any printout:

> This report is CONFIDENTIAL. It is the property of THE ABC COMPANY and shall be disclosed only to authorized persons. The recipient is responsible for proper use and storage of this report, which must be returned to the ABC Technical Library on demand.

2. The phrase "ABC Company Confidential" should appear on any printout that does not contain the statement above.

E. Handwritten Notes; References to Other Documents

1. A researcher may add handwritten notes to a printout if it is clear that the notes serve to explain rather than alter the data. For example, if two numbers printed in a table are multiplied to give a third number in the same or a different table, the researcher might show the formula and a sample calculation in the margin. In addition, a researcher may add handwritten cross-references (*e.g.*, to notebook entries) onto a printout.

2. If a handwritten note on a printout contains substantive information, the person who writes it preferably should sign and date the note. However, since notations that merely help readers interpret data, and cross-references to related information, can be very helpful to anyone reviewing a printout, they are encouraged and do not need to meet any formalities.

3. A witnessed printout or secured file normally contains only data; it does not describe the details of how the experiment was performed. Therefore, it must refer to the applicable test procedure. This can be done by a citation to bound notebook pages, a project report number, or a separate document. References to other documents may be added to a printout or secured file for any other reason. Two examples:

   a. If the experiment is being performed to test an idea described in a lab notebook, the notebook entry should be cited.

   b. If the experiment is being performed to carry out a company directive, government regulation, etc., the directive or regulation should be cited.

4. Many printouts and secured files contain both raw and processed data. Each type of data should be clearly identified, preferably with column headings. The relationship of the raw and processed data should be described in the test procedure.

5. If any unusual or unforeseen results are observed (either during or after a test), which cannot be recorded adequately within the format of the printout or secured file, such observations should be recorded in narrative form in the researcher's bound notebook, and the page number of the notebook entry should be cited in the printout or secured file.

F. Test Dates

Every printout or secured file must include at least one date to identify when the test was conducted. It is preferable to include every important date (*e.g.*, a date when a cell culture was manipulated, and a data-gathering date after the cells were incubated). The test procedure should describe the relationship of all the dates.

G. Signatures and Witnessing

1. Each individual who performed a significant part of a test should be identified, either by separate records, or by signing and dating the printout. When more than one individual conducts an experiment, it is desirable to keep records indicating each individual's contribution to the experiment.

2. Each printout must be signed and dated by a witness who is not likely to be a co-inventor if the experiment leads to a patentable invention. See Section V of *Guidelines for Keeping Research Records*.

H. Report Format

1. Each printout should be maintained as an unburst printout (*i.e.*, as a continuous sheet). If possible, unique computer-generated page identifiers should be printed at the top of each page, indicating the unique number of the printout and the number of that page. The phrase "END OF REPORT" should be printed at the bottom of the last page of each printout. These measures help indicate that the report is a single complete document and that no pages were subsequently added to or deleted from the original printout.

2. It is preferable for headings, page numbers, cross-references, and dates to be printed on the printout by the computer. If this is impractical, the researcher should add all relevant data to the printout, preferably in his/her own handwriting, before signing it.

I. Indexing, Microfilming, Storage, and Security

1. Each group within The ABC Company must use a library-approved method so printouts and secured files can be indexed and located by the Technical Library.

2. Each research group must deliver a copy of each signed and witnessed printout to the Technical Library within a month of its creation. The library will index and microfilm the printouts.

3. If desired, a researcher may obtain a photocopy or an extra computer-printed copy of a printout, for personal use. Such copies should be prominently marked as being for the personal use of the researcher, so that they won't be confused with permanent records.

4. The Technical Library usually produces two microfilm copies of each printout. One set is retained by the library; it can be obtained and read using standard microfilm readers. A second set is normally stored at a secured location elsewhere and is not available for normal use.

5. Any corrections or changes to a printout after microfilming should be implemented by sending a memo indicating the change and the reason for the change to the library. The library will microfilm the memo and index the memo on the microfilm cartridge. Such changes should also be cross-referenced in bound notebooks if appropriate.

6. Printouts and reproductions of printouts must be marked and treated as "ABC Company Confidential."

IV. Secured Electronic Files

1. The *secured file* method of corroboration may be used by a researcher only if the computer operations group for his or her division of ABC has created a procedure for maintaining secured files containing computerized research data. A researcher who wishes to use this method should contact the computer operations group for his division.

2. The previous sections, which relate to printouts, also apply to secured files:

Section III-B, titles and identifying numbers.

Section III-D, cross-references and explanations.

Section III-E, test dates.

Section III-H-1, indexing.

PREPARING AND PROSECUTING THE U.S. PATENT APPLICATION

The previous articles attempted to provide some perspective with respect to the patent system, and discussed the benefits of obtaining patent protection and strategic factors to be considered in determining whether or not to pursue patent protection of an invention. The articles in this section relate to laying the foundation for proving invention and independent development and to the process of preparing and prosecuting a patent application. MAL

WRITING AN INVENTION DISCLOSURE

Michael J. Balconi-Lamica

Michael J. Balconi-Lamica is an attorney with the Intellectual Property Law Department of the International Business Machines Corporation in Hopewell Junction, New York.

An Invention Disclosure *serves a number of purposes. If properly dated, and witnessed, it establishes a date of conception. In a corporate context, it provides the decision-makers the information they need to assess the invention and determine whether to proceed with patent protection. If properly done, it also will communicate necessary information to the patent attorney, such as potential statutory bars to patentability, potential prior art, and the like. There is a very strict duty to disclose all information that might be relevant to patentability to the Patent and Trademark Office. To assure compliance with that duty, it is critical that the patent attorney be made aware of such things as* all *earlier versions or models of invention. Such earlier versions or models may, or may not, be prior art that must be considered. Also, any disclosure of the device to others or possible "offers for sale" should be called to the attorney's attention. In addition, the inventor also should provide the attorney with copies of any literature that is in any way relevant to the issue of patentability.*

The invention disclosure also is intended to aid the patent attorney in identifying the patentable aspects of the invention and in preparing the patent application (in conjunction with "think tanking" sessions with the inventor). In general, from the attorney's perspective, the disclosure materials should include a series of simplified diagrams (e.g., functional block diagrams) of the invention, running from the general to the more specific. It also is important that the attorney be provided with the latest drawings and written descriptions of the invention and any product embodying the invention to, e.g., help ensure compliance with the best mode requirement. The disclosure materials should clearly describe:

- *The problems that are solved by the invention.*
- *Each feature of a product that the inventor considers to be new and different from the prior art.*
- *Each aspect of the product that provides an improvement or advantage over the prior models and/or the competing products. (This is not to say that an invention necessarily has to be better than the prior art to be patentable—it need only be different and nonobvious.)*

- *Each aspect of the product that is anticipated to give an advantage in the mar-ketplace or to be emphasized in promotional materials and advertising.*
- *Any particulars, such as the use of particular circuits, software algorithms or coding techniques, components or values, that provide a special efficiency or advantage.*

With respect to software inventions, it is helpful if the disclosure materials also include:

- *an attempt to relate the program to the physical computer system. For exam-ple, details regarding the organization of data in memory (e.g., a memory map) and all variables (e.g., specific registers or locations in memory correspond-ing to specific variables) are often helpful in assessing the patentability of as-pects of the product, identifying items to be protected, and in the actual preparation of the patent application document.*
- Decision logic *flowcharts at a level of detail sufficient to permit an* average *pro-grammer to generate operative code is similarly helpful.*

The following articles discuss, among other things, the science of writing an in-vention disclosure.   MAL

Abstract

Writing an invention disclosure is an important first step in seeking patent protection for your new method, apparatus, or composition of matter. Whether you are an independent in-ventor or your inventions belong to your employer, the invention disclosure is a written document for communicating your invention to the patent professional, or other party, eval-uating your invention. The invention disclosure is thus an important vehicle or medium for documenting and presenting your invention. With this in mind, the invention disclosure should be written to convey the essence and the importance or value of your invention.

16.1 WRITING AN INVENTION DISCLOSURE

Writing an invention disclosure is a learned skill. Through greater understanding and development of skills for writing an invention disclosure, the inventor can, and generally does, gain a deeper appreciation for the type of information essential to the invention dis-closure. In addition, the inventor gains appreciation for making the invention disclosure suitable for evaluation and patenting purposes.

When writing an invention disclosure, it is important to keep in mind the purpose for writing the disclosure. This purpose is revealed through several subject areas believed es-sential to a well written disclosure:

- identifying the background art;
- identifying the problems in the background art;

- identifying the invention;
- identifying differences between the invention and known alternatives or solutions;
- identifying advantages of the invention as a result of those differences; and
- identifying potential value or use of the invention.

Discussion of each subject area is provided, and in particular, how each subject area is an essential part of the disclosure and how it relates to describing the invention.

16.2 BACKGROUND INFORMATION

Background information is generally contained in the background section of the invention disclosure. The background section provides a description of the general area of the technical art to which the invention pertains and, more particularly, provides information on what is being done in the art. Background information contained in the background section is important for establishing a basis for the invention. This basis is built upon a discussion of problems in the art to which the invention pertains and known solutions to those problems. One manner for identifying and providing background information is by providing citations to patents, publications, and disclosures that the inventor is aware of and which pertain to problems in the art and/or known solutions to those problems.

16.2.1 Problems in the Art

A part of understanding an invention is understanding the technical problem or problems being solved by the invention. This portion of the background section serves to identify and briefly discuss that problem or the specific problems. The emphasis is to highlight the area in the art for which improvement is desired or necessary and to which your invention is directed.

Identifying specific problems in the art conveys those problems, or alternatively, areas for improvement, to the reader of the invention disclosure. The identified problems or areas in the art are those problems or areas that have not been overcome or improved upon, and/or for which a suitable solution or improvement has not heretofore been found. Furthermore, specifically identifying and discussing the problems or areas for improvement in writing assists the inventor in achieving a greater understanding of his or her own invention. This understanding and insight should be conveyed to the reader of the invention disclosure.

16.2.2 Known Solutions

In addition to identifying the problems in the art, known solutions to those problems should be identified and discussed briefly in the invention disclosure. One manner for identifying known solutions is accomplished by providing citations to patents, publications, and disclosures that the inventor is aware of that pertain to the known solutions to the problem. The inventor should keep in mind that, when applying for a patent in the United States, the inventor has a duty to disclose to the U.S. Patent and Trademark Office (PTO) such relevant known solutions and other information, such as, potential offers for sale, all relevant prior art, etc. If there are no known solutions to the problem, what comes closest to a solution to the problem? Identifying and briefly discussing known solutions, and the limitations or shortcomings of those solutions, assists in establishing a basis for the invention.

16.3 DESCRIPTION OF THE INVENTION

This section conveys what the inventor believes to be the invention, the novel features thereof, and discusses how the invention solves the problem or problems in the art. The adequacy of this section will be, in part, a representation of the inventor's ability to communicate in writing what the invention is, and further in part, the inventor's understanding of the invention. This purpose can be satisfied by providing a description using terms that are understandable to a typical person practicing in the area of technology (one skilled in the art) to which the invention pertains and where appropriate, to supplement the written description by including one or more drawing figures.

A well written description, with appropriate drawing figures, effectively communicates the essence of the invention and how the invention solves the problem or problems in the art. The written description and any drawing figures should work together and complement each other. Thus, it may be desirable for an inventor to begin drafting this portion of the invention disclosure by (i) summarizing the crux of the invention using key words or phrases, (ii) selecting a drawing figure, and (iii) writing an appropriate detailed description of the invention in conjunction with the figure.

Summarizing the invention can be accomplished using one or several brief statements. Key words or phrases may be used for briefly describing the essence of the invention. For instance, the summary of the invention for a novel automotive brake mechanism may simply read, "A novel automotive brake mechanism comprises a unique arrangement of multiple brake shoes and linings, the brake shoes and linings being positioned with respect to one another in a staggered relationship to increase the effective surface area of contact with a brake drum for improved braking capability". The summary of the invention for a method may read, "An improved method for manufacturing widgets comprises a widget characteristic detection step interposed at critical points throughout the widget manufacturing process for detecting defective widgets. The widget characteristic detection step monitors characteristics (a), (b), and (c) to provide parameter (d), wherein parameter (d) is representative of the integrity of the previous processing step".

As mentioned above, one or more drawing figures can assist in the description of the invention. Drawing figures are most useful when they highlight and clearly identify the novel features of the invention in connection with other important features necessary for the operability of the invention. A drawing figure may contain a block diagram representation of the invention, a flow chart, or a simplified drawing of an actual device. The figure may also comprise a photograph, where appropriate. In addition, when selecting or generating a figure, it is desirable to keep the figure simple. That is, provide just enough information in the drawing figure to convey the important elements, combination of elements or process steps necessary to show the invention. Furthermore, the figure should show features of the invention that distinguish the invention over the most relevant art.

A briefly detailed drawing figure (*e.g.*, functional block diagram) should be included in lieu of or in addition to a more detailed drawing, such as an engineering drawing. The briefly detailed drawing figure is advantageously drawn to include only features that are essential or otherwise germane to the invention, with sufficient detail to distinguish the invention over the most relevant art. In comparison, a detailed engineering drawing generally contains extra nonessential information, such as, exact part dimensions, tolerances, and other information not germane or key to the invention. Such a detailed engineering drawing containing nonessential information may make understanding the essence of the invention that much more difficult. In some instances, however, the inventor also may want to include the detailed engineering drawing for reference by the patent agent or attorney. Thus, the idea here is to keep each drawing figure simple, to the extent that you can, for figuratively presenting the invention.

After selecting one or more drawing figures for use, you can begin the written description of the invention. To assist in writing this portion of the invention disclosure, think about how you would describe the invention, and in what manner you would describe it, that is, as if you were giving a presentation about the invention. Terminology used in describing the invention should be kept to that which is typically used in the art to which the invention pertains. If acronyms are to be used, be sure to define them. Use of undefined acronyms makes understanding the invention that much more difficult for the patent practitioner or evaluator who ultimately reads the invention disclosure.

As with the drawings, keep the description of the invention simple. Provide enough information to convey and identify the essential elements of the invention and the cooperation between those elements. In addition, references to the drawing figure or figures should be clearly marked and identified, both in the written description and on the respective drawing figure or figures. In this portion of the invention disclosure, the emphasis should be on the novel aspects of the invention as they distinguish the invention over the most relevant art. In addition, identify differences between the known solutions and the invention. If the invention is a new or improved method, provide details about the process steps of the method which distinguish the method over the prior known methods. If the invention is a new or improved device, provide details about the structural features, elements, or combination of elements that distinguish the device over prior known devices.

Be specific with respect to what you, as the inventor, believe are the novel aspects that distinguish the invention over the most relevant art. To further assist in writing this portion of the disclosure, identify and distinguish the novel aspects of the invention, by comparison to known relevant art, for example, and in particular, making reference to information provided in the background section.

The written description of the invention also should include a discussion of implementation and testing of the invention. For instance, has the invention been implemented for its intended purpose? If so, how? What were some of the observations of the implementation? Has the invention been reduced to practice? If so, to what extent?

16.3.1 Advantages

Once the differences have been identified, a further means for describing the invention is to identify the advantages that result from those differences. What specific advantages are gained using the method of the invention over the known methods, that is, in light of the identified differences? What advantages are achieved in view of the differences between the novel device over the known devices? For each advantage, what is its significance? Assuming that the previous sections of the invention disclosure have been completed, as discussed above, identifying advantages should be relatively easy.

16.4 LICENSING OR REVENUE GENERATING POTENTIAL

In today's economic environment, seeking and procuring patent protection on an invention is costly. Providing an indication of any licensing or revenue generating potential of the invention is thus appropriate for the invention disclosure. Pointing out the applicability or value of the invention in the invention disclosure increases the likelihood that the inherent or added value of the invention will be recognized and appreciated.

16.5 OTHER MATTERS

While this article has focused upon the substance of an invention disclosure, other matters should to be addressed in the invention disclosure. For purposes of determining patentability of an invention, an indication of any prior written publications, prior public disclosures, public uses, or offers for sale of the invention should be noted in the disclosure. Furthermore, any proposed such activity should be noted. An appropriate title for conveying the essential nature of the invention (*i.e.*, a method, an apparatus, or a composition of matter) should be selected. Finally, the invention disclosure should be witnessed on each page thereof by someone other than the inventor or inventors.

The task of writing an invention disclosure has been presented from an informal point of view. While the essential portions of a meaningful invention disclosure have been addressed and discussed herein, those readers desiring further information on this subject may refer to the listed reference.

16.6 CONCLUDING REMARKS

As stated earlier, the invention disclosure is an important first step to obtaining patent protection for your invention. The goal and purpose of the invention disclosure is to convey the essence, importance, and value of the invention in writing to the patent practitioner or evaluator reading the disclosure. The invention disclosure also serves to advise the patent practitioner of potential prior art, etc., to ensure compliance with the patent applicant's duty of disclosure to the PTO.

NOTE

J. F. Cottone. "Writing an Invention Disclosure." *IEEE Patents and Patenting for Engineers and Scientists.* pp. 61–64, 1982.

USING ENGINEERING EXPERTISE TO DEVELOP A SUCCESSFUL WORLDWIDE PATENT PORTFOLIO

Peter M. Emanuel

Peter M. Emanuel is the Vice President of Consumer Electronics in the Princeton, New Jersey, Office of General Electric. Recent writings include "Peculiarities of PCT National Phase Filing" (1993) and "A Comparative Survey of Notice Requirements" (1994).

Patents are tools used to meet the goals of the business entity and should be pursued and used intelligently. To take full, but cost effective advantage of the patent system, an interactive team of technologist, patent attorney, and management is imperative.

The following articles describe the nature of the interaction between technologist and attorney.

Mr. Emanuel's article also addresses the strategic filing of corresponding foreign patent applications. MAL

Abstract
Up-to-date and accurate technical information is a crucial element in developing and exploiting a worldwide patent portfolio. Accordingly, engineers and scientists should be intimately involved in the process, and should be active members of teams that make crucial decisions throughout the process. This article explores techniques for effectively using the expertise of engineers and scientists at various steps of the process.

17.1 INTRODUCTION

In developing and exploiting a worldwide patent portfolio, the three most important elements are:

INFORMATION! INFORMATION! INFORMATION!

Engineers and scientists are the best sources of this information.

A flow chart illustrating the process of developing a worldwide patent portfolio appears at the end of this article. The five main steps are:

1. identifying inventions;
2. selecting significant inventions for protection by filing patent applications;
3. selecting countries in which patent applications should be filed;
4. preparing and *prosecuting* the patent applications to ensure that valuable patents are eventually obtained; and
5. periodically reviewing the patent portfolio to weed out those properties that are no longer worthwhile.

The object of obtaining a patent is to obtain the right to either: (a) prevent others from making, using, or selling the invention; or (b) require that others pay a licensing fee before making, using, or selling the invention. The right is obtained when the patent is granted. However, to benefit from the right, you must perform a sixth step of *policing* the patent to determine if others are *infringing* the patent by making, using, or selling the patented invention without authority.

Technical information is required for each of the six activities identified above to ensure that the proper decisions are made and that costly and irreversible mistakes are avoided. Techniques for getting engineers and scientists involved in each of the six activities will now be explored.

17.2 IDENTIFYING INVENTIONS AND SOLICITING THEIR DISCLOSURE

Most companies have invention identification programs that encourage engineers and scientists to disclose their inventions. A requirement to disclose inventions made in connection with company business is typically a condition of employment in most technology based companies. However, as a positive incentive, companies often provide awards when a patent application is filed or when a patent is granted. Companies sometimes also have formal programs for educating scientists and engineers about inventions and patents. Usually, invention disclosure forms are provided to guide inventors in describing the inventions. In view of the widespread use of computers, the forms are often put "on the computer".

Despite formal programs for encouraging engineers and scientists to disclose inventions, often, the message just does not sink in, and many important inventions are lost. Inventors are more often than not simply unfamiliar with what "making" an invention constitutes. Basically, an invention may be made whenever a previously unknown problem is solved, no matter how simple the solution, or when a previously known problem is solved in a new way. As straightforward as this guideline may seem, the academic message must constantly be reinforced by practical experience. Formal programs cannot substitute for close and interactive relationships between the members of the technical staff and a patent attorney. Your patent attorney should be considered to be a part of the technical staff because inventions are integral and inevitable parts of a product developed by the engineers and scientists.

A good start toward developing the kind of relationships that are required is to invite a patent attorney to your technical project review meetings. In addition, patent reviews should be conducted at several milestones of the project, such as at the conclusion of the initial design phase, at engineering sign-off, and again just before product release. Engineering drawings and other documentation should be provided to the patent attorney in advance of the meetings, and the members of the design team should be prepared to describe their contributions.

Members of the technical staff also should consult with a patent attorney whenever technical information is to be disclosed outside of the company because public disclosures can prevent the patenting of an invention, especially in foreign countries. For example, a patent attorney should be consulted before the publication or presentation of a paper, a press release, or meetings at which people outside the company, including vendors and representatives of governmental agencies or industry and professional groups, will be present.

Frequent informal contacts between the technical staff and patent attorneys also should be encouraged. Some of the most important inventions I have ever handled were uncovered while wandering through a laboratory or during lunch time conversations. Such informal meetings are particularly useful for uncovering inventions that are not slated for a specific product or project.

17.3 SELECTING SIGNIFICANT INVENTIONS FOR FILING

Once invention disclosures have been solicited, an orderly procedure should be followed for selecting those inventions believed to be significant enough for filing as patent applications. Significant inventions are those inventions that are likely to have a financial impact on the company in terms of either protecting proprietary products and/or obtaining licensing revenue. It is not financially practical to file patent applications for all inventions. The cost, including attorney and governmental fees, of obtaining only a U.S. patent is typically between $5,000 and $20,000.

Perhaps not surprisingly, an important element in the selection process is the written description of the invention provided in the invention disclosure form. While no decision should be made without contacting the inventor, the written description provides an initial impression of the invention. The written description also often forms the basis of a prior art search, from which the patent attorney determines the *scope* of the invention, *i.e.*, the degree to which the invention is "basic".

An effective written description can be organized in the following way:

- a descriptive title;
- planned use or public disclosure;

- the technical field of the invention;
- the problem to be solved;
- what others have done to solve the problem, or if it is a new problem, the most relevant prior work by others in the field;
- a brief description of the new solution (*i.e.*, its "gist"); and
- a detailed description of one or more implementations of the solution (including the preferred one), with reference to appropriate drawings.

Try to make the description *user friendly*. The description should be long enough to cover the subject, but short enough to keep one's interest. The use of jargon should be avoided.

An invention evaluation or patent review committee is useful in the selection process. Members of the review committee should include a patent attorney and the most appropriate technical experts and managers for the field of the inventions to be reviewed. Gathering technical opinions through the mail or over the telephone is possible. However, periodic meetings are preferable since they produce useful interchanges of ideas.

Abstracts of inventions related to a particular subject should be compiled by the patent attorney and submitted to the patent review committee prior to the meeting. An abstract should contain a brief written description of the gist of the invention, a representative drawing, and an indication of the most relevant prior art and how it may affect the scope of the invention. Portions of the written description submitted by the inventor may be included in the abstract. Preferably, the abstracts should be reviewed by the respective inventors to make sure that they properly represent the inventions. If the subject matter is complex, the inventions should be partitioned into more narrowly defined subject matter groups so that the most relevant technical experts can be called upon for each group. Overhead slides of the abstracts are helpful in focusing discussions during the meeting.

During the invention evaluation meeting, each invention is evaluated and assigned a rating. Exemplary ratings might be: "file immediately"; "file at a later date"; "requires further investigation" (with a specific action indicated); and "do not file". The following factors should be considered in reaching a decision:

- the scope of the invention in view of the prior art;
- the likelihood of use;
- the likelihood of long term use;
- the likelihood of use by others (*i.e.*, whether the problem solved is a common and important problem in the field);
- the likelihood of alternative solutions (considering such factors as cost and the availability of other solutions); and
- the ease of detecting use by others (whether the use of the invention can be detected by inspection of the product itself or from documentation, such as a schematic, or whether a more involved procedure such as testing, is required).

Informing the inventor of the decision is common courtesy and good practice. No matter what the decision is, the inventor should be encouraged to keep the patent attorney informed of any developments that might alter the decision.

17.4 WHERE PATENT APPLICATIONS SHOULD BE FILED

Currently, an individual patent must be obtained in each country where protection is desired (although there has been some effort by way of a Patent Cooperation Treaty and a European Patent Convention to work toward a single patent application and a single examination of the application). Limiting the filing to a single country is often a serious mistake, considering the global nature of business and technology today. On the other hand, the cost of obtaining worldwide patent coverage is extremely high. For example, the cost for obtaining patents for an invention in just twenty foreign countries can easily exceed $40,000. Cost not only mitigates against obtaining patents in every country, but also mitigates against obtaining patents in the same countries for every invention. In short, you can't afford to file everything everywhere! Therefore, a strategy for selecting the countries in which patents are to be obtained should be devised.

The starting point is to decide on a pool of countries from which selections can be made. The following factors should be considered:

- whether the object is to obtain a competitive advantage by preventing others from making, using, or selling the invention, or to obtain licensing royalties, or some combination of the two;
- whether to concentrate on countries in which manufacturing occurs, or on countries that have significant markets for the relevant product;
- what technical and business changes are expected to occur internationally in the next 5 to 10 years;
- what changes are expected to occur within the company in the next 5 to 10 years; and
- the available budget for implementing the strategy.

The first and second factors are related in the sense that obtaining a competitive advantage tends to favor filing in those countries that have significant markets while optimizing royalties favors filing in manufacturing countries. Experience suggests that a judicious mixture of market and manufacturing countries is advisable no matter what the purpose of obtaining patents is. Predicting where significant markets will be tends to be easier than predicting where new manufacturing facilities will be built. On the other hand, keeping track of the number of units that have been manufactured tends to be easier than keeping track of the number of units that have been sold.

A second step in developing a country selection strategy might be to divide the pool of patents into several groups of countries, including a *core* group, containing a minimum number of countries, and successively larger groups, each including the next smaller group and an additional number of countries. When country selection decision for an individual invention is made, the quality of the invention, such as *low*, *moderate* or *high* importance, determines a corresponding breadth of filing, such as *narrow* (or *core* group), *medium* or *wide*. Depending on the nature of the invention, it is advisable to modify the *group* approach by adding or deleting countries on a statistical basis. This ensures that there are enough patents for a reasonable chance of success in countries that are considered less important or speculative at the present time.

The country selection strategy should be periodically reviewed, for example, at yearly intervals, to keep the strategy current. You should not rigidly adhere to a single approach because patent history is filled with examples of mistakes that have resulted from *very clever* schemes.

The same criteria used to select inventions for filing discussed above may be used to select the particular countries in which patent applications are to be filed for those inventions. In fact, it is possible to make the country selections during the invention evaluation meeting, especially since many of the same considerations are involved. However, a separate country selection meeting, at which a patent attorney summarizes the facts presented at the invention evaluation meeting, is preferable because the country selection decision tends to concentrate on business aspects, rather than on technical details of the invention. A separate country selection meeting also avoids using the time of technical personnel unnecessarily. Nevertheless, having a representative of the technical staff, preferably one who also understands the international business picture, present at the country selection meeting is helpful.

17.5 PREPARING AND PROSECUTING A PATENT APPLICATION

Although an inventor may prepare and *prosecute* patent applications for his or her own invention, these specialized activities are better left to a patent attorney. However, the inventor should take an active role in assisting the patent attorney in these activities.

The flow chart at the end of the article indicates the common practice of preparing and filing a U.S. patent application prior to deciding whether to file corresponding applications in foreign countries. The applicant of a U.S. application has a period of one year from the filing date of the U.S. application to file corresponding applications in most foreign countries under international law. The one year period allows further reflection about the invention before the expensive investment in foreign applications is made. The U.S. application forms the basis for any foreign applications.

Preparing a patent application involves drafting a technical description of the invention, usually with reference to accompanying drawings, and a set of *claims* that legally define the scope of the invention. The claims are written in a highly stylized form that sets forth the essential elements of the invention in the broadest possible terms.

In addition to the basic invention, the inventor should be prepared to discuss the following matters with the patent attorney during the preparation of the application:

- the prior art and how the invention differs from it in significant ways;
- different ways in which the invention can be implemented; and
- various ways in which the invention can be modified.

Prior to filing, the inventor will receive a draft of the application, including the claims, for review. This review is required by law and should not be taken lightly by the inventor. The inventor should raise questions or make comments and suggestions, even about the claims.

The *prosecution* of a patent application involves a series of written *Office Actions* (usually two in the United States) from the Patent Office and corresponding written *responses* from the patent attorney. The *Office Actions* usually contain reasons for *rejecting* the application (often based on prior art). The responses contain arguments and amendments of the application, primarily of the claims, as required, to overcome the reasons for rejecting the application.

During the prosecution of an application, the inventor should keep the patent attorney informed as to:

- what modifications have been made to the invention since the application was filed;
- what others (*e.g.*, competitors) working in the same area are doing;
- whether the invention is still considered important enough, in view of commercial or technical developments, and possible amendments to the claims required to overcome rejections, to continue the prosecution; and
- any new prior art that has come to light (by law, this is a *must* and not a *should*).

These same matters should be reviewed again after the application has been *allowed* and before the patent *issue* fee is paid. If new information warrants it, a so-called *continuation* application can be filed to take the new information into account without payment of the issue fee for the original application. However, the issue fee should not be paid if the invention has become commercially or technically obsolete.

The same considerations apply to the prosecution of U.S. and foreign applications. However, the prosecution of foreign applications usually requires a longer time (sometimes years) than the prosecution of the U.S. application. Accordingly, there is more time to refine and develop the foreign applications in light of new information provided by the inventor.

17.6 REVIEWING THE PATENT PORTFOLIO

As earlier indicated, the cost of prosecuting patent applications in even a few countries is significant. In addition, nearly all countries require the payment of periodic fees (or *taxes*) to maintain a patent in force once it is granted. Therefore, periodic review of the patent portfolio, including both patents and applications, in order to *drop* those patents and applications that no longer warrant the payment of prosecution or maintenance fees is a practical necessity. This review requires technical advice to update the information used to make the filing and country selection decisions.

Meetings similar to the initial filing decision meetings are recommended for reviewing the patent portfolio. Meetings for selecting inventions for filing and for reviewing already filed inventions in a given subject matter can be held consecutively since the same technical personnel and considerations most likely will be involved.

During the review meeting, the role of the patent attorney is to focus attention on the inventions that are claimed in the patents and applications, rather than the original implementations of the invention. A common mistake is for technical reviewers to narrowly focus on details of the original implementation of an invention and thereby dismiss the *invention* as being one that is no longer used.

Since a large investment in time and money has already been made, the review decision should be made with extraordinary care. Dropping patents and applications to satisfy momentary budgetary demands is very tempting. However, reinstating a patent or application once it has been dropped is almost impossible. A good guideline for avoiding very serious mistakes is to require a positive reason for dropping a patent or application, rather than a positive reason for keeping the property. A reduction in the number of countries, rather than dropping the property in all countries, is recommended as a prudent compromise.

17.7 POLICING PATENTS

Engineers and scientists should be key members of any team responsible for determining if *others* are infringing a patented invention. Technical personnel are an important resource in gathering marketing information about what is being made, who is making it, how much it costs, and the number being made. Engineers often keep track of what competitors are doing as a part of their design activities. In fact, many companies have a *competitive analysis* group that monitors and studies the products of competitors. Engineers and scientists are usually the best source of any publicly available technical documentation that might describe how a product is constructed, what its features are, and how it operates. They regularly attend technical conferences, seminars and trade shows, and have access to information about components, such as data sheets, which can be used to piece together information about a product. They can also *reverse engineer* a product and devise and perform tests to provide additional information. Finally, technical analysis is required to understand the relationship between a patented technology and that of an allegedly infringing product.

The first person to contact when technical advice is sought in a determination of whether a patented invention is being infringed is obviously the inventor. However, the inventor is only the starting point, and coworkers working on the same or related subject matter also should be consulted. In addition, technical consultants outside of the company may be employed to supplement technical information obtained from employees. Technical consultants are especially important for new subject matter areas for which technical expertise has not been developed within the company. In addition, they can dedicate their time to a patent matter, while an employee usually will have competing priorities. Finally, technical consultants also may have a higher degree of objectivity compared to employees.

The relationship between the technical expert and the patent attorney in determining infringement should be a very interactive one so that each develops some appreciation for the other's responsibilities. For example, proof of infringement requires that each of the elements of the claim defining the invention be matched with a corresponding element of the allegedly infringing product. This requires a judgment as to how components of the product function and cooperate as compared to how the corresponding elements of the claimed invention function and cooperate. The role of the patent attorney is to interpret for the technical expert what the claims mean, while the role of the technical expert is to explain to the patent attorney how the product works. The more interchange there is between the two, the better the result.

17.8 CONCLUSION

There is no substitute for accurate and up to date technical information in the patent business. Obtaining this information from engineers and scientists requires close and interactive relationships between patent attorneys and the technical staff. Formal and informal procedures are required to keep the vital information flowing throughout the process of developing and exploiting a worldwide patent portfolio.

COMMUNICATING WITH A PATENT ATTORNEY

Article 18

Mikio Ishimaru

Mikio Ishimaru is the Director of Technology Law and Associate General Counsel for Advanced Micro Devices, Inc., in Sunnyvale, California. He specializes in high technology law.

Abstract

Patent attorneys are individuals with training both in technology and in law. They act as translators to convert technical information into a superset of legalese called patentese. While a patent attorney can start with a minimalist disclosure, the better the communications, the better the patent and the lower the cost.

It is always a good idea to select a patent attorney who has some expertise in the area of your invention. This is best done by explaining the area of the invention and asking for copies of some patents which the patent attorney has written in that particular area.

Since a patent attorney is under an obligation to keep all invention disclosures confidential, the patent attorney may be told about the invention and asked about ball park costs for the application and subsequent processing involving the patent office. Make sure you will be told beforehand if the costs look like they are to be exceeded.

Patent drafting and processing tends to be more of an art than a science, and different patent practitioners have different communicative styles. As a result, it is a good idea to determine ahead of time how the patent attorney normally likes to proceed in getting the disclosure and in communicating with you, the client inventor.

Since most patent applications follow a standardized format, if you prepare your thoughts and explanations beforehand in this format, it is possible to substantially reduce the time and resultant costs of a patent application. Make sure you have thought your invention through and there are no errors in the information you provide to your patent attorney.

18.1 GENERAL INFORMATION

A U.S. patent is a written document that describes and *claims* your invention. It consists of a detailed technical description, termed the specification, a set of drawings, and a number of *claims* (single sentence statements describing your invention with great legal precision).

B. C. © Johnny Hart. Reprinted with permission.

Preparation of a patent application requires cooperation between you and the patent attorney. It begins with a review by the patent attorney of your written invention disclosure, followed by personal and telephone conferences with you at mutually convenient times and locations. If you have already prepared written material, such as preliminary specifications, other detailed technical documentation, and descriptions of related technology, the patent attorney would like to have copies.

After the application is filed, it will be examined by a U.S. Patent and Trademark Office Examiner who will carry out a patentability search (in a year or so) in the files of the U.S. Patent and Trademark Office, in his or her private files, and in certain computer data bases. The application ordinarily is rejected initially for formal reasons as well as for supposedly being unpatentable because of patents or publications ("applied prior art") uncovered during the search.

The formalities usually can be handled by the patent attorney, but your assistance often will be required in helping to analyze the applied prior art, advise how the language of the claims could be amended if necessary and for the patent attorney to submit an argument in support of the patentability of your invention. This process (called *patent prosecution*) may have to be repeated but hopefully will result in approval of your claims and issuance of a U.S. patent. The entire process usually can be expected to require from one to three years.

18.2 CONTENTS OF A PATENT APPLICATION

It is suggested that the inventor think through the invention in the following standardized format and communicate information to the patent attorney in the sequence of this format:

- Title
- Cross-References to Related Applications
- Background of the Invention
- Summary of the Invention

- The Drawings
- Detailed Description of the Preferred Embodiment
- Claims
- Abstract

18.2.1 Title

The *title* should be short, technically accurate, descriptive of the invention claimed but not too broad. The patent attorney usually will adopt your own terminology.

18.2.2 Cross-References to Related Applications

You should advise the patent attorney of any related patent applications of your own that relate to your invention for inclusion here.

18.2.3 Background of the Invention

The *Background* initially describes the general field of your invention. The historical development of the technology underlying your invention is explained, with emphasis being placed on the problem you solved. A discussion of unsuccessful approaches taken by you or others is particularly helpful. Relevant patents or publications may be identified and discussed in the Background. Care must be taken not to characterize material as being *prior art* unless the patent attorney has confirmed that it is indeed prior art under U.S. law (*e.g.*, the public document is more than one year old).

The Background should be interesting; it should capture the reader's imagination. This section should persuade the reader of your genius and the considerable value of the invention not only to a person skilled in your area of technology, but to a person off the street who might be on the jury if the patent is litigated. The names of competitors and competing products should be supplied to the patent attorney, although this information ordinarily is not included in the Background section.

THE DUPLEX © Glenn McCoy. Distributed by UNIVERSAL PRESS SYNDICATE. Reprinted with permission. All rights reserved.

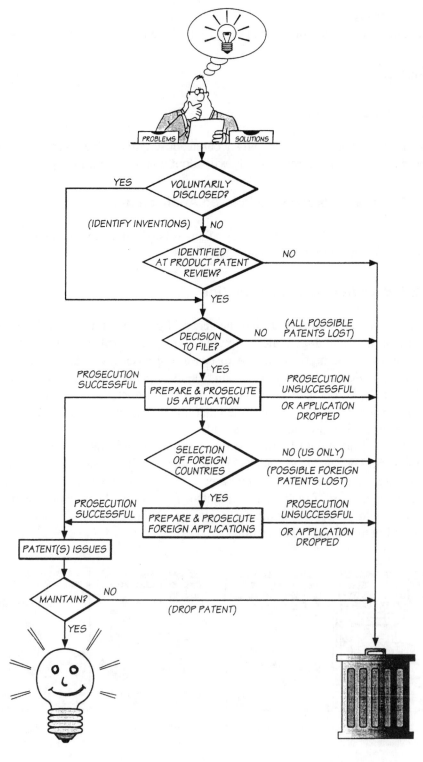

18.2.4 Summary of the Invention

This section is not a true *Summary* but describes the broadest features of your invention. The features should be set out individually in the form of *aspects*. A conclusionary statement at the end of the Summary, describing the advantages of the invention, such as simplified or improved operation, cost reduction, etc., often is helpful.

18.2.5 The Drawings

Except in very rare cases, drawings (technically, a single drawing with one or more figures) are required for patents. Patent drawings are made by professional draftsmen, but you need to provide simple explanatory drawings for them to work from and for the patent attorney to understand your invention.

Liberal use of drawings should be made. The drawings should include a system block diagram corresponding in scope to the broadest features of your invention. More detailed diagrams will correspond to the secondary features. Interact circuitry, signal sources, and timing diagrams should be included liberally to be covered by the narrowest claims. Flow charts or equivalent figures should be included in applications on computer program-implemented methods and systems and in other applications where operating methodology is important.

18.2.6 Detailed Description of the Preferred Embodiment

The *Detailed Description* must provide enough detail to enable a person skilled in your technology to make and use the invention without requiring unreasonable experimentation. But it is not necessary to be so detailed as to enable a competitor to easily make an exact duplicate of the invention.

Trade secrets not directly related or involved with the invention should not be described in the application but should be replaced by publicly known circuits or processes. However, you must always show your "best mode" or best implementation of the invention as of the filing date of the application with the U.S. Patent and Trademark Office. It is not necessary that you explain *how* your invention works as long as a skilled person, following the description, could make and use a workable version of your invention.

A flow chart or equivalent is nearly always sufficient for computer program-implemented inventions. Specific program code ordinarily should not be disclosed in the patent application.

18.2.7 Claims

Claims are single sentence statements that legally define your invention. While the other sections of the application will be written in clear prose, the claims may at first appear to be awkward. Nevertheless, with the patent attorney's help you should be able to comprehend the claims perfectly. The patent attorney will prepare the claims for the application but you can help.

There are two types of claims: independent claims and dependent claims. An independent claim stands on its own. A dependent claim adds to and references an earlier claim. Although no general rule exists as to the number of claims, it is suggested that an application ordinarily will include about three or four independent claims and a total of about twenty claims.

An independent claim has three parts, a preamble describing the invention in very general terms, (*e.g.*, "A system for controlling data transmission in a local area network"), a transitional phrase (*e.g.*, "comprising"), and a body reciting the *elements* or limitations of the invention. You can help the patent attorney by listing the fewest circuit blocks, mechanical or chemical elements, or steps that would define a totally stripped down but workable version of your invention. Each feature that is added to make a commercially viable product should be listed separately. Generally, the fewer the elements, the broader the claim; *i.e.*, the claim covers a greater range of products than described by a claim with many elements.

A claim can define an apparatus or system (apparatus claim), or a method of carrying out some function (method claim). In the broadest claims, a format termed a *means-plus-function* recites the word *means* followed by a desired function. It is interpreted to cover not only the implementation described in the Detailed Description but equivalent implementations as well (although courts have been narrowing equivalents to those in the Detailed Description in recent years).

Method claims as well as apparatus claims often are included when appropriate in the same application as are component-specific claims. Each claim should have a scope different from the others.

Secondary features and nonessential elements are not recited in the broadest claims; dependent claims should contain them. Dependent claims also have three parts, but the transitional phase cross references a different claim(s) (*e.g.*, "as claimed in claim 5"). The application should conclude with at least one *picture claim*, which is an exact verbal description of any commercial embodiment.

18.2.8 Abstract

The *Abstract* is a short paragraph, fewer than 250 words, describing the invention generally and in basic terms. The novel aspect should be included but unnecessary descriptions and laudatory statements should not.

18.3 REVIEWING THE PATENT APPLICATION

When the first draft of the patent application is received, it should be read thoroughly first without making any changes. At this point it is necessary to understand the organizational structure used by the patent attorney and to get a feel for the extent the changes will be required. Always retain the original for your files and make a clean copy of the patent application for your changes.

If only typographical or minor changes are required, the corrections should be made on the copy. For more significant changes, cross out the incorrect sections and rewrite them on a separate page with each section numbered for proper insertion. Drawing changes should be made as shown in the figure below.

Where there are major changes required or concepts have been misunderstood, you should note the areas where the changes are required and plan on a meeting to determine why the patent was drafted in the way it was and/or to explain the problems. Quite often, there may be patent drafting requirements that require the application to be in the form that it is in, or there has been a misunderstanding at such a fundamental level that neither you nor the patent attorney realizes that there has been such a misunderstanding.

While the accuracy of the *Detailed Description* is your primary responsibility, you should also closely review the claims both for accuracy and breadth. Sometimes an examination of the claims will reveal simplifications or improved modifications to your basic invention. In some instances, entirely new concepts may arise out of an examination of the claims.

The patent attorney will arrange for filing the case, and your receipt of a patent office serial number from the patent attorney is an indication that the patent application has been received by the U.S. Patent and Trademark Office.

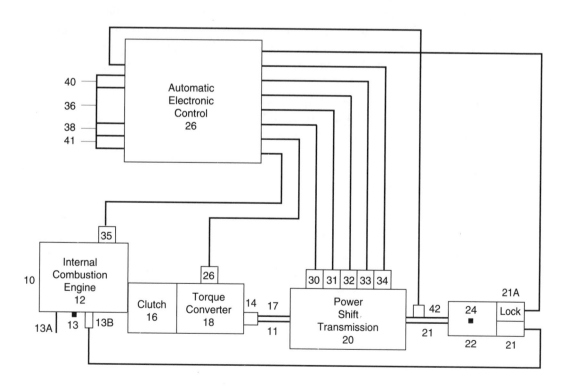

18.4 PROSECUTING THE APPLICATION

Normally, there will be no other activity for one to two years after which the patent Examiner will often reject all or part of the claims in the patent application.

Sometimes the Examiner will find that more than a single examinable invention is claimed in your application. The Examiner will issue an *election requirement* to have you select only one of the inventions for examination. The other inventions can be examined in separate applications, termed *divisional applications* carved out from the original one. Improvements that you make to the invention should be reported to the patent attorney promptly, so that an improvement patent application, termed a *continuation-in-part*, can be prepared, if appropriate.

Depending upon what was previously agreed to by you and the patent attorney, you will be provided with the references cited by the patent office, and sometimes an evaluation of the rejection by the patent attorney.

The patent attorney often will contact you to discuss the various issues raised by the Examiner during prosecution of your application. Your assistance in interpreting the content of the applied prior art and formulating amendments of the claims, if necessary, while retaining the gist of the invention in the broadest possible terms is critical.

You should review the references cited by the patent office with particular attention to those references, usually patents, which are cited as being the most relevant. You should figure out what features or characteristics make your invention functionally and structurally different from the references. These differences can be communicated to the patent attorney either in writing or orally, but if in writing, only the dissimilarities should be discussed since the inventor's correspondence may be discoverable in subsequent litigation to enforce the patent and any comments about similarity may be taken out of context and used as admissions to invalidate your patent.

It should always be kept in mind that all documents you send to the patent attorney and vise-a-versa may show up at trial and, if limiting the invention or minimizing its value, they may prove embarrassing if not lethal to the enforcement of your patent.

18.5 CONCLUSION

In communicating with a patent attorney, it should be realized that the more things are simplified and organized for the patent attorney, the simpler and less expensive will be the entire process in obtaining and enforcing the patent. Try to use the same format that a patent application is normally filed in and understand the purpose of the format.

18.6 ADDITIONAL REFERENCE

Manual of Patent Examining Procedure (MPEP) available from:

Superintendent of Documents
United States Government Printing Office
Washington, D.C. 20402
Tel. No.: (202) 783–3238

THE INVENTION

As Conceived By The Inventor   As Understood By The Patent Attorney   As Described In First Draft

As Described In The Patent Application   As Claimed   As Infringed

GUIDE FOR PATENT DRAWINGS

R. J. Joenk

Dr. Joenk retired recently after 30 years and several careers with IBM, including research in magnetism, editing the *IBM Journal of Research and Development*, publications management and library management. Dr. Joenk was also the editor of the *IEEE Transactions on Professional Communication*. In 1979, he created a special issue of the *Transactions* on "Patents and Patenting for Engineers and Scientists." That issue was updated as a book in 1982, which is the forerunner of this book.

The cost of preparing a patent application often can be reduced if the applicant prepares the drawing for the application. This is particularly true when computer-aided design software is available to generate the figures. The following article discusses the formal requirements for the patent drawing. MAL

Abstract

One or more figures must accompany a patent application whenever the invention can be represented visually. The most representative view will be used on the patent title page and in the *Official Gazette*. All features of the invention that are claimed in the application must be shown in the drawings. Use opaque black ink on durable white paper. Computer-generated drawings are acceptable. Color may be permitted when it is the only practical medium to disclose the work. Photographs also may be permitted. Avoid freehand drawings. These and other instructions are condensed from the U.S. Patent and Trademark Office rules and regulations as amended in the Federal Register, July 20, 1993.

The Patent and Trademark Office (PTO) recently amended its rules of practice regarding patent drawings to adopt international standards and to eliminate unnecessary requirements. The changes were published in the Federal Register, Vol. 58, No. 137, July 20, 1993, pp. 38719–38726, and became effective October 1, 1993. They amend the Code of Federal Regulations, Title 37, Patents, Trademarks, and Copyrights. Known as 37 CFR, it is the codification of the rules and regulations of the PTO; chapter one pertains to patents.

The new rules significantly change the PTO publication "Guide for Patent Draftsmen," last issued in January 1989 and allowed to go out of print due to the changes pending in 1993. It likely will be updated and reissued in 1995 and will be available from the Superintendent of Documents, U.S. Government Printing Office, Washington, D.C. 20402.

The following information and instructions are condensed from the 1989 publication and the 1993 Federal Register. This material is presented in the context of utility patent drawings but also applies to design and plant patent drawings. Special considerations for design and plant drawings also are described.

19.1 DRAWINGS REQUIRED

An applicant for a patent is required by statute to furnish a drawing of the invention whenever the subject matter permits a visual representation, even if it is not necessary for understanding the invention.

Formally, there is only one drawing, but this may consist of several figures or views. The term *drawings* is used to convey this scope.

Drawings may include other forms of illustration such as flow sheets, diagrammatic views, and photographs.

Drawings may be in black and white or color (special circumstances only). Usually the applicant retains the original and submits a high-quality copy, because he or she is responsible for corrections.

19.2 CONTENT OF DRAWINGS

The drawings must show every feature of the invention specified in the claims. However, conventional features disclosed in the description and claims, if their detailed illustration is not essential for understanding the invention, may be shown as graphic symbols or labeled representations that are described in the application.

When an invention is an improvement on an old machine, the drawing should exhibit in one or more views the improved portion, disconnected from the old structure, and, in another view, only so much of the old structure as suffices to show the connection with the invention.

The drawings should be planned so that one of the views is representative and suitable as the illustration of the invention for publication in the Official Gazette and on the title page of the patent.

19.3 STANDARDS FOR DRAWINGS

19.3.1 Paper and Ink

Black and white drawings are normally required. India ink or its equivalent should be used for perfectly black, solid lines. Paper must be white, flexible, strong, durable, smooth, nonshiny, and free from tears, creases, and folds. Use only one side.

Computer-generated drawings are acceptable if they meet the conditions for black and white drawings.

White pigmented correction fluid may be used provided that it is durable and permanent.

Color drawings are accepted on the rare occasions that the PTO first accepts the applicant's petition that color is the only practical medium to disclose the subject. Three sets of color drawings are required. (Note that utility patents are not published in color.)

When an application contains a color drawing (or photograph), the following statement must be included:

> The file of this patent contains at least one drawing executed in color. Copies of this patent with color drawing(s) will be provided by the Patent and Trademark Office upon request and payment of the necessary fee.

19.3.2 Photographs

Photographs are accepted only after approval of the applicant's petition to submit photographs. They must either be developed on double-weight photographic paper or be permanently mounted on bristol board. Details in photographs must have sufficient clarity and contrast to reproduce clearly in the printed patent.

Color photographs must meet the same condition as color drawings, that is, that they are the only practical medium to disclose the subject.

19.3.3 Size of Paper and Margins

All drawing sheets in an application must be the same size. One of the shorter sides of the sheet is regarded as its top. The following sizes are acceptable:

$$21.6 \text{ cm} \times 35.6 \text{ cm} \ (8.5 \text{ in.} \times 14 \text{ in.})$$
$$21.6 \text{ cm} \times 33.1 \text{ cm} \ (8.5 \text{ in.} \times 13 \text{ in.})$$
$$21.6 \text{ cm} \times 27.9 \text{ cm} \ (8.5 \text{ in.} \times 11 \text{ in.})$$
$$21.0 \text{ cm} \times 29.7 \text{ cm} \ (\text{DIN size A4})$$

The following margins are required (all dimensions are cm):

Paper Size	Top	Bottom	Left	Right
21.6 × 35.6	5.1	0.64	0.64	0.64
21.6 × 33.1	2.5	0.64	0.64	0.64
21.6 × 27.9	2.5	0.64	0.64	0.64
21.0 × 29.7	2.5	1.0	2.5	1.5

The area within the margins is called the *sight.* All work must be within the sight. Margin border lines are not permitted.

Two holes, 7 cm apart, may be provided in the top margin. They must be equidistant from their respective sides of the paper.

Security markings, such as "ABC Corp. Confidential," may be placed outside the sight, preferably centered in the top margin.

The sheets of drawings should be numbered consecutively using Arabic numerals. The numerals must be placed within the sight, centered at the top of the sheet, and must be larger than the numerals used as reference characters. The number of each sheet should appear as, for example, 3/5, meaning the third of five drawing sheets.

19.3.4 Identification of Drawings

Identifying information should be placed on the back of each sheet, a minimum of 1.5 cm down from the top. Include the application number or title of the invention, the inventor's name, and the name and telephone number of someone to call if the PTO is unable to match drawings with an application.

19.3.5 Character of Lines

All drawings must be made by a process that gives them satisfactory reproduction characteristics. Freehand work should be avoided.

Every line and character must be durable, clean, black (except for special color items), and sufficiently dense and dark for reproduction. This requirement applies to all lines however fine, to shading, and to lines representing cut surfaces in sectional views. Fine and crowded lines should be avoided.

19.3.6 Shading and Hatching

Shading made by parallel lines should be used if it aids understanding, for example, in depicting curved surfaces and the shadowed side of objects (see Figure 1). The lines

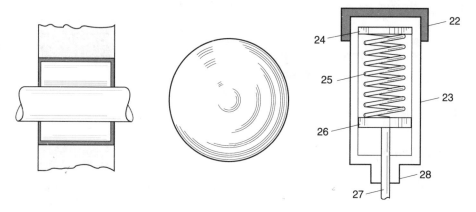

Figure 1   Examples of shading and hatching.

should be fine and few in number and not interfere with legibility. The light should appear to come from the upper left corner at an angle of 45°. Solid black should not be used for surface or sectional shading.

Hatching must be used to indicate sectional portions of an object and should consist of regularly spaced parallel lines at a substantial angle to surrounding principal lines and axes (see Figure 1). Parts of the same item should be hatched the same way.

Different items should be hatched differently. Use hatching in conventional ways to represent various materials (see Figure 2).

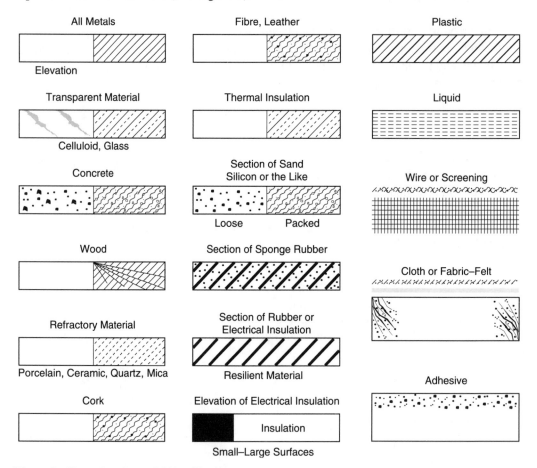

Figure 2 Examples of material identification.

19.3.7 Scale

The scale of a drawing must be large enough to show the mechanism without crowding when the drawing is reduced to two-thirds size for reproduction. All elements of a given view should be in the same proportion. Views of a portion of a mechanism on a larger scale to show details can be provided in a supplementary view.

19.3.8 Numbers and Letters

Reference characters (numerals are preferred) must be plain, legible, carefully formed, and not enclosed in circles or brackets. They must be oriented in the same direction as the view. See Figure 1.

They must not be placed in close and complex parts of the drawing and should rarely cross or mingle with lines. When necessary, a blank space can be left in shaded or hatched areas where a reference character occurs, and the character should be underlined.

When necessarily grouped around a part, reference characters should follow the profile of the part and be placed at the closest point where there is space (see Figure 1). Lead lines should be drawn between the reference characters and the details they refer to. Lead lines should be short and not cross.

Letters and characters must be at least 0.32 cm (⅛ inch) in height—frequently there will be a one-third reduction in size. The English alphabet must be used except where another letter set is commonly used, for example, the Greek alphabet for mathematical symbols.

When the same part of an invention appears in more than one view, it must always be designated by the same reference character, and no character should be used to designate more than one part.

19.3.9 Symbols and Legends

Graphic symbols and labeled representations may be used to depict conventional elements. The elements for which they are used must be adequately described in the application. Known devices should be illustrated by universally recognized symbols (see Figures 3 and 4). Arrows can be used to show direction of movement.

Although descriptive matter is not permitted on drawings, suitable legends with as few words as possible may be used on drawings where necessary for understanding. Lettering must be at least as large as that of reference characters.

19.3.10 Graphic Forms

Chemical and mathematical formulas, wave forms, and tables may be submitted as drawings. Each formula must be labeled as a separate figure. Each group of wave forms must be presented as a single figure using a common vertical axis (with each wave form labeled) and with time extending along the horizontal axis.

19.3.11 Views

There should be as many views or figures as are necessary to show the invention. The views must be numbered consecutively with Arabic numerals preceded by "FIG." (unless there is only one). Several views may be placed on a single sheet. Partial views intended to form one complete view should be labeled FIG. 1A, FIG. 1B, FIG. 1C, and so on.

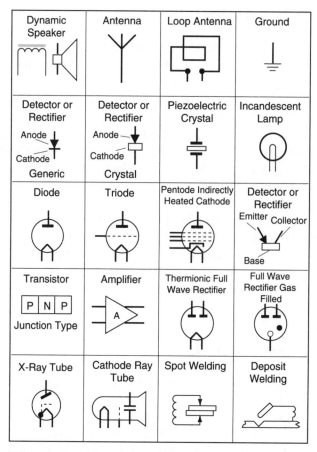

Figure 3   Examples of electrical and electronics symbols.

The views may be plan, elevation, section, or perspective. Detail views or portions or elements on a larger scale also may be used. Exploded views should have the separated parts enclosed in brackets to show the relationship or order of assembly of the parts.

A view of a large machine or device in its entirety may be broken and extended over several sheets if there is no loss in understanding the view.

The plane of a sectional view should be indicated on the general view by a broken (dashed) line, the ends of which are designated by numerals corresponding to the view number of the sectional view. Arrows should indicate the direction in which the view is taken. Views should not be connected by projection lines, nor should center lines be used.

A moved position may be shown by a broken line imposed on a suitable view if this can be done without crowding; otherwise, a separate view must be used for this purpose. Modified or varied forms of construction may be shown only in separate views.

All views on a sheet must stand in the same direction, preferably so they can be read with the sheet held in an upright position. If views longer than the width of the sheet are

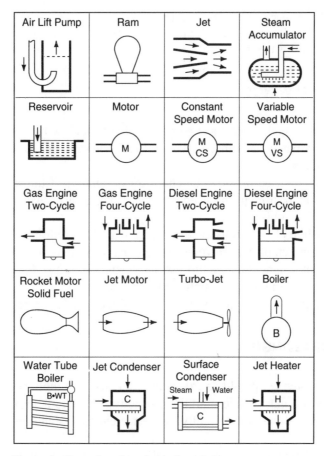

Figure 4   Examples of mechanical symbols.

necessary, the sheet may be turned on its side so that the original top becomes the right side. One view must not be placed on another or within the outline of another.

19.3.12 Copyright and Mask Work Notices

A copyright or mask work notice may appear within the sight of a drawing immediately below the work it refers to. The content of the notice must be minimal, for example, "Copyright 1995 John Doe" or "*M* John Doe." Letter height must be between 0.32 and 0.64 cm ($\frac{1}{8}$ and $\frac{1}{4}$ inch).

If such a notice is included in a drawing, the following statement must appear at the beginning of the patent application:

A portion of the disclosure of this patent document contains material which is subject to copyright (or mask work) protection. The owner has no objection to the facsimile reproduction by anyone of the patent document or the patent disclosure, as it appears in the Patent and Trademark Office file or records, but otherwise reserves all copyright (or mask work) rights whatsoever.

19.4 DESIGN DRAWINGS

A design patent application must be represented by a drawing that complies with the standards for utility patents and that contains enough views to disclose completely the appearance of the article.

Shading must be used to show the character or contour of the surfaces represented. Broken lines may not be used to show hidden planes and surfaces that can't be seen through opaque surfaces of the object.

Black-and-white photographs in compliance with the requirements for utility patents may be submitted in lieu of ink drawings. They must be limited to the design claimed and may not include environmental structure (scenery, studio setting). Photographs and drawings may not be mixed in the same application.

Color drawings and photographs are not permitted in a design patent application.

19.5 PLANT DRAWINGS

Plant patent drawings should be artistically executed in compliance with the standards for utility patents and must disclose all the distinctive characteristics of the plant that are capable of visual representation. Usually, reference characters and view numbers are not needed.

Drawings and photographs may be in color, and must be in color when color is a distinguishing characteristic of the new variety. Color drawings and photographs must comply with the standards for utility patents, and two copies must be submitted.

Article

20

THE BEST MODE REQUIREMENT OF THE U.S. PATENT SYSTEM

Charles F. Hauff, Jr.

Charles F. Hauff, Jr. is an attorney with Snell & Wilmer in Phoenix, Arizona, practicing intellectual property law.

Is it necessary to wait until after an invention has been built and tested before filing a patent application? The answer is a resounding NO!
Filing a patent application is constrained only by two threshold disclosure:

ENABLEMENT. The applicant must be able to provide a description of the invention in sufficient detail to enable a typical person practicing in the relevant technology to make and use the invention; and

BEST MODE. The applicant must disclose what he or she contemplates as the "best mode" (version) of the invention.

If those two requirements can be met, no further development is required before an application can be filed.
The Best Mode *requirement, in effect, means that the applicant must disclose any details known at the time of filing that make the invention more practicable or provide some particular advantage. In other words, if, at the time of filing, the applicant is aware that a particular type of filter circuit makes the invention operate more efficiently, the particular type of filter used must be disclosed.*
However, the Best Mode *is frozen in time upon filing the application. There is no duty to disclose details developed after the date of filing in the application. In fact, addition of new subject matter, e.g., additional detail, to the application after filing is precluded.*
This means that an application can be filed as soon as an enabling *disclosure can be provided; as soon as the invention can be described in sufficient detail to enable a typical person practicing in the relevant technology to make and use the invention without themselves having to be an inventor in the process. So long as the* Best Mode *requirement is met, the invention as disclosed need not be efficient or cost effective, it need only be operational to accomplish its intended purpose.*
If an application is filed early in the development cycle, the Best Mode requirement may be met with relatively few, if any, details beyond those required to provide an enabling *disclosure.*

Post-filing developments may be protected as trade secrets, if their nature and circumstances permit. If there are post-filing developments that are worthy of protection in their own right, patent protection may be pursued through a new continuation-in-part (CIP) application, filed while the original application is still pending. In a CIP application, those claims that are supported by the original (parent) disclosure are treated as if they were filed on the effective filing date of the original application. Claims that include some element or detail that was not disclosed in the original application have the actual filing date of the new application. After a CIP application is filed, the applicant can continue to prosecute the original application, or the original application can be abandoned in favor of the CIP.

There are a number of reasons why it may be desirable to file a patent application early in the development cycle of a product.

The following articles discuss the best mode requirement and patent applications that are filed before the related invention is tested, sometimes referred to by chemical patent attorneys as prophetic applications.   *MAL*

Abstract

A U.S. patent gives to the first, true inventor the right to exclude others from making, using, or selling the patented thing [1]. In return, the inventor must, among other things, set forth the "best mode contemplated by the inventor of carrying out his [or her] invention" [2]. The terms "best mode" and "carrying out the invention" are, however, not defined with precision in the patent statutes. Their meaning, therefore, necessarily depends on the particular facts of each case [3]. An understanding of how these terms are generally interpreted can best be obtained by reviewing how this provision of the law has been applied in individual cases. Thus, this article will first examine several recent court cases that have addressed best mode issues and then conclude with some general observations and practice techniques.

20.1 *DANA CORP. V. IPC LTD. PARTNERSHIP* [4]

In *Dana Corp.*, the patent at issue claimed an internal combustion engine having a particular valve stem seal. The seal comprised a rubber material, which fit tightly on top of the valve guide. The seal purportedly served to prevent oil leakage.

Evidence adduced at trial indicated that the inventor authored a report prior to the filing of the patent application that stated that tests showed a fluoride surface treatment of the rubber seals was "necessary to satisfactory performance of seal [to control leakage]" [5]. Further, the inventor testified in discovery that he questioned why the patent application made "no reference . . . to fluoride treated rubber" [6].

The court held that the inventor contemplated a particular method of manufacture, namely fluoride surface treating of the rubber at the time the application was filed. That method of manufacture, however, was not disclosed in the patent document. Although the method was old, *i.e.* generally known in the art, the court held that because the undisclosed method of treatment was necessary to the invention because it affected how well the invention worked, the patent was invalid for failure to comply with the best mode requirement [7].

20.2 *NORTHERN TELECOM, INC.*
V. DATAPOINT CORP. [8]

In this case, the inventors patented a programmable processor-based batch data entry terminal that provided an improved method of entering, verifying, and storing data to remove source error in data processing. In general, the system enabled the operator to provide entry and verification of data. In particular, as data was keyed in, the operator was guided by screen instructions and certain entries were subject to automatic, as well as visible, checks and edits. The system used a storage area, or buffer, to hold the data as it was entered and, when the buffer held a complete and correct record, the data was transferred to a magnetic tape.

The patent specification indicated that tape cassettes, such as audio cassettes, were desired for use in the invention. The evidence adduced at trial, however, showed that prior to filing the application the company that owned the patent knew that audio tapes were not the best mode of practicing the invention. Rather, the company was using special cassettes that had different yield strength and magnetic characteristics than standard audio cassettes. As a result, the court held that various claims directed to the tape were invalid for failure to comply with the best mode requirement [9].

20.3 *ENGEL INDUSTRIES, INC.*
V. THE LOCKFORMER CO. [10]

The patent in this case related to a system for forming duct sections distributing air throughout a building, *i.e.,* heating or cooling air ducts. In the system, the duct sections are formed with an integral flange engageable with corner connectors such that the sections could be easily joined without the need for conventional rivets or other labor intensive methods [11]. A copy of Figure 1 of the patent is reproduced below.

The patent specification made no reference to crimping of the corners to hold them in place. However, the evidence indicated that the inventors "knew that crimping might be necessary" at the time the application was filed [12]. Moreover, when the system was commercialized, problems arose in handling and transporting duct sections having corners that previously had been connected. To avoid this problem, the company that owned the patent suggested crimping of the corners. The company also sold tools to accomplish the crimping.

Despite this evidence, the Court found the patent claims valid over a best mode charge [13]. The court found that no evidence clearly and convincingly indicated that, at the time of filing, the inventors regarded crimping as a preferred mode of carrying out their inven-

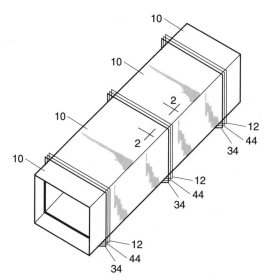

Figure 1 The patent, showing ducts 10 with corner
connectors 34.

tion [14]. Rather, the inventors' preferred mode was to snap in the corners without crimping and this mode was fully disclosed in the specification.

20.4 *WAHL INSTRUMENTS, INC.*
V. ACVIOUS, INC. [15]

The patent here related to reversible and irreversible temperature indicating devices. In general, the patent described a sectional device including two (2) parts between which a layer of temperature indicating material was placed. Various best mode arguments were raised as defenses in litigation the patent owner brought alleging infringement of the patent. For example, the defendant alleged that the patent was invalid for failure to disclose embedment molding of the two (2) parts that was suggested as being preferred by the fabricator of one of the commercial embodiments (an egg timer) of the invention. The inventor, however, testified that embedment molding did not affect how his invention worked.

The defendant also alleged that the best mode of the temperature indicating material was established by a standard commercial product, which the assignee company used to make the original prototypes. Moreover, the defendants alleged that the temperature indicating material had to be fashioned in the form of an insert. While the Court seemed to indicate that such choice was merely because of the reduced cost of the inserts and had nothing to do with the best mode for the invention itself, particularly in view of the fact that the technique was "an ancient art", the Court left open the question of whether those skilled in the art (typical person practicing in the relevant area of technology) would need more information in order to know that the thermochromic inserts on a substrate should be used.

20.5 GUIDELINES

Most often, the best mode requirement is used in a patent infringement action to argue that the patent, or claims thereof, is invalid. Proving a patent invalid and therefore not infringeable provides a complete defense for an accused infringer. Each of the cases discussed in this article resulted from this situation.

Although the best mode defense seemed to be *in vogue* in the late 1980s, recent cases hold this defense in less favor. Nevertheless, it remains an issue that must be considered not only in litigation concerning patents but, perhaps more important, in the preparation of any patent application directed to an invention.

Moreover, best mode determinations made during the preparation of the patent application likely will be subjected to rigorous scrutiny by an accused infringer. In infringement litigation, the inventor(s) most likely will be deposed and questioned about differences between the patent disclosure and other evidence of the best mode or what the inventor suggests may be the best mode. Typically, rigorous questioning is not an aspect of the application preparation process. Therefore, what is discovered in the litigation may be learned for the first time by all involved. It is thus incumbent upon the inventor(s) to provide a full and complete disclosure to the patent attorney of all issues that may have a bearing on the best mode issue.

The following guidelines will assist in ensuring that the best mode is included in the patent:

1. A purpose of the best mode requirement is to restrain inventors from concealing from the public preferred embodiments of their invention. Thus, an inventor's testimony as to why certain aspects of an invention are not described in the patent may be very important in evaluating the inventor's subjective intent [16] (*e.g.,* "it's irrelevant" vs. "I did not want the competition to learn it from me"). As a result, inventors should freely discuss all conceived modes, especially pointing out all preferred modes when the application is being prepared.

2. Compliance with the best mode requirement is governed by the inventors' state of mind with respect to the invention described and claimed in the patent application [17]. Thus, an inventor should carefully review the application in light of the claims to determine whether the description is complete and accurate and to determine whether the preferred mode is clearly set forth.

3. An accused infringer must prove a best mode defense by clear and convincing evidence. In this context, contemporaneous documents, particularly those created by the inventor, tend to have great weight [18]. Thus, all documents relating to the invention should be thoroughly reviewed for evidence of *preferred, desired,* or *advantageous* aspects not described in the specification.

4. While technical details apparent to the typical person practicing in the relevant area of technology (person of ordinary skill in the art) need not be included in the patent specification [19], if such a person cannot divine the most advantageous way to use

an invention from the specification, the best mode requirement is not met [20]. Thus, care must be taken at the time of filing not only to assess the content of the prior art, but also the level of ordinary skill in the art.

5. While decisions regarding reducing cost of components of a device may not affect the best or preferred mode for the invention [21], in general, such information should be disclosed to the patent attorney so that it can be fully evaluated.

6. While patent specifications typically do not include production or manufacturing specifications [22], the particulars of making a prototype or commercial embodiment may be relevant to the best mode and should be disclosed to the patent attorney so that it can be fully evaluated [23].

7. While there is no absolute requirement that names for sources of materials be provided (unless the name of the source would not be known or easily available) [24], sources should normally be provided for materials and/or elements of preferred embodiments, where known.

8. The best mode requirement relates to *carrying out* the invention [25], thus, care should be taken to ensure that not only the invention is fully and accurately described, but also that sufficient detail of matters relating to the use of the invention, particularly preferred uses are likewise set forth. For example, if you invented a new internal combustion engine, the best mode requirement would require divulging the fuel on which it would run best [26].

9. In the context of biotech inventions, while antibodies (or other microorganisms) that are difficult to screen may not need to be deposited in a depository [27], deposit should be considered and its advantages (*e.g.*, avoiding an issue in enforcement of the patent) and disadvantages fully considered.

20.6 CONCLUSION

The statutory obligations imposed on the inventor by the best mode requirement are not without ambiguity. Thus, the guidelines set forth in this article are not absolute; rather, they are suggestions to encourage and facilitate dialogue between patent attorneys and inventors with regard to best mode issues. In many instances, the *right answer* is not clear, even from a rigorous review of pertinent case law. However, in cases where an issue arises, it may be prudent to err on the side of over-inclusion to avoid potentially problematic, and likely costly, issues if the patent is litigated and compliance with the best mode requirement challenged.

NOTES

[1]   35 U.S.C. §271.

[2]   35 U.S.C. §112.

[3]   See, *Wahl Instruments Inc. v. Acvious,* 21 U.S.P.Q.2d 1123, 1126 (Fed. Cir. 1991).

[4]   *Dana Corp. v. IPC Ltd. Partnership,* 8 U.S.P.Q.2d 1692 (Fed. Cir. 1988) cert. denied, 490 U.S. 1067 (1989).

[5]   *Dana Corp.,* 8 U.S.P.Q.2d at 1695.

[6]   *Id.*

[7]   *Id.* at 1696.

[8]   *Northern Telecom. Inc. v. Datapoint Corp.,* 15 U.S.P.Q.2d 1321 (Fed. Cir. 1990).

[9]   *Northern Telecom,* 15 U.S.P.Q.2d at 1328.

[10] *Engel Industries, Inc. v. The Lockformer Co.,* 20 U.S.P.Q.2d 1300 (Fed. Cir. 1991).

[11] *Engel,* 20 U.S.P.Q.2d at 1301.

[12] *Id.* at 1303.

[13] *Id.* at 1304.

[14] *Id.*

[15] *Wahl Instruments. Inc. v. Acvious,* 21 U.S.P.Q.2d 1123 (Fed. Cir. 1991).

[16] See, *Wahl,* 21 U.S.P.Q.2d at 1128.

[17] See *e.g. Engel,* 20 U.S.P.Q.2d at 1303.

[18] See, for example, *Dana Corp.,* 8 U.S.P.Q.2d at 1695.

[19] *W. L. Gore & Associates. Inc. v. Garlock. Inc.,* 220 U.S.P.Q. 303, 306 (Fed. Cir. 1983) cert. denied, 469 U.S. 51 (1984).

[20] *Chemcast Corp. v. Arco Industries Corp.,* 16 U.S.P.Q.2d 1033 (Fed. Cir. 1990).

[21] *Wahl,* 21 U.S.P.Q.2d at 1130.

[22] *Christianson v. Colt Industries. Operating Corp.,* 3 U.S.P.Q.2d 1241, 1254–55 (Fed. Cir. 1987) vacated on other grounds 486 U.S. 800 (1988).

[23] See *e.g., Wahl* 21 U.S.P.Q.2d at 1127; see also Dana Corp., 8 U.S.P.Q.2d at 1695.

[24] *Wahl,* 21 U.S.P.Q.2d at 1130.

[25] 35 U.S.C. §112, first paragraph.

[26] *Randomex Inc. v. Scopus Corp.,* 7 U.S.P.Q.2d 1050, 1054, n.1 (Fed. Cir. 1988).

[27] *Scripps Clinic & Research Foundation v. Genentech, Inc.,* 18 U.S.P.Q.2d 1001, 1002 (Fed. Cir. 1991); see also *Amgen Inc. v. Chugai Pharmaceutical Co., Ltd.,* 18 U.S.P.Q.2d 1016, 1024–25 (Fed. Cir. 1991).

<table>
<tr><td>Article</td></tr>
</table>

| Article **21** | # PROPHETIC PATENT APPLICATIONS: WHEN SHOULD YOU FILE, AND HOW? |

Patrick D. Kelly

Patrick D. Kelly serves as "Of Counsel" for Haverstock, Garrett & Roberts in St. Louis, specializing in medical technology, including the use of computers in medicine. He also is an inventor and the President of JFKM Research, LLC, which is studying anti-viral topical lubricants that may be able to slow the spread of AIDS and other sexually transmitted diseases.

Abstract

For several reasons, it almost always is advisable to file a patent application on a promising idea as soon as possible. Sometimes, it may even be advisable to file an application before any research is done, or before certain experimental results or software become available. This article explains why it can be safer in some situations to file even before the physical work is done, and it offers guidance and examples showing how to maximize the chance of success if this approach is taken.

21.1 INTRODUCTION

Suppose you have a great idea for an invention. It's not a simple consumer product; it's a research-intensive project that might take months. You describe it to your employer, but they're busy with other things, and expressly waive their rights. You can do whatever you want with your idea, but you'll probably need help. You'll need funding, and you might have to talk with some technical people who have certain specialties. What do you do? How do you get started?

If you want to publish your idea with no data, to see if you can generate some interest in it, there are ways; a few journals (Medical Hypotheses is an example) and countless electronic networks and bulletin boards are happy to print or post theories and proposals with little or no supporting data, and Research Disclosures will publish anything for a fee, like a scientific vanity press. But premature publication can preclude patent protection, and publishing an idea without patenting it can doom an idea to gathering dust on library shelves. If no company can profit from it, no company will invest in it.

If you tell people about your idea while hunting for collaborators or support, you risk giving it away. And you might warn competitors already working on the same idea that they'd better move quickly. They can nod and say it's an interesting idea, and as soon as you leave, put more pressure on everyone to work harder and get a patent application filed as soon as possible. For an example, see *La Jolla Biologists Troubled by Midas Factor,* Science 213: 623 (1981).

You can send a letter to a company that makes one of the components you plan to use in your invention, telling them you have an idea that could increase sales of their device or compound, and offering to tell them more in confidence. But unless you have a well-established reputation (*e.g.,* you're a professor at a major university), they'll probably respond by saying they're reluctant to enter into confidentiality agreements, and you'll have to tell them something about your idea, with no safeguards, before they'll consider signing a secrecy agreement. They might suggest that you should file a patent application and then show it to them. But how do you file a patent application if you've got no data, and no way to get data without funding and support?

You can file a "Disclosure Document" with the U.S. Patent and Trademark Office if you want, for a filing fee of only $10.00, but you'd better realize the limitations of that approach. It's comparable to having a letter notarized, or having a co-worker sign and date a lab notebook as a witness. The only thing a Disclosure Document can do is prove you started working on your idea before the official date given to the document. It doesn't offer any legal protection beyond that. The best use of a Disclosure Document, if you want to go that route, is to establish the earliest possible date for the initial write-up, and then contact a patent attorney to start working on a patent application.

But this leads back to the question: how do you file a patent application if you've got no proof that your idea works? If you haven't even started to build or test it yet?

One answer is this: you can file a *prophetic* patent application—prophetic as in *prophesy.* It predicts the future, instead of reporting the past.

There is another term that inventors working with prophetic applications should know about: *parent application.* The first patent application filed on a new idea will usually give the inventor at least two years or more to do research on the idea. After some hard data become available or a working prototype has been completed, the first application can be superseded by a *continuation-in-part* (CIP) application with the newly gathered information. When the CIP application is filed, it cites the first application and claims a *priority date* of the first application. From then on, the first application is referred to as the *parent application.* It was the first one filed, and the others are its descendants.

This is a key point. Anyone who wants a solid, enforceable patent that will stand up in litigation should seriously consider filing a first application as quickly as possible, even if it is only prophetic and has no data; the reasons for this urgency are discussed below. After the first filing, research needs to be done, and if the idea works as anticipated, the inventor and his patent attorney should consider filing a CIP application containing proof that the invention works. If they file a CIP application with the new data, the first (prophetic) application turns into a parent application. If done properly, this approach can give the best of both worlds; it creates the earliest possible filing date, and it creates a patent with solid evidence that the invention actually works, which can help strengthen the patent against possible challenges.

It should also be recognized that any good patent must be prophetic to some extent. It is stupid to limit patent claims to the earliest data, or to only one version of an invention when any scientist or engineer could suggest ways to create alternative versions that will achieve the same result. When an inventor sees a draft of a patent claim covering his or her invention, he or she must begin trying to figure out how competitors might try to avoid the claim while achieving the same result. If an inventor can think of any way to avoid the claims, even if the "non-preferred embodiment" doesn't work as well, he or she should work with the patent attorney to try to cover that option, even though the inventor hasn't actually built or tested it yet. This is essential to obtaining good patent coverage, and it requires predictions that go beyond just reporting what has already been done.

But returning to the main topic of this article, there is a special class of patent applications and issued patents based entirely on hypotheses, library research, and discussions, unsupported by hard data or actual results. These are the truly prophetic patents. They can be frustrating, but they also can be fascinating. If the facts are right, if the words are handled properly, and—most important of all—if the predictions turn out to be accurate, these applications can mature into patents that are as enforceable as any other patent.

21.2 WHY FILE EARLY? WHY NOT WAIT?

There are powerful incentives to file a patent application as soon as possible. Competitors may be working on the same idea, and whoever files an application first has major advantages over others who file later. The United States uses "interferences" to determine who wins, if competing patent applications are filed, and in these battles, the "senior party" (the one that filed first) has several major advantages. Most other nations use a "first-to-file" system, so there isn't even a contest; whoever filed the first competent application will win.

In addition, there is a constant danger that a research article or other item will suddenly appear in print, creating more prior art that must be overcome.

Finally, there is yet another powerful incentive for early filing. As discussed below, the patent law requires an inventor to disclose the "best mode of carrying out the invention" known to the inventor on the day the application is filed. The inventor cannot get a valid patent by disclosing an early model or process that has already been superseded by a better version the inventor wants to keep secret. In exchange for 17 years of patent protection, an inventor must reveal, in the application, the best mode that is known on the day of filing. This is a rigid requirement, and there is only one good way to exploit it: file a patent application as soon as possible, then do more research after the application is filed. If an initial prophetic application is approved and allowed by an examiner and then issues as a patent, any improvements discovered after the early filing date can remain as trade secrets.

For all of these reasons, one of the clear-cut goals and obligations of good patent practice is to file applications promptly.

How promptly? In the opinion of this author, an application should be filed, or at least seriously considered and discussed, as soon as two criteria can be met.

First, there should be a *reasonable expectation of success for the invention, i.e.,* the invention will work for its intended purpose. The italicized phrase comes from a case, *In re O'Farrell,* 7 USPQ2d 1673 (1988), decided by the Court of Appeals for the Federal Circuit (the CAFC, which has exclusive jurisdiction over all patent appeals). In the *O'Farrell* case, the CAFC held that a certain invention involving genetic engineering was unpatentable because it was *obvious* under 35 USC §103. If allowed, that patent would have become a major force in the field of genetic engineering; it would have been worth tens or even hundreds of millions of dollars. But the inventors waited too long before filing an application, while various publications (including their own articles in scientific journals) advanced the general state of knowledge in the field. In the words of the CAFC, "For obviousness [which destroys patentability] under section 103, all that is required is a reasonable expectation of success".

If the general state of knowledge in a certain field is approaching a point where an invention might be declared *obvious* under 35 USC §103 if more relevant articles appear and become prior art against an invention, then the risk factor grows larger with each week's delay. Therefore, in light of *O'Farrell,* it would appear to be reasonable and even advisable to file an application as soon as a level of "reasonable expectation of success" is reached, even if the hands-on research hasn't been finished or even started yet.

A *reasonable expectation of success* doesn't require a high degree of certainty. If you think there's a 50–50 chance that an invention will work, then it is reasonable to start covering the bases and protecting your investments, in case it does work. If it doesn't work as hoped, you can quietly abandon an application; unless it was also foreign-filed in countries that publish all applications, no one else needs to know a patent application was ever filed. If based on an honest "I think this is likely to work" belief, this tactic is not abusive or fraudulent; instead, it's common practice.

The second criterion for deciding when to file is this: you must be able to describe your idea in enough detail to teach others how to make and use it. That level might be reached while research is still in progress, before any final results are available, or it might be reached before any hands-on research even begins.

So, if you get a flash of insight about how to do something better than anyone else has ever done it before, the question is not, "Have you done it yet?". Instead, the relevant questions are, "Do you have a valid reason to expect that it will succeed?" and "Can you describe it in enough detail to teach people how to do it now, without having to rely on hoped-for breakthroughs in the future?". If the answers are yes, you may be ready to start working on a patent application.

Keep in mind also that the U.S. Patent and Trademark Office works on a timescale measured in months and years. If a patent examiner doubts a prophetic claim, the examiner can issue an Office Action demanding proof. But if this happens, the proof usually isn't required until at least a year after the application is filed; more commonly, the first deadline for actual proof is at least 18 to 24 months after an initial filing. So an inventor usually has at least a year or two to complete the research, after filing the first application. That doesn't count the extra years that can be obtained by appealing a rejection, or by filing a follow-up application containing data gathered after the first application was filed.

For all of the foregoing reasons, the presumption is in favor of early filing. If a project will take months to complete, then ask yourself, why not file for patent coverage now? Why not at least try to protect yourself the best you can, while you're doing the research? If you work with innovation, at the cutting edge of technology, you need to be heads-up, pro-active, and even pre-active, instead of waiting to find out what others have done and then reacting. You might be playing against opponents you don't know about and can't even locate yet, so the sooner you get some points on the board, the better off you'll be.

21.3 MECHANICS, CHEMISTRY, PHARMACOLOGY, OR COMPUTERS?

In the mechanical field, patents usually don't contain examples or experimental data. They contain drawings, and it is not difficult to draw a machine or device that hasn't been built, if the inventor has a clear idea of how the parts should fit together. The actions of gears, levers, and other mechanical components are generally predictable, so it is not difficult to obtain prophetic patents on mechanical devices. Indeed, it is often impossible, from reading a mechanical patent, to tell whether a device has actually been built or tested; the specification simply states that the various components interact in such-and-such a manner. If a mechanical device doesn't work as claimed, the patent simply becomes worthless.

Prophetic patents in chemistry are more difficult to obtain, because they could hinder research. If a patent could be obtained on a new molecule or mixture merely by making the substance without having to prove its utility, anyone else who later discovers a valuable use for that substance could be prohibited from using the compound for that valuable purpose. That would give chemists and chemical companies an unfair way to lock up new areas of chemistry merely by synthesizing new compounds, and it would discourage research on those compounds by anyone else.

In pharmacology, prophetic patents are very difficult to obtain. There is a presumption that a minor change in molecular structure can generate unpredictable effects in living organisms. Amino acids offer an example; two molecules with exactly the same chemical formula can have totally different effects in living organisms, if one is the D isomer and the other is the L isomer. As another example, penicillin works well in mice, rats, and rabbits; no one would have predicted that it is relatively toxic to guinea pigs. Therefore, if someone wants a patent on a new drug, they must prove the drug works as claimed. Tests on humans are usually not required; tests can use lab animals (*Campbell v. Wettstein,* 167 USPQ 376, 1973) or even, in some situations, in vitro tests using cell culture (*Nelson v. Bowley,* 206 USPQ 881, 1980).

In terms of predictability, most inventions involving computer hardware or electronics would probably be regarded as closer to mechanics than to chemistry. However, inventions involving things such as semiconductor materials, quantum or subatomic physics, or chemical treatment of electronic devices are closer to the chemical field, and might need proof that they work as claimed.

Prophetic patents involving software need careful attention to balance several competing goals. On one side, there does not appear to be a limited-resource need for prophetic software patents; anyone with enough resources to write the necessary code and file a patent application on a software invention can simply run the software and make sure it works. Since enhancements might be developed during the process of writing and testing, and since the enhancements might add important value to a patent, these factors point toward writing and testing the code first, then filing an application. However, two other factors point in the opposite direction. First, competitors might be working on similar software, and whoever files an application first will be in better shape for a contest between them. Second, the code itself might need to be disclosed under the "best mode" requirement, if it is available on the day the application is filed. However, if the code has not been completed and is not available on the day of filing, then it obviously cannot be disclosed. If the narrative descriptions accompanied by flow charts and other supporting information are adequate to support the patent application without requiring a complete listing of the code, then the inventor can get a patent while keeping the code itself (developed after the application is filed) as a trade secret.

21.4 GENERAL REQUIREMENTS

Any patent application must satisfy several requirements. Every component, reagent, or step necessary to create or use the invention must be known and available to the interested public. Any necessary information must be in the application, or it must be widely known in the art; it can't be hidden in an obscure publication so that only a few people know about it (*In re Howarth,* 210 USPQ 689 (1981)).

In addition, as noted above, the application must disclose the best mode of carrying out the invention, known or contemplated on the day the application is filed. This requirement is not the place for brinkmanship games; don't try to get as close as possible to the line. Instead, disclose anything you think would be helpful to someone trying to figure out the invention. During the life of a patent, the best mode will probably advance far beyond any ideas you have before you've done any research, and if you hold back a relevant piece of information, you will probably be accused of committing fraud if anyone wants to challenge your patent. Keep your eye on the ball; if your goal is to get the best possible patent, then fully disclose the best mode on the day of filing. The only way to beat this requirement is by filing an application as soon as possible, then doing more research after that.

The patent law (35 USC §112), requires that any patent application (including a prophetic application) describe how to make the invention (assemble the components, synthesize the compound, etc.), in words or drawings that can be followed by people skilled in that art. This doesn't require an encyclopedic survey of the entire field of art; the teachings of the application can be supplemented by information generally known in an industry or field of research. To minimize the risk of disputes about what is or is not known, it is often a good idea to cite two or three standard treatises or review articles that cover the field, in addition to citing the most relevant items of prior art.

A patent application also must assert at least one utility for the invention. You cannot simply state, "Here is a machine; the components interact in such-and-such a manner". The description must go on to state, "This machine can be used to do such-and-such a task". This is an important requirement, and inventors should approach it with caution bordering on fear; you need to say something positive about utility, but if it turns out to be a false or overbroad prediction, it might come back to haunt you.

If the legal requirements are met, the filing of a patent application is called a constructive reduction to practice. The regulations governing proceedings before the Patent and Trade Office (*e.g.,* 37 CFR 1.131) and numerous court decisions state that an actual reduction to practice is not required; a constructive reduction (*i.e.,* a written application that satisfies 35 USC §112) is enough.

The requirement that a patent application must teach people how to accomplish the desired goal, using available resources, explains why people can't patent ideas that can't be accomplished yet. The most famous example is Arthur Clarke, who proposed geosynchronous satellites. When he published his article in the 1940s, there was no way to get rockets or satellites into space (let alone position them in geosynchronous orbit). Since neither Clarke nor anyone else could accomplish what he proposed, it was nothing more than a vision of a distant goal, and it could not be used as the basis for a patent application. Clarke's article could, however, be used as prior art against other patent applications that tried to claim various aspects of geosynchronous satellites.

21.5 ROUTINE v. UNDUE EXPERIMENTATION

An invention cannot be patented unless the conception (the mental creation of a complete and workable idea) is complete and only "routine experimentation" will be required to reduce it to practice. This standard must be applied in light of the following factors:

1. There is no fixed time limit on experimentation. An experiment might take months to complete. For example, to test a plant growth regulator or a treatment for Alzheimer's, it might require crops or large animals to age to the point of senescence. That's okay, as long as (1) the time is reasonable under the circumstances, and (2) the experiments can be carried out by technicians following instructions that require only "routine experimentation" without requiring "undue creativity".

2. Obviousness (over prior art) and enablement (whether the text of an application adequately teaches the invention as claimed) are both determined by evaluating the level of "ordinary skill in the art". However, the level of "ordinary skill" can be very high. If an industry widely uses scientists with PhD's for research, then scientists with PhD's constitute an ordinary level of skill in that industry.

3. It is not necessary for a method to succeed 100 percent of the time in order for that method to be patentable. For example, in biotechnology, nearly any method of creating a new plasmid or genetically engineered cell will not succeed in every single cell. However, if the method is performed on thousands or millions of cells, some

number of cells in the test population will be successfully transformed. If a second procedure can be described for screening the population and isolating the desired cells without undue effort, then the two procedures (the transformation procedure, followed by the screening procedure) working together can teach those with skill in the art how to practice the invention. Screening standards that don't require predictability are set forth in court decisions such as *In re Wands,* 8 USPQ2d 1400 (1988).

Two important decisions by the PTO Board of Appeals that raise questions of routine versus undue experimentation are *Ex parte Jackson* (217 USPQ 804; 1982) and *Ex parte Forman* (230 USPQ 546; 1986). Although both are in the field of biotechnology, they offer good examples of principles that need to be considered when drafting entirely prophetic applications, or semi-prophetic applications based on early and limited experimental results.

Jackson involved three strains of bacteria which the applicant had discovered in natural settings, which were sufficiently different from other bacteria to justify calling them a new species. Some of Jackson's claims would have covered a certain process involving any strains from the new species. The Board refused to allow those claims, and limited the claims to processes using strains that had been discovered and deposited by Jackson. In the Board's opinion, Jackson had not taught others how to go out and find more strains of that species in nature.

The *Forman* decision involved a bacterial hybrid that carried antigens from two different types of disease-causing bacteria, which could serve as an oral vaccine against both types of bacteria. The disclosure was limited to hybrids obtained through bacterial conjugation, a somewhat unpredictable sexual process, rather than through controlled genetic engineering. Since an element of luck was involved in getting the desired hybrids through sexual unions between bacteria, Forman could not persuade the Board that any scientist with ordinary skill would be able to carry out the necessary steps using sexual conjugation, and the Board held that Forman's broad claims were not allowable.

Regrettably, the *Forman* decision criticized Forman and his coworkers for not being able to predict which specific strains would have the desired characteristics at the end of a conjugation procedure. That line of analysis is questionable in view of more recent decisions which indicate that the ability to predict is not always necessary if effective ways are disclosed for screening and isolating cells having the desired traits.

The *Forman* decision is cited frequently, because it lists eight factors that are relevant in deciding whether it would require undue experimentation for others to make or use an invention, to the broadest extent of the claims, based on the disclosures in an application. Those factors are:

1. the quantity of experimentation necessary;
2. the amount of direction or guidance presented in the application;
3. the presence or absence of working examples;
4. the nature of the invention;
5. the state of the prior art;

6. the relative skill of those in that art;
7. the predictability or unpredictability of the art;
8. the breadth of the claims.

It's worth noting that neither Jackson nor Forman were "prophetic" applications. Both contained detailed, extensive examples and experimental results. The question was whether those examples could support predictions that other scientists would be able to extend those results to the broadest limits of the claims.

This emphasizes a point made above: to some extent, every patent is prophetic. It's one thing to say, "Here's what I did". It's different to say, "If other scientists repeat my work, they'll get similar results". The second sentence is a prophesy, rather than a report of what has already happened. But it's no different than what scientists say whenever they've discovered something of interest. No matter how extensive your lab data might be, any claim that others will get the same results is only a prediction.

Bear in mind that any prediction made in an issued patent can be analyzed and picked apart in the harsh glare of hindsight, under highly adversarial conditions. If any predictions in an application turn out to be incorrect or couldn't be carried out by the inventor within a reasonable time limit, competitors are likely to either ignore the patent or attack it in court.

21.6 GAMBLERS AND SHARPSHOOTERS

In some ways, prophetic patents are for gamblers; they can be fascinating and fun if you enjoy taking chances, and they sometimes win. But unlike gambling, the risks can be minimized through planning and hard work. And unlike gambling, the biggest risk of all may be to delay while you wait for more data. Others might be working on the same idea, and the state of knowledge in the field might be getting dangerously close.

If you have a good idea and enough determination to carry it through, early filing of a patent application, even if no hard data are available yet, may be the best way to cover yourself while you gather data. If you take that route, think about asking one or more scientists and patent attorneys who aren't involved to try to shoot holes in your application, either before you file it or shortly afterward. Analyze every technical scenario and every word in the claims. What will happen if your idea works, but only partly? Will any gaps destroy the patent, or can you find a way to draft functional language that will leave out nonfunctioning embodiments? Is there a way to shift some of the claims away from chemistry or pharmacology, toward hardware? Can you avoid or minimize any objections that might be raised under the eight guidelines in the *Forman* decision? Those are some of the questions.

Most of all, steer clear of shotgun approaches. Use a rifle, and aim it carefully. This isn't a game of throwing slop against a wall to see if anything sticks, or an effort to get something for nothing. Instead, it's a way to protect investments while doing research. Study the prior art carefully, think about discussing your ideas with some experts as soon as you've filed your first application, and be ready to revise and refile it if any new data or additional insights will let you improve upon your first attempt.

INVENTORSHIP: WHO QUALIFIES, AND HOW?

Patrick D. Kelly

Patrick D. Kelly serves as "Of Counsel" for Haverstock, Garrett & Roberts in St. Louis, specializing in medical technology, including the use of computers in medicine. He also is an inventor and the President of JFKM Research, LLC, which is studying anti-viral topical lubricants that may be able to slow the spread of AIDS and other sexually transmitted diseases.

As noted in some of the earlier articles, U.S. law requires that an application for a patent be in the name of the actual inventor. The entity (one or more persons) named on the patent as the inventor must have, in fact, invented the invention claimed in the patent and not derived it from another.

Care must therefore be taken to apply for the patent in the name of the correct inventors. There are presently provisions for correcting certain errors in the named inventorship of a patent. However, it must be shown that any errors in naming the inventors arose "without deceptive intent". Thus if, for example, the director of research of a company, who had nothing to do with an invention, is named as an inventor or co-inventor, the patent may be invalid for failure to name the correct inventorship.

Ownership of the invention is a separate and distinct issue. Care must be taken to ensure that there is no question as to the ownership of inventions—particularly in situations where vendors and consultants are involved.

These aspects of patent law are discussed in the following articles. MAL

Abstract

Anyone who might be named as inventor or co-inventor on a patent should know the basics of how the patent law controls inventorship. Most decisions are fairly easy, but some require shades of gray to be force-fit into black or white categories. The patent statute is silent on who is an inventor, so court decisions in contested cases have become the law, in the form of legal precedents. This article explains the basic rule of inventorship, which requires a contribution to the *conception* (the complete mental embodiment) of at least one claim. That standard often can be applied flexibly to achieve the goals of the people involved, and this chapter recommends several procedures for reaching fair decisions and minimizing resentment in close cases.

22.1 INTRODUCTION

Every scientist, engineer, or other researcher should understand how the patent law governs inventorship. The U.S. patent law requires that the inventors be accurately named. The patent application includes a sworn oath by the inventors stating that they believe themselves to be the true inventor(s). No one who signs an oath under penalty of perjury should do so without understanding what he or she is signing.

About 80 to 90 percent of the time, inventorship decisions are easy, because the facts are clear. But the other 10 to 20 percent of the time, where two or more people contributed at different levels, difficult problems can arise. A remark or question in a lab or hallway, during a conference, or over a lunch or drink might elicit a suggestion that can range anywhere from mildly helpful to absolutely essential. Difficult questions also arise among people with different roles in a research department; a director will suggest an area of research, a senior scientist will study it and develop a plan of approach, a technician will fill in details and carry out the actual work, and an outside consultant may look over everyone's shoulders and offer advice. The senior scientist/principle investigator will almost always qualify, but the research director, the technician, and the consultant will fall into various shades of gray. Those shades of gray must be force-fit, somehow, into black-or-white, yes-or-no categories when it's time to decide inventorship. Someone either is or is not a co-inventor; no shades of gray are allowed.

In a sense, the law of inventorship is easy. It's the law of co-inventorship that's difficult. From here on, this analysis will assume that two or more people worked together on an invention and their level of contribution was unequal. That's where the problems arise.

22.2 GENERAL RULE: YOU MUST CONTRIBUTE TO CONCEPTION

For better or worse, the patent statute (35 USC 116) and the regulations (37 CFR 1.41) are both silent on who should be listed as an inventor. The rules say, "A patent must be applied for in the name of the actual inventor or inventors", but the rules are totally silent on the question, "Who is an actual inventor?".

Since the statute and regulations don't offer any guidance, the law is controlled by court decisions, which act as legal precedents. Most (but not all) of the court decisions say that in order to qualify, someone must contribute to the conception of an invention.

22.3 CONTRIBUTION

How much of a contribution must someone provide to a conception? There is no fixed requirement, no magic percentage. It must be a *significant* contribution, but significance will depend on the facts of the case. For example, if twenty or thirty (or even a hundred) different insights and experimental results had to be combined properly in order for all the pieces to fit together, one could argue quite reasonably that someone who supplied just one of those insights would qualify, if that insight played an important role in solving the puzzle. Stories are common of someone working on a problem for months or even years, and then suddenly solving it after a chance remark or a two-minute discussion provoked a key insight or suggested a key experiment. Out of politeness, most contributors who didn't put in any time-consuming effort on the project usually decline an invitation to be added as a co-inventor, if such an invitation is offered, but such contributors could and sometimes should be included.

However, a contribution is usually disqualified if it has already been patented or is in the public domain. An inventor can use any and all information that is publicly available, without having to give inventorship credit to any authors or inventors of the information being used. Rather than listing them as co-inventors, their work must be cited as prior art against the invention. If an article in a scientific journal provides a crucial insight into how to improve a machine or method described in that article, the author of the article is not a co-inventor of the improved machine or method, even though his or her published article played an essential role in contributing to the conception of the invention.

However, if information that was not publicly available is used, the presumption points in the opposite direction, and the person who provided the information is likely to deserve co-inventorship.

For example, suppose an outside inventor contacts your company with an idea for a hyperwidget. Your company did not sign a confidentiality agreement with him; he submitted the idea without any contract to protect him, hoping to get your company interested. You are asked to evaluate it, and when you study it, you realize it could be redesigned in a way the outsider never thought of, to make it even better.

The facts of this example indicate (rather strongly, in this author's opinion) that the outsider made a key contribution to the conception of the improved hyperwidget. If he had not shown your company his hyperwidget, in a nonpublic manner, you and your company never would have created your improved version. Therefore, he apparently contributed to the conception of the improved version.

If he is trying to patent his own version, this creates a fairly clear rule. If you saw his version before his patent issued, and before any other public disclosure, then he did you the favor of providing you with advance, unpublished information (even though it might not have been covered by a written confidentiality agreement). He may therefore be a co-inventor. However, if you see his version only after his patent was issued or after some other public disclosure, he is not a co-inventor; instead, his work must be treated as prior art.

22.4 CONCEPTION:
THE *MERGENTHALER* STANDARD

The following is a widely-used legal definition of conception, from an early decision that is quoted with approval in any number of more recent decisions:

> The conception of the invention consists in the complete performance of the mental part of the inventive act. All that remains to be accomplished in order to perfect the act or in-

strument belongs to the department of construction, not invention. It is, therefore, the formation in the mind of the inventor of a definite and permanent idea of the complete and operative invention as it is thereafter to be applied in practice that constitutes an available conception within the meaning of the patent law.

Mergenthaler v. Scudder, 11 App. D.C. 264, 1897 C.D. 724 (Court of Appeals, District of Columbia, 1897).

The first sentence of this definition is excellent; it is clear, direct, and reliable, so long as you understand that a conception requires more than just envisioning the desired result. Having a goal is not enough, no matter how clearly the goal can be stated, unless the inventor can describe how the goal can be achieved in sufficient detail to teach other people how to do it. All of the necessary components, tools, reagents, and techniques must be available, and the work must be capable of being carried out by someone skilled in the art who is properly instructed on what to do and how to do it. Such work may require skill, diligence, perseverance, and even cleverness, but it must not require a high level of insight or creativity. If an unanticipated insight, a level of genuine creativity, or a markedly high degree of cleverness (beyond the level of *ordinary skill*) is required to overcome obstacles that the first inventor did not describe or anticipate, then whoever supplies the insight or creativity may deserve recognition as a co-inventor.

The first sentence is fine, but the second and third sentences from *Mergenthaler* suffer from several important problems if one tries to apply them to modern research. For one thing, the second sentence (which was written in the 1800s) does not recognize that any dividing lines between construction and invention are often blurred or nonexistent in research today. Nearly any research-oriented company or university will have a research department in which ideas for inventions are actually built, tested, and reduced to practice, and the choice of which particular experiments to run, and which types of analytical procedures and equipment to use, can have a major impact on whether the researchers notice the unexpected results that lead to the invention. Those decisions concerning which experiments to run, and how to run them, are both constructive and creative, and they create a broad transition zone between the mountains of invention and the foothills of construction, making it impossible to draw any clear line to separate invention from construction.

More problems in the *Mergenthaler* standard become apparent when one considers the phrase, "a definite and permanent idea of the complete and operative invention as it is thereafter to be applied in practice." In real life, a conception is usually regarded as complete (indeed, an actual reduction to practice is also complete) by the time someone has finished making a prototype that works and can accomplish the desired result. But that doesn't mean the working prototype will be "definite and permanent", "complete", or "thereafter to be applied in practice". Those terms ignore what usually happens during refinement, follow-up testing, and development of a lab discovery into a commercial product. In all seriousness, how many early prototypes can qualify as "permanent"? If courts began applying *Mergenthaler's* "definite, permanent, and complete" standards rigorously, it would cause a great deal of trouble and consternation in the patent system.

Other court decisions that are generally consistent with *Mergenthaler* contain language such as, "An inventor may use the services, ideas, and aid of others in the process of perfecting his invention, without losing his [exclusive] right to a patent" (*e.g., Hobbs v. United States,* 171 USPQ 713 (1971) and *Shatterproof Glass Corp. v. Libbey Owens Ford Co.,* 225 USPQ 634 (1985)). However, since inventorship standards are defined by court decisions while the statute is silent on this issue, it is possible to locate other court decisions that contain somewhat different language and reach different results, such as the following:

> The conception of the entire device may be due to one [person], but if the other [person] makes suggestions of practical value, which assisted in working out the main idea and making it operative, or contributes an independent part of the entire invention, which is united with the parts produced by the other and creates the whole, he is a joint inventor, even though his contribution be of comparatively minor importance and merely the application of an old idea.
>
> *Monsanto v. Kamp,* 154 USPQ 259 (D.D.C., 1967)

In any event, the most important goal of the patent system is to promote innovation and progress, and the rules of inventorship should be applied with that goal in mind.

22.5 THE 1984 CHANGES

In November 1984, Congress passed Public Law 98–622, which made a number of changes in the U.S. patent statute, including major changes affecting the law of co-inventorship. The unmistakable purpose of the 1984 amendments was to make the patent system more flexible and better suited to coping with the complexities of innovation.

Before November 1984, when a patent application was filed, every co-inventor had to be a co-inventor of every claim. This followed from the idea that a patent application can claim only one invention (which isn't strictly true; a single patent can sometimes claim, for example, both a method and an apparatus or compound). This problem could be solved only by filing multiple applications. If Smith created a new piece of hardware that used a sub-assembly or a special technique developed by Jones, it was often necessary to file two or three applications: one naming Smith as sole inventor, one naming Jones, and one naming both of them, each with claims limited to that particular person's contribution. Since a typical application costs hundreds of dollars in filing fees and thousands of dollars in attorney fees, people (especially independent inventors, start-up companies, and universities) were under a great deal of pressure to file a single application if they could. Under that pressure, can the patent attorney make a sound argument that Jones' contribution either didn't rise to the level of inventorship, or else applied, somehow, to everything Smith did? Decisions like that, which are tempting ways to save money, can unravel if an opposing attorney later discovers them and attacks them during a lawsuit.

The 1984 law changed all that. The revised section now reads, in part:

Inventors may apply for a patent jointly even though (1) they did not physically work together or at the same time, (2) each did not make the same type or amount of contribution, or (3) each did not make a contribution to the subject matter of every claim of the patent.

The only requirement is that each listed co-inventor must be a co-inventor of at least one claim.

By creative drafting of the claims, it is probably possible to add nearly anyone who was substantially involved in the development of the invention, if that's what the client(s) or the company wants. For example, if a technician contributed by optimizing the process parameters in a particular reaction, then a claim can be narrowly drawn to that particular step, using those particular parameters. If the technician is a valid co-inventor of that particular claim, he or she can be legitimately named as a co-inventor on the patent application. If the goal is clear, an attorney can try to develop the best strategy to reach that goal.

If a patent application claims more than one invention, the examiner can require the claims to be divided into two or more applications. This is a very common practice; most applications that claim both (1) a method and (2) an apparatus or compound usually receive a 'restriction requirement,' which will require the applicant to choose one group of claims (the method claims, or the apparatus or compound claims). One group of claims is elected, and the nonelected claims are put in the freezer, for storage and later use. A *divisional* application with the nonelected claims can be filed later, with a new filing fee, at any time while the original application is still pending.

The list of inventors on an application should be reviewed (1) whenever an election is made after a restriction requirement is received, and (2) after a Notice of Allowance is received (since the claims may have been amended during prosecution to focus on different aspects of the invention). Inventorship should be revised whenever necessary to include the inventors of only the elected or allowed claims.

In addition, if more than two or three inventors are listed on any application, it's a good idea to consult with your patent attorney regarding putting a memo in the file explaining what each person contributed, to make it easier to defend or revise any inventorship decisions if the need arises. Challenges won't arise until years later, and it can surprise anyone to see how differently people will remember what happened, when personal recognition is at stake.

There is a point of uncertainty in the law and the regulations. The regulation adopted by the Patent and Trademark Office to implement 35 USC §116 is in Title 37 of the Code of Federal Regulations, Section 1.45. Paragraph 1.45(c) says:

> If multiple inventors are named in an application, each named inventor must have made a contribution, individually or jointly, to the subject matter of at least one claim of the application . . .

Some patent attorneys believe this requires all co-inventors to be co-inventors of at least one specific claim, such as Claim 1. However, most attorneys don't agree with that interpretation. If Smith is an inventor of claims 1 through 9, and Jones is an inventor of claims 10 through 20, the rule (as written) apparently is satisfied, and the question becomes: can all of claims 1–20 be properly joined in a single application?

22.6 CONTINUATION-IN-PART APPLICATIONS

The 1984 amendments also made another important change to the law of inventorship. If an improvement is made to an invention that is already described and claimed in a pending patent application, the improvement can be claimed as a second invention by filing a second application, called a *continuation-in-part* (CIP) application, which cites the first (*parent*) application. A CIP application has, in effect, a dual filing date: any claim directed to subject matter that was adequately described in the parent application is entitled to the benefit of the first filing date, and any claim directed to new information is covered by the second filing date. CIP's give inventors an incentive to bring improvements to the attention of the public, rather than patenting a basic invention and then keeping any subsequent improvements secret.

CIP applications offer a major advantage: a parent application is not regarded as *prior art* against a CIP application. The teachings of the parent cannot render the improvement unpatentable under the obviousness standard, because the CIP gets to piggy-back on the parent with respect to any information that was contained in the parent. However, any publications describing the original invention or offers for sale dating more than one year prior to the CIP filing date may still be prior art with respect to the new matter.

Before the 1984 amendments, CIP applications suffered from a major limitation: every inventor named on the parent application had to be an inventor of the CIP application. If not, the CIP could not take advantage of the parent case; it would have to be filed on its own, and it would have to be patentable despite the parent application being regarded as prior art. For example, suppose Smith and Jones create a process and file a patent application. A new researcher, Wilson, then joins their lab, and with the guidance of Smith and Jones, he improves the process and increases its yields. Under the old law, the improvement would have to stand or fall on its own; it would have to be patentable over the prior art of Smith and Jones.

The 1984 amendments changed that. Now, 35 USC §120 says that a CIP application can be filed so long as at least one inventor on the parent case is also a co-inventor of the CIP. This means that Smith, Jones, and Wilson can all file a CIP application on the improvement together (or, Smith and Wilson can file the CIP alone, if Jones was not involved in the improvement). That's the way it should be; if the improvement was an advance in the art, the inventors should be encouraged by the patent system to tell the public about it without sacrificing their rights.

22.7 WORKING IN DIFFERENT LOCATIONS, AT DIFFERENT TIMES

Since 1984, 35 USC §116 (quoted above) has stated explicitly that two or more people can be co-inventors, even though they did not work in the same location, or at the same time.

The standards of inventorship carry legal duties that depend on contribution to conception rather than employment status, and those obligations must be obeyed even when they inconvenience a company. It is prudent, if a company deals with consultants or vendors in ways that might lead to patentable inventions, to use a standard clause in consulting or vendor agreements, requiring assignment of inventions created during the course of performance of the contract.

22.8 INTERNAL PROCEDURES: DECIDING CO-INVENTORSHIP

As noted above, inventorship decisions often require shade-of-gray facts to be labelled either black or white. The best way to minimize any unfairness or resentment created by a less-than-ideal result is by making sure the procedure used to reach the decision was fair.

In this author's opinion, the patent attorney should take full and exclusive responsibility for inventorship decisions; the final decision on who is and who isn't an inventor is a matter of law. The decision, however, is based upon facts; the patent attorney should be given the opportunity to talk to each person who might deserve consideration as a possible co-inventor.

The sequence of names has no legal significance. There is no special legal status for the first inventor. However, while all of the inventors' names are on the face of the patent, the inventive entity shown in bold print at the top of the patent typically lists only the first-named inventor, with the remaining inventors represented by the abbreviation *et al.*

22.9 EXTERNAL PROCEDURES: CORRECTIONS AND LAWSUITS

The list of inventors can be amended, using a *certificate of correction*, at any time while an application is pending or after a patent issues, so long as there was no deceptive intent on the part of the inventor, attorney, or assignee (35 USC §116 and 256; 37 CFR 1.324). During a lawsuit, a court can order a correction of inventorship, provided that all parties have been given notice and opportunity for a hearing.

If two or more people are at absolute loggerheads regarding co-inventorship of a patent, and if each side is represented by an attorney, they should consider referring the dispute to an independent, impartial attorney who doesn't represent either side. For example, if an outsider submits an idea to a company, and a company employee modifies the idea and thinks the improved version should be his alone, it might be impossible for the outsider and the company to agree on who owns what. If this type of problem arises, both sides can refer the question to an impartial attorney who doesn't work for either side, who can investigate the matter and give each side a fair chance to present its case, and then issue a written decision, in a manner comparable to a mediator or arbitrator. This will provide an adequate basis for filing an application, and it will protect the inventor(s) and/or company against any accusation of deliberate deception. If the loser wants to fight the decision, either in court or by filing his own patent application and demanding an interference proceeding in the Patent Office, he can do so.

22.10 WHAT DO THE 1984 CHANGES REALLY MEAN?

The underlying theme behind the 1984 amendments was that the courts should not spend their time on inventorship issues, unless a genuine question of deliberate deception has been raised.

This is not to say that anyone can ignore the requirements of the law. Anyone listed as a co-inventor must still contribute to the conception of at least one claim. A technician who carried out instructions, or a manager who provided resources and encouragement, will not qualify unless he or she actually contributed to the conception of at least one claim.

But anyone who works with innovation should realize that the 1984 changes created new opportunities for researchers and removed some of the obstacles that prevented legitimate co-inventors from receiving recognition.

Article 23 | OWNERSHIP OF INVENTIONS

C. Douglass Thomas

C. Douglass Thomas is a Patent Attorney with the Hewlett-Packard Co.

Abstract

It can be financially rewarding to be the owner of inventions or patents. Initially, it is the employee-inventor who owns the invention or patent. However, the employee-inventor may be obligated to assign rights to the invention or patent to his or her employer. In any case, advanced planning can be beneficial to both employer and employee.

23.1 HAVE YOU MADE AN INVENTION?

Whenever you discover or create something new, you probably say you have made an invention. Indeed, Webster's dictionary defines *invent* as: to originate as a product of one's own contrivance. Even so, the patent laws have a more limited notion of invention, known as a patentable invention. To be a patentable invention, the invention must meet all the requirements of the patent laws. For example, the invention must be new, useful and nonobvious to one skilled in the art. Hence, not all inventions are patentable inventions.

In any case, if the invention turns out to yield a marketplace advantage, the owner of the invention will be first in line to reap the financial rewards. The balance of this article will discuss who the owner is and why.

23.2 INITIALLY INVENTORS OWN THE INVENTION AND ANY PATENT ISSUING THEREON

Inventions are initially owned by the employee-inventor. Determining who the inventors are can, however, be a difficult task [1]. In any case, it is the employee-inventor, not the employer, who initially owns the invention. This is not so with works of authorship protected by the copyright laws (or mask works of a semiconductor chip product [2]), because in this case title vests directly with the employer (*e.g.*, software programs, drawings) [3].

© 1992 Hugh Cadzow

23.3 OWNERSHIP OF INVENTIONS
AND PATENTS MAY BE TRANSFERRED
FROM THE INVENTOR(S) TO OTHERS
BY VARIOUS METHODS

Even though the ownership of an invention originally vests with its inventors, inventors who are employed by corporations or universities are usually under some contractual or statutory obligation to relinquish some or all of their rights to the invention.

23.3.1 Common Law—Nature of Employment

Rights to one's invention in the absence of any state or federal legislation or any contractual agreements are determined by common law (court decisions that have precedential effect). The common law for ownership of inventions has been summarized by the Supreme Court of the United States as follows:

> One who is employed to make an invention, who succeeds during his term of service in accomplishing that task is bound to assign to his employer any patent obtained. The reason is that he has only produced that which he was employed to invent. His invention is the precise subject of the contract of employment. A term of the agreement necessarily is that what he is paid to produce belongs to his paymaster. On the other hand, if the employment be general, albeit it covers a field of labor and effort in the performance of which the employee conceived the invention for which he obtained a patent, the contract is not so broadly construed as to require an assignment of the patent [4].

Thus, absent some contractual arrangement, an employee's discovery generally belongs to the employee, unless the discovery is within the scope and purpose of employment.

For example, an employee employed as a buyer (order clerk) for a supplier of aircraft hardware, including nuts, bolts, screws, washers, O-rings, and cotter pins, was found to be a general employee (*i.e.,* not hired to invent) and, therefore, not required to assign his invention relating to a self-sealing fastener to his employer. On the other hand, if an employee is hired to invent something or solve a particular problem (*e.g.,* design engineer), then any inventions of the employee relating thereto would belong to the employer.

Further, just because an individual is hired as a consultant does not necessarily mean he or she is not hired to invent. In addition, a president or other officer of a company likely will be found obligated to assign his or her inventions to the company because state corporation laws require that officers owe undivided loyalty to the company.

23.3.2 Common Law—Shop Rights

Even when the employer is not entitled to the invention, the common law may give the employer some limited rights to use the invention. In particular, when the employee-inventor uses work time and/or employer's facilities, equipment, or materials in perfecting the invention, the employer is given a nonexclusive and nontransferable royalty-free license (referred to as a *shop-right*) to use an employee's patented invention. An employer having a *shop-right* can make use of the employee's patented invention (*e.g.,* make, use, and sell products incorporating the invention) without compensating the employee.

23.3.3 Assignment of Rights to Employer

For obvious reasons, employers want the rights to inventions and discoveries (and other forms of intellectual property) their employees have made. By controlling intellectual property rights, the employer can enjoy a competitive advantage over competitors, prevent competition from former employees, and yield greater profits.

To obtain control over intellectual property rights (including inventions and discoveries), most companies require assignment of such rights to the company in their employment agreements [5]. Most employment contracts contain specific provisions that obligate an employee to assign to their employer all inventions made while performing their job. The following paragraph is taken from the standard employment agreement of a Fortune 500 Corporation (CORP.) and is representative of such provisions:

> This Agreement concerns inventions and discoveries (whether or not patentable), designs, works of authorship, mask works, improvements, data, processes, computer programs and software (hereinafter called "Proprietary Developments") that are conceived or made by me alone or with others while I am employed by CORP., and that relate to the research and development or the business of CORP., or result from work performed by me for CORP. Such Proprietary Developments are the sole property of CORP., and I agree:
> a. to disclose them promptly to CORP.;
> b. to assign them to CORP.; and
> c. to execute all documents and cooperate with CORP. in all necessary activities to obtain patent, copyright, mask work and/or trade secret protection in all countries, CORP. to pay the expenses.

In essence, when you sign such an agreement as a condition of employment, you have agreed to assign away all rights to any inventions you may, in the future, make (if such inventions relate to the business of the company or result from work performed for the company). In this case, CORP. is said to have equitable title to your inventions. You have legal title to your inventions until you actually assign the invention to CORP. as you have contractually bound yourself to do. Note, with copyrights and semiconductor mask works, if an employee creates the work in the performance of his or her job, it's automatically the CORP.'s property and no assignment is necessary to transfer legal title.

There are, however, some limitations on employer's rights to your inventions. These limitations come from three sources: assignment provisions, courts, and state legislatures.

Assignment provisions typically do not require assignment of every invention an employee might make. For example, the representative assignment provision, provided above, requires that (i) the invention be conceived or made while an employee, and (ii) that the invention relate to the R&D or business of the CORP. This second limitation may not be much of a limitation if the CORP. is a multinational corporation with a wide range of diverse businesses.

Some companies assert rights to post-employment inventions of employees. In particular, some employment agreements include *holdover* provisions that require employees to assign inventions made after termination of employment if the invention made is a result of work done during employment. Typically, these clauses attempt to include inventions made one or two years after termination of employment. These *holdover* provisions are not favored by the courts because of their negative impact on the public and their hindrance on the employee's ability to obtain other employment. As a result, courts will only enforce *holdover* provisions that are fair and reasonable. For example, if an employee, in making an invention, does not use trade secrets or other proprietary information acquired while an employee, then a *holdover* provision would likely be unenforceable. Hence, the employee would retain ownership of the invention.

The laws of several states [6] also limit the ability of companies to force the assignment of your rights to inventions or discoveries in certain cases. In particular, overbroad assignment agreements required by employers will be unenforceable to the extent they are against public policy. The states with such specific legislation have made it clear what they deem against public policy. Generally speaking, as a result of such legislation, an employee-inventor will (despite an assignment provision to the contrary) retain title to inventions developed on his or her own time without using employer's equipment, materials, facilities, or trade secrets, unless the inventions relate to an employer's actual or reasonably anticipated business, or result from work performed by the employee for the employer.

23.3.4 Sale of Some or All Invention Rights to Another

In any case, whether the employee retains title or the employer acquires title, the owner of the invention or discovery may license or assign some or all of the patent rights to another. Assignments must be recorded in the U.S. Patent and Trademark Office. Thus, you can search the chain of title to a patent much the same way you do with real estate.

23.4 SUMMARY

Employers and employees alike can protect their ownership rights by some advanced planning. Employers should have an assignment provision in the employment contracts of all employees. The assignment provision should not be overbroad. Employees, on the other hand, who wish to make inventions apart from work, should work on those inventions only at home and without using the employer's materials, equipment, or proprietary information. By doing so, the employee eliminates any *shop rights* of the employer and reduces the likelihood that an assignment provision (if any) would encompass the invention. If the employee cannot avoid using the employer's materials, equipment, or proprietary information, the employee should attempt to obtain the employer's written permission beforehand. Employees of smaller companies may also desire to negotiate the terms of such assignment provisions before accepting employment (large companies will not negotiate).

NOTES

[1] Inventorship determinations are discussed in detail in the article of this edition entitled "Inventorship: Who Qualifies, and How?" written by Patrick D. Kelly.

[2] Mask works are protected by the Semiconductor Chip Protection Act, 17 U.S.C. §900, et seq.

[3]   Computer programs are protectable by both copyright law and patent law. Hence, although an employer owns a copyright to an employee-created computer program, an employee may still own patentable inventions lurking within the computer program.

[4]   *United States v. Dubilier,* 289 U.S. 178, 53 S.Ct. 554, 17 U.S.P.Q. 154 (1933).

[5]   As for government employees, Executive Order 10096 governs. Executive Order 10096 provides that the government shall obtain title to all inventions made by any government employee (1) during working hours, or (2) with a contribution by the government of facilities, equipment, materials, funds, or information or time of other government employees on duty, or (3) which bear a direct relation to or are made in consequence of the official duties of the inventor.

[6]   California, Illinois, North Carolina, Minnesota, and Washington.

PATENT EXAMINATION IN THE U.S. PATENT AND TRADEMARK OFFICE

Article 24

Al Lawrence Smith

Al Lawrence Smith is the Patent Examining Group Director of the U.S. Patent and Trademark Office. As Group Director, he manages a staff of 100 engineers and scientists engaged in the examination of patent applications. He is the originator of telephonic prosecution, whereby the examiner initiates an interview to reach agreement to place an application in condition for allowance, and he is the originator and writer of the "Helpful Hints" column, which appears in the Official Gazette of the Patent and Trademark Office.

The application has been prepared and filed with the Patent and Trademark Office (PTO). Then what?

When a patent application is filed with the PTO, it is assigned a serial number for identification and accorded a filing date. The application is then classified as to subject matter and assigned to a Patent Examiner having expertise in the particular technological area of the invention. The Patent Examiner then conducts an investigation, searches the PTO files to determine if there is any relevant prior art in addition to that supplied by the applicant, and mails what is known as an "Office Action" to the applicant's attorney.

The Office Action, in essence:

- lists all of the references considered by the Examiner;
- states any objection as to the form of the application or claims; and
- states as to each claim any substantive rejections, together with a detailed explanation as to precisely why the examiner considers the claims unpatentable.

Typical substantive rejections are to the effect that the claim is deemed anticipated, i.e., that all of the elements of the claim are thought to be disclosed by a single prior art patent or publication, or "rendered obvious" by a patent or publication or combination of prior art patents or publications.

After receiving the Office Action, the attorney typically forwards it, with copies of the references cited, to the inventor for review and comment. The inventor and/or attorney then analyze the Office Action and references. The analysis should identify:

- any errors in the positions taken by the examiner in the Office Action, e.g., erroneous characterization of the references;

250

- *for each claim, and each rejection, the differences between the subject matter described in each individual reference and (1) the* claim language *and (2) the preferred embodiment described in the specification;*
    If the examiner has rejected a claim as obvious over a combination of references, identify any reasons why the references cannot be combined as suggested by the examiner, and establish or confirm that the references do not suggest that it would be desirable to make the modification or combination of features suggested by the examiner; and
- *assuming for the purposes of argument that it is permissible to combine or modify the references as suggested by the examiner, the differences between the modified or combination references as suggested by the examiner and (1) the claim language, and (2) the preferred embodiment described in the specification.*

The attorney then drafts a response to the Office Action (assuming one is necessary). The response is typically due within three months of the mailing date of the Office Action, although up to three months additional time can be obtained through payment of extension fees. The response must answer each and every issue raised by the examiner by traversing (arguing against) the examiner's positions, amending the claims, or canceling the claims (that is, accepting the examiner's rejection). In effect, the attorney negotiates with the examiner to determine the exact scope of the claims to which the inventor is entitled.

It must be stressed that the language of the claims is controlling in arguing against a rejection; differences between the references cited and the preferred exemplary embodiment described in the specification are not typically relevant to the rejection. The response must explain to the examiner how the specific language of the claims is distinguished from the references. The claims, however, can be amended to include any detail described in the specification. That is the purpose of identifying the differences between the preferred embodiment and the prior art.

Assuming that an agreement is reached with the Examiner with respect to the exact scope of the claims, the application issues as a patent. If no agreement can be reached, an appeal can be taken to the Board of Patent Appeals and Interferences, and ultimately to the Federal courts.

In the following article, the Patent and Trademark Office provides some valuable insight into the examination process. MAL

Abstract

The patent examining staff of the U.S. Patent and Trademark Office includes about 1850 engineers and scientists. The examination of an application for patent consists primarily of studying the invention as disclosed, searching through the prior art, and communicating the decision to grant or refuse a patent. Refusal is typically based upon lack of novelty, obviousness, inoperativeness or lack of utility, and/or insufficiency of disclosure. The examiner's correspondence is specific in applying the relevant sections of the patent law, the pertinent prior art, and the examiner's reasoning, and includes copies of the pertinent patents and publications. Upon receipt of the applicant's response, which typically includes amendments and arguments, the application is reexamined and a final decision is communicated to the applicant. The examiner will assist the applicant in properly defining the invention in patentable terms if the invention is deemed patentable.

24.1 INTRODUCTION

Article I, Section 8, of the United States Constitution provides:

The Congress shall have the power to promote the progress of science and the useful arts by securing for limited times to authors and inventors, the exclusive right to their respective writings and discoveries.

Acting under that provision, Congress enacted the patent laws and established the Patent and Trademark Office (PTO) to administer the granting of these exclusive rights in the form of patents.

In the fiscal year ending September 30, 1993, the PTO received 188,369 patent applications and granted 107,332 patents. Typically, two-thirds of the applications become patents. Patented inventions provide a valid advancement of technology, and it is important that these patents be published as early as possible, so as to maximize their effect on industrial progress and their potential benefit to the inventors. The primary mission of the PTO, then, is to issue valid patents and to issue them in the shortest possible time.

The average application pendency time is typically 18 months (from filing to patent grant and/or abandonment). This seems to be the minimum period for Office efficiency and effective prosecution by the inventors and their attorneys. For many years, the average pendency was about 24 months. As the result of a major pendency-reduction campaign, the pendency was reduced to below 19 months in 1989. At this time, the pendency is about 19 months. The PTO's goal is to maintain an average pendency of between 18 and 19 months.

The PTO has a staff of about 1850 patent examiners, all of whom hold degrees in Engineering or Science, and many of whom also hold law degrees and/or advanced technical degrees. Each of these examiners is assigned to handle a relatively narrow segment of technology and becomes exceptionally knowledgeable in that particular art.

24.2 THE PATENT EXAMINATION PROCESS
IN GENERAL

The examination of a patent application is a unique effort requiring highly specialized knowledge and skill. A Patent Academy, plus about seven years of on-the-job training, prepares each examiner for the award of Primary Examiner status, with full and independent authority to grant or deny a patent.

The thought process required in the examination of a patent application is extremely complex. While reading the specification and drawings for an understanding of the invention, the examiner is also drawing conclusions as to what is known or suspected to be old, as well as trying to recognize what is new. The examiner's mind retains what is being read, while simultaneously planning the actual search that will be made in the files of prior art patents and publications. Efficient prosecution demands that the examiner's attention be directed toward the application disclosure as a whole, not merely to the claims. Otherwise, patentable subject matter may be overlooked. This open-minded approach must continue as the examiner conducts the search, and even while writing the letters rejecting the application throughout the prosecution. Such letters, or "Office Actions", are not considered complete until every effort has been made to identify and indicate any patentable subject matter.

The PTO examiners conduct a search for each application to determine whether the invention is new and unobvious. The search files are massive, containing more than 30 million documents. The more than 5 million U.S. patents are not only found in their original classified locations, but they also are cross-referenced into related subclasses, adding about 10 million additional documents. The PTO also has more than 13 million foreign patents and copies of articles from professional journals and the like. All of these documents are filed according to a continuously updated classification system which categorizes all technology into about 434 classes and 132,000 subclasses of subject matter. A large Scientific Library of over 120,000 volumes of technical texts, abstracts, periodicals, etc., and on-line computer access to numerous commercial databases are other resources used in the examiners' searches.

Unless a prior disclosure of precisely what has been invented is discovered during the search, the examiner must decide whether the invention would have been obvious to a person skilled in the art (the person of ordinary skill in the relevant technology) in view of the prior art disclosures found in the search. More controversy springs from questions as to the obviousness of subject matter than from any other source in the prosecution of a patent application. Reasonable people can, and often do, disagree as to what is, and what is not, obvious.

As indicated earlier, the PTO's primary mission is to issue valid patents as promptly as possible in order to promote technological growth. Thus, the examiners must have a positive attitude, rather than an adversarial attitude; and they must be willing to assist the inventors in defining their inventions in patentable terms as quickly as possible, if they are deemed patentable.

24.3 OVERVIEW OF EXAMINATION AND PROSECUTION

The examiner's examination of the application consists primarily of a study of the application for adequacy of disclosure, operability of the invention, compliance with formal and legal requirements, and a search through the prior art to see if the invention is new.

The applicant is notified in writing of the examiner's decision by an "Office Action", which is mailed to the attorney or agent and which typically sets a three-month period for response. The reasons for any adverse action regarding patentability, as well as any formal objections or requirements, are stated in the Office Action. Copies of information or cited references (prior patents, sections of the law, etc.) are included to aid the applicant in deciding whether to continue the prosecution of the application. If the applicant fails to respond, the application is held abandoned, and the applicant is so notified.

If the examiner finds that the invention as recited in the claims is not new, the claims are "rejected". The claims also may be rejected if they differ somewhat from what is found to be old, but the difference is not considered sufficient to justify a patent. It is not uncommon for some or all of the claims to be rejected in the first Office Action. Relatively few applications are allowed *as filed*. Thus, it is wise not to give up when a first letter of rejection arrives.

After the first Office Action, if adverse in any respect, the applicant, if he or she wishes to continue prosecution, must reply in writing within the time allowed, and may request reconsideration, with or without amendment. Extensions of the response time can be granted for a fee, but the maximum response period is six months, as set by statute. To be entitled to reconsideration, the applicant must respond to every requirement and every ground of objection and rejection stated in the Office Action. The applicant's response must be a bona fide attempt to advance the case to final disposition. A mere allegation that the examiner has erred will not be accepted as a proper response or reason for reconsideration. Specific arguments are required. The applicant must point out clearly the patentable features of novelty that the claims recite in light of the state of the art as disclosed by the cited prior art references. The applicant also must explain how any amendments to the claims that have been submitted avoid such references.

After a response is submitted by the applicant, the application is reexamined and reconsidered; and the applicant will again be notified if the claims are allowed or rejected, in the same manner as after the first examination. The second Office Action usually will be made final, whereupon the applicant's response is limited to an appeal in the case of a rejection of the claims. At this stage in the prosecution, further amendment is restricted, but not impossible. Response to a final rejection or action must include cancellation of, or appeal from the rejection of, each claim rejected, and if any claim stands allowed, compliance with any requirements or objections as to form. Another option available to the applicant is the filing of a "Continuation" application, which, if filed before the patenting or abandonment of the prior application, will receive the benefit of the filing date of the prior application. A continuation application provides the opportunity for further prosecution of the same invention before the patent examiner.

If the examiner concludes that all of the claims are allowable, the applicant is so notified by the mailing of a form entitled, "Notice of Allowance and Issue Fee Due", which sets a three-month period for payment of the issue fee. The patent is granted about three-and-one-half months after the PTO receives the issue fee.

Interviews with examiners may be arranged, but an interview does not remove the necessity for a written response to an Office Action within the required time. The action of the PTO is based solely on the written record. Interviews are available only after the first Office Action is received. They can be held only in the examiners' offices, and only during regular office hours. Interviews are generally requested by the applicant's attorney or agent to (1) seek clarification of the examiner's reasoning, (2) better explain the novelty and advantages of the invention, (3) display a model, (4) come to a meeting of the minds on the issues for appeal, and/or (5) negotiate mutually acceptable language to define the invention in patentable terms.

If two or more inventions are claimed in a single application, and are of such independent or distinct nature that a single patent may not be issued for both of them, the applicant will be required to elect one of the inventions and restrict the application to that one. The other invention may be made the subject of a separate application called a "Divisional" application, which, if filed while the first application is still pending, will be entitled to the benefit of the filing date of the first application.

If the inventor discovers an improvement over the invention disclosed in the application, this new subject matter cannot be added to the application. However, the inventor may file a *continuation-in-part* (CIP) application, before the first application becomes patented or abandoned, and receive the benefit of the filing date of the first application for all subject matter carried forward into the CIP application.

If the examiner persists in the rejection of any of the claims in an application, or if the rejection is made final, the applicant may appeal to the Board of Patent Appeals and Interferences in the PTO. This Board consists of the Commissioner, the Deputy Commissioner, the Assistant Commissioners, and a number of Administrative Patent Judges. Normally, each appeal is decided by only three members of the Board. An appeal fee is required with the Notice of Appeal. A brief to support the applicant's position then must be filed along with another fee. The examiner then prepares a brief, called the "Examiner's Answer". The applicant is entitled to an oral hearing if desired, also for a fee. If the decision of the Board of Patent Appeals and Interferences is still adverse to the applicant, the applicant has a choice of appealing to the Court of Appeals for the Federal Circuit, or filing a civil action against the Commissioner of Patents and Trademarks in the United States District Court for the District of Columbia.

Occasionally, two or more applications are filed by different inventors claiming substantially the same patentable invention. Under the United States *First-to-Invent* system, the inventor who was last in filing an application may be the one who is awarded the patent, provided that it can be proven that his or her later-filed invention was conceived before the invention of the earlier-filing adversary. The inventor who filed last also must show continued diligence in reducing his or her invention to practice. In this situation, since the patent can only be granted to one of them, the examiner will institute an "Interference Proceeding" to determine priority of invention, *i.e.,* who is the first inventor and thus entitled to the patent. Interference Proceedings may also be instituted between an application and an issued patent, provided that the patent did not issue more than one year prior to the filing of the conflicting application. Each party to an Interference Proceeding must submit evidence of facts proving when the invention was made. In view of the necessity of proving the various facts and circumstances concerning the making of the invention, inventors must be able to produce credible evidence. If no evidence is submitted, a party is restricted to the date of filing of his or her application as the earliest date; in which case the inventor who was first to file would receive the patent grant, based solely on the relative filing dates. The priority question is determined by a panel of three members of the Board of Patent Appeals and Interferences based on the evidence submitted. From the decision of the Board, the losing party may appeal to the Court of Appeals for the Federal Circuit for review, or may file a civil action against the winning party in the United States District Court. Because of this rare possibility of an "Interference Proceeding", inventors are cautioned to keep good shop notes and to date their entries, and to have them witnessed, dated, and signed periodically by two friends.

Inventors may also avail themselves of the PTO's "Disclosure Document Program", whereby they send a description of their invention to the PTO, along with a $10 fee, to be held by the PTO as evidence of their date of conception. This "Disclosure Document" is not a patent application and does not establish a "filing date". It would only come into play as evidence in an "interference" situation. If a patent application is not filed on the invention within two years, the Disclosure Document is destroyed.

24.4 TYPICAL GROUNDS FOR REJECTION, AND APPLICANT'S RESPONSES

The Patent Law provides that the applicant, the inventor, "is entitled to a patent" if the statutory conditions for patentability are met. Thus, it is incumbent upon the examiner to cite the authority and evidence upon which refusal is based. The examiner does this by "rejecting" the claims. Such rejections must include the applicable sections of the statute and rules, the supporting evidence, and the examiner's reasoning where appropriate or necessary. The Patent Law is codified in Title 35 of the United States Code, and the Patent Rules are codified in Title 37 of the Code of Federal Regulations.

The law also provides that, in order to be entitled to *a patent,* the invention as presented in the application must be new and useful, and must be adequately described such that any person skilled in the art could make and use the invention. The application must conclude with *claims,* which are definitions of the subject matter that the applicant regards as the invention. These *claims* are required to be in a particular form and must be so clear and specific that any artisan would be able to determine just what would infringe the claims. The claims are the operative part of the patent. Patentability and infringement are judged by the language and features recited in the claims.

24.4.1 Lack of Utility

If the examiner determines that the invention as described in the application is inoperative, the examiner will reject on the ground of lack of utility. Applicant's recourse is typically the presentation of a working model, test results, and/or testimony of experts.

24.4.2 Nonenabling Disclosure

If the examiner deems the applicant's disclosure of the invention insufficient to enable a person skilled in the relevant technology to practice the invention, the examiner will reject on the ground of nonenabling disclosure. Applicant's recourse is to attempt to persuade the examiner that the omitted details, structure, steps, or features are so well known and/or conventional in the particular art that the skilled artisan would readily apply them in the making or using of the invention.

24.4.3 Improper Claims

If the claims are vague, indefinite, confusing, etc., they will be so rejected. Applicant's recourse is to amend the language of the claims such that the scope of protection is clearly defined.

24.4.4 One Invention—One Patent

If the examiner finds that any of the claims in an application also appear in a "recently-granted" patent to the "same applicant", the examiner would reject those application claims on the ground of double patenting. A second patent may not be obtained on the very same invention because the seventeen-year term of a second patent would begin and end after that of the first patent, and the inventor's exclusionary rights would thus be effectively extended beyond the statutory maximum term of seventeen years.

The applicant's recourse in this situation is to cancel the rejected, essentially-duplicate, claims. As an alternative, the applicant could amend the claims by adding a feature that is "disclosed" in the second application, but that is not "claimed" in the earlier patent; in which case there would be no extension of the rights on the "same invention". It is the "claims" that define the scope of the exclusionary rights. However, if the additional feature is one that would be obvious, and which would not "patentably" distinguish the application claims from the claims of the earlier patent, the claims would be rejected on the ground of "obviousness-type double patenting". The aim here is to prevent prolongation of the patent term, by prohibiting claims in a second patent that are not patentably distinct from claims in an earlier patent. The applicant's recourse to overcome an obviousness-type double patenting rejection is the filing of a "terminal disclaimer", which disclaims the terminal period of the second patent's term that would extend beyond the expiration date of the first patent.

If that same inventor's first patent was granted "more than one year prior to the filing of their second application", the examiner's rejection would cite a section of the law known as the "statutory bar" provision. The applicant's recourse here is limited to cancellation of any essentially duplicate claims so rejected. Of course, any rejection may be appealed to the Board of Patent Appeals and Interferences.

24.4.5 Lack of Novelty and Loss of Right

If, in searching the prior art, the examiner finds a single prior patent or publication that "discloses" every feature recited in the applicant's claims, the examiner would conclude that the claimed invention lacks novelty. The examiner would reject the claims as being either "anticipated by" or "clearly anticipated by" that patent or publication.

The applicant's recourse depends first upon whether the claim is held to be "antici-pated by" or is held to be "clearly anticipated by" the cited prior art, *i.e.,* by the prior patent or publication. If the claim is rejected as being "clearly anticipated by" by the cited refer-ence, applicant's recourses generally are: (1) cancel or amend the claim; (2) request that an Interference Proceeding be instituted if the patent was less than one year old; or (3) attempt to prove by affidavit that the invention disclosed, but not claimed, in the patent is inopera-tive. Of course, any rejection based on prior art may be traversed by applicant explaining why, in his or her view, the invention as claimed is patentably distinct from the reference; however, this approach is rarely successful in the face of a "clearly anticipated by" rejection.

If every claimed feature and function is not blatantly and clearly shown in the refer-ence, the claim would be rejected as being only "anticipated by" (as opposed to "clearly an-ticipated by") the reference, *e.g.,* where the examiner regards the reference's rubber gasket as anticipating a "biassing means" recited in the claim, which biassing means is actually a coil spring in the applicant's disclosure; or where the examiner regards a claimed feature as being "inherent", though not disclosed or discussed, in the reference. In this instance, the ap-plicant may cancel or amend the claims or merely present test results or arguments in an at-tempt to convince the examiner that the reasoning used in the Office Action is without merit.

When rejecting claims in an application, the examiner construes the language of the claims in the broadest possible sense to ensure that the patent is appropriately limited, even to the point of rejecting the claims on nonanalogous prior art totally unrelated to the appli-cant's intended field of endeavor. For example, a claim reciting the features of a "javelin" might be rejected as being anticipated by a "toothpick", since size is generally irrelevant to patentability.

The applicant's recourse depends also upon the nature and dates of the prior art cited by the examiner. If the publication or patent date of the reference is more than one year prior to the applicant's "application filing date", the reference is a statutory bar, even if the prior patent or publication is applicant's own. The applicant has a duty of candor and good faith in dealing with the PTO, which includes a duty to disclose to the examiner all information known by the applicant, or by applicant's representative or assignees, to be material to patentability of the claimed invention. Also, if the examiner cites evidence of public use or sale, or even an "offer" to sell the invention, even if by the applicant himself, more than one year before the "application filing date", the applicant is "statutorily barred" from receiv-ing a patent under the "loss of right" provision in the law.

If the publication or patent date of the reference is prior to, but "less than one year" prior to, the application filing date, the examiner would reject by presuming that the appli-cant's filing date is the "date of invention". The examiner would conclude that the earlier-dated prior disclosure of the reference established prior public knowledge, or a date of "invention" by another earlier than that of the applicant. At this point the applicant's date of invention is only "presumed" to be the filing date for purposes of rejection. The appli-cant may be able to prove an earlier date of invention. If the reference is a patent, which "discloses" but "does not claim" the same invention, the applicant can, if the facts justify, submit an affidavit as to facts establishing that the claimed subject matter was invented prior to the "filing" date of the reference patent. This is called a *swearing back* affidavit and is provided for in the PTO Rules. Under the present law, only activity in the United States may be used to show facts leading toward completion of the invention.

If the reference is a patent, which "claims" substantially the same invention as does the applicant, a "swearing back" affidavit would not be permitted. However, an Interference Proceeding may be requested to determine which inventor is the first inventor and thus entitled to the patent rights.

The examiner would also reject the claims if the reference is a patent to another inventor that was "granted after" the applicant's filing date, but was "filed prior to" the applicant's filing date. Here again, applicant could use a *swearing back* affidavit to overcome the reference and avoid the rejection—unless the applicant and the patentee are "claiming" the same invention—in which case an Interference Proceeding would be available to determine priority of invention between the two parties.

24.4.6 Obvious to One of Ordinary Skill in the Art

If the examiner finds a prior art reference, which in-and-of-itself does not anticipate the applicant's claims, but concludes that the claimed differences did not require the exercise of inventive faculty, the examiner would reject the claims under the "obviousness" section of the statute. The examiner may apply the disclosure of a single reference or combine the teachings of multiple references in showing that the applicant's invention "would have been obvious to one of ordinary skill in the art to which the subject matter pertains". Since the inventor is "entitled to a patent" unless the examiner can show that application of the statute provides otherwise, the examiner bears the burden of proving that the invention is not patentable, and must present enough evidence to establish a prima facie case of obviousness of the claimed invention.

The types of evidence available to the examiner include: (1) prior art references; (2) admissions by the applicant; and (3) affidavits by the examiner and/or the applicant.

Prior art references that are legally available as evidence for this purpose are only those specifically spelled out in the Patent Law. Admissions are typically statements in the record by the applicant to the effect that something is old or well known in the art, or acknowledgements of prior use or sale of the invention by the applicant. Affidavits can be made by examiners if they have personal knowledge of the prior existence of something (rarely used), or by the applicant when attempting to establish certain data or information as fact.

In using the evidence to reject the claims, the examiner must consider:

1. the scope and content of the prior art;
2. the difference between the claimed invention and the closest prior art; and
3. the level of ordinary skill in the art.

Accordingly, the examiner's rejection would typically state, *e.g.,* "Claims 1 to 10 are rejected under 35 USC §103 as being unpatentable over Jones", or "unpatentable over Jones in view of Thomas and Walters". The examiner would then explain (1) what the Jones reference discloses, (2) what the difference is, *i.e.,* those features recited in the applicant's claims that are not disclosed by Jones, and (3) why it would have been obvious to one of ordinary skill in the art to modify Jones' teachings, specifically, how the Jones invention would be modified and why the artisan would have been motivated to so modify Jones' teachings as to yield the applicant's claimed invention.

When the examiner applies a combination of references, *e.g.,* "A in view of B and C", reference "A" is generally considered the *primary* reference, which discloses all except some details of the applicant's claims; and references "B" and "C" are the *secondary* references, which disclose those claimed details that are not shown in the primary reference. The examiner must show that there is some teaching, suggestion, or motivation for combining the features of the references. Otherwise, the examiner's rejection could be justly challenged as being based on "hindsight" prompted only by the applicant's disclosure of the combination of the features.

Applicant has several recourses in challenging a rejection based on "obviousness". The most typical, and often successful, arguments are:

1. Even as modified or combined, the resultant teachings still omit one or more of the applicant's claimed features.
2. The proposed modification of the primary reference destroys the intended operation, or purpose, of the primary reference's invention.
3. The proposed modification or combination results in an inoperative device.
4. The combined references are from nonanalogous arts that are so diverse that only through hindsight would someone find and combine them.
5. A *swearing back* affidavit is presented which demonstrates that the applicant invented the claimed invention prior to the date of the cited reference(s).
6. The prior art never recognized the "problem", or the "cause of the problem", cured by applicant's invention; and, thus, the invention as a whole is unobvious, even if the solution is, through hindsight, obvious.

The U.S. Supreme Court has ruled that certain "secondary considerations" bear on the legal conclusion of obviousness. Accordingly, the applicant also can attempt to rebut the examiner's showing of obviousness by presenting factual evidence of "secondary considerations", such as commercial success of the invention, or truly unexpected results, or the satisfaction of a long-felt need. These forms of evidence can be quite persuasive, particularly where the examiner's showing of a motivation or suggestion to modify or combine references is weak. However, evidence that merely proves that the applicant's invention is "better" than the prior art is usually insufficient, alone, to demonstrate unobviousness of an invention. There is no requirement in the Patent Law that a patentable invention be "better". It is only required that it be "new, useful and unobvious".

24.5 CONCLUSION

It must be recognized that this is a very brief introduction to the highly complex field of patent examination and prosecution. Patent practice is extremely complicated, which is why inventors are strongly encouraged to employ the services of registered patent attorneys or agents to file and prosecute their patent applications.

The primary role of the patent examiner is to examine patent applications and grant patents for inventions that satisfy the statutory requirements of novelty, usefulness, nonobviousness, and sufficiency of disclosure. They deny patents on inventions that do not add to the nation's technological wealth of knowledge.

The Patent and Trademark Office exists to serve the nation through the promotion of technological, industrial, and economic progress, by granting to inventors, for limited times, the exclusive right to their discoveries, but only if they are patentable under the law.

U.S. MAINTENANCE FEES— PATENT VALIDITY BY CHOICE NOT CHANCE

Marc Sandy Block

Marc Sandy Block is currently an Intellectual Property Law Counsel for two divisions of the International Business Machines Corporation. Other publications include articles in various bar journals and the *Journal of the Patent Office Society.*

Unexpected and surprising results should come from your patented invention, not your patent maintenance program.

Abstract

You created a pioneering invention, negotiated a patent application through the intricate passages of the patent system, and are finally granted a patent. As you look forward to your royalties, you realize that your patent comes in "installments". To keep your patent in force for its full life span of 17 years, you must pay periodic maintenance fees. This article will acquaint you with maintenance fee basics, some problems you might face, and some measures to take to manage your maintenance fees.

25.1 BASICS OF MAINTENANCE FEES

25.1.1 Due Dates

If you own a U.S. utility patent [1] granted on an application filed on or after December 12, 1980, three successive maintenance fees must be paid to keep your patent in force. Associated with each fee is a *window* period extending from 3 to 3.5 years after the patent is granted for the first fee and from 7 to 7.5 years for the second fee and from 11 to 11.5 years for the third fee. You can pay each fee within its associated window or you can pay during a six-month grace period following each window. If you pay within the grace period, however, you are subject to a surcharge in addition to the maintenance fee.

By way of example, if you received your patent on February 1, 1990, you can pay the first maintenance fee between February 1, 1993 and August 3, 1993 with no surcharge. (Because August 1, 1993, the date 3.5 years after the patent grant, is a Saturday, payment can be made on Monday, August 3rd—the next day that is not a Saturday, Sunday, or District of Columbia holiday.) By paying the surcharge, you can make payment during the grace period August 4, 1993 through February 1, 1994.

25.1.2 Small Entity Status

Referring to Figure 1, which lists relevant maintenance charges, your basic fees and grace period surcharge depend on whether you are a "small entity", as defined by the U.S. Patent and Trademark Office (PTO). You qualify as a "small entity" if you are an independent inventor, a nonprofit organization, or a "small business concern". A "small business concern" is defined in the law [2] and generally includes businesses having no more than 500 employees, assuming they do not transfer rights under the patent to someone who is not a small entity. When you qualify as a "small entity", your maintenance fees for a patent are reduced by 50 percent [3]. To establish your status as a small entity, you must send in a verified statement claiming the status before or when you make a payment. The PTO has forms you should use. Small entity status established during prosecution (when seeking a patent) carries over for maintenance.

25.1.3 Fee Schedule

Until recently, the rules distinguished between (1) patents based on applications filed between December 12, 1980, and August 26, 1982, and (2) patents based on applications filed on or after August 27, 1982. Not only did fees differ, but the small entity discount did not apply to applications filed in the earlier period. The fees changed on December 16, 1991, to provide one fee schedule (including the small entity discount) for all patents filed on or after December 12, 1980.

25.1.4 PTO Requirements

The PTO rules are specific about how and when to pay maintenance fees [4]. To accept your fee, the PTO requires that you provide the patent number and the application serial number. For a reissue patent, the patent number and serial number should correspond to the reissue (and not the original) patent. As noted in Figure 2, other information should also be provided [5].

While you can pay maintenance fees for more than one patent at a time, you cannot mix maintenance fees with other PTO fees. When submitting maintenance fees for more than one patent, the PTO suggests that you list the patents covered in chronological order (oldest at the top). If the payment made is inadequate, the PTO applies the payment received to the patents in the order listed. Contrary to the PTO suggestion, you might wish to list the patents in order of decreasing importance to your business, just in case there is some error, or insufficient payment.

MAINTENANCE FEE AMOUNTS
(Effective October 1, 1992)

Maintenance Fees are due for maintaining an original or reissue patent filed on or after December 12, 1980, except a design or plant patent.

FEE CODE	PAYMENT YEAR	FEE DUE	SMALL ENTITY
183/283	Due 3.5 Years	$ 930.00	$ 465.00
184/284	Due 7.5 Years	$ 1,870.00	$ 935.00
185/285	Due 11.7 Years	$ 2,820.00	$ 1,410.00

SURCHARGE

186/286		$ 130.00	$ 65.00

PETITION SURCHARGE AFTER EXPIRATION

187	$ 620.00
188	$ 1,500.00

EXPLANATION OF INFORMATION REQUESTED

1. Patent Number- The Patent Number of the patent on which a maintenance fee is being paid. Required by 37 CFR 1.366. For a reissue patent the original patent number, patent date and filing date should also be included between parentheses in the same box as the reissue patent data giving the reissue patent number, reissue patent date, and reissue application filing date respectively.

2. Fee Code- Patent and Trademark Office Fee Code listed above. Used by Office to credit fees to appropriate fee category.

3. Maintenance Fee Amount- Amount listed in 37 CFR 1.20 for maintenance fee being paid.

4. Surcharge Amount- If the maintenance fee is paid after the due date, a surcharge is required in the amount indicated in 37 CFR 1.20 (k)-(m).

5. U.S. Application Serial Number- The United States Serial Number of the United States application for patent on which a maintenance fee is being paid. Required under 37 CFR 1.366(c). The two digit series code should be included as part of the serial number. All applications filed January 1979 thru December 1986 have a Series Code 06/. All applications filed January 1987 thru present have a Series Code 07/.

6. Patent Date- The issue date of the patent on which a maintenance fee is being paid.

7. Application Filing Date- The United States filing date as defined in 37 CFR 1.362(c).

8. Payment Year- An indication should be made as to whether the maintenance fee being paid is that required to be paid by 4, 8, or 12 years after the patent date to prevent expiration of the patent.

9. Small Entity- Maintenance fees paid on patents based on applications filed on or after August 27, 1982 should also indicate by a "Yes" or "No" whether small entity status is being claimed.

Figure 1   An example of a schedule of maintenance fees.

MAINTENANCE FEE TRANSMITTAL FORM

U.S. Department of Commerce
Patent and Trademark Office

Address to:
Commissioner of Patents
and Trademarks
Box M Fee
Washington, D.C. 20231

I hereby certify that this correspondence is being deposited with the United States Postal Service as first class mail in an envelope addressed to "Commissioner of Patents and Trademarks, Box M Fee, Washington, D.C. 20231" on _____
Name of person signing _____
Signature _____

Enclosed herewith is the payment of the maintenance fee(s) for the listed patent(s).
1. ☐ A check for the amount of $_____ for the full payment of the maintenance fee(s) and any necessary surcharge on the following patent(s) listed.
2. ☐ The Commissioner is hereby authorized to charge $_____ to cover the payment of the fee(s) indicated below to Deposit Account No. _____.
3. ☐ The Commissioner is hereby authorized to charge any deficiency in the payment of the required fee(s) or credit any overpayment to Deposit Account No. _____.

*Information required by 37 CFR 1.366 (c) (columns 1&5). Information requested under 37 CFR 1.366(d) (columns 2-4 & 6-9)

ITEM	1 PATENT NUMBER*	2 FEE CODE	3 MAINTENANCE FEE AMOUNT	4 SURCHARGE AMOUNT	5 U.S. APPLICATION SERIAL NUMBER*	6 PATENT DATE [mm/dd/yy]	7 APPLICATION FILING DATE [mm/dd/yy]	8 PAYMENT YEAR	9 SMALL ENTITY?
1									
2									
3									
4									
5									
6									
7									
8									

Sub-totals - Columns 3 & 4

Total Payments

Use additional sheets for listing additional patents

(For Office Accounting Use Only)

*Respectfully Submitted:
_____
(Payor's Name)

_____
(Payor's Signature)

_____
(Payor's Telephone Number)

PAYOR NUMBER (if assigned) _____

FEE ADDRESS _____
_____
_____
_____

NOTE: All correspondence will be forwarded to the "Fee Address" or the "Correspondence Address" if no "Fee Address" has been provided. 37 CFR 1.363

*(WHERE MAINTENANCE FEE PAYMENTS ARE TO BE MADE BY AUTHORIZATION TO CHARGE A DEPOSIT ACCOUNT, FORM PTO-1536 SHOULD REFLECT BOTH THE PAYOR'S NAME AND SIGNATURE IN THE BOTTOM LEFT CORNER THEREOF.)

Burden Hour Statement

This form is estimated to take five minutes to complete. Time will vary depending upon the needs of the individual case. Any comments on the amount of time you are required to complete this form should be sent to the Office of Information Systems, Patent and Trademark Office, Washington, D.C. 20231, and to the Office of Information and Regulatory Affairs, Office of Management and Budget, Washington, D.C. 20503. DO NOT SEND FEES OR COMPLETED FORMS TO THIS ADDRESS. SEND TO: Commissioner of Patents and Trademarks, Box M Fee, Washington, D.C. 20231.

Figure 2 Sample Maintenance Fee Transmittal form

When payment is made, use a "Certificate of Mailing" or mail by U.S. Post Office Express Mail [6]. With either of these approaches, the PTO regards the payment as being made on the date of mailing. Payment should be addressed to:

Commissioner of Patents and Trademarks

ATTN: Box M Fee

Washington, D.C. 20231

When payment is credited, the PTO sends a receipt for the maintenance fee. The person tracking the maintenance fee payments should also track these receipts (or debits to your PTO deposit account) and provide an appropriate inquiry to the PTO if such proof of payment is not received in a reasonable time period.

To avoid maintenance fee problems, you might be thinking about paying all your maintenance fees up front. The PTO does not accept prepaid maintenance fees. If you have a PTO deposit account, can you authorize the PTO to debit maintenance fees before they come due? The answer is "no". The PTO will debit, on request, only maintenance fees that are currently due.

25.2 POTENTIAL PROBLEMS

The following illustrate some of the problems that can arise when paying maintenance fees.

One problem may involve your manner of payment. The PTO prefers a certified check, post office money order, or U.S. currency. You can also pay through your deposit account at the PTO (if you have one), provided the balance will cover the fee. A personal check drawn on a U.S. bank can be used if it is immediately negotiable.

If the check is not signed or if there are not sufficient funds, the check will not be considered payment. Or if the information provided is inconsistent, payment may not be credited.

A more subtle problem may arise in that the PTO can adjust the maintenance fees, as frequently as once every three years, to track the Consumer Price Index (CPI). Fee changes beyond the CPI may be authorized as well. In 1989, for example, fees jumped nearly 70 percent to help reduce the budget deficit. So the fees indicated in Figure 1 may change when your payment is due.

If you license a party who does not qualify as a small entity, you must indicate the status change to the PTO and the full maintenance fee (without the 50 percent reduction) must be paid. Failure to do so makes the payment improper.

The PTO may refuse to accept a payment made before the patent expires [7] for various reasons. If so, the PTO permits you to petition to have the refusal reconsidered [8]. If the petition is granted and the PTO was in error, you might be entitled to a refund of the petition fee. So your petition should include a refund request.

It may happen that payment is missed and the grace period runs out. On October 12, 1992, patent laws relating to delayed payments set new requirements [9]. Instead of requiring a showing of "unavoidableness" in all instances as in the past, the new law also authorizes the PTO to accept delayed payments that are "unintentional".

In either case, you must submit a petition and pay a petition fee in addition to the maintenance and surcharge fees otherwise due. If your petition is based on an "unintentional" delay, the fee (coded as 188 in Figure 1) is considerably greater than for an "unavoidable" delay (coded as 187). In either case, no discount is available for small entities.

You can, at any time, petition to show that a delayed payment was "unavoidable" by showing that "all reasonable care was taken to ensure that the fee would be paid timely". An error in a docketing system (that keeps track of maintenance fees) could possibly justify a finding of unavoidableness if it is shown that the system was properly designed and operated, and that the patentee took steps to make sure that the patent was entered into the system [10].

Justifying delay as "unintentional" can only be raised within 24 months after the grace period ends. After that you must show "unavoidableness".

Any attempt to justify a delayed payment should fairly represent the facts. As in all communications with the PTO, misrepresentations or fraudulent statements used to maintain a patent can carry serious consequences [11].

When the grace period ends, the patent is considered expired. If you petition the PTO to accept your late payment as unavoidable or unintentional, and the PTO accepts the delayed payment, your patent is reinstated. If your petition is denied, you can file yet another petition to have the matter reconsidered [12]. If, on reconsideration, your payment is accepted and the PTO determines that the initial refusal was due to PTO error, your petition fee may be refunded.

Your reinstated patent is then treated as if it had never expired, with one significant exception. If others took action during the hiatus between the end of a grace period and acceptance of a delayed payment, you might be limited or precluded from enforcing your patent against them. For example, suppose your competitor manufactured 1000 units of a new product (covered by your patent's claims) during the hiatus and sold the units after your delayed payment was accepted by the PTO. You would likely be unable to succeed in an infringement action against your competitor for those units.

Similarly, if an individual made an item (covered by your claims) during the hiatus and continued using it after the PTO accepted your delayed payment and reinstated your patent, you would have difficulty in enforcing your rights. But what if a competitor has capitalized a business during the hiatus but does not start making the "infringing" product until after reinstatement? In this and other situations, the court is authorized to do equity (or what seems fair) [13].

25.3 TIPS

There are a number of steps you, as a patent owner, can take to properly maintain the patents in your portfolio.

First, you or a maintenance fee administrator (such as your patent attorney) should have a system for tracking maintenance payments that are due. Make sure that the system is well-designed and that you can verify that your patents are properly entered. A similar suggestion applies to foreign patents that also require maintenance fees in their respective countries.

In addition, you should prepare a patent portfolio financial plan that is periodically updated. The plan balances costs for acquiring new patents with costs for maintaining granted patents. The plan should prioritize the value of your various patents to help determine which patents (if any) should be permitted to lapse. To make sure your valuable patents are maintained, communicate your findings to your administrator and have your administrator advise you of fee changes as they take effect. Make sure your administrator has your current address.

Depending on the economic climate or fee changes announced by the PTO, you might advise the administrator to make payment early or late in the permissible pay period.

The PTO provides notices concerning maintenance fees. An Official Gazette published by the Government identifies patents for which fees are due. Also, if you do not pay a fee within its window period, the PTO will send a notice to the "fee address" generally during the grace period. However, the PTO has clearly stated that these notices are just a "courtesy". Failure by the PTO to provide a notice or PTO errors in the notice do not relieve you of the responsibility to pay the fees in a timely manner.

Because rules and fees change, you need to have current information when paying your maintenance fees. The Patent Maintenance Division of the PTO periodically publishes a Customer Information Package that can keep you up-to-date.

25.4 CONCLUSION

Maintenance fees will never rise to the top of a patent owner's list of favorite topics. But the wise patent owner should know enough to ensure that any loss of rights is by choice rather than chance, and by forethought rather than forfeit.

NOTES

[1] Maintenance fees in the United States apply to utility patents. They do not apply to design patents nor plant patents (*i.e.*, patents on asexually reproduced plants protectible under the law). A utility patent is what you normally think of as a *patent*—namely a patent on a machine, article of manufacture, composition of matter, process, or some improvement thereof.

[2] The patent statute is found in Title 35 of the U.S. Code. The patent statute provides authorization for the PTO to make rules to administer the laws. Such rules relating to patents and the PTO are generally found in Title 37 of the Code of Federal Regulations (hereafter "CFR"). The precise definition of what business entities qualify for the reduced fee is set forth in 37 CFR 1.9. The definition of "small business concern", as copied from the U.S. Small Business Administration, is "an entity which (including affiliates) has no more than 500 employees and has not assigned, licensed, or obligated itself to transfer rights in the invention to a party who would not qualify for the reduced fees". Details about what constitutes "employees" and "affiliates" are outlined in 37 CFR 1.9 and 13 CFR 121.12.

[3] The 50 percent reduction is set forth in Title 35 of the U.S. Code at section 41(h), (35 U.S.C. §41 (h)).

[4] See 37 CFR 1.366.

[5] One such piece of information is the *payor number*. If you wish to designate someone to receive fee notices and pay your maintenance fees, you can send the PTO a *fee address*. The fee address is the name and address of your designee (which can be you). That fee address is given a *payor* number by the PTO and should be identified with your fee payments to expedite processing. If no one is designated, notices are sent to the *address for correspondence* used during patent prosecution.

[6] See 37 CFR 1.8 for Certificates of Mailing and 37 CFR 1.10 for Express Mail submission of papers to the PTO.

[7] A patent "expires" for nonpayment of the first, second, or third maintenance fee exactly four years, eight years, or twelve years after the patent is granted. Although expiration normally coincides with the end of the grace period, the grace period (but not the expiration) may include extra days if the last day of the grace period is a Saturday, Sunday, or District of Columbia holiday.

[8] See 37 CFR 1.377.

[9] See CFR 1.378(b) and (c).

[10] See 1046 Official Gazette 28–37; Notice of July 30, 1984, commenting on Rule 378.

[11] For example, see 18 U.S.C. §1001 for criminal penalties.

[12] See 37 CFR 1.378(e).

[13] Specifically, 35 U.S.C. §41(c) (2) states that:

> No patent, the term of which has been maintained as a result of the acceptance of a payment of a maintenance fee under this section shall abridge or affect the right of any person or his successors in business who made, purchased, or used after the six month grace period but prior to the acceptance of a maintenance fee under this subsection anything protected by the patent, to continue the use of, or to sell to others to be used or sold, the specific thing so made, purchased, or used. The court before which such matter is in question may provide for the continued manufacture, use, or sale of the thing made, purchased, or used as specified or for the manufacture, use or sale of which substantial preparation was made <during the hiatus> . . . to the extent and under such terms as the court deems equitable for the protection of investments made or business commenced <during the hiatus>.

OBTAINING PATENT PROTECTION OUTSIDE OF THE UNITED STATES

In today's global economy, a product may be marketed all over the world. There are also potential competitors all over the world, ready and able to copy any successful unpatented product they come across.

However, patents are limited in geographic extent. For the most part (other than in Europe), each country has a separate patent system that pertains only to activities that have a nexus to that country. For example, a U.S. patent will protect against manufacture, use, and/or sale of infringing products within the United States. This encompasses infringing products being imported into the United States from abroad and infringing products being manufactured in the United States and exported abroad. However, a U.S. patent has no application to situations where both the manufacture and the sale occurs outside of the United States. To protect against such situations, corresponding patents must be obtained in at least one strategic foreign country. Factors to consider in determining whether or not to pursue corresponding patents in a particular country include:

- *Is there a significant market for products using the invention in that country or is it likely one will develop in the future?*

- *Is it likely that there will be significant use of the invention or manufacture of products using the invention in that country?*
- *Are significant potential competitors or potential licensees located in the country?*

The strategy of pursuing corresponding foreign patents is discussed in more detail earlier in the book in Article 17, Using Engineering Expertise To Develop a Successful World-Wide Patent Portfolio.

It also is important to review the issue of pursuing patent protection in a particular country in the context of its intellectual property laws and the differences from U.S. law. Inventions that may be patentable in the United States may not be patentable in various other countries. For example, the United States provides a one-year grace period in which an application may be filed after a publication describing the invention. Most other countries provide no such grace period; they require absolute novelty. (This subject is dealt with earlier in the book in Article 12, Avoiding the Loss of Patent Rights.*)*

The converse is also true; it may be possible to obtain patent protection in countries outside of the United States on inventions that are rendered unpatentable in the United States by some peculiarity of U.S. law not found in the laws of the other country. For example, internal use of an invention by the inventor's company more than a year in advance of filing a patent application can be a statutory bar to patentability in the United States. It is not a bar to patentability in various other countries. It also may be possible to obtain broader and more significant patent protection in various countries than in the United States under some circumstances.

The differences between the intellectual property laws of the various countries and corresponding U.S. law can be subtle, but significant. It may be desirable to consult expert counsel from the individual countries during the decision making process, as well as in pursuing patents in that country.

This section of the book addresses the different vehicles for pursuing patent protection around the world and provides a comparison between the intellectual property laws of a number of countries and those of the United States.
MAL

272

Article 26

HOW TO FILE A PATENT IN FOREIGN COUNTRIES

Arnulf Huber

Arnulf Huber is a European Patent Attorney with the firm of Uexkull & Stolberg in Hamburg, Germany. He is registered to practice before the German Patent and Trademark Office as well as the European Patent Office.

Abstract

Patents can be filed in other countries besides the United States as (a) individual national patent applications, (b) a European Patent by using the European Patent Convention (EPC) covering 16 member states, or (c) an International Application by using the Patent Cooperation Treaty (PCT).

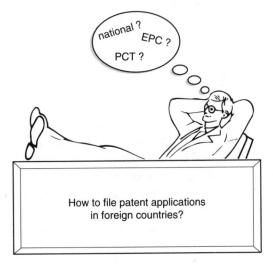

26.1 INTRODUCTION

It is generally accepted that patented inventions constitute a significant business value. This value is a function of the size of the market where the invention is patented. In other words, the invention is more valuable if it is patented both in the United States and in foreign countries to cover the larger market. However, since no such thing as a *world patent* exists, the inventor must apply for patent protection in each foreign country separately, in order to obtain a national patent in that country. Due to variations in the law of each country and also due to varying standards of living, it is both costly and time consuming to obtain national patents for an invention for which patent protection has already been applied in the United States. Although filing of separate national patent applications in each foreign country appears to be the logical way for obtaining patent protection abroad, there are other ways to achieve this goal: The European patent application and the International patent application.

Before discussing the aspects of national, European, and international applications, I should point out that foreign filings are only possible if (a) the invention has not been disclosed to the public prior to filing a patent application in the U.S. Patent and Trademark Office and (b) if the foreign applications are filed not later than one year ("priority year") from the filing date of the U.S. application. Both of the above requirements must be met. Foreign applications cannot be filed if the invention already has been used or published in the United States prior to filing of the U.S. patent application, in spite of the fact that such prior (public) use does not bar the inventor from obtaining a patent in the United States.

Before deciding how to apply for patent protection in foreign countries, the inventor or his assignee should establish where the markets are. Normally two factors define the markets for inventions: the size of the market and the standard of living in each of these markets. For the foreseeable future, the following markets outside of the United States appear to be of major commercial interest: Japan and South Korea of the Asian market; Canada and Mexico of the North American market; and Germany, Great Britain, France, Italy, and Spain of the European market.

26.2 NATIONAL PATENTS

If an inventor or a company decides to file foreign applications along the traditional route of national patent applications, orders should be given to file the individual patent applications well before the end of a 12-month period ("priority year") after the filing of the U.S. patent application, which allows the applicant to claim the original U.S. filing date. This gives the foreign patent agent time to prepare a translation into the respective national language from the U.S. patent application and to refer back to the U.S. attorney, in case additional information is required. One should always allow the foreign agent two months for preparing such national translations because many words are technical terms that cannot be translated directly into, *e.g.,* Japanese or German. Quite often ambiguities occur that appear to be clear to the writer of the English language text, but are not so to the translator of the foreign language. Other problems come from typographical errors, *e.g.,* inclined . . . inklined . . . ink lined. It is hard to believe how often such typographical errors occur and what serious problems they create for both the translator and the foreign agent during the prosecution of the foreign patent application.

The costs for filing individual national applications are normally in the same order of magnitude as the filing of the U.S. application, primarily because of the additional costs of translating and revising the application.

Once the foreign national application has been filed, the foreign legal system will process the application according to the laws of the respective country. Thus, wherever patents are examined, the national examiner will raise objections, which normally vary significantly from the objections raised by his counterparts in other countries. This makes it necessary to change the language of the claim and thus, when the national patent has issued, each patent may have a different set of claims and a different scope in each country.

26.3 EUROPEAN PATENTS

In 1979, a number of European states formed the European Patent Convention (EPC), which issues identical patents for each member state. In 1993, there were 16 member states to the European Patent Convention: Austria (AT); Belgium (BE); Switzerland (CH); Germany (DE); Denmark (DK); Spain (ES); France (FR); Great Britain (GB); Greece (GR); Ireland (IE); Italy (IT); Luxembourg (LU); Monaco (MC); The Netherlands (NL); Portugal (PT); and Sweden (SE).

Instead of filing national patents in any one of the above states, one can file a European patent application at the European Patent Office (EPO), which has its headquarters located in Munich, Germany. The applicant can select any combination of the above-mentioned EPC member states, and, although he can later cut down on the number of states, he cannot add any additional ones. Thus, it is recommended to designate all possible EPC states at the time of filing (in spite of the fact that this adds to the costs), if the applicant is not sure about the markets for the invention.

The European Patent Office (EPO) charges to the applicant a filing fee for each patent application plus designation fees for each selected state. In 1994, this fee was $210 per state, which was the minimum designation fee; the maximum designation fee for all 16 states amounted to $3360. An average for 5 states may be $1050. In addition to the EPO fees, there are agency fees charged by European patent attorneys, and these fees are normally in the same order of magnitude.

Additional costs include the search fee (about $1300) and claims fees for each claim over 10. The claim fee amounts to approximately $60; it can be substantial if the number of claims of a U.S. application is not reduced prior to filing in the EPO. As you may know, U.S. applications tend to have a significant number of claims in an attempt to claim the invention from every possible aspect, and because the U.S. system does not allow for claims that depend on more than one other previous claim. Since such a restriction does not apply to the EPO, it is generally possible to reduce significantly the number of claims prior to filing in order to save costs. It should, therefore, always be the inventor's or the applicant's goal to reduce the number of claims down to 10 when filing the application in the EPO, because the first 10 claims are free. It has been shown that in 90 percent of the European patents issued, the number of claims was ultimately reduced to 10 or fewer, even if filed with a larger number of claims originally.

Since the European patent application can be filed in the English language, there are a number of advantages, vis-á-vis individual national filings:

- Since no translation is required at the time of filing, the order to file a European patent application can still be given close to the end of the priority year. The foreign agent should not have problems filing a patent application in the EPO if he receives the specification, claims, and drawings (where applicable) less than one month before the end of said priority year.

- The European patent application will be processed and examined in English, thus enabling the inventor to understand the Examiner's arguments and to follow the proceedings.

- When the European patent issues, the claims are identical for all designated states and the inventor or applicant need not speculate about the kind of patent protection in each of the designated states.

However, after the EPO has issued the European patent, the applicant will have to validate this patent nationally in each state where he wants to have patent protection. At this point, he can pare down on the number of the selected states, if he so wishes. But wherever he wants to have a patent, he will have to appoint a national agent and perform through this agent certain steps before the respective national Patent Office. In addition, translations of the European patent must be prepared for those states where English is not an official language. The costs for such translations may be substantial because it is not simply a question of translating an English language text into a foreign language, but it is the translation of a legal document, which restricts the translator's freedom and requires more than ordinary skills of translation.

Although the costs for a European patent application appear to be high compared to a national patent application, it is generally considered that the break-even point for a European filing is with the designation of four EPC states. Thus, whenever the inventor or applicant desires to obtain patent protection in four or more EPC member states, the filing of a European patent application is certainly the best way of doing it.

26.4 INTERNATIONAL OR PCT APPLICATIONS

Another instrument of filing foreign application is the Patent Cooperation Treaty (PCT) whereby patent applications can be filed internationally. Through the PCT, an inventor can file an International Application at the U.S. Patent and Trademark Office and specify an even larger number of states than in the EPO. In 1994, there were 55 member states to the Patent Cooperation Treaty. It should be noted that the EPC states can be selected in the international (PCT) application both as one region (EPC), or as individual national states (*e.g.,* U.S., JP, DE, FR, GB, IT).

Although the filing of international PCT applications appears to be quite simple, a number of errors may be made if one is not really an expert in this field and some of these errors can never be remedied. If such errors occur, the International PCT Application will be lost irrevocably and no patent can be obtained in one or all of the selected PCT states. For example, if one forgets to mark the box for Japan, the application will be lost for this country because Japan does not allow for any correction of the PCT filing documents. The international PCT application is of most utility when the applicant:

- is very close to the end of the priority year for filing foreign applications, *i.e.,* probably within ten days or fewer to the end of this year, or
- wants to delay the payment of some of the national filing fees and translation costs for eight to eighteen months. An experienced U.S. attorney always should be consulted when filing a PCT application. Otherwise the damage could be tremendous.

A PCT filing also can be a source of value, particularly when corresponding applications are expected to be filed eventually in many countries. The PCT search may uncover prior art that would limit the scope of allowable claims so that it may no longer be worth filing the patent application broadly or at all. The search and preliminary examination afforded by the PCT also sometimes make it possible as a practical matter to dispose of at least some aspects of the prosecution of the patent in a single proceeding thus sparing the attorney the necessity of providing the same argument repeatedly in many different national prosecutions.

26.5 CONCLUSION

If one considers the filing of patent applications in foreign countries, one should do this well before the end of the priority year, preferably ten months after the filing date of the corresponding U.S. patent application. The foreign filings should be effected individually; only for last-minute-situations the applications should be filed by way of the Patent Cooperation Treaty (PCT). If there are three or more West-European member states among the desired countries, it is likely that these are members to the European Patent Convention (EPC). In such a case, the European patents should be obtained through the European Patent Office.

Article
27

DIFFERENCES BETWEEN U.S. AND AUSTRALIAN INTELLECTUAL PROPERTY LAWS

Trevor N. Beadle

Trevor N. Beadle is a registered Patent Attorney and a member of the firm Carter Smith & Beadle practicing in their Melbourne Office. He is a Fellow of the Institute of Patent Attorneys of Australia.

Abstract

This article provides a comparison of Australian intellectual property laws to the law applicable in the United States.

27.1 INTRODUCTION

The Australian intellectual property laws have many broad similarities to the law applicable in the United States enabling the grant of patents for a wide range of inventions as well as the protection of trademarks, designs, copyright, and copyright-style protection for new integrated circuits.

The major differences are:

- Australian law is based on first to file rather than first to invent;
- A system of deferred examination has been adopted with the proviso that the Commissioner of Patents can direct an Applicant to request examination;
- Modified Examination involving amendment of an application to correspond to an equivalent patent in the United States, Canada, Europe, or New Zealand;
- Pre-grant Opposition is still available in Australia;
- Post-grant reexamination can be requested; and
- Petty patents having a term of only six years are available.

The Australian intellectual property laws are otherwise quite similar to the U.S. laws requiring enforcement of intellectual property rights through the Australian Court system.

The Australian intellectual property system is based on the intellectual property laws in force in the United Kingdom at the turn of the century. However, from the 1950s, Australia has adopted a number of intellectual property provisions that are uniquely Australian, although there is government support for the harmonization of Australian intellectual property law with those of other countries.

While each of the branches of the Australian intellectual property law can be regarded as being broadly similar in general thrust to the equivalent laws of the United States, there are a number of specific differences. The Australian intellectual property laws operate to grant valid intellectual property rights to all applicants, irrespective of their country of origin. The legal system, by means of which those intellectual property rights are enforced, is independent and regularly decides disputes between parties without any bias in favor of the local party.

In common with the laws of the United States, the intellectual property laws of Australia are principally divided into laws relating to patents, trademarks, designs, and copyright. The law relating to each of these branches is defined by separate legislation. Disputes relating to Secret Use and Confidential Information are decided under the Common Law, and there is no specific legislation covering such matters. Australia has "Anti-Trust" legislation in the form of the Trade Practices Act, which is sometimes used to prevent unfair competition not covered by the Trade Marks legislation or by the Common Law of Passing Off. Australia also has specific legislation relating to the protection of integrated circuits, and this legislation will be briefly discussed later. The emphasis of this article will be on Patents and related protection in Australia.

27.2 PATENTS

Apart from one significant difference, the Australian patent system is basically similar to the U.S. patent system, and most inventions that are capable of patent protection in the United States would be capable of patent protection in Australia. Thus, using the case of software related inventions as a topical example, the Federal Court of Australia recently held in *International Business Machines Corporation v. Commissioner of Patents* (22IPR417) that the claimed invention need only involve the production of some commercially useful effect in order to be patentable. This test of patentability is now adopted by the Australian Industrial Property Office (Patent Office) and replaces the previously adopted test used by the U.S. Patent Office, which was considered and criticized by the U.S. Court of Appeals for the Federal Circuit in *Arrhythmia Research Technology Inc. v. Corazon Lr Corp*, 22 USPQ2d 1033, which indicated that the test was no longer appropriate.

27.3 EARLY PUBLICATION

In common with most countries other than the United States, Australian patent applications are published as a matter of course, before grant, once 18 months have elapsed from the earliest priority date.

27.4 NOVELTY AND INVENTIVE STEP

In common with the U.S. law, Australia requires an invention to be novel and inventive over matters already known in a particular field. The novelty and obviousness tests applied in Australia are broadly similar to those applied in the United States with the notable exception that Australian law does not provide the twelve-month "grace period" provided by U.S. law. Thus, Australian law is based on the principle of "first to file" rather than on the U.S. principle of "first to invent". However, Australian law does provide for the filing of so-called Provisional Patent Applications, which may contain only a limited description of the invention. The Provisional Application has a restricted life of twelve months and must be followed by the filing of a Complete Application, containing a full description of the invention, within the twelve-month life of the Provisional Application. Patent applications based on overseas applications must be filed with a Complete Application.

27.5 EXAMINATION

Australian law also requires patent applications to be examined. Recent changes introduced by the extensively amended Australian Patents Act 1990 require that the Examiner should not only consider the issue of novelty but also consider the issue of inventive step or obviousness having regard to what was known in a particular field before the filing date or before the International Priority date in the case of an application based on an International or overseas filing. However, in considering the question of inventive step or obviousness, the Australian Examiner is, unlike the U.S. Examiner, not entitled to combine patent or other literature in considering what is inventive in a particular industry, unless one piece of literature contains a clear cross reference to the other piece of literature in a manner that would have directed the person skilled in the relevant industry to read that other piece of literature effectively as a single document. Australian Examiners are entitled to combine proven common general knowledge in a particular industry in Australia with a piece of pertinent literature provided the literature would be reasonably expected to have been found, understood, and regarded as being relevant by a skilled person in the relevant industry. Although there has not been any significant experience with examination under the amended Act, the above tests provide Australian Examiners with far more onerous tests than those faced by U.S. Examiners. It is expected that inventions that may not be regarded as being patentable in the United States on the ground of obviousness would in many cases satisfy the inventive level test in Australia.

Unlike the U.S. law, examination in Australia is not performed as a matter of course. Australia adopted a deferred examination system with the uniquely Australian variation that the Commissioner of Patents is able to direct an applicant to request examination within a predetermined time to enable the Patent Office to examine patent applications in a more orderly manner. If examination is not requested by the applicant within the predetermined time after direction or within five years of the date of filing in Australia, the application lapses. A request for examination must be accompanied by the prescribed fee and the applicant has the option of choosing Ordinary Examination or Modified Examination. Modified Examination is a process in which the patent application is amended to correspond to an equivalent patent issued in an English language form. Thus, Modified Examination can be based on a corresponding U.S. patent, a European patent (if written in the English language), a Canadian patent, or a New Zealand patent to name the major possibilities. Modified examination is also uniquely Australian and appeals to many U.S. based applicants. However, the Australian Patent profession has some reservation concerning the desirability of Modified Examination, particularly when based on U.S. patents. Patents granted on the basis of Modified Examination must be interpreted according to Australian law, and Australian Courts will, in many instances, interpret the amended specification in a manner quite different from U.S. Courts. Thus, professional advice should be sought before deciding to request Modified Examination.

27.6 OPPOSITION

Australia is one of the last English-speaking countries to retain pre-grant opposition. The Australian opposition system allows any person to oppose the grant of a patent on the ground that the invention claimed is not novel or is not inventive or that the specification of the patent application is not adequate in some material respect. The opposition process involves the filing of a Notice of Opposition followed by the filing of a Statement of the Grounds and Particulars of the opposition, which outlines the nature of the opposition to the application, followed by the service of evidence in support of the grounds of opposition. The applicant has the right to serve evidence in answer to the evidence in support, and if evidence in answer is served, the opponent has the right to serve evidence in reply. The preceding summary of the opposition procedure is highly simplified. If further information is required, an Australian patent attorney should be consulted.

27.7 GRANT

If there is no opposition to an application following its acceptance by the patent Examiner, or if the opposition is decided in favor of the applicant, the application proceeds to grant on payment of a sealing fee.

27.8 ANNUITIES

Australian law requires the payment of patent annuities on an annual basis from the third year following the filing of an application. The patent annuity fees increase in a relatively linear manner on an annual basis. An Australian patent has a maximum term of sixteen years from the date of application. Only pharmaceutical patents can be extended for four years if a significant delay in regulatory approval can be shown.

27.9 REEXAMINATION

The amended Patents Act 1990 introduced for the first time the availability of a reexamination process for patent applications filed under the amended act. Australian practitioners have had no direct experience with the Australian reexamination procedure but it will operate in an essentially similar manner to the U.S. reexamination procedure.

27.10 PETTY PATENTS

Australian law provides for the grant of a petty patent, which has a term of only six years. Petty patent applications are automatically examined and no pre-grant opposition is possible. However, a form of post-grant opposition is available within the first year of grant of the patent.

27.11 LITIGATION

Litigation of Australian patents is before the Federal Court of Australia, or any other prescribed Court, including the Supreme Courts of the various States. The Supreme Courts are Courts of first jurisdiction in Australia. Appeals from decisions of a prescribed Court are to the Full Court of the Federal Court with final appeal to the High Court of Australia only in cases authorized by the High Court. Patent litigation in Australia is essentially similar to patent litigation in the United States with most infringement actions being coupled with attacks on the validity of the patent. However, all Australian patent litigation is traditionally heard by a single judge and, while jury trials are not prohibited in the Supreme Courts, patent litigation is invariably heard by a judge. Litigation in Australia is significantly less expensive than litigation in the United States, and the court procedures in Australia are under review in an endeavor to reduce the cost of litigation, although there is still a considerable way to go. Typical Australian costs per party range from about $50,000 to $500,000, with higher costs being possible where the matter is particularly complex and bitterly fought.

27.12 DESIGNS

The Australian Designs Act provides for the registration of designs applied to articles and relating to their shape and configuration or pattern and ornamentation. Australian law specifically allows the registration of functional shapes so the registrability of designs is not limited to ornamental considerations as is the tendency with the patenting of designs in the United States. Design registrations are relatively quite limited in scope, and Australian Courts usually only find infringement where the alleged copy is very similar to the registered design. It may be of interest to readers to know that printed circuit board designs are registrable under the Australian Designs Act.

27.13 COPYRIGHT

The Australian Copyright Act automatically protects copyright in relation to literary or artistic works, including computer programs, whether in written or electronically stored form. Where an artistic work is susceptible to industrial application and the corresponding design is not registered under the Australian Designs Act, and is capable of registration, copyright in the industrial application of the artistic work is no longer enforceable once the design has been industrially applied and sold or offered for sale in Australia. For this reason, it is important to consider whether a design registration should be obtained before industrial application and sale or offer for sale in Australia.

27.14 INTEGRATED CIRCUITS

The Circuit Layouts Act 1989 provides automatic copyright-style protection for all new integrated circuits first commercially exploited in Australia or in an eligible foreign country. The eligible foreign countries include the United States since similar legislation provides protection for integrated circuits. From the commencement of this Act, integrated circuits are no longer registrable under the Australian Designs Act, although, as mentioned above, printed circuit board designs are registrable. Original circuit layouts are automatically protected by the Act and unauthorized copying of the layout constitutes an infringement under the Act. Such infringement is actionable in an eligible Australian Court.

DIFFERENCES BETWEEN U.S. AND CANADIAN INTELLECTUAL PROPERTY LAWS

Jeffrey W. Astle

Jeffrey W. Astle is an Associate with the Patent and Trademark Institute of Canada.

Abstract

This article provides a brief review of some aspects of the Canadian patenting system and describes where it deviates significantly from the U.S. system. Also discussed are other forms of intellectual property protection available in Canada.

28.1 PATENTS

Conveniently for American inventors, the Canadian patent law system is similar in many respects to the U.S. patent law system. Some differences, however, are noteworthy.

Substantial and significant amendments made to Canada's Patent Act on November 19, 1987 [1] converted Canada's patent system from a "first-to-invent" patent system (similar to the U.S. system) with a generally applicable two-year grace period, to a "first-to-file" patent system with a modified absolute worldwide novelty requirement. With the conversion of the patent system came an optional deferral of examination of the patent application and a laying open of the patent application making the application available for public inspection. For the most part, the amendments were made so that Canada's patent laws conformed with the requirements of the Patent Cooperation Treaty (PCT). The effect of these amendments is discussed below.

28.1.1 Historical

The patent law of Canada is based upon its Patent Act [2]. Canada's current Patent Act is derived from the 1869 patent statute [3] which was generally modelled after the U.S.' patent statute of 1836 [4]. The Patent Act today is the product of many amendments made over the years; however, with its roots in the 1836 American statute, the law of patents and patenting in Canada shares many similarities with U.S. patent laws.

28.1.2 Rights Afforded to Applications Previously Filed in the United States or Other Countries

Both Canada and the United States are adherents to international reciprocal patent treaties. In Canada, this is relevant for the purpose of determining who was the "first-to-file" a patent application, as well as for determining which prior art references are applicable for examining a patent application.

When a patent application filed in Canada claims priority from an originating U.S. application filed within the preceding twelve months, the corresponding Canadian application is deemed to have a "priority" date of the U.S. application; for the purposes of prosecuting the Canadian application, it is as if the application was filed on the date that the U.S. application was filed.

28.1.3 Requirements for Obtaining a Patent in Canada

Requirements for obtaining a Canadian patent are categorized and described in the following paragraphs:

28.1.3a The Applicant

Unlike the United States (save for exceptional cases when an applicant is unavailable or uncooperative), the applicant for a patent in Canada may be the inventor or an assignee of the inventor. When the applicant is an assignee, an original or notarized copy of the assignment of the Canadian rights to the invention must be filed with the Canadian Patent Office, evidencing the assignee's rights. In Canada, a valid assignment must include a witness to the inventor's signature.

28.1.3b The Subject Matter

Most subject matter acceptable for patenting in the United States is acceptable for patenting in Canada. Worthy of note, however, are differences with respect to the patentability of lifeforms, methods of medical treatment, and computer software.

Lifeforms

Certain classes of lifeforms may be patentable in Canada.

The United States has blazed trails with respect to the patentability of lifeforms; Canada, on the other hand, has not chosen which trail it will ultimately follow. At present, Canada's law relating to the patentability of man-made lifeforms remains unclear. A recent Supreme Court of Canada decision that rejected a patent application for a variety of soybean for insufficient disclosure avoided answering the question of whether such lifeforms are patentable in Canada [5]. Therefore, it is not known whether a man-made lifeform may be acceptable subject matter for a patent in Canada, even if adequate disclosure can be made. Where, however, a simple lifeform was capable of being described as possessing uniform properties and characteristics (*i.e.,* a microbial culture), as opposed to its varied characteristics as a multi-celled lifeform, patent protection has been obtained in Canada [6].

For new varieties of some plant species, one might consider filing for protection under Canada's Plant Breeders' Rights Act [7] as an alternative to pursuing patent protection.

Methods of Medical Treatment

Inventions relating to a process or method of treating living humans or animals by surgery or therapy have been held to be unpatentable subject matter. The courts have ruled that such a method does not produce a result that is in relation to trade, commerce, or industry or a result that is essentially economic. For example, a method of medical treatment that lies in the field of professional surgery cannot be considered an "art" or "process" within the meaning of the Act [8]. Articles or apparatuses that are designed for use in the treatment of humans or animals, or diagnostic methods, may be patentable [9].

Computer Software

Where computer software produces a useful end result beyond simply solving an algorithm, it may be patentable in Canada.

Generally, the Patent Act provides that "no patent shall issue . . . for any mere scientific principle or abstract theorem" [10]. On this basis, Canada's Federal Court of Appeals has held that a patent may not be obtained for computer software that simply utilizes a computer to perform mathematical calculations [11]. Patents have been granted where the use of the computer software is applied to a physical system (*i.e.,* an elevator system and a strategy to provide priority service to one floor) [12].

Canada's Copyright Act [13] provides means of obtaining protection for computer software as a "literary work".

Copyright subsists in a work once it is created. Registration is not required, but offers certain presumptions such as ownership and the existence of copyright and is therefore useful in litigation. Copyright rights typically last for fifty years following the death of the author.

28.1.3c Requirements for Patentability

Corresponding to the requirements for patentability contained in the U.S. patent law found in 35 U.S.C. §§101, 102, and 103, the Canadian patent law has required that the claimed subject matter of a patent application satisfy three criteria: novelty, utility, and nonobviousness.

Novelty

In both the United States and Canada, the novelty aspect of patentability requires that an invention be demonstrably different from the "prior art". The prior art comprises patents, technical articles, public disclosures, etc., relevant to the invention. The determination of what comprises the prior art differs significantly in Canada.

In the United States, citable prior art includes all non-trade secret information known by others in the United States, or patented or described in a printed publication anywhere, before the invention was invented by the inventor. Prior art further includes anything patented or published anywhere, or in public use or on sale in the Unites States, more than one year prior to the filing date of the inventor's patent application. This is a "first-to-invent" system.

In Canada, citable prior art consists of any invention described in another patent application filed in Canada having a filing date or priority date preceding the earliest of the filing or priority date of the subject application, as well as any information available to the public anywhere, prior to the earliest of the filing date or priority date of the subject application. One exception to this is that knowledge available to the public in the one year period prior to the actual filing date of the patent application, which has been derived, directly or indirectly, from the inventor, is not considered part of the prior art. This is Canada's "first-to-file" system [14].

Utility

Utility, that is, the requirement that the invention accomplishes some desired objective, is comparable in both the United States and Canada.

Nonobviousness

Nonobviousness, the requirement for an inventive step (that "spark" of ingenuity), is implied, but not defined in Canada's Patent Act. The test for nonobviousness in Canada has been judge made. As a result, with the recent conversion to a first-to-file system in Canada, there may be room for argument as to what comprises citable prior art for this aspect of patentability. Statutory amendments enacted, but not yet in force, indicate that the prior art applicable in determining nonobviousness will be information available to the public anywhere prior to the earlier of the priority or filing date of the application, with the exception of information available to the public anywhere which was disclosed, directly or indirectly, by the applicant, unless it was available to the public more than one year prior to the Canadian filing date of the application [15].

As a result of Canada's first-to-file provisions, where a previously filed foreign application cannot be relied upon for a priority date, a patent application must be filed in Canada in a timely fashion.

28.1.4 The Application

The format of a U.S. patent disclosure and claims is generally acceptable for filing in Canada. In Canada, applications may be filed in the English or French language.

28.1.5 Differences in Prosecuting a Canadian Patent Application

All Canadian patent applications are laid open for public inspection shortly after eighteen months from the earliest of the priority or filing date of an application [16]. Unlike the

United States, Canada only maintains the secrecy of a patent application until it is laid open. A Canadian patent application may be withdrawn and secrecy of the subject-matter maintained by providing a timely request to the Canadian Patent Office [17].

As a result of the laying open of a patent application in Canada, where a patent ultimately issues from a laid-open application, a patent owner may sue one who has infringed the claims of a laid-open patent application for "reasonable compensation" from the laid-open date to the date of issue of the patent and for regular damages (or other remedies) from the date that the patent issued [18]. The differences between "reasonable compensation" and regular damages have not yet been determined by the Courts.

Annual maintenance fees must be paid for pending patent applications and issued patents from the second to the nineteenth anniversaries of the Canadian filing date [19]. In the United States, maintenance fees are payable only on the three and one-half, seven and one-half and eleven and one-half year anniversaries of the date of issue of a patent to maintain the patent in force.

In the United States, the examination of patent applications is not deferred. An applicant for a patent in Canada may defer examination of the application for up to seven years from the date of filing [20]. By deferring examination, an applicant may direct its attention to prosecuting the U.S. patent before pursuing prosecution of the corresponding Canadian application. Further, once the U.S. patent issues, a voluntary amendment to the claims of the corresponding Canadian application incorporating the claim amendments made during the prosecution of the U.S. application will very often result in the expedited allowance of the Canadian application.

A U.S. patent may remain in force for seventeen years from the date of issue. An issued Canadian patent remains in force for twenty years from the filing date of the Canadian patent application [21]. Therefore, while an applicant is not prejudiced by delays in obtaining issuance of a U.S. patent application, the longer a Canadian patent application remains pending during examination, the less time the resulting patent will be in force.

Recent amendments to the Patent Act included a provision permitting filing prior art protests to pending applications. Any person may, in reference to a pending patent application, file with the Canadian Patent Office prior art that that person believes would have a bearing on the patentability of any claim of the pending patent application [22].

28.2 OTHER FORMS OF INTELLECTUAL PROPERTY PROTECTION

Protection for aesthetic features applied to functional objects may be protected under Canada's Industrial Design Act [23].

An application for an industrial design must be filed within one year from publication of the design in Canada. An industrial design registration will provide exclusive rights for an initial period of five years, which may be maintained for an additional five years upon payment of a government fee.

Another available form of intellectual property protection is provided by Canada's recently enacted Integrated Circuit Topography Act [24], which provides protection for the three-dimensional configuration of chips and semiconductor chips. Protection of an original circuit design has a duration of ten years. Application within two years of commercial use of the design is necessary.

NOTES

[1] R.S., 1985, c.33 (3rd. Supp.).

[2] R.S., 1985, c.P–4, as amended by R.S., 1985, c.33 (3rd Supp.); S.C., 1992, c.1; S.C., 1993, c.2; S.C. 1993, c.15.

[3] Patent Act, S.C., 1869, c.11.

[4] 5 Stat. 117.

[5] *Pioneer Hi-Bred Ltd. v. Canada* (Comm'r of Patents), [1989] 1 S.C.R. 1623.

[6] *Re Application of Abitibi Co.* (1982), 62 C.P.R. (2d) 81.

[7] S.C., 1990, c.20.

[8] *Tennessee Eastman v. Commissioner of Patents* (1972), 8 C.P.R. (2d) 202 [S.C.C.].

[9] *Re Application for Patent of Goldenberg* (now Patent No. 1,244,344 (1988), 22 C.P.R. (3d) 159.

[10] Patent Act, s.27(3).

[11] *Schlumberger Canada Ltd. v. Commissioner of Patents* (1981), 56 C.P.R. (2d) 204 [F.C.A.] leave to appeal to S.C.C. refused.

[12] *Re Application for Patent of Westinghouse Electric Corporation* (No. 1) (1985), 9 C.P.R. (3d) 202.

[13] R.S.C., 1985, c.C–42.

[14] Patent Act, s.27.

[15] S.C., 1993, c.15.

[16] Patent Act, s.10.

[17] Patent Act, s.10.

[18] Patent Act, s.55.

[19] Patent Act, ss.27.1 and 46.

[20] Patent Act, s.38.1.

[21] Patent Act, s.44.

[22] Patent Act, s.34.1.

[23] R.S.C., 1985, c.I–9.

[24] S.C., 1990, c.37.

DIFFERENCES BETWEEN U.S. AND EUROPEAN/U.K. INTELLECTUAL PROPERTY LAWS

Matthew Read

Matthew Read is a European and U.K. Chartered Patent Attorney and a partner in the firm of Venner Shipley & Co. in London, England. He has been a contributor to the AIPLA Journal in relation to U.K. and EPC developments concerning the patentability of software-based inventions.

Abstract

Differences between European and U.S. patent laws can give rise to practical difficulties when it is desired to extend patent protection from the United States into Europe. Features of the European Patent Convention are discussed and compared with U.S. patent law. Also, a comparison is made between U.S. and U.K. law for designs, copyright, mask works, and trademarks.

You may be asking yourself—why should I bother to read this? What is the point of studying U.K. intellectual property law, apart from a perverse interest in how the law would have been if the United States had lost the War of Independence.

As I sit in my office in the heart of the City of London, within a stone's throw of St. Paul's Cathedral, I am very clear as to the answer to this question. The United Kingdom has now become part of Europe. Europe is a major world trading block with a population greater than that of the United States and a similar geographical area. Many high-tech companies are based in Europe, so United States corporations need to protect their technology here in order to maintain a competitive edge. Many major U.S. corporations file patent applications in Europe, and this forms a substantial part of my workload.

Europe as a trading block consists of a collection of European countries, each with their own national laws, operating within the Treaty of Rome, so as to provide a single trading area known as the European Union. In a number of areas, the laws of the individual European countries have been harmonized. One of these areas is patents. However, it is important to remember that each country maintains its own national identity and its own laws.

29.1 PATENTS

Each European country has a Patent Office for granting its own national patents under its own laws and procedure. Additionally, as part of the European harmonization process, a European Patent Office (EPO) has been established, which allows a single application to be processed for up to 17 European countries (as of March 1994). The application can be processed in English, French, or German at the choice of the applicant. Before the advent of the European Patent Office, individual patent applications had to be filed in each country of interest, which required a translation into each of the local languages and the payment of Official Fees to each Patent Office concerned. This was very expensive. The European Patent Convention (EPC) allows a single application to be processed which, for U.S. applicants can be filed in English, with a substantial saving in fees. The EPC system does not grant a single patent for Europe but instead results in the grant of a bundle of national patents in the countries concerned, which are then maintained by the payment of renewal fees to the individual national patent offices.

This brings me to the first major difference between the U.S. and European systems. For Europe, it is necessary to choose between the EPC or National Route; in the United States, you only have one Patent Office.

The relative merits of filing individual national applications or a single application at the EPO are discussed in more detail in Article 25. However, if you are interested in three or more European countries, a European Application at the EPO is generally cheaper than individual national applications.

29.1.1 Novelty Requirements

It is common ground that for a valid patent, an invention needs to be new. The definition of novelty, however, varies from country to country and whenever patent attorneys from different countries meet, they usually end up arguing about the relative merits of their national novelty requirements. We British take a broad view since patents have been part of our history for hundreds of years, prior to the Industrial Revolution, and in those days, the Sovereign granted patents for many different monopoly rights, for example the supply of saltpetre, oil of blubber, and other commodities. It was only with the advent of the Industrial Revolution that it was considered necessary for a patent to be for a novel invention.

U.S. law takes a very commonsense view of novelty based upon the date of conception of the invention. Thus, in U.S. litigation, much consideration is given to the date at which the inventor actually conceived the invention. In contrast, for the EPC, United Kingdom, and most other countries of the world, the date of filing the patent application at the Patent Office is the critical date; no consideration is given to the date of conception as such. The U.K. and European "first-to-file" system is in some ways unfair to an inventor who is slow to file a patent application but is much simpler to administer than the U.S. system because there is no requirement to review the inventor's notebooks or other papers to determine the date that the invention was actually conceived.

The first-to-file system always has been a feature of U.K. law and there are some interesting cases from many years ago when inventors would, in a race to obtain a filing date after the Patent Office had closed for the day, attach the patent application to a brick and throw it through the Patent Office window in the presence of a witness.

The U.S. novelty requirements are generally less onerous than the corresponding EPC and U.K. requirements. Under U.S. law, a person shall be entitled to a patent unless the invention was known or used by others in the United States or patented or described in a printed publication in the United States or in a foreign country either prior to the applicant making the invention or more than one year prior to filing the U.S. application. The more onerous so-called "absolute" novelty requirement of the laws of the United Kingdom and most European countries stipulates that the invention must not be part of the "state of the art", which comprises all matter which has been made available to the public anywhere in the world by written or oral description, by use or in any other way. Thus, unlike in the United States, use anywhere can be a bar to novelty.

U.S. law also includes a user-friendly feature not found in the laws of the United Kingdom or other European countries. This is the so-called one-year grace period. Under U.S. law, the inventor has a period of one year from his or her own public sale use or publication of the invention to file a patent application at the U.S. Patent Office. There is no corresponding one-year grace period in the Patent Laws of the EPC countries. Therefore, use of the one-year U.S. grace period can have disastrous consequences for a U.S. inventor who wishes to extend his or her patent protection abroad, as I will now explain. For most U.S. inventors, patent applications abroad are filed under the Paris Convention. This International Convention, to which most major industrial countries are a party, allows applicants to file corresponding applications abroad within one year from the initial filing date in their own country. The foreign applications are entitled to "claim priority" from the first filed application so that the foreign applications have an effective filing date that is the same as the initially filed application.

Consider now the following example:

U.S. Inventor A devises an improved semiconductor device which is disclosed at a trade show in the United States [.] Product literature is released. There is great commercial interest and a U.K. manufacturer shows interest in a license deal. Two months later, a U.S. patent application is filed. Nine months later a corresponding EPC patent application is filed designating the United Kingdom, France, and Germany, claiming priority from the U.S. application.

Since the European application was filed within 12 months from the U.S. application, a valid priority claim can be made under the Paris Convention and hence the effective filing date of the European case is the same as that of the U.S. application.

The U.S. application has been validly filed since it was filed within the one-year grace period under U.S. law. However, the corresponding European application is invalid. No recognition is made of the U.S. grace period under the various European laws and so the disclosure of the invention at the trade show constitutes part of the "state of the art" as regards the novelty of the European application. Hence, the European application is incurably invalid and the inventor has irrevocably lost the right to patent protection in Europe, which could have disastrous consequences for the proposed license deal since there are no patent monopoly rights to license.

The moral of this story is that a patent application must always be filed before publicly disclosing the invention, if foreign patent protection is to be obtained.

29.1.2 Continuation-In-Part Application

Another user friendly feature of U.S. law is the so-called *continuation-in-part* (CIP) application, which is a further patent application that builds on a previously filed or parent application, and usually includes additional information about the invention. Great care has to be taken if the CIP application is used to build corresponding foreign applications. Under the Paris Convention, it is only possible to file corresponding foreign applications based upon the first application for protection filed within 12 months from the original filing date in the United States. Therefore, for a CIP application filed more than 12 months after the original U.S. application, it is only possible to direct foreign application to the new matter of the CIP. It is not possible to obtain claims directed to the original idea disclosed in the parent U.S. application even though the idea disclosed in the parent U.S. case has not been published. The 12 month rule of the Paris Convention prevents valid foreign protection being obtained. It may seem that I am highlighting a rather esoteric difference in the laws, but this problem often arises because U.S.-based applicants frequently try to use a later filed CIP application to extend protection abroad. Usually, however, only very narrow protection indeed can be obtained in this way.

29.1.3 Secrecy

U.S. patent applications remain secret until the date of grant. In contrast, U.K., EPC and most other European national applications are published after 18 months from the earliest priority date. This is an automatic step in the application procedure and is intended to provide early disclosure of the content of the application. Thus, in practice, if an EPC application is filed under the Paris Convention, say 11 months after the original U.S. filing, the EPC application will be published 7 months thereafter, *i.e.,* 18 months from the original U.S. filing date. This can be an important consideration if it is desired to keep an invention secret for commercial reasons.

29.1.4 Patentability of Computer Software

The position under the EPC and in the United Kingdom is generally similar to that in the United States and software-based systems are often patentable. However, the method of analysis is somewhat different. Programs for computers are excluded from patentability under U.K. and EPC statutes, but this is only in respect of the program as such and if software is embodied in a system that produces a novel technical effect, it will be patentable. Mathematical methods and methods of presentation of information are not patentable. The upshot of this is that software packages such as accounting systems and wordprocessors, generally speaking are not patentable, but systems that give rise to a technical effect, such an image enhancement by pixel data processing or microprocessor controlled machinery, are patentable. Generally, if your U.S. attorney advises that a U.S. patent can be obtained, it is highly likely that corresponding patent can be obtained in Europe/United Kingdom.

29.2 OTHER FORMS OF PROTECTION

From Mike Lechter's introduction, it will be appreciated that patents are only a part of the entire intellectual property picture since protection also can be obtained in respect of designs, copyright, mask works, and trademarks. In Europe, so far, harmonization has only been achieved in respect of patents. A treaty has been drawn up for trademarks and probably will be implemented eventually. No progress has been made in respect of designs or copyright. These matters will be considered below, but solely in relation to the United Kingdom.

29.2.1 U.K. Registered Designs

A U.K. Registered Design corresponds to a U.S. design patent and protects the appearance of an article. The novelty requirements for a U.K. Registered Design is based on an old, imperial concept of novelty, which can be quite useful for a U.S. applicant. The novelty requirement is "local", which means that only disclosure of a design in the United Kingdom is considered pertinent. Thus, publication of a design in a document in the United States, which does not reach the U.K. shores, is not relevant.

Also, a design that has been manufactured in fewer than 50 samples even if published in a document remains new as far as the filing of a Registered Design is concerned.

Usually, for U.S. applicants, a U.S. design patent is filed first, and then corresponding applications are filed abroad under the Paris Convention. For designs, the convention period is six months (rather than 12 months for patents). However, if the six-month deadline is missed, in many instances, it is still possible to file a valid non-convention Registered Design Application in the United Kingdom due to the unusual novelty requirements. Also, some of the other European countries provide a period of grace for filing designs, so it is always worthwhile checking the law in the countries of interest even if the six-month convention period has passed.

29.2.2 U.K. Copyright

U.K. Copyright Law has recently been amended. For designs made prior to the amendment, three dimensional articles are entitled to copyright protection in certain circumstances. This copyright is based on the original engineering drawings for a product, which is infringed by copies that are themselves made by copying an article validly made from the drawings. This is an automatic right of protection. This copyright applies to designs produced before August 1989 and extends to engineering drawings made in the United States.

For designs made after August 1989, a new form of protection has been introduced known as the Unregistered Design Right. This replaces copyright for three-dimensional articles, which gave rise to much difficulty. The Unregistered Design Right is akin to copyright and provides automatic protection for the appearance of articles designed after August 1989. Unfortunately, the Unregistered Design Right does not extend to designs made in the United States unless the original design was first marketed within the European Community.

Consequently, automatic copyright style protection for three-dimensional articles has effectively ceased for U.S. designs produced after August 1989. Thus, if protection is required, a Registered Design Application must be filed.

For designs made before that date, copyright protection continues but for a term of 10 years only *i.e.* until August 1999, with licenses being available as of right to third parties from August 1994.

29.2.3 Computer Software in the United Kingdom

U.K. Copyright subsists in U.S. originating software products. They are deemed to be "literary works" and are afforded the same kind of copyright protection as books and other written matter. The U.K. Copyright Act includes a very broad definition of literary work, which includes the usual forms of programming within its scope. Protection is automatic and there is no registration procedure.

29.2.4 Mask Works in the United Kingdom

U.S. originating mask works are provided with automatic protection. U.K. law treats them in the same manner as an Unregistered Design Right. Protection is automatic without a registration procedure and the duration is normally 10 years from the date of first marketing but with a maximum term of 15 years from creation.

29.2.5 U.K. Trade Marks

Trademarks are registered at the U.K. Trade Marks Registry, in much the same way as trademarks are obtained in the United States. There are some esoteric differences between the two trademark systems but as a practical matter, if a trademark can be obtained in the United States, it is highly likely that a corresponding trade mark can be registered in the United Kingdom.

DIFFERENCES BETWEEN U.S. AND JAPANESE INTELLECTUAL PROPERTY LAWS

Shusaku Yamamoto

Shusaku Yamamoto has over twenty years of practice as a patent attorney. He is the founding member of the Shusaku Yamamoto Patent Law Offices in Chuo-Ku, Osaka, Japan. Mr. Yamamoto is well versed in both Japanese and U.S. patent law. He is the author of numerous publications and has lectured at corporations throughout the world. He is also a member of the Licensing Executives Society and other international professional organizations.

Abstract

This article provides a comparison of Japanese Intellectual Property laws to the law applicable in the United States.

30.1 INTRODUCTION

Since 1979, the U.S. Government has actively pursued a policy of strengthening its laws protecting intellectual property rights with the intention of maintaining its position as the world's economic leader. The founding of the U.S. Court of Appeals for the Federal Circuit in Washington, D.C., in 1981 to specialize in patent matters and the broad application of the doctrine of equivalents, all of which cause a pro-patent age in the United States, form part of that policy.

To effectively achieve that policy, the U.S. Government has strongly demanded that Japan harmonize and remove the significant differences between U.S. and Japan's intellectual property laws, especially patent laws and their application.

This is desirable not only to American companies but to Japanese companies in view that nowadays, with the advent of economic globalization, boundaries between countries are disappearing. Japan is pressed to eliminate the peculiarities in its patent laws and application and to resolve the outstanding significant issues between the United States and Japan such as the long pendency period before a patent is granted, narrow claim interpretation, etc.

Only significant differences in patent laws between Japan and the United States are discussed here, and in light of recent amendments to the Japanese patent practice effective retroactive to January 1, 1988, and amendments to the patent law, which came into force on January 1, 1994.

30.2 FIRST-TO-FILE SYSTEM

One of the fundamental differences between the U.S. and Japan's patent systems is that Japan has adopted the first-to-file system. This means that in cases where more than two applications are filed with regard to the same invention, the patent is granted to the applicant who files first. The filing date is the date on which the application is deposited at the Post Office. Japan does not have the first-to-invent system of the United States. Accordingly, there are no interference procedures in Japan, which involve lengthy and costly debates over who is the first to invent.

In cases where both applications are filed on the same day, directed to the same invention, the applicants have to decide among themselves through negotiations as to who will receive a patent. If no agreement can be reached, then both applications are rejected, thus making it likely that an agreement will be reached. In cases where a party who steals an invention from the inventor or the successor files an application thereon, the application is rejected. Even though the application is granted as a patent by mistake, the patent will be invalidated by the Board of Appeals (Board) of the Japanese Patent Office (JPO).

In the United States, the first person to invent is determined according to conception and reduction to practice in the United States. Acts occurring outside the United States, other than filing a priority patent application, have no effect in determining the date of invention. This discriminates against foreign inventors who invent outside the United States and are limited to their foreign priority date when attempting to establish the first date of invention, and is one of the major issues in international harmonization.

30.3 GRACE PERIOD

As in the United States, if a disclosure of the invention has been published anywhere in the world, that publication can be an effective prior art reference against a Japanese application. However, the publication will not be considered a prior art upon which the application can be rejected if the application was filed within six months of the date of the publication [1]. This grace period is one year in the United States.

There is unfortunately a 1989 Supreme Court decision to the effect that, if a foreign (*e.g.*, United States) patent was issued before the inventor or the applicant files the counterpart Japanese application, that U.S. patent constitutes an effective prior art reference against the Japanese application even though the Japanese application was filed within the six-month grace period from the publication date of the U.S. patent [2].

In my view, it is very strange that such a Japanese counterpart application, even though filed within the six-month grace period, will be rejected as a result of the publication of the foreign patent obtained by the same inventor or applicant. In light of the movement toward worldwide harmonization of patent laws among the JPO, the U.S. Patent and Trademark Office (PTO) and the European Patent Office (EPO), it is likely that this decision will not be applied by the JPO or the court in future decisions. In the United States, such a publication of a foreign patent will not be an effective prior art reference against the U.S. application if the application was filed in the PTO within one year of the publication of the foreign patent.

30.4 THE LAID-OPEN SYSTEM (KOKAI)

In Japan an application is "laid-open" to public inspection 18 months after the effective filing date of the application (*i.e.,* the date of mailing at the Post Office or the priority date of the basic application, whichever is earlier). The invention becomes publicly known at this time even though a patent may not have actually issued on the application. This is different from the U.S. system where an application is kept secret until a patent actually issues. A laid-open application can be used as a prior art reference against applications filed anywhere in the world after the Japanese laid-open date.

Once an application has been laid-open (Kokai), the applicant is entitled to provisional protection of the claimed invention in return. However, this is limited to the right to collect money compensation from an unauthorized person who commercially worked the invention. The amount of compensation is only equivalent to what the applicant would normally be entitled to receive for the working of the invention had it been patented. To exercise this right, the applicant must first send a warning letter to the other party. Liability to pay compensation starts from the day the other party receives the warning letter. The letter may be sent anytime after Kokai, but the right to obtain compensation may not be exercised (*i.e.,* the applicant cannot sue to recover the compensation) until after the application has been published for opposition purposes later.

30.5 REQUEST FOR EXAMINATION SYSTEM

Unlike the United States where the PTO examines an application on its own accord, in Japan, it is necessary to make a request for examination of the application. This request can be filed by any person within seven years from the actual filing date in Japan. Allowing persons other than the applicant to file a request for examination prevents deliberate delay by the applicant to the detriment of another party who has a similar invention which he wants to commercialize and who needs to know whether or not the pending application will ultimately be granted. After the request is made, the JPO will examine the application. If no request is made, the application is deemed withdrawn.

30.6 PUBLICATION FOR OPPOSITION SYSTEM (KOHKOKU)

If the JPO examiner accepts the application, it will be published for opposition. This publication is referred to as a Kohkoku. Upon Kohkoku, the applicant has a conditional patent right, *i.e.,* the exclusive right to work the invention for a maximum period of 15 years from the date of the Kohkoku. This is, however, subject to the life of the patent not exceeding 20 years from the effective filing date of the application. Therefore, if the request for examination was delayed for the full seven-year period and the examination process took three years before Kohkoku was made, the life of the patent will be only ten years, not 15 years, from the date of the Kohkoku. However, in the United States, the life of a patent is 17 years from the date of issue of the patent, regardless of how many years the application process took.

30.7 PRE-GRANT OPPOSITION SYSTEM

An opposition can be filed to a published application (Kohkoku). The opposition can be filed by any person within three months of the Kohkoku. An opposition brief containing full arguments and evidence in support can be filed within 90 days after the three-month opposition period has passed. If the application is rejected as a result of the opposition, and that rejection becomes final and conclusive, the applicant loses the exclusive right to make, use, and sell the invention. Further, the exclusive right shall be deemed not to have been created from the beginning; therefore, if the applicant or his authorized users had meanwhile exercised his exclusive rights granted under the Kohkoku, he has to compensate the other party for any damages that he has thereby caused.

Such a system where a patent issues only after a published application is opposed is one of the causes of the backlog problem in Japan. In the interest of international harmonization of patent laws, this will, in the near future, be changed to a system where a patent issues before the opposition period.

There is no opposition system in the United States. However, a reexamination system exists, which is similar to the post-grant opposition system of the EPO. Although a third party may request the PTO to reexamine the patent, this is different from the opposition system because he may only initiate the reexamination; he cannot participate in the substantive reexamination of the patent by the PTO.

30.8 DISCLOSURE REQUIREMENTS

Disclosure requirements in Japan are somewhat similar to those in the United States. The application must contain a disclosure of the invention and a statement of the objective, structure, and effect of the invention to such an extent as to enable those skilled in the art to easily carry out the invention. The best mode is not a requirement in Japan, although required in the United States. This can cause problems if an application was filed first in Japan and then filed in the United States claiming priority based on the Japanese application. This is because the later U.S. application is often prepared to conform in all respects to the Japanese application on which priority is claimed.

The claimed subject matter must be supported by the disclosure. This requirement was especially strict in Japan with respect to chemical cases, which require specific examples supporting the scope of the claims and not merely a broad, general statement of the invention disclosure. Previously, in cases where the application did not satisfy this requirement, the claims were required to be restricted to the specific examples disclosed in the specification; otherwise, the application was rejected because of insufficient disclosure of the invention. This is one of the major problems causing serious trade friction between Japan and the United States.

For the purpose of harmonization, Japan has reformed the JPO Manual of Patent Examining Procedure (Japan MPEP) by relaxing the disclosure requirement. In the new Japan MPEP issued on June 21, 1993, which follows the U.S. position, the disclosure requirement will be satisfied even though the claims are drafted beyond the disclosure of the invention in the specification, provided the concept of the claimed invention corresponds with what has been disclosed in the specification, and the objective, structure, and effect of the claimed invention are described in the specification. This means that applications that disclose a broad, general statement of the invention and specific examples supporting only part of the scope of the claims will no longer be rejected.

The new Japan MPEP confirms a 1983 Tokyo High Court decision [3]. It is also revolutionary because this practice will be retroactive to 1988 and all patent applications filed since 1988 will have the benefit of this new, relaxed disclosure requirement.

30.9 AMENDMENTS

Amendments to the claims, specification, and/or drawings can be filed only at the following times:

- within one year and three months from the effective filing date;
- when a request for examination is filed;
- within three months from the date the applicant was notified by the JPO that a third party had filed a request for examination;
- when responding to the first official action;
- when responding to the second and subsequent official actions; and
- when appealing to the Board of Appeals of the JPO against the examiner's final rejection.

Under the prior laws, amendment of claims may be made relatively freely. This is no doubt to compensate for Japan's first-to-file system where claims may have been drafted hastily and the application filed in a rush. Thus, claims may be enlarged, and even if the amendment of the claims, specification, and/or drawings introduce new matters into specification that have not been described in the originally filed specification and drawings, the amendment will be permitted so long as it does not change the gist of the invention disclosed in the originally filed specification.

However, each amendment results in a fresh prior art search by the examiner; therefore, to cut down on delays and to accord fair treatment between an application that has been excessively amended and one that has not, the new patent law effective on January 1, 1994, has drastically restricted the scope of permissible amendments. Amendments can be made only within what has been explicitly disclosed in the originally filed specification and drawings, and new matters cannot be introduced. Even if an application with such amendments receives a patent, such a patent can be invalidated before the JPO Board. Moreover, in the last two of the above-listed situations, amendments to the claims are limited to the following: (i) a cancellation of claims; (ii) a restriction of the scope of claims; (iii) a correction of errors in the description; and (iv) a clarification of ambiguous descriptions. The same applies to amendments made after the decision to publish the application for opposition.

With the new restrictions on amendments, it is more essential than ever that well drafted specification and claims of a quality high enough to cover broad claims, yet be acceptable to the JPO, be filed right from the beginning.

30.10 *SUBMARINE PATENTS* IN THE UNITED STATES

In the United States, although applications may not be amended to introduce new matter that was not disclosed in the originally filed specification, such new matter can be easily introduced into the specification by filing continuation-in-part (CIP) applications. There is no limit as to the number of CIP applications that may be filed so long as they are filed while the parent application is still pending. As a result, the patent application can be kept pending for many years, especially since there is no restriction that a patent's life may not exceed 20 years from the date of application, as in Japan [4].

Moreover, because the United States does not have a laid-open system, the invention remains secret until it is actually granted as a patent [5]. For these reasons, a surprisingly old, low technology invention suddenly emerges, submarine-like, as a patent and this damages companies that have meanwhile developed more advanced technologies without knowing that such a submarine patent existed [6]. This is also one of the major issues between Japan and the United States.

30.11 APPEALS BEFORE THE JPO BOARD

30.11.1 Invalidation of Patent

The validity of an issued patent can be challenged. A validity question is examined and decided only by the JPO Board. If the defendant counterclaims for invalidity during an infringement suit, he has to file a separate invalidation appeal to the Board. Meanwhile, the rest of the suit is stayed. The Board's decision is made in light of novelty and unobviousness requirements similar to those in the United States. Questions of sufficiency of the disclosure of the invention also are addressed. Validity challenges can be made even after the expiration of the patent.

In the United States, validity challenges may be made in the PTO or in the courts. A challenge in the PTO is made by requesting reexamination of a patent on the grounds that new prior art disclosing the invention has been found. More commonly, a validity challenge is made in a court as a counterclaim by a defendant in a patent infringement suit. It also can be brought in an action for declaratory judgment by a party who has been threatened by the patent owner with infringement. The declaratory judgment makes it possible for an infringer to take the initiative by seeking the court's decision that the patent is invalid and thus not infringed.

30.11.2 Correction of Patent

In Japan, after the patent has issued, the claims of the patent can be corrected by filing a Correction Appeal, but it cannot be substantially enlarged or changed. In contrast, the United States has a reissue patent system that is available to correct errors made without any deceptive intention by the applicant. Where a reissue application is filed within two years of the issue date of the original patent, any claim of the original patent may be enlarged provided the additional subject matter had been disclosed in the granted patent. However, broadened claims (and in some cases, even narrowed claims) may not be enforceable against third parties who have relied upon the original claims.

30.11.3 Appeal against a Final Rejection

If, after examination, a final rejection is sent out by the examiner, an appeal can be filed in the Board within 30 days of receipt of the final rejection. If an appeal is filed together with an amendment to the rejected claims, the application is transferred to the Examination department where the amendment is first examined by an examiner. If the examiner maintains his position, then the application is retransferred to the Board where the application is examined by three Appeal examiners.

In the United States, after a final rejection, the applicant no longer has any right to unrestricted further prosecution. This is the same in Japan under the new patent law, which allows, for example, amendments to be made by adopting suggestions made by the examiner and/or by canceling claims. An applicant, who has been given a final rejection, can file an appeal to the examiner's decision in the Board of Appeals of the PTO. He also can re-file the application to continue prosecution before the examiner.

30.12 CLAIM INTERPRETATION

The technical scope of a patented invention depends on the claim language [7]. Claim interpretation is carried out based not only on the specific language in the claims but also on amendments and/or remarks submitted to the JPO during the prosecution of an application. In fact, claims are not interpreted beyond the applicant's intention at the time of filing the application. This means that claim interpretation is made according to the actual, express description of the invention in the specification, which makes claim interpretation in Japan narrow. This is also one of the major harmonization issues between the United States and Japan.

As discussed above, the new Japan MPEP was drastically changed to allow as broad claims as possible even when they are drafted beyond the disclosure of the invention in the specification. The effect of the invention can be submitted to the JPO by arguing the superiority of the invention in the remarks with or without experimental data unless the effect of the invention is disclosed in the specification. Courts in Japan will follow that policy of the JPO, and it is expected that claim interpretation in Japan will become broader.

30.13 PRIOR USER RIGHT

Ideally, a patent should be given to an inventor who made the invention first; therefore, patent rights should be given on a first-to-invent basis rather than a first-to-file basis. However, Japan adopted a first-to-file system as a matter of administrative policy. To compensate the defects of the first-to-file system, Japan allows the person who used the invention first a nonexclusive license. This provision does not exist in the United States, nor is it needed.

The prior user can employ this right to avoid infringement liability provided the following conditions are met: (1) the prior use was in Japan; (2) the prior use was made without knowledge of the contents of the invention claimed in the patent application; and (3) the prior user must have worked the invention commercially or made substantial preparation therefor [8]. Generally, the prior user's volume of activity will not be limited, but only the particular scope of his activity can continue.

30.14 PRIOR ART REFERENCES

Japanese Patent Law Section 29(1) states that inventions that are described in a publication distributed in Japan or elsewhere prior to the filing of a patent application shall not be patented. Such publication would be a prior art reference. On the other hand, the United States' 35 USC § 102(e) provides that A's invention will not be patented if it was described in a patent granted on an application filed by B in the United States before A's invention was made. This section has been interpreted to mean that in cases where B had first filed a foreign application and then filed an application in the United States claiming priority based on the foreign application, the actual filing date in the United States will be used to determine whether B's granted patent can be used as a prior art reference rather than the earlier date of B's foreign application. Under 35 USC § 102(e), accordingly, where B's application on which a patent is granted was filed in the United States, even though the priority date of B's application is earlier than the date of A's invention, B cannot use his patent as a prior art reference to defeat A's patent application [9]. This is also a disputed issue in the international harmonization of patent laws.

30.15 DOCTRINE OF EQUIVALENTS

A court in Japan may give the patent claims a scope of equivalents such that activities that are not literally within the wording of the claims may still be infringing. However, the claim interpretation by courts in Japan is very narrow and the Japanese concept of equivalents, used mainly to resolve the vagueness of claims, is totally different from that used by the Court of Appeals for the Federal Circuit (CAFC) in the United States.

Under the doctrine of equivalents, both the U.S. and Japanese courts will take the position that an accused product comprising A, B, and D is an infringement of a patented invention comprising A, B, and C, if D performs substantially the same function in substantially the same way to obtain the same result that C does [10]. However, a great difference in the adoption of this doctrine is the CAFC will consider whether the substitution of C for D as an element in the patented product or process would be considered obvious to those skilled in the art at the time of patent infringement [11], whereas a Japanese court will consider whether it would be considered obvious at the time of the filing of the patent application [12].

Obviously, it would be easier to find infringement under the U.S. doctrine of equivalents rather than under the Japanese version. Japanese courts are generally reluctant to admit the doctrine of equivalents and tend to restrict its scope to the choice of design. At the same time, the CAFC, which has tended to interpret claims excessively broader based on the doctrine of equivalents, is now moving toward a narrower application of the doctrine of equivalents [13]. For example, prior art will restrict the range of equivalents [14], further, a copyist is prevented from evading patent infringement by making insubstantial changes [15].

30.16 DUTY OF DISCLOSURE

Although the new Japan MPEP says that all information, such as prior art references, material to the patentability of a claim should be disclosed in the specification, a failure to disclose will not cause a rejection of the application. This is so even where the failure to disclose was intentional, because the concept of "fraud" on the Patent Office does not exist in Japan. This is very different from the U.S. patent law and practice where a failure to disclose will cause the application to be rejected [16] or affect the validity and enforceability of the patent if it becomes issued [17].

30.17 COMPULSORY LICENSES

Unlike the United States where a system of compulsory licensing does not exist, in Japan a compulsory license can be provided for any person who intends to *work* a patented invention (use the invention in a commercial product) when the patented invention has not been worked by the patent owner or the licensee for more than three consecutive years in Japan under Section 84(1).

A compulsory license also is provided for the owner or exclusive licensee of a patent that is an improvement of another person's patented invention, and he cannot use his own invention without infringing the earlier patent under Section 92(1).

A compulsory license also is provided when the working of the invention is especially necessary for the public interest under Section 93(1).

The parties who intend to work the patented invention under Sections 84(1) and 92(1) will first have to negotiate with the patent owner, and it is only if the latter refuses to voluntarily grant the license that the parties can file a request with the Commissioner of the JPO for an arbitration decision [18].

The party who intends to work the patented invention under Section 93(1) can request the Minister for International Trade and Industry for an arbitration decision only when the patent owner or the exclusive licensee refuses to grant the license voluntarily [19].

There have been nine requests filed so far under Section 84(2), seven under Section 92(2) and none under Section 93(2) as of January 1, 1989. However, no arbitration decision was issued on any request because they were all either settled or withdrawn before arbitration decisions were issued. Requests are settled or withdrawn before arbitration decisions are issued because the request procedures are complicated and time-consuming.

30.18 NATIVE-LANGUAGE FILING

Currently in Japan, patent applications must be filed in the Japanese language. Any documents to be filed with the JPO must be translated from the native language into Japanese. Translation errors will affect the scope of protection because corrections of mistranslation that introduce a new matter into the specification will not be allowed.

However, with the conclusion of the current phase of the U.S.-Japan Patent Harmonization talks, a Mutual Understanding was signed on January 20, 1994, between the respective Commissioners of the U.S. and Japanese Patent Offices. As a result, Japan will, by July 1, 1995, permit foreign applicants to file patent applications in English, if followed by a Japanese translation filed two months later. Further, up to the time allowed for replying to the first substantive Office Action, any corrections of mistranslations will be accepted.

30.19 INFRINGEMENT

Working a patented invention (using the invention in a commercial product) without authorization is a direct infringement of the patent. The making, using, importing, or selling of articles that form part of the patented invention constitutes infringement only if the article is usable only for the production of the patented product. This type of infringement is known as contributory infringement [20]. However, if that article has alternative commercial noninfringing uses, even though it can be used as part of the patented product, there is no contributory infringement regardless of whether or not that article was used, sold, and imported with the intention of using it to make the patented product [21].

On the other hand, in Japan the concept of active inducement of infringement does not exist. In the United States, it would be infringement if the seller indicates in the instructions of an article that it is particularly suitable for use in the patented product even in cases where such an article has alternative commercial noninfringing use [22]. In Japan, this would not be infringement.

Similarly, if a product patented in the United States were manufactured outside the United States by A, and A sells the product to importer B knowing that B would sell it in the United States (thus infringing the patent), A would be liable for infringement as an active inducer of B's act of infringement [23]. If this situation occurred in Japan involving a Japanese patent, A would not be liable for infringement.

30.20 UTILITY MODEL LAW

Japan has a petty patent protection system under utility model law. Conversion of a patent or design patent application to a utility model application and vice versa is permissible within certain specified time limits. Utility model protection is not available for processes. The duration of a utility model used to not exceed 15 years from the filing date of the application, but under the new law that is effective from January 1, 1994, this has been reduced to six years from the filing date.

To expedite the examination for both patent and utility model applications, the new law prescribes that a utility model application will be examined only on formalities and no substantive examination will be made. A public appraisal report system is introduced whereby any person can request the JPO to prepare an appraisal report of the utility model application. Such a request is published in the official gazette.

The owner can exercise his rights only if he sends a warning letter together with the appraisal report, if any, to the alleged infringer.

Amendments after filing the application and before the utility model issues can be made only within the scope of the disclosure of the invention in the originally filed specification and drawings. New matter cannot be introduced. After issuance, only deletion of claims are permissible. The correction of errors in the description and the clarification of an ambiguous description are not permitted after issuance.

When an infringement lawsuit has been filed by the utility model owner, and if the defendant counterclaims to invalidate the utility model, the defendant can request that the suit be stayed until the invalidity decision becomes final and conclusive.

When the utility model right that has been exercised is determined to be ineffective, the owner is presumed to have been negligent in filing his infringement suit. However, the owner can overcome this presumption of negligence by producing evidence that he has carefully ascertained the validity of the patent, for example, he had made vigilant searches for prior art at the time of filing of the application for the infringement lawsuit and/or he had obtained a validity opinion from attorneys.

NOTES

[1]   Japanese Patent Law Section 30(1).

[2]   *Hoechst Aktiengesellschaft v. The Commissioner of the JPO,* Supreme Court decision dated November 10, 1989, which held that the term "disclosure in a printed publication" appearing in Section 30(1) refers to an act by which the inventor or the applicant makes the invention public or known, with his active intention of making it public or known. Turning to disclosure through a foreign laid-open application, there is merely a passive intention in admitting a third party's [*i.e.* the foreign Patent Office in publishing the application] act of making the invention public or known. Therefore, the disclosure represented by the laid-open application does not fall within the term "disclosure in a printed publication" in Section 30(1) and the six-month grace period consequently does not apply.

[3]   *Akira Takano v. The Commissioner of the JPO,* Tokyo High Court decision dated August 16, 1983, which held that: ". . . however, claims indicate the subject matter the applicant regards as the invention to be patented and the statement on the claims should be indispensable for the structure of the invention. Accordingly, it is apparent that the invention on which the applicant seeks a patent through the filing of the application should be grasped and examined based on the statement on the claims. In cases where the invention grasped from the statement on the claims mismatches the objective, structure, and/or effect of the invention disclosed in the specification, it is permissible that the specification is rejected because of lack of the disclosure requirement; however, it is not reasonable that regardless of the statement on the claims, the invention on which the applicant seeks a patent is grasped and examined based on only the statement of the objective and effect of the invention disclosed in the specification."

[4]   This will soon change because, as a result of the Mutual Understanding signed on January 20, 1994, by the respective Commissioners of the U.S. and Japanese Patent Offices, a bill was introduced by Sen. Dennis DeConcini to establish a 20-year patent term beginning on the date the application is filed.

[5]   *Supra,* note [4]. This bill also provides for the publication of a patent application 18 months after it is filed.

[6]   One good example of a submarine patent is that filed by Jerome Lemmelson on December 24, 1954, under Serial No. 447,467 entitled "Controlling system and methods for scanning and inspecting images". It was finally patented on June 2, 1992, under U.S. Patent No. 5,119,190—some 37½ years after it was first filed! For further reading on the potentially devastating effect of "submarine patents", see Stewart Yerton's "The Sky's The Limit", The American Lawyer, May 1993, page 64.

[7]   Japanese Patent Law Section 70.

[8]   Japanese Patent Law Section 79.

[9]   *In re Hilmer* 149 USPQ 480 (CCPA 1966).

[10] The United States authority is *Graver Tank & Mfg. Co., Inc., et al. v. The Linde Air Products Company No.2,* 339 U.S. 605, 85 USPQ 328 (1950). The Japanese authority is *Badische*

Anilin und Soda Fabrik v. Sekisui Chemicals Industrial Co., Ltd. & Ors. Case No. Showa 35 (yo) 493, decided on May 4, 1961.

[11] *Atlas Powder Co. v. DuPont De Nemours & Co.,* 224 USPQ 409 (Fed.Cir. 1984).

[12] *Badische Anilin, supra,* note [8].

[13] The case which turned the tide is *Wilson Sporting Goods Co. v. David Geoffrey & Associates,* 14 USPQ2d 1942 (Fed. Cir 1990).

[14] *Supra,* note [11]. It was held that prior art restricts the range of equivalents. The doctrine of equivalents would not be applied to allow a patentee a hypothetical claim wide enough to cover the accused product, if such a claim could not have been obtained from the USPTO in the first place because of prior art.

[15] *Valmont Industries Inc. v. Ranke Manufacturer Company Inc.,* 25 USPQ2d 1451 (Fed. Cir. 1993), which also held that the intention of the copyist should be considered; therefore, if there was an intention to infringe, the doctrine of equivalents should be applied broader, and vice versa.

[16] United States 37 CFR 1.56.

[17] Such conduct by the patentee was first treated as obtaining a patent by "unclean hands", *Precision Instrument Manufacturing Co. v. Automative Maintenance Machinery Co.,* 324 U.S. 806, 814–816 (1945). Subsequently, this is now treated as being an "unenforceable" patent under 35 USC §282, *J.P. Stevens & Co., Inc. et al. v. Lex Tex Ltd., Inc.,* 223 USPQ 1089 (Fed. Cir. 1984).

[18] Japanese Patent Law Sections 84(2) and 92(2).

[19] Japanese Patent Law Section 93(2).

[20] Japanese Patent Law Section 101, United States 35 USC §271(c).

[21] *Supra,* note [17].

[22] United States 35 USC §271(b).

[23] *Supra,* note [22].

BIBLIOGRAPHY

Kohsaku Yoshifuji, *Patent Law Outline* (9th Edition).

Donald S. Chisum, *Patents.*

Manual of Patent Examining Procedure published by the U.S. Department of Commerce, Patent and Trademark Office.

Shusaku Yamamoto, "Functional Descriptions in Claims and the Disclosure of Patent Specification", Journal of Patent Management, Vol. 34, No. 1, 1984.

KOREAN AND U.S. INTELLECTUAL PROPERTY LAWS

Paul S. Stevens

Paul Stevens is a California attorney who has been resident in Korea and of counsel to the Koreana Patent & Law Firm in Seoul for three years. Other published articles include *"Amgen v. Chugai Pharmaceutical*—The EPO Case in Korea" and "Trade Secret Protection in Korea".

Abstract

This article provides guidance to companies and individuals planning to do business in Korea's intricate society. It discusses the background and philosophy governing the development of Korea's intellectual property laws and contrasts them with the laws of the United States. It introduces Korea's laws covering patents, trade secrets, trademarks, copyrights, computer programs, and mask work. The process of obtaining and enforcing patent rights in Korea is explained, with particular emphasis on aspects of Korean law that are troublesome for foreign inventors.

31.1 INTRODUCTION

An understanding of the differences between Korean and U.S. intellectual property laws begins with an appreciation of the fundamental differences between the cultural and legal philosophies of the two countries. The United States has a strong tradition of individual rights; there is no question whether an individual may own intellectual "property" such as an invention or a copyright. Consequently, an individual who creates an invention may practice that invention as a trade secret, maintaining secrecy forever under full protection of the common law. The inventor may alternatively choose to seek a patent—a monopoly right to exclude others from using this invention for a limited time—in exchange for revealing the invention to the public. Unauthorized use of inventions clearly is culpable conduct, and strong laws discourage such infringement of "rights".

Traditionally, Korea followed a Confucian ethic, which saw little culpability in one person's use of another's ideas, no matter how obtained, because society's right to useful ideas superseded an individual's "selfish" desire for profit. The idea of private rights to intellectual "property" simply never occurred to Koreans until it was introduced from abroad in the early twentieth century.

With this background, when intellectual property laws were first enacted in Korea, they emphasized the "development of national industry" through invention, not the idea that individuals had rights to intellectual property [1]. Further, the laws were not understood and routinely ignored. Thus, as Korea rapidly developed and its economy became international, perceptions that Koreans have a cavalier attitude regarding foreign-owned intellectual property (IP) rights have grown, and foreign businessmen are now reluctant to transfer their hard-earned know-how.

Meanwhile, rising labor costs have squeezed Korea out of low technology, labor intensive industries and into competition with technologically advanced nations. Korean business and government officials, increasingly desperate for new technologies and concerned with the lack of domestic research and development spending, are reevaluating the nature and necessity of IP protection [2].

Accordingly, Korea has recently revised its legal system covering all areas of intellectual property, with the expressed aim of raising its level of protection to that of the most advanced countries [3]. Today, a comprehensive set of laws is in place extending IP protection to both foreign and domestic innovators, and Korea has joined the World Intellectual Property Organization (WIPO) (1979), the Paris Convention for the Protection of Industrial Property (1980), the Patent Cooperation Treaty (PCT) (1984), the Universal Copyright Convention (UCC) (1987), and the Budapest Treaty on the International Recognition of Microorganisms (1988).

31.2 PROTECTION OF INVENTIONS

Korea, like the United States, offers patent or trade secret protection for inventions. Korea also recognizes a form of petty patent unavailable in the United States, called utility models.

31.2.1 Trade Secret

Trade secret protection was essentially unavailable in Korea until January 1, 1993. Before that date, trade secrets could be protected only by contract, but even limited contractual protection was difficult to obtain because of Korean governmental restrictions on the parties' freedom to establish the terms and conditions of contracts [4]. Further, while contractually you might have been able to prevent disclosure of your secret, you had no legal claim against third parties who received the secret in violation of the contract, since contracts create duties and obligations only as to the contractees.

Trade secrets are now specifically protected under Korean statutory law, which defines a trade secret as "a production method, marketing method, or other technical or business information useful for business activities, which is not publicly known and has independent economic value and is kept secret with considerable effort" [5]. As in the United States, possession of a trade secret gives you no right to prevent the independent development and use of the secret by others, but if your trade secrets are unfairly disclosed or acquired, you can bring an action for damages and an injunction preventing use of the secrets. Proving trade secret infringement, however, will be difficult, because Korean courts do not have strong powers to require production of evidence. Moreover, you will likely have to make your secret a part of the public record in order to sue for misappropriation of it, an obvious hindrance in the sense that benefits arising from the exploitation of trade secrets continue only as long as the secret remains a secret.

31.2.2 Patent and Utility Model Rights

Ownership of either a regular patent or a utility model "patent" in Korea gives you the exclusive right to work your invention, that is, to manufacture, use, sell, import, or commercially display your invention, and, if your invention is a process, products produced by the process [6]. A third party who wishes to work your invention must receive your permission to do so, unauthorized use constitutes infringement.

The right to work is far different from the U.S. patent right to exclude others from your invention. In America, you bear no obligation to allow access to your patented invention—your invention is private property, and you may exclude others from using your invention just as you may exclude others from using any of your personal possessions. In contrast, the right to work in Korea conceptually includes a working requirement—a duty either to use the invention to the extent reasonably required by society, or to make it available for others to use. If your invention is not continually worked, *i.e.,* is not used in commercial products, for a period of three years or more without justification, you may be compelled to allow others to use it by grant of a license through arbitration [7]. If the nonworking of your patent continues for a period of two years after the grant of such compulsory license, your patent right may even be canceled [8].

Compulsory licensing is also possible in Korea where your invention is an improvement over and requires use of the entirety of a third party's patented invention [9]. Again, in the same situation in the United States, the third party bears no obligation to allow you use of the invention. However, in Korea, the third party may be compelled to grant you a license if your invention constitutes a "substantial" technical advance over the third party's invention [10].

31.2.2a Patentability of Inventions

A patent may be obtained in Korea for a novel, nonobvious, and industrially applicable invention that is "the highly advanced creation of technical ideas utilizing rules of nature" [11]. As a practical matter, this definition of patentable invention encompasses the categories of subject matter considered patentable in the United States, *i.e.,* "any new and useful process, machine, manufacture or composition of matter, or any new and useful improvement thereof" [12]. Creation of living microorganisms, chemical products, food, drink, and computer-related inventions—all are patentable in Korea under similar standards as in the United States. In addition, Korea provides for the patenting of asexually reproducing plants, including tubers, tuberous roots, and bulbs [13]. "Design" patents for protecting the ornamental value of an article, *i.e.,* the shape of a bottle, are available under the Korean Design Law.

Not patentable in either Korea or the United States are abstract ideas, physical phenomena, or products or laws of nature themselves. You may not obtain a patent for a mathematical algorithm, or for discovering a new plant found in the wild. Korea further excludes from patentability inventions of substances manufactured by the process of transformation of the atomic nucleus [14], methods for diagnosis, treatment, mitigation, or prevention of human disease, and methods for the promotion of human health using medicine. The patentability of bioengineered animals in Korea remains an open question, although several applications are pending in the Korean Industrial Property Office (KIPO).

Coexisting with patents in Korea are a form of petty patent called utility models. Utility model rights are offered only in the manufacturing arts, and are available for "low-grade" novel and nonobvious inventions of "an industrially applicable device which relates to the shape or structure of articles", such as a baby carriage or a lawnmower; processes may not be claimed [15]. Utility Model rights cost less to obtain than patent rights, but have a shorter duration—ten years from the date of publication of an application, but no more than fifteen years from the application date for a utility model versus fifteen years from publication but no more than twenty years from the application date for a patent [16]. In most other respects, utility models and patents receive similar treatment, and the discussion herein of Korean patents and patenting should be understood to apply equally to utility models, unless otherwise noted.

Inventions of a device, *e.g.,* a lawnmower, are theoretically eligible for either patent or utility model protection in Korea—which one depends on the level of "inventiveness". A patent requires a high degree of inventiveness, a utility model requires a low degree. However, since there is no specific standard for determining the degree of inventiveness, the line between utility models and patentable inventions is blurred in practice. In this connection, a patent application can be converted into a utility model application, and vice versa.

31.2.2b Novelty

Novelty is the most fundamental requirement for issuance of a patent. *Nonnovelty, i.e.,* prior public exposure of the substance of an invention, necessarily means a patent applicant is offering nothing new to the public. Why should the public give a patent monopoly for an invention they already know about?

Ancillary to the novelty issue is the concept of priority of invention. An invention can be new only once; where two or more inventors file separate patent applications claiming the same invention, which of them is entitled to a patent? In the United States, the focus is on determining the first actual inventor; priority of invention will be given to the applicant who can establish the earliest acts of invention in the United States, and who has not thereafter suppressed, abandoned, or concealed the invention ("first-to-invent" system). Korea, on the other hand, establishes by legal fiat that the date of invention is the date of application; the patent will be awarded to the first applicant ("first-to-file" system) [17].

The first-to-file and first-to-invent systems differ in many respects, but none is so important as is their respective treatment of novelty. The United States allows you, as an inventor, a one-year grace period during which you can file an application and avoid the novelty-destroying effect of any earlier public disclosure of the invention by establishing a date of invention prior to the public disclosure [18]. Accordingly, if you publish details of your own invention within one year prior to applying for a patent, you will not be barred from obtaining a patent in the United States by your own public disclosure [19]. You may even benefit from the publication in establishing an early date of invention. Even where a third party publishes the same invention, you may still obtain a U.S. patent so long as you file an application within one year of the disclosure and can establish a date of invention prior to the public disclosure [20].

Although Korea does offer a grace period, it is only six months in duration and is significantly limited in scope. Korea's first-to-file system focuses on the date of application. Any public disclosure of an invention prior to the application date necessarily renders the invention nonnovel. Consequently, Korea's grace period applies only to situations where you have an excusable reason for your own prior disclosure, *e.g.,* where you have publicly disclosed your own invention unintentionally or in certain scientific meetings or government-approved exhibitions [21]. Any third party's independent public disclosure of the same invention before your application date absolutely destroys novelty, regardless of your true date of invention. Thus, if you accidentally publicize an invention, a third party thereafter independently publishes the same invention, and you then file a patent application, you are not entitled to a patent; the invention lacks novelty on the date of application. Similarly, if you publicly disclose an invention and, thereafter, a third party beats you to the patent office, it may be that neither of you can receive patent—the third party because of your publication, and you because of the third-party's first filed application [22].

Despite its rigidity, the first-to-file system offers one clear advantage—certainty. While you can never prove a date of invention earlier than your patent application date, neither can anyone else. You do not need to keep massive documentation of every step of the inventive process for the purpose of a possible interference, *i.e.,* the drawn-out and expensive U.S. procedure that determines whom among two or more competing inventors was the first-to-invent. Interference procedure is unnecessary and does not exist in Korea.

Inventors who lose the "race" to the patent office are not altogether without protection. Prior user rights will be granted to those inventors who can establish commercial use, or preparations toward such use, of the patented invention in Korea before the effective filing date of another's patent application [23]. Such prior users do not infringe the patent by using it themselves.

31.2.2c Patent/Utility Model Application Process

The first step in obtaining a patent in Korea is filing a patent application disclosing your invention as shown in Figure 1. Your application will thereafter be subject to substantive examination by the Korean Industrial Property Office (KIPO) to determine whether it meets the requirements for patent, *e.g.,* novelty, nonobviousness, first-to-file, etc. In contrast to the

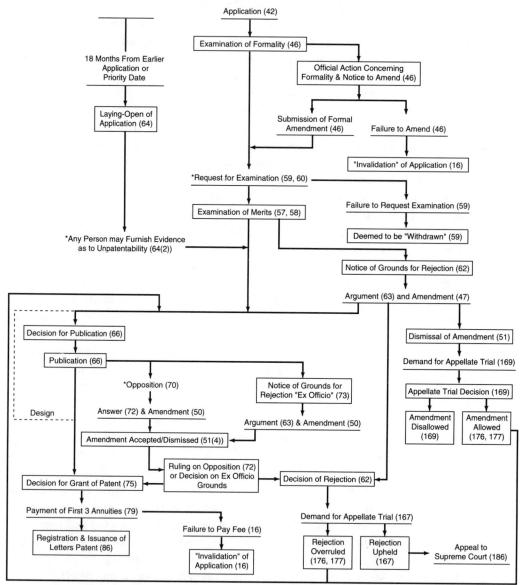

Figure 1   An overview of the patent application process in Korea

United States, the applicant in Korea can be either the inventor or an assignee [24]. Foreigners not living in Korea must appoint an agent living in Korea to prosecute their patent application, *i.e.,* represent them during the various stages of pendency of their application [25].

To mitigate the harshness of the novelty requirement, Korea, like most countries including the United States, will grant an application priority date retroactive to the first filing of your application in another country that is an adherent to the Paris Convention or Patent Cooperation Treaty (PCT). Such claim of priority protects you against public disclosure or patent applications made after your priority date, *i.e.,* your first application date in a foreign country, and before your actual Korean application date. However, it will not benefit you if your invention has been published even before the priority date. In such situations, since novelty has been destroyed before the earliest application date, you may obtain a patent in Korea only by operation of its "excusable conduct by the inventor" grace period.

The two methods by which you may claim priority in Korea are:

1. By the Paris Convention route, you must file an application in Korea within one year of its first filing date (the priority date). Thereafter, the priority document, *i.e.,* an official copy of the first filed foreign application, must be submitted within 16 months of the priority date [26].
2. By the Patent Cooperation Treaty (PCT) route, you must file an application with any PCT receiving office in any country within 1 year from the first filing date (the priority date). Korea must therein be designated as a receiving state of the PCT application. Thereafter, an exact translation of the PCT application must be submitted in Korea within 20 months of the priority date (or 30 months if you request an international preliminary examination within 19 months from the priority date and name Korea as an elected state to receive the results of the preliminary examination) [27].

Whichever way you choose to file your patent application in Korea, be aware that it will be laid-open, *i.e.,* the filing particulars and all claims and drawings will be published, 18 months from the application date, or, if you claimed priority, the priority date [28]. This early publication of pending applications accelerates access to information contained in the patent application and permits identification of unpatentable inventions sooner. In this regard, any person may submit to the KIPO evidence as to the unpatentability of an invention [29]. In contrast, the U.S. Patent Office keeps your application confidential until the date of patent grant. The patentability issue is solely between you and the U.S. Patent Office and you can retain trade secret protection for an invention until a patent issues.

Early publication of patent applications in Korea's laying-open system does not mean you are without protection against unauthorized use of your invention. After the laid-open date, you may request compensation from any person payable from the date they work (begin using) your invention either knowing it to be the subject of your patent application or having been so warned [30]. However, you may not receive such compensation unless and until your patent application is published after substantive examination for patentability [31].

Examination of your application is not automatic in Korea, as it is in the United States. A Request for Examination must be made within five years (three years for a utility model) of the actual Korean filing date or, in a PCT case, the date the application was filed in a PCT receiving office [32]. If a Request for Examination is not made within five years (three years for utility model), the application will be deemed to have been withdrawn [33].

Your application will usually be examined about two or three years after a Request for Examination. However, some applications are eligible for preferential examination, most particularly those applications that are being worked (*i.e.,* the invention is being used) by an unauthorized third party after laying open of the application [34].

On examination, your application is either preliminarily rejected or published for opposition. A preliminary rejection is issued where the Examiner considers your application unpatentable. You are given the opportunity to amend your application to comply with what the Examiner considers patentable or to argue against the rejection [35]. Thereafter:

1. If you succeed in persuading the Examiner to change the preliminary ruling, your application is published [36].
2. If the Examiner remains unpersuaded as to patentability, a final rejection is issued. You may appeal a final rejection all the way through the Supreme Court [37].
3. If you have amended your application, but the Examiner believes your amendment "changes the gist" of the claimed invention, *i.e.,* adds new matter which was not disclosed in your originally filed application, the Examiner will reject the amendment. If you appeal the rejection of an amendment, the examination of your application will be stayed until your appeal is concluded [38].

An Examiner's decision to publish your application results in publication of your entire application, followed by a two month nonextendable period for opposition [39]. If no opposition is filed, the Examiner makes a final decision to grant the patent [40].

In an opposition, any third party may interject itself into the patenting process by submitting evidence of unpatentability of an invention to the Examiner and further arguing as to unpatentability [41]. For example, a third party may oppose your patent application on the ground that your invention is not novel, or it is obvious, or even, perhaps, it is stolen property. Such third party intervention is impossible in the United States, where your patent application is secret until grant of a patent.

Where an opposition is filed, the Examiner must issue a written decision on the opposition before making a final decision either to grant or reject the patent [42]. If the application is rejected, you may appeal the rejection [43]. On the other hand, if the patent is granted, an opponent may not appeal the grant. His only recourse will be to seek to invalidate the patent after it issues.

31.2.2d Infringement

You may claim a remedy for infringement in Korea only after the publication of your patent application. You may commence litigation after the publication of the application even though a patent has not yet been granted, *i.e.*, after the application is published for opposition but before a decision to grant is made [44]. However, if your application is not granted, you are liable for damages caused to another party by the litigation.

Policing of a Korean patent is best done by your sales agent or associate in Korea who is aware of what is happening in the marketplace. If patent infringement is suspected, you may send a warning letter to the accused infringer. A warning letter creates a presumption that an infringer who continues to infringe has an intent to infringe, which usually induces an out-of-court settlement.

An accused infringer will often request a "trial" for either a determination of scope or for invalidation. Both trials are held in the Korean Industrial Property Office (KIPO) independently of and parallel with patent infringement litigation.

In contrast with U.S. practice, your patent in Korea may not be invalidated by a court at law in an infringement action, even if there exist reasons for invalidation of your patent right, *e.g.*, nonnovelty at the time of filing, obviousness, etc. Only a trial board of the KIPO sitting in a separate invalidation trial has the power to invalidate your patent.

The scope trial also distinguishes the Korean patent system from that of the United States. Scope trials also are held in the KIPO and theoretically define the limits of a patented invention vis-a-vis an opposing invention. However, the scope trial decision is merely advisory, and has no binding effect on the court at law, which has jurisdiction over your infringement litigation. Nevertheless, a scope trial decision is oftentimes persuasive, because the KIPO has technical expertise whereas court judges rarely have a technical background.

Obtaining sufficient evidence to prove patent infringement is difficult in Korea. Certainly no broad discovery procedure exists as in the United States. In this regard, while the court can order the production of evidence, the defendant can refuse to produce the evidence. Damages also are difficult to prove in Korea. However, a patent owner can claim, as damages, an amount equivalent to a royalty for a patent license [45]. Also, the court can order the infringer to produce documents necessary for the assessment of the damage caused by the infringement.

As in the United States, the patent owner can obtain a preliminary injunction [46]. It takes about three months for such injunction if the infringement is obvious. In addition, a patentee or exclusive licensee in Korea may file a criminal complaint against an accused infringer, who faces possible liability of up to five years in prison or a fine up to about U.S.$25,000 [47].

31.3 OTHER INTELLECTUAL PROPERTY RIGHTS

31.3.1 Trademarks and Servicemarks

Korea grants trademark or servicemark protection for characters, figures, or signs, or any combination thereof, which are capable of distinguishing one's goods or services from those of another [48]. In contrast with the United States, protection does not extend to color or three dimensional marks.

To be protected under the Korean Trademark Law, foreigners as well as Koreans should follow statutory procedures for application, examination, and registration. The registration requirement is based on a first-to-file system, which contrasts with the first-to-use system of the United States [49]. However, partial protection is available even for unregistered foreign trademarks, insofar as an application for a trademark will be rejected if it is the same or similar to an unregistered famous foreign trademark [50]. Moreover, unauthorized use of such a famous mark is forbidden under the Korean Unfair Competition Prevention Law.

31.3.2 Mask Work

An Act concerning Layout Design of Semiconductor Integrated Circuits, which is substantially similar to U.S. mask work law, became effective in Korea on September 1, 1993. Under the new law, layout designs having originality, *i.e.*, semiconductor chip mask designs known as "mask work" in the United States, may be protected in a fashion similar to Korean patents. The effects of the layout design right, however, do not extend to what is called "reverse engineering", *i.e.*, duplication of the layout design for the purpose of teaching, analyzing, or evaluating the layout design or for the purpose of private and noncommercial use. "Innocent" infringers are treated in the same fashion as in the United States—good-faith purchasers will be liable for a reasonable royalty on each unit of infringing layout design, semiconductor integrated circuit, or semiconductor chip that they import or distribute for commercial purposes only after they have notice that the units constitute infringement.

In marked contrast with U.S. mask work protection, compulsory licensing of the layout design right in Korea is possible as it is under Korean Patent Law. Further, while Korea recognizes the same U.S. term of 10 years from the earlier of the date of registration or first commercial exploitation, Korea further adds the caveat "but no more than 15 years from time of creation".

31.3.3 Copyright and Computer Programs

Copyright protection is available in Korea for the original creation of literary, scientific, and artistic works.

With respect to foreign works, protection extends only to works first published after October 1, 1987, although de facto retroactive protection has been granted to all printed materials copyrightable under the U.S. Copyright Act that were created or published since 1977 in the United States [51]. While authors may, for the sake of more thorough protection, register their works in Korea, the copyright itself is attributed to authors on the date of creation regardless of any formalities. Registration of a copyright is not a prerequisite to instituting an infringement action.

Computer program copyright is explicitly available under the Korean Computer Program Protection Law (CPPL) enacted in 1987. Software is afforded protection under the same circumstances as under the Copyright Law. Moreover, U.S. programs created or published since 1982 enjoy de facto protection under the CPPL.

31.4 CONCLUSION

Recent revisions of Korea's intellectual property laws and regulations indicate that Korea is working toward international standards in the protection of intellectual property rights. Nevertheless, the application of Korea's intellectual property laws remains unclear. Not only are the laws relatively new and counter to custom, but little guidance can be found in Korean judicial decisions since relatively few cases have been litigated in a country where lawsuits are frowned upon because they disrupt the essential social harmony. The Korean government does appear deeply committed to addressing intellectual property rights issues, so innovators can anticipate full protection of their intellectual property rights in the future.

NOTES

[1] Old Korean Patent Law, Article 1.

[2] Jee-Hye Park, "The President's Economic Initiative," Journal of the American Chamber of Commerce in Korea, vol.27, no. 3, p. 11, May/June 1993.

[3] Recent Developments in Intellectual Property Rights of Korea, Korean Ministry of Trade and Industry Publication, Jan. 1993.

[4] Intellectual Property Rights in Korea, American Chamber of Commerce and EEC Business Group Publication, March 1991.

[5] Korean Unfair Competition Prevention Law, Article 2(2).

[6] Korean Patent Law, Articles 2, 94.

[7] *Ibid.*, Articles 107–113.

[8] *Ibid.*, Article 116.

[9] *Ibid.*, Article 138.

[10] *Ibid.*

[11] *Ibid.*, Articles 2, 29.

[12] 35 United States Code Section 101.

[13] Korean Patent Law, Article 31.

[14] *Ibid.*, Article 32(1).

[15] Korean Utility Model Law, Articles 2, 4.

[16] *Ibid.*, Article 22(1); Korean Patent Law, Article 88. Contrast with the U.S. patent term of 17 years from grant. The U.S. patent term creates the problem of the *submarine patent, i.e.* a patent on basic elements of a technology which, due to delays in patent prosecution, "surfaces" long after the technology has become established.

[17] Korean Patent Law, Article 36; Korean Utility Model Law, Article 7.

[18] 35 U.S.C. Section 102.

[19] *Ibid.*

[20]   *Ibid.*

[21]   Korean Patent Law, Article 30.

[22]   Theoretically, a third party may learn of your invention through a six-month grace period publication and then file a patent application based on your disclosure, thus barring you from receiving a patent. However, Korean Patent Law Article 33 provides that only an inventor or his assignee may obtain a patent. If an "unentitled" person files an application before the inventor or his assignee, the true inventor may claim benefit of the unentitled person's filing date (Article 34).

[23]   Korean Patent Law, Article 103.

[24]   *Ibid.*, Article 33.

[25]   *Ibid.*, Article 5.

[26]   *Ibid.*, Article 54.

[27]   *Ibid.*

[28]   *Ibid.*, Article 64.

[29]   *Ibid.*, Article 64(2).

[30]   *Ibid.*, Article 65.

[31]   *Ibid.*

[32]   *Ibid.*, Articles 59, 60.

[33]   *Ibid.*, Article 59.

[34]   *Ibid.*, Article 61.

[35]   *Ibid.*, Articles 62, 63.

[36]   *Ibid.*, Article 66.

[37]   *Ibid.*, Article 62.

[38]   *Ibid.*, Article 51.

[39]   *Ibid.*, Articles 66, 70.

[40]   *Ibid.*, Article 75.

[41]   *Ibid.*, Article 70.

[42]   *Ibid.*, Article 72.

[43]   *Ibid.*, Article 167.

[44]   *Ibid.*, Article 68.

[45]   *Ibid.*, Article 128.

[46]   *Ibid.*, Article 126.

[47]   *Ibid.*, Article 225.

[48]   Korean Trademark Law, Article 2.

[49]   *Ibid.*, Article 8.

[50]   *Ibid.*, Article 7.

[51]   Recent Developments in Intellectual Property Rights in Korea, *supra,* p. 19.

[52]   *Ibid.*

Article
32

DIFFERENCES BETWEEN U.S. AND SCANDINAVIAN/FINNISH INTELLECTUAL PROPERTY LAWS

Knut Feiring

Knut Feiring is the Managing Director of Oy Kolster Ab, an intellectual property protection firm in Helsinki, Finland.

Abstract

This article, which primarily discusses patent legistation, provides a comparison of Intellectual Property laws of Denmark, Finland, Norway, and Sweden to laws applicable in the United States.

32.1 GENERAL REVIEW

The four Nordic countries, *i.e.,* Denmark, Finland, Norway and Sweden, all have copyright laws and other legislation for protection of intellectual property such as literary, artistic, and musical works, computer programs, etc., and also modern legislation for protection of industrial property such as inventions, trademarks, designs, utility models, and integrated circuit layouts.

The individual countries offer the different forms of protection indicated in Table I.

Table I Industrial property protection available in the Nordic countries

	DENMARK	FINLAND	NORWAY	SWEDEN
Patent law	yes	yes [1]	yes	yes
Trademark law	yes	yes [2]	yes	yes
Design law	yes	yes [3]	yes	yes
Utility model law	yes	yes [4]	no	no
Integrated circuit law	yes	yes [5]	yes	yes

[1] Law No. 550/67 of December 15, 1967 as last amended by Law No. 387/85 of May 10, 1985.

[2] Law No. 7/64 of January 10, 1964 as last amended by Law No. 996/1993.

[3] Law No. 221/71 of March 12, 1971 as last amended by Law No. 802/91 of May 10, 1991.

[4] Law No. 800/91 of May 10, 1991.

[5] Law No. 32/91 of January 16, 1991.

32.2 DIFFERENCES BETWEEN U.S. AND NORDIC PATENT LAWS

32.2.1 General Remarks

The patent laws of the four Nordic countries have been harmonized in all essential respects since 1968, and the laws have been revised to essentially correspond with the Patent Cooperation Treaty (PCT) and with the European Patent Convention (EPC). The Nordic countries are members of the PCT and the EPC as indicated in Table II.

Table II Membership of the Nordic countries in the PCT and EPC

	DENMARK	FINLAND	NORWAY	SWEDEN
PCT, phase I	yes	yes [6]	yes	yes
PCT, phase II	yes	yes [6]	yes	yes
EPC	yes	no	no	yes

[6] Decree No. 58/80 of September 26, 1980.

The main differences between U.S. and Nordic patent laws are described in the following paragraphs.

32.2.2 Type of Law

U.S.
The United States is a common law country where the law is continually influenced by case law.

Nordic
The Nordic countries are civil law countries with fixed laws.

32.2.3 Right to Patent

U.S.
First-to-invent principle. The first and true inventor in the United States is entitled to the patent.

Nordic
First-to-file principle. The inventor who first files a patent application (or a person to whom the invention is assigned) is entitled to the patent.

32.2.4 Novelty Requirement

U.S.
Restricted novelty is required. Printed matter published anywhere in the world and oral public disclosure and sale in the United States more than one year prior to the date of filing will destroy novelty.

Nordic
Absolute novelty is required. Printed matter and oral public disclosure and sale anywhere in the world prior to the date of filing will destroy novelty.

32.2.5 Grace Period

U.S.
The grace period is twelve months. Publication or sale of an invention by the inventor within twelve months before filing a patent application does not destroy novelty.

Nordic
There is no grace period. Publication by the inventor or others destroys novelty.

32.2.6 Fields of Technology

U.S.
Inventions in practically all fields of technology are patentable.

Nordic
Inventions relating to plant and animal varieties, biological processes for the production thereof, methods of therapy on humans, second medical indications, and computer programs are not patentable. Microbiological processes are patentable. In Finland, pharmaceuticals and foodstuffs are patentable only after January 1, 1995.

32.2.7 Effect of Priority Date

U.S.
A U.S. application claiming priority from an application filed abroad (*e.g.*, on March 1, 1993) is not effective against an application filed by another in the United States (*e.g.*, on July 1, 1993) between said foreign priority date and the filing date (*e.g.*, February 1, 1994) of the U.S. application claiming said foreign priority date. (The Hilmer rule)

Nordic
A non-Nordic priority date has the same effect in the Nordic countries as a Nordic priority date. An application filed in a Nordic country (for example, on February 1, 1994) and claiming priority from an application filed in any country (for example, on March 1, 1993) is effective against an application filed by another in the Nordic country (for example, on July 1, 1993) between said priority date and the filing date of the Nordic application claiming the priority.

32.2.8 Effect of Prior Art

U.S.

Whole contents approach. The whole contents (description, claims, and drawings) of an earlier application can be cited against a later application in considering novelty and obviousness.

Nordic

Modified whole contents approach. The whole contents of an earlier unpublished application can be cited against a later application only in considering novelty, not in considering obviousness. For example the invention of an application filed in a country prior to the invention of an earlier application was published (became available to the public) must only be novel but does not need to be nonobvious with respect to the contents of said earlier application.

32.2.9 Publication of Applications

U.S.

Applications are published only after grant.

Nordic

Applications are published (made available to the public) 18 months after the filing date or priority date, whichever is earlier.

32.2.10 Opposition Procedure

U.S.

There are no provisions for third parties to oppose the grant of a patent. There is, however, a reexamination procedure that can be initiated by a third party after the grant of a patent.

Nordic

Pre- and post-grant opposition procedures are provided. In Finland and Norway, an application is laid open for opposition purposes in the Patent Office for three months before grant; in Denmark and Sweden for nine months after grant.

32.2.11 Prosecution Time

U.S.

Compact prosecution. A decision of grant or final rejection should be reached within a certain period of time, typically about 18 to 19 months. The second office action is typically made "final" after which no new issues can be raised.

Nordic

Unlimited prosecution. No set period of time within which the examination of an application must be started or completed. Normally, only two office actions are issued.

32.2.12 Elimination of Double Patenting

U.S.

Terminal disclaimer. Overlap between the claims of applications of the same applicant can be avoided by causing the term of a later patent to expire at the same time as an earlier patent.

Nordic

Overlap between the claims of applications cannot be eliminated by terminal disclaimers.

32.2.13 Rights of Prior User

U.S.

No rights of prior user. The patent is granted to the first inventor who did not abandon, suppress, or conceal the invention.

Nordic

A person who uses an invention before another person has filed an application relating to the same invention has the right to continue using the invention without being subjected to infringement damages or required to pay royalties.

32.2.14 Term of Patent

U.S.

The patent term is 17 years from the date of grant.

Nordic

The patent term is 20 years from the filing date.

32.2.15 Infringement

U.S.

Compensation for infringement is limited to a period of six years prior to the filing of the complaint. Parties pay their own attorney fees.

Nordic

Compensation is limited to five years prior to institution of infringement proceedings, unless action for compensation is brought within one year of the grant of the patent. Also attorney fees can be recovered from the losing party.

32.2.16 Compulsory Licenses

U.S.
Working (use in a commercial product) of the invention is not required and compulsory licenses are not granted.

Nordic
A compulsory license can be granted if the invention has not been worked (used in a commercial product) within three years of the grant and four years of the filing of the application.

32.2.17 Invalidity and Amendment of Patent

U.S.
The Patent Office can reexamine a granted patent upon a request by the Patentee, by a third party, or on its own initiative. The validity of a patent also can be tested in the Federal Courts.

Nordic
Restriction (limitation of scope of claims) or invalidation of a patent is decided by a court.

32.2.18 International Trade Commission (ITC) Procedure

U.S.
An administrative action against unfair methods of competition can be brought before the International Trade Commission.

Nordic
No corresponding procedure is available.

32.2.19 Telefax Filing

U.S.
Telefax filing is not accepted.

Nordic
A filing date and number can be obtained simply by filing a request that references a previous application by indicating country, filing date, filing number, applicant's name, and priority date (if priority is claimed).

32.3 OTHER FORMS OF INDUSTRIAL PROPERTY PROTECTION

Trademarks and trade dresses can be protected under trademark law in all four Nordic countries on the basis of registration or use.

The appearance of an article or ornament can be protected under design law in all four Nordic countries.

"Small" inventions that do not reach the level of nonobviousness required of patentable inventions can be protected under utility model law in Denmark and Finland.

Semiconductor chip mask works can be protected under integrated circuit layout law in Denmark, Finland, and Sweden.

DIFFERENCES BETWEEN U.S. AND SOUTH AFRICAN INTELLECTUAL PROPERTY LAWS

Llewellyn Parker

Llewellyn Parker is an intellectual property partner with the firm of John & Kernick in South Africa. He is a member of the South African Institute of Intellectual Property Law and deals with general patent matters although his interests are biased toward biotechnology.

Abstract

This article deals with the major differences between the intellectual property laws of the United States and South Africa. Most of the important differences are found in the patent laws of the two countries and several of these differences are examined. In addition, the novelty requirements relating to South African registered designs are discussed. These novelty requirements enable a valid design to be registered despite prior use in the United States, provided there has been no description in a printed publication.

33.1 INTRODUCTION

The term Intellectual Property covers a number of proprietary rights. The owner of these rights can use them to prevent conduct that would give other persons an unfair or unlawful trade advantage. Like the United States, South Africa has a number of statutes or acts that define and regulate various forms of intellectual property. A brief resume of the more important acts will be presented before considering some of the more pronounced differences between the U.S. and South African systems and particularly between the laws governing patents.

33.2 THE SOUTH AFRICAN PATENTS ACT OF 1978

This Act came into force on January 1, 1979, and provides that a patent may be granted for any new invention that involves an inventive step and that is capable of being used or applied in trade or industry or agriculture [1]. Unlike its U.S. counterpart [2], the South African act expressly provides that the following are not patentable:

- Discoveries [3];
- Scientific theories [3];
- Mathematical methods [3];
- Literary, musical, or artistic works or other aesthetic creations [3];
- Schemes, rules, or methods for playing a game, performing a mental act, or doing business [3];
- The presentation of information [3];
- A program for a computer [3];
- Varieties of animals or plants essentially biological processes for producing animals or plants [4]; and
- Methods of treatment of the human or animal body by surgery or therapy or of diagnosis [5].

Most of the differences between the intellectual property laws of the United States and South Africa are evident in the patent systems of these two countries.

33.3 THE SOUTH AFRICAN DESIGNS ACT OF 1967

This Act and its regulations govern the grant and administration of registered designs. A registered design relates to any design applied to an article insofar as the design (1) appeals to and is judged solely by the eye and (2) is not dictated by function. Any design feature dictated solely by the function the article is intended to perform or any method or principle of construction is not protectable [6].

The duration of a South African design is 15 years as opposed to 14 years for a U.S. design. The major difference between South African and U.S. designs is their novelty requirements. For a U.S. design, the novelty requirement is the same as for a patent [7]. The novelty requirements for a South African design are less stringent. The criteria are that a substantially similar design should not be:

- used in South Africa;
- described in any publication in South Africa;
- described in a printed publication anywhere; and
- registered in South Africa [8].

The less stringent South African design novelty requirement is important. Where a product is developed and used in the United States, as long as it has not been described in a printed publication or used in South Africa, it can be registered in South Africa and a monopoly obtained irrespective of the length of time used in the United States. By the same token, a South African touring the United States can purchase an item, return with it to South Africa, and register the design.

33.4 THE SOUTH AFRICAN COPYRIGHT ACT OF 1978

Like its U.S. counterpart [9], the South African Copyright Act provides protection for original literary works, musical works, artistic works, cinematograph films, sound recordings, broadcasts, and program-carrying signals [10]. Unlike the U.S. act however the South African act specifically provides for the protection of computer programs [11] which were previously treated as literary works [12]. The act defines a computer program as:

> . . . a set of instructions fixed or stored in any manner and which, when used directly or indirectly in a computer, directs its operation to bring about a result; [13].

The act also reserves, inter alia, for the copyright owner the exclusive right to make or authorize the making of an adaptation of the computer program [14]. An adaptation of a computer program is defined [14] to include a version of the program in a programming language, code, or notation different from that of the program or a fixation of the program in or on a medium different from the medium of fixation of the program [14]. The above provisions relating to adaptations will, it is envisaged, cover many reverse engineering and code conversion practices.

Another important difference between the U.S. and South African systems is that (except for cinematograph films, which are governed by a separate act [15]) South Africa has no provision for the registration of copyright. Accordingly an owner of copyright must, in legal proceedings for infringement of copyright, prove the date on which the allegedly infringed work was reduced to a material form, that the author was a qualified person in terms of South African law, and he or she is the owner of the work.

33.5 THE SOUTH AFRICAN PLANT BREEDER'S RIGHTS ACT OF 1976

This act provides protection for new varieties of specified species of plants in much the same way as the United States plant patents. Unlike patents and designs, an application is examined and samples for testing purposes are usually required. The examination process usually takes between three and five years during which time the variety may not be commercially exploited. The duration of monopoly granted varies according to the plant variety.

33.6 COMMON LAW RIGHTS AND UNLAWFUL COMPETITION

South African common law rights include a broad category of conduct, which is generally termed unlawful competition. This conduct falls within the law of "delict", which is equivalent to the United States law of "torts".

For conduct to constitute unlawful competition, the following requirements must be met:

- the conduct must be unlawful;
- the conduct must result in actual damage or the likelihood of damage to the person affected by the unlawful conduct; and
- the conduct must interfere with a right or legal entitlement of the person affected.

Because no statute regulates unlawful competition, the courts decide on the merits and facts of each case whether a particular conduct is unlawful competition. Some established categories of unlawful competition are:

- Passing-off: a misrepresentation by one person that his or her goods or services are those of another person. The wronged person must have a reputation in his or her own goods or services as a result of extensive use in South Africa.
- Misuse or disclosure of confidential or secret information.
- Misrepresentation about one's own products.
- Misrepresentation about a competitor's products or business.

33.7 DIFFERENCES BETWEEN U.S. AND SOUTH AFRICAN PATENT LAWS

The South African Patents Act is, to a large extent, based on the patents act of the United Kingdom and consequently the many differences between the U.S. and United Kingdom patent laws are also manifest as between the U.S. and South African patent laws. The most pronounced differences are the following:

33.7.1 Novelty Requirement

To obtain a patent in South Africa the invention must be new [1]. New is defined as not forming part of the "state of the art" immediately before the priority date of any claims to the invention [16]. The "state of the art" includes all matter which has been made available to the public anywhere in the world [17] and also includes inventions used secretly and on a commercial scale within South Africa [18].

With the exception of section 102(b) of USC 35, the novelty requirements of South Africa and the United States are similar. Section 102(b) provides that an inventor may disclose the subject matter of the invention up to twelve months before applying for a patent in the United States. Should this be done, a valid patent could not be claimed in South Africa. Such a disclosure would destroy the novelty of the invention for South Africa has an "Absolute Novelty System".

33.7.2 Duration of Patents

The duration of a South African patent applied for after December 31, 1978, is 20 years from the date of application, subject to payment of the prescribed renewal fees [19]. Renewal fees are payable annually from the expiration of the third year from the date of application.

The duration of a United States patent is seventeen years from the date the patent is granted, subject to payment of renewal fees which are due three, seven, and eleven years from the date of grant.

A reason for this difference in duration may be due to the often prolonged prosecution period that precedes the grant of a U.S. patent. In South Africa a patent usually proceeds to grant between nine and twelve months after the date of application.

In South Africa, patents applied for before January 1, 1979, are dealt with in terms of the repealed Patents Act of 1952. This act provided that the patent term was sixteen years. Where a patentee can show that inadequate remuneration was derived from the patent during its normal term, the term of the patent can be extended by a further five years.

The current South African patents act, unlike the U.S. patents act (with respect to drugs) and unlike its predecessors, has no provision for the extension of term of a patent although the idea of incorporating such a provision for drug-related inventions is being considered.

33.7.3 Examination and Prosecution

The difference in the examination and prosecution procedures between the United States and South Africa is perhaps the most important difference between the two countries. In the United States, patent examiners examine the application to determine whether the alleged invention is novel and nonobvious. This is usually followed by a prosecution phase where the inventor attempts to convince the examiner that the invention is indeed novel and nonobvious. This procedure is lacking in South Africa.

The result of this lack of substantive examination in South Africa is that patents of dubious inventiveness are often granted. Where legal proceedings for infringement of a patent are instituted, the infringer usually counterclaims alleging invalidity of the patent on the grounds that it lacks novelty and an inventive step and must prove this.

33.7.4 First to File as Opposed to First to Invent

The United States is a "first to invent" system.

Section 135 of the U.S. code provides that a Board of Patent Appeals and Interferences shall determine questions of priority of inventions whenever an application for a patent is made which would interfere with a pending application or an unexpired patent. This first to invent system grants the rights to an invention to the first inventor irrespective of the date of filing.

South Africa is a first to file system in that the rights to an invention go to the inventor who first files for a patent.

33.7.5 Legal Costs

In South Africa, a legal representative may not accept a case on a contingency basis. The rationale is that this supposedly aids in maintaining the independence of the legal practitioner. However, this means that the litigants must have sufficient funds to cover the legal representative's costs before the case can be accepted. Accordingly most litigants tend to settle out of court rather than incur the costs of litigation.

Additionally, a litigant who achieves substantial success in legal proceedings is usually awarded costs. This also tends to discourage the institution of legal proceedings for the nuisance value thereof without a sound economic reason. In general, the successful litigant should recover approximately 60 to 70 percent of the actual costs incurred.

NOTES

[1]   Patents Act of 1978, section 25(1).

[2]   United States Code, Title 35, section 100.

[3]   Patents Act of 1978, section 25(2).

[4]   Patents Act of 1978, section 25(4)(b).

[5]   Patents Act of 1978, section 25(11).

[6]   Designs Act of 1967, section 1.

[7]   United States Code, Title 35, section 171 read with section 102.

[8]   Designs Act, section 4(2).

[9]   United States Code, Title 17, section 102.

[10]   Copyright Act of 1978, section 2(1).

[11]   Copyright Act, section 2(1)(i).

[12]   Northern Office Micro Computers vs Rosenstein 1981 (4) SA 123(c).

[13]   Copyright Act, section 1.

[14]   Copyright Act, section 11B.

[15]   Registration of Copyright Films Act of 1977.

[16]   Patents Act, section 25(5).

[17]   Patents Act, section 25(6).

[18]   Patents Act, section 25(8).

[19]   Patents Act, section 46(1).

EXPLOITING INTELLECTUAL PROPERTY

The intellectual property has been secured. Now, what can be done with it?

The previous sections of the book dealt with extracting information from the patent system, strategic considerations, and securing intellectual property rights. This section of the book addresses some of the issues of financing, marketing, and otherwise making money from intellectual property. MAL

Article
34

FORMS OF ENTITIES FOR EXPLOITING INTELLECTUAL PROPERTY

Bradley S. Paulson

Bradley S. Paulson is an attorney practicing in corporate and securities, export, and franchising law with Meyer, Hendricks, Victor, Osborn & Maledon, P. A., in Phoenix, Arizona.

There are a number of ways in which intellectual property can be exploited. For example, a patent can be used to maintain product differentiation, preventing the competition from copying an aspect or feature of the company's product. It also can be licensed to other companies for use in specified products, territories, marketing channels, or fields of endeavor. Sometimes, for a variety of reasons, the intellectual property can best be exploited through a dedicated new company. Many a new business has been built around intellectual property, created for the specific purpose of exploiting the intellectual property.

One of the initial questions that must be addressed in those situations is the form of business entity to be created. The following article discusses the pros and cons of the different forms of business entities.   MAL

Abstract

Choosing a form by which to conduct a business is an important decision for an entrepreneur starting a new enterprise, or continuing an existing business. This article will outline the practical choices for forms of business entities by which intellectual property may be exploited and will examine general legal considerations and consequences associated with the various choices. This article also provides an overview of the incorporation process and an analysis of the merits and features of joint ventures.

34.1 CHOICE OF ENTITY

The choice of entity can have significant consequences, not only for the manner in which the business will be operated, but also for the degree of financial risk to which the owners will be exposed. Five practical choices of entity exist: (1) a sole proprietorship,

(2) a general partnership, (3) a limited partnership, (4) a corporation, or (5) a limited liability company.

34.1.1 The Sole Proprietorship

The *sole proprietorship* is the fundamental form by which an individual may conduct business. The sole proprietorship is not a legal entity distinct from its owner, and no organizational documents are needed to commence operation as a sole proprietorship. The owner, after obtaining any necessary approvals for conduct of the particular business, merely commences operations. The net income or losses are passed through directly to the sole proprietor. A sole proprietorship terminates when the owner ceases operations.

Generally, neither the creation nor the termination of a sole proprietorship will constitute a taxable transaction. Upon termination, the owner remains liable for any obligations of the business. Since a sole proprietorship is not a separate legal entity, transfer of the business is accomplished by selling the assets of the business. For federal income tax purposes, the transfer is treated as a sale of each asset. Accordingly, the sale price must be allocated among the respective assets. Depending on the tax basis of the respective asset, each separate sale could result in income or loss for the owner.

The sole proprietorship can be a useful business form for an individual starting a new business, especially a part-time business. However, despite being simple to start or terminate, a sole proprietorship can pose difficulties in planning a transfer of the business and in estate planning for the owner. In addition, because the business is not a separate legal entity, the sole proprietorship exposes the owner to personal liability for obligations of the business. This exposure may be partially offset by procuring liability insurance.

34.1.2 The Partnership

The *partnership* is the basic noncorporate form in which two or more persons can conduct an enterprise. The owners may be individuals, corporations, estates, trusts, other partnerships or other entities. The partnership itself is not a distinct legal entity. As a result, the partners, are personally liable for partnership liabilities. Generally, if two or more persons associate themselves to carry on a business, they will be deemed to be operating as a partnership. The "partnership agreement" sets forth the rules for governance of the partnership. Even if no written agreement exists, the law may deem the existence of an oral partnership agreement among the partners. Further, to the extent a written or oral partnership agreement does not address an issue of partnership governance, state partnership law provides assumptions for the operation of the partnership. For example, state laws generally provide that the business affairs of a partnership are governed by a majority vote of all of the partners. As a result, unless the partnership agreement provides to the contrary, the partnership will not have centralized management and control. Many partnership agreements provide that a managing partner will have authority for day-to-day operation of the business, but reserve major policy for the determination of the collective partners.

The partners own an equity interest in the partnership, and the partnership agreement may require additional capital contributions under certain conditions. Transferability of a partnership interest is usually prohibited without the consent of the other partners, since partners want to have control over the composition of the partnership. For income tax purposes, the partnership itself is not taxed. Income, losses, deductions, and credits pass through directly to the partners, who are taxed according to their respective share of the partnership. The partnership agreement needs to provide for appropriate division of the foregoing among the partners. The death or withdrawal of a partner may terminate the partnership, unless the partnership agreement allows the surviving partners to continue the partnership business.

For federal income tax purposes, the partnership is a more advantageous form of entity than the corporation. The partnership's primary advantages are: (1) partners may deduct partnership losses, whereas stockholders cannot deduct corporation's tax losses; (2) a partnership is not subject to the potential double taxation threat applicable to corporations; and (3) because individual income tax rates generally are lower than corporate tax rates, the income of a partnership may be taxed at a lower rate than the income of a corporation. The principal administrative advantage of a partnership is that it is simpler to organize and less expensive to operate than a corporation. The principal disadvantage of a partnership is the unlimited liability of each partner for liabilities of the partnership, including liability for the acts of other partners acting as agents of the partnership.

The partnership is a useful form for joint ventures. Corporations often choose to enter into joint ventures with other corporations in the form of a partnership, because the corporations already enjoy limited liability and the partnership form of the joint venture will offer simplicity in organization, operation, and termination.

34.1.3 The Limited Partnership

The *limited partnership* is similar to the partnership in form, except that limited partnerships have one or more "limited partners." A limited partner is an investor whose liability for partnership obligations is limited generally to his investment. However, limited partners may not participate in managing the business; participation will destroy the limited liability. Every limited partnership must have at least one "general" partner who is responsible for managing the business and has unlimited liability for partnership liabilities.

34.1.4 The Corporation

A *corporation* is a separate legal entity from its owners (stockholders) and has the characteristics of limited liability, centralized management, free transferability of interests, and continuity of existence.

Stockholders of a corporation have limited liability in that their liability for corporate obligations is limited to the amount of their investment. Ownership of the corporation is represented by shares of stock. Several types and classes of stock may be employed to allocate different degrees of control and investment risk. Classes of common stock ordinarily represent potential growth and the classes of preferred stock ordinarily represent a more predictable return on investment. Common stock usually has greater voting rights than preferred stock, which may not have any voting rights.

A corporation has centralized management in that, although it may be owned by many stockholders, its business affairs are managed by a board of directors, who delegate duties to officers of the corporation. Corporate policy is established by the board of directors, which delegates responsibility for the day-to-day operation of the corporation to the president and his subordinate officers.

Relative to other forms of business entities, corporate interests offer the greatest liquidity. Transfers of corporate interests are effected by merely transferring the stock certificates. In closely held (few stockholders) or smaller corporations, the stockholders may have contractual restrictions on their ability to transfer shares. In addition, the federal and state securities laws generally restrict the timing, volume, and manner of sales of securities in certain circumstances. If the transfer of stock is by sale, the selling stockholder realizes capital gain or loss to the extent of the difference between the amount realized for the stock and the stockholder's tax basis in the stock. Tax basis generally equals the cost of the stock.

Unlike other forms of organization, the corporation has continuity of life. A corporation will perpetually continue in existence unless terminated by liquidation or merger. The death or departure of its principals does not result in termination of the corporation.

The corporation offers more protection against personal liability than partnerships or sole proprietorships. It is advantageous if liquidity of interest is desired or if the business is expected to continue indefinitely. The corporate form is the preferred vehicle for raising capital due to the liquidity of the investment and the limitation on liability. The use of stock options and stock awards are also a relatively inexpensive method of compensating and incentivizing employees. A principal disadvantage of the corporate form is that it requires observance of many legal formalities and involves greater expense and administrative burden than is associated with noncorporate entities. The potential for double taxation also presents a significant disadvantage. Corporate revenues are taxed as income to the corporation, and dividends distributed to stockholders are again taxed as personal income to the stockholder.

34.1.5 The Limited Liability Company

The *limited liability company* (LLC) is a recent creation that is attracting increasingly greater attention as an alternative form for doing business. The LLC combines two of the most desirable corporate attributes—centralized management and limited liability for investors—with the most desirable partnership characteristic: pass-through treatment for federal income tax purposes. The U.S. Internal Revenue Service has ruled that unincorporated organizations operating as LLCs are classified as partnerships for federal tax purposes because they lack the corporate characteristics of liquidity of interest and perpetual existence. Accordingly, the LLC is not taxed on income, but rather the individual owners are taxed for their proportionate shares of income. There is no risk of double taxation as with a corporation. LLCs have not been used extensively, probably due to uncertainty over whether limited liability will be accorded in states that do not have an LLC statute. As more states adopt LLC legislation, LLC usage should increase.

34.2 THE INCORPORATION PROCESS

Since many entrepreneurs and ventures are likely to select the corporate form of doing business, the following is a general overview of the incorporation process. Corporations are fictitious entities created by state law and therefore must observe certain formal requirements for legal recognition. The corporation laws in each state vary in detail but they generally follow a similar pattern. A corporation is created by the preparation and filing of a document entitled the "Articles of Incorporation" (or "Certificate of Incorporation" in some states). This is the fundamental document governing the relationships between the various interests—the officers, directors, stockholders, and creditors. It is often required that the articles of incorporation state a purpose for which the corporation is organized.

Most corporation statutes require that a corporation signify its incorporated status by including in its name words such as "Corporation," "Corp.," "Ltd." or "Inc." Each state secretary's office maintains a list of all domestic corporations and all foreign corporations registered to do business in the state. By statute and under common law principles of unfair competition, corporations may not adopt a name that is deceptively similar to the name of an existing corporation either incorporated under the laws of, or duly qualified to do business in, a state. By perusing the state secretary's list, an entrepreneur or his counsel can see whether a given name has already been taken. If multi-state operation is contemplated, certain agents—for example, the CT Corporation System—will search the rosters of the important commercial states to see if a given name is available. It is usually possible to reserve a name in most states for up to 90 days.

State statutes generally regulate the type of consideration for which corporate stock may be issued. Many states prohibit the issuance of stock in consideration for promissory notes or future services. The reason for this prohibition is to ensure that a corporation receives adequate capital in exchange for its stock. The corporation statute typically authorizes the directors or stockholders to adopt bylaws. Bylaws specify the procedural rules of governance of the corporation; *e.g.,* they specify how meetings of directors and stockholders are called, what constitutes a quorum for meetings, what number of votes are necessary to adopt a proposal, how directors may be replaced, etc. State corporation laws also specify rules for corporate governance, but defer to a great extent to the bylaws of the corporation.

The articles of incorporation also must identify the aggregate number of shares of stock, and different series of stock, that the corporation has authority to issue. If the stock of the corporation is divided into different classes or series, the designation of each class or series and a statement of their relative preferences, limitations, and rights in respect of such classes or series must be identified.

The incorporation process is relatively inexpensive. A nominal filing fee must accompany the filing of articles of incorporation in most states. In addition, a corporation must file an annual report with the state each year, which also requires a nominal filing fee.

34.3 BUSINESS ALLIANCES

An attractive method for firms to share resources in a business alliance is the *joint venture*. A joint venture may mean many different things to different parties. A joint venture may be a permanent marriage between two firms, or a joint project that is limited in scope. It may refer to a distinct entity that is established to operate on behalf of two or more joint venturers, or may refer to a loose relationship between two or more parties pursuing a common goal. Regardless of the scope of a joint venture, or the vehicle through which it operates, joint ventures hold enormous potential. Established corporations are particularly interested in marriages with small, high-tech companies. It is often the case in the research and development arena that some of the most innovative "breakthrough" ideas originate from small businesses, not the research laboratories of giant companies. High-tech start-up companies account for an enormous amount of innovation, but their resources are limited.

There are many issues that potential venture partners need to consider when creating a joint venture. First, they should decide whether to create a separate joint venture entity. As noted earlier, a partnership is often a preferred choice of entity for joint ventures. Even if joint venturers do not create a distinct partnership entity, they may be deemed to be operating as a partnership under applicable law. By cooperating in a joint venture without creating a formal joint venture entity, the parties continue their separate identity of business operations, without transferring assets to a distinct entity. By avoiding transfers of real and personal property to and from the joint venture entity, state and local transfer taxes and other regulations restricting transfer may be avoided. By continuing to operate as separate entities, the joint venturers may avoid some troublesome management issues. The maintenance of separate assets and operations also avoids complicated problems of disentangling assets when a joint venture entity is dissolved. On the other hand, a compelling reason for forming a separate joint venture entity is to engender stability and permanency; with a separate joint venture entity, the parties' commitment to work together and resolve problems may be strengthened by the formal arrangement. A separate vehicle also provides an additional layer to shield against liabilities arising from the joint venture.

Regardless of whether or not a separate joint venture entity is formed, a joint venture agreement must be prepared to provide the answers to several critical business issues, including control of the venture, funding responsibilities, division of profits, ownership of technologies developed and other benefits of development efforts, termination procedures, and other resource allocating issues.

With respect to control of the joint venture, it is important for the board of the joint venture, if it is a separate entity, or a committee composed of representatives of each side, if it is not a separate entity, to be vested with the power to make decisions on behalf of the joint venture. A joint venture cannot be successful if it does not have a central decision making apparatus, but rather is caught in a tug-of-war between the decision makers of the various joint venturers. Beyond control issues, other responsibilities must be divided. For instance, if a large company were to partner with a start-up, high-tech company, the start-up might be responsible for performing research and development and the large company might be responsible for providing the resources for sales, marketing, and distribution of products developed. If the products are to be manufactured by the start-up company, it will undoubtedly need investment from a large company to purchase equipment and facilities. On the other hand, the large company might be in a position to manufacture the products more economically.

Many joint ventures may be in the form of a larger company purchasing an outright interest in a start-up company, giving both parties a stake in the ongoing success of the enterprise. The larger company may purchase a smaller company or a certain product line or technology outright and continue a relationship with the seller such that the seller continues to participate in the management of the project. The parties should anticipate that they may have disputes over the direction of the project. Consultants may be employed to settle disputes. Another directional method commonly used to resolve disputes is a buyout provision. Under such a provision, a party has the option to buyout the interest of the other party for a price (which may be based on a formula) established in their agreement. A system of accounting must be agreed upon (especially if tracking milestones for additional investment or performance on behalf of the joint venturers is intended). Both parties will benefit from agreeing on as many of these points as possible when they initially enter into their joint venture agreement.

When appropriate, firms should consider joint ventures with universities and other not-for-profit institutions in order to benefit from their research facilities and resources. Most major universities maintain a patent office that licenses university-developed technology. One risk of joint ventures with universities is that university research rarely yields a ready-for-market product; refinement will be necessary for commercial exploitation.

TECHNOLOGY INCUBATORS AND FINANCING

Robert J. Calcaterra
Kathryn W. Calcaterra

Robert J. Calcaterra is the Chief Executive Officer and President of the Arizona Technology Incubator (ATI) in Scottsdale, Arizona. ATI is a nonprofit corporation jointly funded by private and public sources, charged with starting up and nurturing new technology-based businesses in the Greater Phoenix area. Dr. Calcaterra is also CEO and President of the Arizona Technology Venture Fund, a seed venture capital fund that will invest in new start-up companies in the state.

Kathryn W. Calcaterra is the Administrator of the NASA Technology Transfer Center within the Arizona Technology Incubator. This Center serves as NASA's representative in the state for the transfer of technology from federal research laboratories to the private sector.

Abstract

This article provides a brief description of the history and nature of business incubators and some financing sources available to incubators' client companies. The authors outline leading causes for the failure of start-up companies, criteria for successful incubators, and benefits available to client companies through incubators.

35.1 INCUBATOR HISTORY

Business incubators are multiple-tenant facilities that provide useful shared services and assistance to start-up companies, thereby increasing the companies' probabilities of success. Companies with common needs share business and technical support services, experiences, and resources. The incubator provides access to a network of experts who are familiar with the problems of new businesses and can provide management assistance, customers, and investors to entrepreneurs and to managers of start-up firms. The kinds of experience and counsel accessible through this network is not often available to or affordable for early stage companies.

In 1983, there were about 50 business incubators in the United States and Canada. Currently, there are approximately 500 incubators, which have been opening at the rate of one per week since 1986. Of these, some 60 incubators target technology products or processes as their client companies [1].

Incubators' physical facilities average about 24,000 square feet, and about 80 percent of them are affiliated (at least informally) with one or more colleges or universities [2]. Most occupy rehabilitated buildings. The primary objective of these nurturing enterprises is economic development. They are established to create new businesses that will provide more jobs in a specific geographic region. Business incubators are remarkably cost effective tools for economic development. They can create jobs for less than $2,000 per job, while other development methods cost five to 10 times as much.

35.2 THE NATURE OF INCUBATORS

Starting a company from the ground up is not an easy task. Small Business Administration statistics show that 50 percent of new businesses fail after three years, and that 80 percent fail after five years [3]. Inexperienced potential business owners need affordable facilities and services plus practical advice concerning the start up and operation of their companies in order to increase their probability of success. The National Business Incubation Association claims that 80–90 percent of its nurtured companies survive at least five years [4].

Although incubators share a general economic climate and some attributes, their organizational structure, financial backing, and client focus vary widely. Some incubation facilities are funded publicly through federal, state, city, or a combination of public resources. Others are privately funded enterprises, which are organized to make a profit for their investors. Still others are organized as public/private partnerships whose funds are provided by various governmental agencies as well as by donations from private corporations and individuals. These partnerships may be either nonprofit or for-profit.

The organizational structure of individual incubators reflects the nature of their funding sources. Those funded publicly or by public/private partnerships usually have a board of directors that hires a professional staff to operate the facility and provide business advice and counsel to the client companies. Unfortunately many of the privately funded incubators are primarily real estate enterprises that involve shared facilities and some office services but do not facilitate company development and job growth.

Many incubators specify specific target client populations; *i.e.,* minority businesses, service providers, or technology products or processes such as computer software, biotechnology, or medical items. Narrowing the target population helps incubator management personnel design specific programs to meet the specialized needs of their clients. In addition, clusters of companies in specific niches often attract customers and funding sources that are useful for many of the incubator's clients.

35.3 CRITERIA FOR SUCCESS

National Business Incubation Association studies [5] show that the causes of incubator failures are consistent and are concentrated in three primary areas.

1. client finance: the limited availability of equity capital or excessive short and long term debt leads to a high failure rate for incubator client companies;
2. incubator finance: inadequate funding for operations, facility improvement, and maintenance contributes to incubator failure. This is exacerbated by a tendency for funding entities to discontinue donations after two to three years; and
3. quality clients: the inability of incubator client companies to obtain investment and sell their products can lead to nonpayment of rent and fees as well as the inability of the incubator to graduate clients in a timely fashion.

These causes of failure are interrelated. If any two—or all three—happen at the same time, a snowball effect can occur. In other words when tenants are unable to acquire financing, they fail to pay rent and service charges, thus creating a bad debt problem for the incubator. This lost income makes it difficult for the incubator to cover its own expenses and makes fundraising very difficult. When an incubator manager spends a majority of his time raising money to cover the incubator's operating costs, he has less time to spend advising client companies and recruiting qualified businesses into the facility.

Incubators organized as public/private partnerships provide the strongest framework for such enterprises as long as the support is broad based and financial support is committed for at least five years. The most successful partnerships include financial and manpower participation from four essential support elements:

1. Government: city, county, and state agencies. Federal funds are more difficult to acquire;
2. Research university/college, which provides a source of potential clients as well as a network of expert technical and business advice;
3. Large industry: utility companies and major corporations; and
4. Service industry: law, accounting, and public relations firms.

Participants from these elements provide the incubator with contributions but equally importantly with a network of interested, experienced professionals who can be called on to provide counsel, advice, and potential customers and suppliers to client companies. To be successful, an incubator must graduate companies that are producing marketable products, processes, or services for profit. To help start-up businesses achieve this goal, technology incubators offer these benefits to their clients:

- a database of potential financial investors;
- a local and national network of business and technical experts, many of whom offer their services pro bono or at reduced costs;

- strategic plan and business plan development advice;
- immediate decision-making and problem-solving counsel;
- management team building introduction and advice;
- training seminars in management, marketing, and finance;
- negotiations assistance;
- accounting services;
- marketing research; and
- secretarial services including facsimile and copy machines.

35.4 CLIENT FINANCING

As mentioned earlier, the financial success of client companies is essential to the incubator's success; therefore, a major goal of the incubator is to help identify and acquire financial resources for its tenants. That leads to the obvious question: Which comes first? The chicken (client company) or the egg (financing)? Ideally in this instance, a highly qualified chicken comes first. Technology incubators usually have an experienced admissions committee to evaluate the technologies and potential for success of the companies applying for admission. They look for:

- a committed management team willing to listen to advice and counsel;
- existence of a niche market in which the company can attain a dominant position with a high gross margin; and
- a competitive advantage as a result of a proprietary position or unique skill, knowledge, or network. Once admitted to the incubator, a start-up company's management team, with the help of incubator staff, will write a business plan. A well researched and written business plan is a key tool in attracting investment. Searching for appropriate money to back start-up enterprises is a time consuming and often discouraging task. However, many sources of investment capital exist: venture capital, angels, receivables financing, debt (although this is highly unlikely for a fledgling company), SBICs (small business investment companies licensed to obtain debt capital from the Small Business Administration), SBIR and STTR grants (Small Business Innovation Research and Small Business Technology Transfer Research), and strategic alliances or partnerships with larger companies.

Relatively new on the investment scene are capital networks. For a fee, these programs offer electronic access to their local databases of investment sources. They often liken themselves to a dating service; *i.e.,* they match a company with one or more potential funding sources. Any relationship that results from the introduction is up to the participants to work out. Capital network programs in the Boston area and in Texas have been very successful in the last few years. Proponents of these networks are promoting a regional database to serve start-up companies in the Southwest. The ultimate goal is to provide a nationwide electronic network of capital investment.

Acquiring investment capital from these or any other sources is difficult and laborious. Consequently, some incubators are establishing their own seed loan and investment funds to provide nominal capital for their client companies to cover expenses during business plan development, market research, and product introduction beta testing as well as during the search for first round financing. In return for this investment (ranging from $10,000 to $25,000 per company), the incubator accepts a negotiated interest percent or an equity position in the client company. Money for the seed fund is raised from public and private sources specifically for investment and does not come from the incubator's operating funds.

35.5 CONCLUSION

Successful business incubators can provide new companies with the vital, nurturing environments they need to survive the taxing start-up process. To be a long term success, an incubator should be a financially sound public/private partnership with strong ties to a major research university. An incubator with a specific target client population can design its business development services to address problems and attributes of a particular industry.

There are two primary intangible benefits afforded industry specific incubator clients. First is the network of experienced supporters to solve problems and provide customers and investment sources. Second, incubator clients share a synergy and sense of purpose that help them face the tribulations of starting a new business. In regularly scheduled meetings directed by incubator staff, clients brainstorm to solve common problems; they encourage each other; they share their networks.

More tangibly, successful incubators provide their clients with networks of potential funding sources. The best nurturing enterprises can create sources of investment. In addition, incubator staff members offer advice and counsel on how to convert an introduction to a potential investor into an actual capital investment. The incubator provides a solid framework for success in a very difficult business climate.

NOTES

[1]   Dinah Atkins, Executive Director, National Business Incubation Association, One President St., Athens, Ohio 45701.

[2]   Scott D. Schroeder and Richard Greenberg, *The State of the Business Incubator Industry 1989* (Athens, Ohio: National Business Incubation Association, March 1990), pp. V–VI.

[3]   J. A. Timmons with L. E. Smollen and A. L. M. Dingee, Jr., *New Venture Creation: Entrepreneurship in the 1990s,* Third Edition (Homewood, IL: Irwin, 1990).

[4]   Schroeder and Greenberg, p. 22.

[5]   Schroeder and Greenberg, pp. 27–30.

BIBLIOGRAPHY ON BUSINESS INCUBATION

The following publications can be ordered from the National Business Incubation Association, One President Street, Athens, Ohio 45701.

The State of the Business Incubation Industry 1991. Athens, Ohio: 1992.

Elizabeth Levy, Terry G. Williams, and Dr. Richard T. Meyer. *The 1991 National Census of Public and Private Seed Capital Funds.* Atlanta, Georgia: Emory University Business School, 1991.

Candace Campbell of the Hubert H. Humphrey Institute of Public Affairs, University of Minnesota. *Change Agents in The New Economy: Business Incubators and Economic Development.* Charles Stewart Mott Foundation, 1988.

Raymond W. Smilor and Michael D. Gill, Jr., of the IC2 Institute, University of Texas at Austin. *The New Business Incubator: Linking Talent, Technology, Capital and Know-How.* Lexington, Massachusetts: Lexington Books, 1986.

Article 36

THE PROS AND THE CONS OF INVENTION MARKETING

Richard C. Levy

Richard C. Levy is president of Richard C. Levy & Associates, in Bethesda, Maryland, a product development firm specializing in toys and games. He is author of the highly praised *Inventor's Desktop Companion*, published by Visible Ink Press. His most recent patented inventions include Playskool Baby's *One-Plus-One* pacifier, Remco's *Switchblade* transforming vehicle, and *Blirds*, a plush line from Ganz.

Don't be surprised if you learn about your patent from an invention marketing company before the PTO advises you. Many invention marketers subscribe to the PTO's Official Gazette as an inexpensive way to obtain a qualified mailing list of inventors and often beat the Office to the punch.

Anyone who has been awarded a patent over the past twenty-five or thirty years has no doubt received a letter that began with the fateful words, "Dear Inventor: A number of manufacturers have invited us to send them descriptions of your invention . . ."

After 18 years of experience inventing and licensing original concepts to industry, and having licensed over 80 products to firms ranging from Hasbro and Mattel to P&G, I have formed an educated opinion about the writers of such letters (a/k/a Front Money Frauds), as well as like companies that take out "Inventions Wanted" ads on late night radio call-in shows (*e.g.,* Dial 1-800-I HAVE AN IDEA), in magazine and newspaper classified sections, and on night-time and mid-day television programs.

My position on these so-called invention marketing companies is that they are most often nonperforming, paracreative slugs who, like California condors, make their nests in caves high on cliffs, just out of reach (of the law). And like the vultures they resemble, they kill for food (monetary fees), slowly soaring the skies looking for inexperienced, starved, and frustrated creatures such as inventors who are seeking an easy way to cash in on their million dollar ideas.

Fortunately, the Attorneys General in dozens of states are trying to make these predators as endangered a species as the North American land bird they resemble. So too is the U.S. Federal Trade Commission. And numerous states (*e.g.,* California, Illinois, Minnesota, North Carolina, Ohio, South Dakota, Tennessee, Texas, Washington, and Virginia) have enacted protective legislation on behalf of resident inventors.

Fred Hart, Outreach Inventor Liaison, at NIST's Office of Energy Related Inventions, describes as "pure and simple garbage" the work done by most invention marketing services.

It is almost a guarantee that if you engage the services of an invention marketing company that you'll get ripped off.

Jim Kubiatowicz, former director of product development at Spearhead Industries, says of invention marketing companies, "They scare the living daylights out of me. They're leeches. They prey on novices."

If you have a complaint against an invention marketing outfit, file it with your state attorney general. The AG's office will tell you if previous complaints have been received about the same marketer.

If you would like to know whether a specific invention marketing company has been cited by the U.S. Federal Trade Commission, the easiest way to learn is by filing a Freedom of Information request. Send it to Office of FOIA, The Federal Trade Commission, Washington, DC 20580.

If you would like to see a sample of protective inventor legislation, request a copy of Minnesota's Invention Services Legislation 325A.02 or Virginia's Chapter 18, 59.1–209. These are excellent examples of how such legislation should be written.

Are there reputable invention marketers? Yes, of course. But none that I have ever seen advertise in the mass media. The best handle a few choice inventors and take No up front money. I repeat for emphasis, No up front money.

Pros pay their own marketing expenses and receive as payment a percentage of any rewards the invention might generate. Their percentage can run from a third to a half of an inventor's future royalties on a specific invention. If the marketer performs, in my opinion, there is nothing out of line with a 50 percent cut.

A reputable and active marketing company will be able to show you a track record of successful placements and put you in touch with satisfied clients.

So where can one find reputable assistance? The best way I know is to get recommendations from corporate executives in the very industry you target. For example, if you want to license a game to Milton Bradley, ask someone in Milton Bradley's R&D department for the name of an agent the company deals with on a regular basis. Who better to recommend an honest broker than a company that benefits from the broker's work.

Ask fellow inventors. Word spreads fast about bad apples. Many inventor organizations maintain files on sleazy invention marketing services and often write them up in their newsletters.

It is a misconception that there is an easy dollar to be earned. In a land of instant millionaires; very few folks actually make a lot of money. Even though the market is big, the competition is ferocious. Remember, nothing is as easy as it looks, and everything takes longer than you think.

Caveat Emptor!

Article 37

LICENSING TECHNOLOGY

Vance A. Smith

Vance A. Smith is a principal in the intellectual property law firm of Camoriano and Smith in Louisville, Kentucky. He has written and negotiated over 300 license agreements involving companies residing in more that 40 different countries. Mr. Smith has been actively involved in the Licensing Executives Society and the Licensing Executives Society International.

After a concerted effort, an exclusive right to intellectual property has been obtained. Why would a company then be willing to permit (license) others to use its intellectual property?

There are a number of reasons. Some of these reasons, such as obtaining a royalty income in return for use of the intellectual property, are obvious. This is particularly so where the company is not using the licensed technology itself; or the company is unable or unwilling to meet the demand for products using the licensed intellectual property by itself:

- *The company may not have the capital to expand its production facilities or it may have other product lines to which it must devote all of its resources.*
- *It might not be practical or economical for the company to export product into a particular geographic area, or to establish its own manufacturing facilities in that area.*
- *The company might not have the resources or contacts to develop a necessary distribution system in the area.*

Other reasons for licensing intellectual property, however, are not necessarily obvious:

- *Having an additional source for a given product may increase the market acceptance of the product.*
- *The company itself might use the licensed product as a part in another product, or sell the licensed product as part of an overall line of products, but find it uneconomical or impractical to manufacture the licensed product itself. By licensing another party that can economically manufacture the product, the company can ensure a source of supply. The fact that the product also may be available to the company's competitors is offset by the compensation paid to the company by the licensee.*

> • *Licensing a local in a given geographic area to manufacture one product may create a market in that geographical area, or at least increase market acceptance for other products of the company.*   MAL

Abstract

Licensing of technology involves the transfer of technical information and intellectual property rights such as patents, trade secrets, confidential know-how, and trademarks through a contractual arrangement called a license agreement. While the negotiations and preparation of license agreements may be complex, provisions specifying grant limitations, payment terms, and other conditions are common to almost all license agreements. Some of the more common provisions and the rationale behind them are described in this article.

37.1 INTRODUCTION

The licensing of intellectual property is a significant recurring activity among large and small businesses in our modern world. The increase in this phenomena can perhaps be best understood in the following context:

37.1.1 Downsizing

Due to the downsizing of many large companies to meet international competition and ensuing cutbacks in research and development, large companies are becoming more aware of the technical contributions and capabilities of the smaller sized companies. They have become more amenable to "licensing in" technically compatible developments to supplement their slackening research and development efforts and to receive the rights to intellectual property that serve to facilitate the transfer of developed and developing technology among businesses.

37.1.2 More Technology

Despite the cutbacks in R&D, it is estimated that over 90 percent of all scientists and engineers who have ever lived are alive today. Largely through their efforts, the development of technology is progressing at a blurring pace, increasing the magnitude of technology available for licensing.

37.1.3 Many Different Technologies Needed

To be an expert on all aspects of technologies that go into the making of a complex product or machine or the development of a process is an impossible task for any single company. The many technical disciplines have created what amounts to a scientific Tower of Babel. Companies are finding it simpler and more economical to license the fruits of the special technical expertise of other companies or universities to supplement their own technical development efforts. It has become popular today to form "alliances" among companies to develop products and processes with follow up license arrangements to facilitate the use of the newly developed, cross disciplinary technology.

37.2 GENERAL DISCUSSION

To take advantage of the growing opportunities for transfer of technical development information, the developers of technology must ensure that the technology is protected to the greatest extent possible by intellectual property rights. Patents should be sought on key aspects of the technology and care should be taken that rights to foreign patents are preserved. Other aspects of the technology more appropriate to trade secret protection should be treated in a confidential manner. Liberal use should be made of copyrights, design patents, mask works, and trademarks where appropriate. Enhancing technology with good intellectual property rights will make the technology much more valuable in dealing with any potential licensing partners.

Licensing is perhaps best defined as the transfer of proprietary rights to intellectual property from an owner of the rights to a third party in such a manner that the third party can legally use all or a portion of those rights. By licensing the intellectual property rights, the third party can then utilize the technology protected by the rights. Transfer of rights can be total as where one party sells or assigns a patent to the other. In this circumstance, the assignor of the rights has given up all rights to the patent and cannot legally continue to make, use, or sell products covered by the patent. The transfer, however, can be partial such as in the case where the third party is granted a nonexclusive license to make, use, or sell products under the patent. Under a nonexclusive license, the owner still retains certain rights under the patent including the right to provide a nonexclusive license to others.

Numerous and flexible forms of transactions fall within the licensing spectrum defined at one end by total transfer of rights and at the other end by a limited and controlled transfer. Due to the flexibility and wide range of choices permitted, licensing is an extremely attractive and essential part of many business strategies today. In some instances, licensing allows companies having limited resources to penetrate geographically distant markets using licensees located in the market regions to make and sell products. In other instances, proprietary technology otherwise doomed to lie fallow can be licensed to others for consideration. Companies that wish to quickly diversify their product lines without top to bottom product development may find that it makes economic sense to license the right to make and sell products developed elsewhere. The business reasons for using licensing are legion in number.

37.3 DISCUSSION OF SOME COMMON
IMPORTANT PROVISIONS

A typical licensing agreement can be long or short, the length often depending upon the depth and extent of the negotiations preceding the written agreement. Because of the relative long duration of most licensing agreements, clauses should be drafted to anticipate contingencies that have a significant probability of occurring and would impact heavily on the activities set forth in the license agreement. Additionally, many licenses involve various types of intellectual property including confidential know-how, patents, trademarks, copyrights, mask works, and utility and/or design patents, all of which require individual treatment. For example, when rights to proprietary know-how are being transferred, it is often necessary to set forth in intricate detail provisions governing the transfer and the rendering of technical assistance (a form of technology transfer) to implement the use of the know-how by the licensee. As a general rule, licensing agreements are tailored to the particular situation at hand and influenced heavily by the negotiations. Some of the common major provisions are described in more detail in the ensuing paragraphs.

37.3.1 Grant

The grant includes the language defining the exact rights being transferred to the licensee and the limitations imposed on the use of the rights once the agreement is executed. For example, the grant may provide to the licensee the exclusive right to make, use, and sell products employing the proprietary technology or covered by the patents of the licensor. The exclusive license precludes the licensor from either making, using, or selling the products or licensing the proprietary technology or patents to another party. Another example of a limited grant is the field of use restriction that, for example, may limit the right granted to the licensee to sales of the products to specified industries. A nonexclusive license, another form of a limited grant, would allow the licensor to retain the right to license other parties or the right to make, use, or sell the products itself.

The grant may be limited in geographical scope. Businesses wishing to preserve certain regions for their own use may grant a third party rights limited to specified territories outside of the preserved region. This type of license is frequently employed by companies having limited resources to exploit proprietary technologies on a broad geographical scale when the window of opportunity for commercialization of the proprietary technology has a small time duration. Additionally, companies may wish to ensure the products embodying their technology enjoy widespread commercial popularity, perhaps securing a long-term market success before a competitor obtains a market share.

Other limitations to the grant may involve granting exclusive rights to manufacture in a specified territory but nonexclusive sale rights in a broader geographical territory. Many licenses granted to licensees located in the European Union (formerly the European Economic Community) have exclusive manufacturing rights in the home country of the licensee and nonexclusive sales rights in the remainder of the European Union countries. The rules and laws of the European Union Commission and Treaty of Rome establishing the Union discourage (but do not preclude) grants of exclusivity by severely limiting the term, *i.e.,* the time period, of the exclusive license grant.

There are many other variations of grants that are used in license agreements that are limited in substance only by the imaginations of the parties negotiating the agreements. The grant embodies the essence of the marketing strategies of the parties and can involve extensive negotiations. The parties should strive to word the language of the grant so as to avoid later conflicts.

37.3.2 Consideration for the Grant

There are endless ways in which the licensor can be paid ("consideration") for the transfer of intellectual property rights. This payment is not based upon an exact formula but represents what the parties consider to be a fair return. The licensor wants to share in the profits made by the licensee selling products or using processes that pertain to the transferred intellectual property rights. Yet the sharing must be equitable to both parties. Usually the licensee assumes most of the risks and thus gets the "lion's share" of the profits. Because profit is an elusive concept to define in a license agreement, the parties generally prefer to use a royalty that is based upon the gross selling price of a product manufactured under the intellectual property rights. For example, if the major intellectual property transferred is a patent, then often the licensor is paid at specified time intervals an agreed-to percentage of the selling price of the product covered by one or more claims of the patent. The exact percentage of the royalty ultimately agreed upon by the parties depends to a great extent upon the following: the perceived value to the licensee of the intellectual property rights; what is being transferred to the licensee; whether the grant is exclusive or not; the extent of territorial limitations; the contributions of each party; and the risk being assumed by the licensee.

For example, if the rights are solely limited to patent rights, then the royalty percentage will likely be less than in the situation where additional rights are transferred such as confidential know-how embodying substantial technology. Exclusive rights demand higher royalties than nonexclusive rights. If the licensor provides significant know-how and technical assistance teaching the licensee how to utilize the know-how, then the negotiated royalty percentage will likely reflect the higher contribution by the licensor.

The payment also can be a flat sum for each product sold. Many licensors prefer to avoid flat sums, particularly if it is likely that the sales price will rise during the term of the license. Additionally, when a process for making a product is licensed, the parties may find it more palatable to calculate the royalty based upon volume of product made or some through-put calculation appropriate for the particular process.

37.3.3 Minimums

Licensors often are concerned about the licensee's dedication to market products under the license, particularly when the grant is exclusive and the term of the agreement is long. In such instances, the licensor is concerned that lack of motivation on the part of the licensee may lead to diminished royalties. Unless a protective mechanism is included in the agreement, the licensor may be left in the unenviable position of having negotiated away all rights to the intellectual property and yet receiving little royalties. To encourage good faith efforts in marketing, licensors often include a clause setting forth an annual minimum royalty payment. Minimum royalties come into play only when sales of the licensee actually do not support the payment of a royalty reaching the minimum royalty level. This provides modest income protection for the licensor. Other solutions may involve a reversion of the transferred rights if the royalty actually paid continues below a specified minimal level. When a reversion occurs, the licensor has the right to find another licensee or make and sell the licensed products itself.

37.3.4 Continuing Obligations of the Parties

License agreements are often considered executory agreements since the agreements often have performance obligations that continue long after the agreement is initially entered into between the parties. Some executory obligations are discussed below.

37.3.4a Technology Transfer Provisions

When know-how is to be transferred under the license, the license agreement should have provisions setting forth in detail how and when the technology is to be transferred. The licensee often is provided the right to visit the facilities of the licensor where the technology is being used to gain experience in how to best utilize the technology. The licensor also may be required to provide a defined number of hours of its qualified employees' time to consult at the facilities of the licensee.

37.3.4b Confidentiality Obligations

When exchange of confidential information is required under the agreement, the parties also will agree to maintain the information in confidence and use the information only for the purposes permitted by the agreement. This is a particularly important provision when key aspects of the technology can be protected only by the preservation of the confidentiality of the information. Often, the confidentiality provisions specifically state that the obligation to maintain confidentiality survives the termination of the agreement itself.

37.3.4c Improvements

Frequently when substantial technology is transferred, the parties may agree to share knowledge of improvements that each party makes during the term of the agreement. Thus, as each party reaches an agreed-to stage in the development of improvements to the technology, the other party may be given the right to use the improvements including any intellectual property rights covering the technology commensurate with the limitations imposed by the grant. These rights to improvements are often called *grantbacks*. This sharing of the fruits of continuing research and development is often an essential part of the business strategies of each of the parties as it provides some assurance the technology will remain competitive.

37.3.4d Infringement Responsibilities

The parties must determine who is going to be responsible for enforcing the licensed intellectual property rights that may be infringed by a third party during the term of the agreement. Often the parties share the responsibility. Where the license is exclusive, frequently the licensee shoulders a significant part of this burden. In nonexclusive arrangements, the licensor usually remains responsible.

37.3.4e Boiler Plate Provisions

Many license agreements contain standard provisions, which are called *boiler plate* provisions. Most of them are couched in language to ensure that the parties are not held liable in certain situations. These should be drafted and reviewed carefully and not given short shrift in the negotiating process. For example, often waiver of warranty provisions are found in this part of the agreement. Such waivers can have a dramatic effect on the obligation of the licensor if the technology does not perform as expected. Provisions prohibiting assignment of the agreement to third parties are often included. An assignment prohibition may be a critically damaging provision if the licensee is purchased by a third party where the reason for the purchase is the manufacture and sale of the very products under license.

37.3.5 Term and Termination of the Agreement

All license agreements should set forth the duration of the agreement, *i.e.,* the *term* and conditions under which the agreement may be terminated prior to the end of the term.

37.3.5a Patent Licenses

The parties to a pure patent license typically set the term of the agreement to expire upon the expiration of the licensed patent. Any effort to pay royalties beyond that date can subject the parties, particularly the licensor to governmental scrutiny. Care must be exercised when considering extending royalty payments beyond the patent term.

37.3.5b Mixed Licenses

In agreements involving mixed intellectual property rights, negotiating the term of the agreement can be complex. If, for example, the life of the patent is perceived to be shorter than the life of the confidentiality of the transferred know-how, it is likely that the parties may want to establish a term of the agreement substantially longer than the term of the patent. However, governmental limitations on doing this often exist such as in the European Union and many developing countries. Some governments even provide fixed terms for mixed agreements.

Many of the developing countries, such as Brazil, have governmental policies and regulations that limit license grants to certain time periods. After the expiration of a specified time period, the licensee has the free and usually unencumbered right to use the proprietary technology as it wishes without any further consideration flowing to the licensor. Thus, licensors must consider carefully the constraints imposed by governmental regulations as a factor in its global marketing strategy before entering into a licensing agreement.

Often royalty rates must be reduced as patents under license begin to expire to satisfy government regulations and, of course, the licensee's concern that the intellectual property rights are becoming less valuable. Since trademarks and copyrights have altogether different terms that vary from country to country, mixed licenses will undoubtedly be of significantly increased complexity.

37.3.6 Breach and Termination

Provisions in most all but the simplest of license agreements permit one of the parties to terminate the agreement due to a significant and unremedied breach of the agreement by the other party. In anticipation of breaches, the parties must consider the following when negotiating a license agreement: how confidential information is to be treated after termination; whether the licensee will be able to fill orders already entered for licensed products; and what to do with the inventory of licensed products in the licensee's possession.

37.3.7 Conclusion

The specific situations of the parties dictate whether or not some of the provisions mentioned above (or others not mentioned) should be included or not included. Careful and well thought out negotiations determine the precise wording of each included provision. It is also important to have a check list of various licensing provisions available when considering licensing as a business strategy. Good check lists for licensing may be found in some of the publications in the reference bibliography.

BIBLIOGRAPHY

Szczpanski, Steven Z. *Eckstrom's Licensing in Domestic and Foreign Operations,* v. 1. Clark Boardman: New York, New York, 1990.

Goldscheider, Robert. *Eckstrom's Licensing in Domestic and Foreign Operations: The Forms and Substance of Licensing.* Clark Boardman: New York, New York, 1990.

White, Edward P. *Licensing: A Strategy for Profits.* KEW Licensing Press: Chapel Hill, NC, 1990. (Available by writing the Licensing Executives Society, 638 Prospect Avenue, Hartford, CT 06105-4298.)

Goldscheider, Robert. *Technology Management: Laws/Tactics/Forms.* Clark Boardman: New York, New York, 1988.

PATENTS, DATA RIGHTS, AND SOFTWARE IN U.S. GOVERNMENT CONTRACTING

Frank J. Bogacz and Robert M. Handy

Frank J. Bogacz is a Senior Intellectual Property Attorney for Motorola dealing with IP issues in government contracting. He currently covers patent, copyright, trademark, and licensing legal issues for Motorola's Government and Systems Technology Group. He has one U.S. patent.

Robert M. Handy is Group Intellectual Property Counsel for Motorola, Inc., responsible for IP issues and licensing related to Motorola's Government and Systems Technology businesses, including Motorola's new global satellite cellular telecommunications project known as the IRIDIUM System.

The U.S. Government can be a substantial customer of a company. It also can be a source of funding for Research and Development. However, there are dangers to the uninitiated in doing business with the government. The unwary can literally give away valuable intellectual property rights. The following article discusses the treatment of intellectual property in government contracts and points out some of the pitfalls.   MAL

Abstract

Intellectual Property (IP), *e.g.,* inventions, technical data, software, patents, copyrights, trade secrets, documentation, etc., is involved in almost every U. S. Government contract. The ownership of rights to the IP generated by a contractor before as well as during a Government contract depends on the applicable procurement regulations and the particular facts and circumstances of the contract. The Federal Acquisition Regulations (FAR) and Defense Federal Acquisition Regulations Supplement (DFARS) that apply to IP are described and the rights of ownership or licenses of various kinds that may be retained by the contractor or acquired by the government are explained. Generally the government gets at least unlimited rights in the "foreground" IP developed under the contract, and may acquire some rights to and even ownership of a contractor's preexisting "background" IP, depending on the circumstances. What must be done to prevent the Government from acquiring unlimited rights or ownership of a contractor's background IP is explained.

38.1 INTRODUCTION

The intellectual property (*e.g.*, inventions, works of authorship, technical data, software, etc.) that a Government contractor creates may be divided into two categories, background intellectual property and foreground intellectual property. Background intellectual property rights are generally those rights that the contractor has established prior to entering into a Government contract. Foreground intellectual property rights are those rights that are established during the term of the contract as specified by the U.S. Government procurement regulations. Intellectual property created by the contractor during the term of the Government contract but not funded by the contract may become background or foreground intellectual property, depending on the particular circumstances and the scope and deliverables of the contract. A key question is, as between the contractor and the Government, who has what rights in this intellectual property. Typically, background intellectual property rights belong to the contractor and foreground intellectual property rights belong to the Government. But, this is not always so and the outcome depends significantly on the details of the transaction. The federal government procurement regulations treat patents, copyrights, and trade secret technical data somewhat differently.

38.1.1 Patents in Government Contracting

What patent rights do the Government and the contractor each obtain under a Government contract? The answer is governed by the Federal Acquisition Regulations (FAR) for most U.S. Governmental agencies. Certain agencies such as NASA and the Department of Energy have their own patent regulations. In addition, each Government agency may have a subset of regulations, which it may include in a contract under certain circumstances. For example, the Department of Defense uses the Defense Federal Acquisition Regulation Supplement (DFARS), which differs in some respects from the FAR. However, the most common regulations dealing with ownership of inventions and patents in a Government contracting situation are: (1)FAR 52.227–11 (the –11 clause); (2)FAR 52.227–12 (the –12 clause); and (3)FAR 52.227–13 (the –13 clause).

No matter who obtains title to an invention made on a contract, an important question is, what subject matter is included. As with most government regulations, it is essential to understand clearly the definitions of the various terms used in regulations. Title is obtained in a "subject invention". A "subject invention" is an invention conceived or first actually reduced to practice in the performance of work under the contract. This is a two-pronged test. If the invention satisfies either prong, it is a "subject invention": (1) Was the invention conceived in performance of work under the contract, or (2) was the invention first actually reduced to practice in performance of work under the contract?

Small Businesses: The –11 clause [1] is used by the U.S. Government when contracting with small businesses. This provision provides that the contractor/inventor retain title to inventions subject to a royalty free license to the U.S. Government for the Government's purposes. Thus, the contractor is permitted to retain title for commercial use to any patent on any "subject invention" made on the contract.

Other Than Small Businesses: The −12 clause [2] is used with contractors which are not small businesses and provides that the contractor may elect to retain title to any "subject invention" made "on the contract". Similar to FAR 52.227–11, the FAR 52.227–12 clause provides that the Government obtains a nonexclusive, irrevocable royalty free license under any patent on any "subject invention" for any Government purposes. The contractor may elect to retain title to the patent for any non-U.S. Government sales (*e.g.,* sales to foreign governments) and for commercial products. One difference between FAR 52.227–11 and 52.227–12 is the amount of time the contractor has to elect to retain title to the inventions made under the contract, *i.e.,* two years after disclosure under 52.227–11 versus only eight months under 52.227-12.

The Federal Acquisition Regulations provide that U.S. Government agencies are to use FAR 52.227–12 unless certain exceptions apply. The −12 patent rights clause is to be used when the contracting agency is the Department of Defense, the Department of Energy (DOE) or NASA, even though DOE and NASA also have their own regulations.

Acquisition by the Government: The −13 clause [3] provides that the Government obtains title to any "subject invention" and that the contractor/inventor obtains only a royalty free nonexclusive license to the commercial rights. The paragraph 13 patent rights clause is typically used where work is to be done outside the United States by a foreign corporation or is required by a treaty or executive agreement or is in best interests of the United States for foreign policy concerns. Some examples are encryption and bomb technologies.

So as can be seen from the above, the full range of ownership possibilities can exist. The FAR 52.227–11 and −12 clauses allow the contractor/inventor to elect to retain title to "subject inventions" while the Government obtains a license right for its purposes. However, the contractor may elect not to retain title and give title to the "subject invention" to the Government. A contractor may desire not to retain title to "subject inventions" since the obligation to timely file a patent application results. The other end of the spectrum is the −13 clause which allows the Government to retain title and the contractor/inventor to retain only a nonexclusive license for its own purposes. In either case, the Government is not obliged to file a patent application. Under the −11 and −12 clauses, the Government may file only if the contractor elects not to file or fails to timely file.

Under the −11 and −12 patent clauses, the contractor may elect to retain title to "subject inventions". In order to obtain title to "subject inventions", the contractor must follow a procedure of providing notification to the Government, electing to file and timely filing of the U.S. patent applications. The contractor must file a written report identifying the inventions to the Government and electing to retain title. The contractor must at its own expense provide for the filing of the patent applications in the U.S. Patent and Trademark Office. There are time limits associated with each of the events mentioned above. Should the contractor elect not to retain title to a "subject invention" or should the contractor fail to timely perform one of the actions mentioned above, title to the invention passes to the Government and the contractor will obtain only a nonexclusive license. Keep in mind that even if the contractor obtains title to the invention, the Government can assign a security classification to the patent application before or after it is filed, thereby placing it in limbo until the security classification is lifted.

How do you tell if an invention was conceived in performance of work under the contract? Conception includes the mental act of realization of a complete and operative invention. The mental act of conception must be corroborated with written evidence. Examples of conception might be a schematic drawing of a circuit or a flow chart detailing the steps of a particular method to be performed by a computer.

What does "in performance of work under the contract" include? This includes any work done by the contractor pertinent to the statement of work of the contract, performed while the contractor has the Government contract. Thus, the time span begins on the date on which the contract is signed by both parties and ends when substantially all the contract deliverables have been accepted by the Government.

If the invention was conceived in performance of work under the contract, the invention is a "subject invention". If the conception of the invention has taken place outside of work performed under the contract, as for example, in connection with a separate development effort unconnected with the contract, the invention is outside the first prong of the test, but may still be a "subject invention".

The second prong of the "subject invention" test is, has the invention been first actually reduced to practice in performance of work done under the contract. What does first actual reduction to practice include? There is a three-part analysis to determine whether there has been actual reduction to practice.

1. A first actual reduction to practice means that an actual reduction to practice occurs for the first time, under the contract. A reduction to practice includes the production of an operative physical embodiment of the invention. Drawings alone will not suffice.

2. An actual reduction to practice also includes the step of showing workability of the invention. Workability means the existence and testing of the invention under its normal working environment. For simple inventions merely constructing them and visual inspection may satisfy the workability requirement.

   Laboratory testing alone may not be sufficient to establish workability. In cases involving components of aircraft that must perform in varying environmental conditions such as pressure, vibration, heat, cold, sun, wind, and precipitation, courts have held that actual flight testing is required [4]. Although a few exceptions to the aircraft rule exist, generally this rule has been upheld by the courts [5].

   Computer simulation alone may not be effective to establish workability. Computer simulations may be used to evaluate the probable workability and utility of an invention. However, the courts have not clearly decided the issue of whether computer simulation will satisfy the workability requirement [6].

3. The last part of the reduction to practice test is that some practical utility must be identified for the invention. This step is relatively straightforward and most inventions satisfy this requirement.

So, for the invention to not become a "subject invention" and for the contractor to retain it as background intellectual property, the invention must pass both prongs of the test,
that is: the invention must be both conceived and first actually reduced to practice before
the contractor has the contract or completely outside the contract. Commercial products
with embedded inventions generally satisfy both prongs of the "subject invention" test and,
therefore, the contractor is entitled to retain its full right in any such inventions that may be
used in government contracts. However, if the invention is included in the deliverables (*i.e.,*
the contract cannot be performed without it) and it is first actually reduced to practice during the term of the contract (even though not funded by the contract), it will still be a subject invention. This is often overlooked.

The reduction to practice test speaks of first actual reduction to practice. The patent
laws of the United States permit inventors to file patent applications and obtain patents without having an actual reduction to practice. The filing of a patent application is a constructive
reduction to practice. The constructive reduction to practice accomplished by the filing of a
patent application is not a first actual reduction to practice and will not satisfy the requirements of the "subject invention" test. As a result, even though a contractor/inventor has an
issued U.S. patent, this background intellectual property right may be swept into the definition of a "subject invention" if the invention embodied in the patent has not been first actually reduced to practice prior to obtaining the contract. Therefore, a contractor/inventor may
unwittingly give the Government a license (or title) to a patent it has as background intellectual property simply by actually reducing this invention to practice on a Government contract. This is an example of how background intellectual property rights may be lost to the
Government by accepting a Government contract. If the −13 clause is included in the contract, the contractor/inventor may lose title (ownership) to the invention and patent under the
circumstances described above.

The phrase "in performance of work under the contract" noted above deserves further
discussion. In research contracts where there is a broad statement of work, the performance
test is satisfied if the item was conceived contemporaneously with contract performance
and was within the contract scope or resulted directly from contract performance. Thus, inventions that are merely peripheral to the main purpose of the contract effort may be swept
in and become "subject inventions". For example, a court held that a crash helmet developed on a contract concerning aviation medicines was made in performance of work under
the contract. This was due to the very broad statement of work included in the contract [7].

To be swept into a contract there must be a foreseeable nexus between the invention
and the work to be performed under the contract. To be excluded from being a "subject invention" in a development contract: (i) no research thereon must be covered by the contract; (ii) the item embodying the invention must not have been a foreseeable item to be
developed under the contract; and (iii) the work on the contract must not be closely carried
out with the development of the item. It is to be noted that in such cases the Government
has the burden of proof by preponderance of the evidence that the item was a "subject
invention".

What happens if the Government or its contractor infringes your patent? Title 28 USC
1498 provides that the Government may not commit the tort of patent infringement. How-

ever, a patentee can institute a claim against the Government in the U.S. Court of Claims. Recovery is limited to a reasonable royalty for use of the inventor's patent. The inventor may not obtain an injunction, treble damages or costs against the Government. However, it may be possible in certain circumstances to obtain attorneys' fees.

A Government contractor is authorized to infringe a U.S. patent if reasonably necessary to comply with the contract terms by the Authorization and Consent clause (FAR 52.227–1). However, financial responsibility for such infringement may still fall on the contractor if the contract is for commercial off-the-shelf products. FAR 27.201–2 provides that the Authorization and Consent clause will be used in all contracts, except when small purchase procedures apply. The Authorization and Consent clause may, however, be used even in those situations.

There are two versions of the Authorization and Consent clause, the main version and "Alternate 1". The main version of the Authorization and Consent clause should be used in all non-research and development contracts. Under this provision, financial responsibility for the infringement is determined by whatever infringement indemnity clause is included in the contract. When the Government is buying a substantially "commercial" product already developed by the contractor, the contractor is usually required to provide an indemnity (see FAR 52.227–3). "Alternate 1" should be used in research and development contracts. Usually, for R&D contracts, the Government will waive the indemnity (*e.g.,* see FAR 52.227–3). Even if the Authorization and Consent clause is not specifically inserted in the contract, the courts often will imply their insertion in the contract [8].

38.1.2 Data Rights and Government Contracting

What are the rights of the contractor and the U.S. Government in technical data? What is technical data? Technical data is recorded information of a scientific or technical nature. Examples of technical data include documents relating to research, experimental, developmental or engineering work; or information used or usable to define a design or process or to produce, procure, support, maintain, or operate items covered by the contract. Specific examples of technical data include research and engineering data, engineering drawings, specifications standards, technical reports, and computer software documentation, but not the software itself.

As with patents, technical data exist in two forms. Background technical data is data in which the contractor has a proprietary interest and may have certain intellectual property rights. Foreground technical data is data that is developed on the particular Government contract.

Typically a contractor has a background position with respect to intellectual property associated with the products it manufactures. Generally such valuable technical data constitute trade secrets. Trade secrets are any valuable information not generally known to the public that give the contractor a competitive advantage and that the contractor treats as a secret.

The rights of the Government and the contractor in either foreground or background technical data are generally set forth in FAR 52.227–14 or DFARS 252.227–7013. Typically a contractor retains ownership in background technical data, if that technical data was "developed" with its own funds prior to contract award. The contractor would retain title to this background data and the Government could, under appropriate circumstances, be awarded some set of Limited Rights in this background data. On the other hand, if technical data were developed with contract funds on the contract (*i.e.,* foreground data), the Government generally obtains Unlimited Rights to such foreground data even though the contractor usually retains title to this foreground data.

Unlimited Rights means that the Government may do whatever it pleases with the technical data, including disclosing the data to others without any restriction. The contractor retains title to such foreground technical data, but the Government has the unfettered right to destroy its trade secret value and place such data in the public domain.

The Government may obtain Limited Rights in technical data when the contractor agrees at contract formation time to deliver such technical data with Limited Rights. Limited Rights are a defined set of rights that inhibit the Government from disclosing such technical data without specific safeguards and only upon the permission of the contractor. The uses to which the Government may put such technical data are limited and the contractor retains title to such data. The contractor must mark the data with the appropriate Limited Rights legend required by the FAR or DFARS (depending on which applies) or there is an automatic default whereby the government obtains Unlimited Rights [9].

Where the contractor has partially developed and paid for the technical data and the Government has partially paid for the development of the technical data, the Department of Defense Federal Acquisition Regulations Supplement (DFARS) provide for "Government Purpose License Rights". The contractor can limit the Government's rights to Government Purpose License Rights only in a contract with the Department of Defense. Government Purpose License Rights are typically negotiated in a range between Limited Rights and Unlimited Rights. Typically the Government is granted Government Purpose License Rights for a time certain period, usually five years after which it receives Unlimited Rights.

The last kind of rights granted to the Government are Restricted Rights, which apply only to software. Restricted Rights are predefined in the regulations [10] and limit the actions of the Government with respect to software and in certain cases software documentation. In order for the contractor to limit the Government to Restricted Rights, the software must be background software "developed" off the contract. A more detailed discussion is provided in Section 38.1.3 of this article.

What rights in technical data does the Government obtain under Unlimited Rights [11]? The Government obtains the rights to use, duplicate, or disclose technical data in whole or in part in any manner and for any purpose whatsoever and has the right to permit others to do so. This includes the right to distribute the data to other companies to provide the same or similar equipment or services using this data. The Government obtains Unlimited Rights when it pays for the development of an item. Therefore, if Government funds are used to develop the item, the Government has Unlimited Rights in technical data associated with the item. The contractor does retain title to any such technical data subject to the Government's ability to destroy the trade secret quality of such technical data.

What does Limited Rights in technical data mean [12]? Limited Rights are the rights to use, duplicate, or disclose technical data in whole or in part by or for the Government with the express limitation that such technical data may not, without the written permission of the contractor furnishing the data, be released outside the Government or used by the Government for manufacture. It may be used by a party other than the Government for emergency repair and overhaul. It may be released to a foreign Government when that is in the foreign policy interest of the U.S. Government. Any such releases are subject to a prohibition against further disclosure.

When does the Government obtain Limited Rights in technical data? The Government obtains Limited Rights in technical data when the contractor has "developed" it "exclusively at private expense" and agreed to deliver it to the Government as a contract deliverable, and when the contractor properly marks the technical data so delivered. Thus, a contractor who agrees to deliver certain background technical data must ensure that the technical data is an item that has been developed "exclusively at private expense". This means that no government funds may be used to "develop" the item or service and the resulting technical data. Often a contractor has technical data in an item that is not "developed" off the contract as defined in the regulations. In such cases, the contractor may wish not to agree to deliver such technical data; may not take the contract until such technical data is "developed"; or may negotiate at contract formation time with the Government for Government Purpose License Rights treatment for such data funded by both the contractor and the Government. Further, unless the contractor marks such proprietary data with an appropriate legend, the Government may still obtain Unlimited Rights in the contractor's background proprietary technical data [13].

What rights does the Government obtain under Government Purpose License Rights? The Government obtains the rights to use, duplicate, or disclose the technical data in whole or in part and in any manner, only for Government purposes, and to permit others to do so only for Government purposes [14]. Government purposes include disclosing to other companies for competitive reprocurement but do not include permitting others to use such technical data for commercial purposes.

What does it mean for an item to be "developed" [15]? The item must exist and be workable. The item must be constructed or the process must be practiced. Workability means that the item is analyzed and tested sufficiently to demonstrate to a person reasonably skilled in the applicable art that there is a high probability that the item will work as intended. The item need not be at the stage where it could be offered for sale or sold on the commercial market nor must the item be actually reduced to practice within the mean of the patent laws as stated above.

Why is it important to determine whether an item is developed on or off the contract, with Government funds or contractor funds? If an item is "developed" on the contract, the Government gets Unlimited Rights in the associated technical data. If the item is developed off the contract, the Government normally obtains only Limited Rights or Restricted Rights in delivered items.

What does "exclusively at private expense" mean [16]? The term "exclusively at private expense" means that no part of the development of the item was paid for by the Government and that the development was not required for the performance of a Government contract. Independent research and development and bid and proposal effort are considered to be a private expense. Indirect costs are considered to be Government funded when the development is required for the performance of a Government contract even though the contractor may have funded that portion of the work with nongovernment funds. This is sometimes overlooked by contractors.

What is "required for the performance of a Government contract" [17]? Required for the performance of a Government contract means that the development was specified in the contract or the development was accomplished during, and was necessary for, performance of the contract, *e.g.,* it is a deliverable or essential to a deliverable.

Where are restrictive legends required? To avoid giving Unlimited Rights to the Government, the contractor must ensure that any technical data that is delivered under the contract is marked with the appropriate restrictive legend. If unmarked data is delivered or if the data is delivered with the wrong markings, the Government gets such data with Unlimited Rights. If unmarked or if company proprietary information is submitted, the Government may return it to the contractor for appropriate marking, however the Government is not under any obligation to do so. Thus, the burden is on the contractor to make sure that the technical data is correctly marked.

In order to preserve rights in technical data, the contractor must mark the technical data with a Limited Rights legend or a Government Purpose License Rights legend, as the case may be. The Limited Rights legend is shown in Appendix 1. The Government Purpose License Rights legend is shown in Appendix 2. The legends in Appendices 1 and 2 are only for the Department of Defense Federal Acquisition Regulation Supplement (DFARS). For protecting data rights subject to a Federal Acquisition Regulations (FAR), the Limited Rights notice of Appendix 3 should be used. Note, these notices are for technical data and not for software, which is governed by a different set of regulations (*e.g.,* "Restricted Rights").

38.1.3 Computer Software in Government Contracting

Computer software is treated differently than technical data under the Government Procurement Regulations. Again, as with data, if computer software is made on a contract, the Government receives Unlimited Rights in such computer software. In the Government procurement regulations, computer software documentation is sometimes treated as software.

Computer software is defined differently by the FAR and the DFARS Regulations. Under the FAR, computer software is defined as computer programs, computer data bases, and documentation thereof. However, these terms are not themselves defined in the FAR. Under the DFARS, computer software is defined as computer software and computer data bases only. Computer software and computer data bases are defined in detail in the DFARS.

In the DFARS, a computer is a data processing device capable of accepting data, performing prescribed operations on the data and supplying the results of these operations. Under the DFARS, a computer program is a series of instructions or statements in a form acceptable to a computer, designed to cause the computer to execute the operations. A computer data base is a collection of data capable of being processed and operated on by a computer.

Under the FAR, computer software documentation is included in the definition of computer software and is given the same treatment. Under the DFARS, however, computer software documentation is treated separately, but may be accorded the same treatment under certain circumstances, for example, in connection with Commercial Computer Software.

The FAR 52.227-19 purports to deal with "Commercial Computer Software", but does not define the term. However, it does define the term "Restricted Computer Software", which corresponds approximately to what we ordinarily think of as Commercial Computer Software. In the FAR, Restricted Computer Software means any computer program, computer data base, or documentation thereof, that has been developed at private expense and either is a trade secret, is commercial or financial and confidential or privileged, or is published and copyrighted.

Under the DFARS, Commercial Computer Software means computer software that is used regularly for other than Government purposes and is sold, licensed, or leased in significant quantities to the general public at established market or catalog prices. Under both the FAR and the DFARS, Commercial Computer Software and in some instances related documentation is accorded special treatment. That special treatment is typically a Restricted Rights treatment. This means that the Government will obtain only certain specified rights in the Commercial Computer Software and/or its related documentation.

What rights does the Government obtain in the computer software? Both the FAR and the DFARS provide for the Government obtaining Unlimited Rights or Restricted Rights in computer software depending on the circumstances. The DFARS provide the further option of the Government obtaining Government Purpose License Rights in mixed funded technical data and software documentation but not in computer software itself. (See the discussion of Government Purpose License Right under the Technical Data Section 1.2.)

When does the Government obtain Unlimited Rights in computer software? Generally, unless otherwise agreed in writing, the Government obtains Unlimited Rights in computer software when the Government pays for the development of the computer software. More specifically, the Government obtains Unlimited Rights in computer software which:

1. results directly from performance of experimental, developmental, or research work done on any Government contract;
2. is required to be originated or developed under a contract or generated as a necessary part of a contract;
3. constitutes a computer data base prepared under a Government contract which includes Government supplied information or information in which the Government has Unlimited Rights or which is in the public domain;
4. is prepared or required to be delivered under any Government contract which constitute corrections or changes to Government furnished computer software; and
5. is publicly available or released by a contractor without restrictions.

When does the Government obtain Restricted Rights in computer software? The Government obtains Restricted Rights in computer software when that software has been "developed exclusively at private expense". As is the case with data rights, "developed exclusively at private expense" means that no part of the cost of the development was paid for by the Government and that the development was not required for the performance of a Government contract, *e.g.,* a deliverable or essential for a deliverable. Independent research and development and bid and proposal costs are considered to be "at private expense". However, all other indirect costs are considered Government funded when the development was required for the performance of a Government contract. These indirect costs are considered funded at private expense when development was not required for the performance of a Government contract. These are DFARS definitions only.

What rights does the Government obtain under Restricted Rights in computer software? For both the FAR and DFARS, the Government obtains at least the rights to:

1. use the computer software on the computer for which it was acquired, even if that computer is transferred to a different Government installation;
2. use the computer software on a backup computer, if the computer for which the software was acquired is inoperative;
3. copy the computer program for archival or backup purposes (under the FAR all computer software, including documentation, may be reproduced for this purpose); and
4. modify or combine the computer software with other software as long as the derivative software is subject to the same Restricted Rights as the original computer software.

In addition, under the FAR the Government can adapt the computer software for its purposes. Further, under the FAR, as a fifth right, the government may disclose and reproduce the computer software for use by the Government's support service contractors for any of the purposes mentioned above. The above rights apply to commercial as well as non-Commercial Computer Software.

For the Government to obtain only Restricted Rights in computer software, it is necessary that the computer software be "developed at private expense" by the contractor. To be "developed" means that the computer software must exist and be workable. Workability means that the computer software has been analyzed and tested sufficiently to demonstrate to a reasonable person skilled in the applicable art that there is a high probability that the computer software will work as intended. The computer software need not be at the stage where it could be offered for sale or sold on the commercial market, nor must the computer software be actually reduced to practice. "Developed" is a lower standard than "actually reduced to practice" for patents. (See Patents Section 1.1). "Exclusively at private expense" means that no part of the development was paid for by the Government and that the development was not required for the performance of a Government contact. Failing either branch of this test gives the Government Unlimited Rights.

Although the DFARS provide for Government Purpose License Rights for technical data, no Government Purpose License Rights are available for computer software even in situations where there is mixed funding of the software; the definition of technical data to which the Government Purpose License Rights apply under the DFARS excludes computer software.

Generally unless the computer software is marked with an appropriate restrictive legend, the Government will obtain Unlimited Rights in such improperly marked or unmarked computer software, even if the computer software was "developed exclusively at private expense". Therefore, marking the computer software and documentation to be delivered by the contractor to the Government is as important as who paid for the development of the software. Simply put, the contractor loses its rights or gives the Government Unlimited Rights in any software which is not appropriately marked and is delivered to the Government under a Government contract.

For appropriate marking of computer software and associated documentation, a distinction between Commercial Computer Software and non-Commercial Computer Software is necessary. For the DFARS "Commercial Computer Software" is computer software that is used regularly for other than Government purposes and is sold, licensed, or leased in significant quantities to the general public at established market or catalog prices. The sales of significant quantities to the general public requirement is generally satisfied if 55 percent to 75 percent of the sales of the computer software are to non-U.S. Governmental entities [18]. The FAR does not define any specific criteria for when computer software is Commercial Computer Software, but does define "Restricted Computer Software" as mentioned above. Computer software other than "Commercial Computer Software" or "Restricted Computer Software" is non-Commercial Computer Software.

For software delivered under the DFARS to retain its status as Commercial Computer Software, the legend shown in Appendix 4 must be affixed to the software and to the related computer software documentation. In this particular circumstance, the computer software documentation is treated as having been delivered with Restricted Rights also. The documentation must also reference the Restricted Rights to be accorded to the software.

For software delivered under the FAR to retain its status as Commercial Computer Software (*i.e.*, "Restricted Computer Software"), it must be marked with the legend shown in Appendix 5. The contractor also may provide its standard commercial license agreement with the understanding that the minimum rights that the Government obtains in the Restricted Computer Software cannot be limited by the license agreement more than what is already provided in the FAR for "Restricted Computer Software rights". These minimum Restricted Rights are given at FAR 52.227–19 and listed above. Since computer software documentation is included in the FAR definition of Restricted Computer Software, the documentation also must be marked with this legend and will be accorded the Restricted Computer Software rights treatment given to the software itself.

Since contractors routinely mark their software with a copyright notice, even though the software is unpublished, the legend in Appendix 6 also must be affixed to the computer software and its documentation.

Non-Commercial Computer Software under the DFARS, (*i.e.*, computer programs and computer data bases) must be marked with the legend in Appendix 7. The corresponding computer documentation must be marked with the legend in Appendix 1 since computer documentation is treated as technical data rather than computer software under the DFARS. It is to be noted that a license agreement is required for specifying the rights in the computer software the Government is to receive and that the contractor may not limit the Government's rights more than what is provided under Restricted Rights in DFARS 252.227–7013 (a)(17).

Non-Commercial Computer Software under the FAR, (*i.e.*, computer programs, computer data bases, and documentation thereof) may be marked with the Restricted Rights notice given in Appendix 8. Where the notice of Appendix 8 is impractical to be used (*i.e.*, will not fit), the Restricted Rights notice of Appendix 9 may be used in its place.

Thus, in order for a contractor to give the Government only Restricted Rights, the following items are required:

1. an agreement that is incorporated into the contract stating the identity of the computer software to be delivered with Restricted Rights;
2. a license agreement specifying the rights to be accorded the Government, except for Commercial Computer Software under the DFARS;
3. marking the computer software and/or documentation as appropriate with the proper restrictive legend; and
4. reference the software rights limitations in the computer documentation.

The existence of the different required marking legends under the FAR and DFARS is a frequent source of confusion. But it is important to select the correct marking because of the automatic default to Unlimited Rights if the incorrect marking is used.

Following are a few practical suggestions for the marking of computer software with restrictive legends. Mark the computer software disk itself with the appropriate restrictive legend. Display the appropriate restrictive legend upon the initial screen or upon several introductory screen displays, if the software is so adapted. Mark the package in which the software is delivered with the appropriate restrictive legend. Embed the appropriate restrictive legend in the software as comments to be displayed if the software is printed or listed.

What about Copyrights? Where software is developed with Government funding, the contractor may retain copyright in such computer software, but must request permission from the contracting officer. The contractor must acknowledge the Government's sponsorship in such software.

NOTES

[1] FAR 52.227–11 (Short Form).
[2] FAR 52.227–12 (Long Form).
[3] FAR 52.227–13.
[4] *Gaiser v. Linder,* 253 F.2D 433, 1958.

[5]   *Bendix Corp. v. United States,* 220 Ct.Cl. 507, 1979.

[6]   *McDonnell Douglas Corporation v. United States,* 670 F.2D 156, 1982.

[7]   *Mine Safety Appliances Company v. U.S.,* 364 F 2D 385, 1966.

[8]   *G. L. Christian v. United States,* 312 F.2d 418; 160 Ct. Cl. 1 (1963).

[9]   See FAR 52.227–14(f) and DFARS 252.227-7013 (b) and (c).

[10] See FAR 52.227–19 and DFARS 252.227-7013 (c).

[11] See FAR 52.227–14 and DFARS 252.227-7013(a)(19).

[12] See FAR 52.227–14, Alternate II and DFARS 252.227-7013(a)(15).

[13] FAR 52.227–14, Alternate II and DFARS 252.227-7013 (b).

[14] See DFARS 252.227–7013(a)(14) and (b)(2).

[15] See DFARS 252.227–7013 (a)(10).

[16] See DFARS 252.227–7013 (a)(12).

[17] See DFARS 252.227–7013 (a)(16).

[18] See FAR § 15.804 (f) (2) (i).

SECTION

VII

TAKING STOCK OF INTELLECTUAL PROPERTY AND COPING WITH THIRD PARTY PATENTS

Intellectual property rights relating to new developments have been secured. A licensing program is instituted with respect to selected intellectual properties. Time marches on. The company enters into contracts both as the provider and as the recipient of product and services. Products evolve. Circumstances change. Intellectual property rights can be affected by those changes, both as to scope and applicability to the company's business. Liabilities can be created.

How can a company realistically assess and evaluate its actual intellectual property position? How can it minimize potential liabilities and exposure to third party claims of intellectual property infringement?

The following articles address those issues. MAL

EVALUATION OF PATENTS AS ASSETS

Daniel J. Noblitt

Daniel J. Noblitt is an attorney specializing in intellectual property law with Meyer, Hendricks, Victor, Osborn & Maledon, P.A., in Phoenix, Arizona. He has a degree in Electrical Engineering, with areas of concentration in digital and microprocessor-based systems and electroacoustics.

Abstract

After a patent has issued, it does not exist in a vacuum. The patent must be evaluated to determine its scope of protection for current products and its effectiveness for deterring infringers. The results of this evaluation affect the competitive position of the company, the company's attitude toward the competition, and the likelihood of attracting investors. Patents can be evaluated by examining the patent's scope and comparing it to relevant products. In addition, the patent's disclosure and the prior art should be reviewed to ensure that all legal requirements have been satisfied to confirm the validity of the patent. If problems should arise, the company must determine the best course of action for resolving these problems and proceed quickly before rights are lost.

39.1 INTRODUCTION

For many companies, especially entrepreneurial, technology-oriented firms, know-how and proprietary technology are the most valuable assets the company owns. Ideas and technology available only to a single competitor often make the difference whether a young company will survive and thrive or fade and disappear in a competitive market. It is this same technology that attracts investors willing to bet that the proprietary technology will push the company to the front of the pack.

Experienced CEOs and investors realize that, unlike most tangible assets, the value of technology varies directly and widely with the degree of legal protection it commands. As long as the legal protection endures, competitors can be kept at bay and forced to take a license, risk litigation, or try to compete without the advantage of the technology. If the protection fails, however, the competitive edge provided by the technology is lost, and company's fortunes and the investor's funds may well follow.

Generally, the most effective and reliable protection for proprietary technology is provided by patents. Although patents are well known, the protection they afford varies with their quality and scope. Indeed, the protection provided by a patent may not only vary, but cease to exist altogether if the patent is invalid. If crucial technology is covered by a weak or invalid patent, the company's competitive advantage may be virtually annihilated.

Although a weak or invalid patent may destroy the power provided by proprietary technology, many pitfalls can be foreseen. With some investigation and analysis, chinks in the technology's legal armor may be identified and analyzed before they are attacked. Although every weakness may not be fatal, knowledge of such potential hazards is essential to making wise choices.

The primary inquiry addresses whether the patents owned by the company provide protection for the vital technology. The scope of protection must be determined to establish whether alternatives or simple variations of the technology may be practiced without infringing the patent and circumventing the company's rights. Other matters, such as validity and confirmation of ownership, also must be addressed for a thorough analysis.

39.2 ABOUT PATENTS

A patent generally constitutes a deal between the federal government and an inventor. The only way to promote invention and entice inventors into disclosing their secrets is to provide an incentive. So the deal is this: if the inventor comes up with something new and useful and is willing to disclose it, the government will allow the inventor to prevent anyone else from making or selling the patented subject matter for 17 years. After that, anyone can use it.

Utility patents, which are by far the most common, can cover products, processes, or products made by processes. A patent comprises two principal sections: the disclosure and the claims. The disclosure describes the invention in detail, usually with reference to a set of drawings. The claims, on the other hand, define the scope of the legal protection and constitute the heart of the patent. If the claims are too narrow, competitors can design commercially viable products without infringing the patent. If the claims are too broad, they risk including previously known technology and being rendered invalid. But if the patent protects the invention so that the competition must infringe the patent or market an inferior product, the patent can be a powerful asset.

39.3 THE MAIN QUESTION: DOES THE PATENT COVER THE PRODUCT?

39.3.1 The Product

The main issue relevant in assessing a patent is, "Does the patent cover the commercial product?" The claims of a patent are infringed only by a party that makes or uses each element, or its substantial equivalent, of the claimed apparatus or process. To infringe a patent, an accused device or technique must include each and every limitation cited in the claims. If a single claim limitation is not included or performed in the accused apparatus or process, no infringement has occurred.

Perhaps the most important consideration is the product itself. Many patents are filed and prosecuted during the early stages of a product's life. As time passes, the product is often improved and features change. The final product is frequently much different from the prototype upon which the patent was based. Consequently, the claims must be revisited with an eye toward the most current version of the product to ensure that the coverage of the claims is not simply outdated.

39.3.2 The Claims

In construing a claim, the patent's disclosure, its prosecution history (correspondence between the Patent and Trademark Office and the inventor or his representative), other claims in the patent, and material that was invented and known prior to the patent's filing date (commonly referred to as the prior art) must all be considered. The starting place, however, is the language of the claim itself. An effective claim should describe a unique and necessary feature of the company's product or service that provides the company with a competitive edge. If the claim is not directed to a unique and necessary feature, a competitor can avoid infringing the patent by incorporating the important aspects of the product and eliminating those that are claimed.

The description in the claims should be as general as possible. Unnecessary limitations allow a competitor to avoid infringing the patent simply by changing one or a few of the enumerated details. Even if the claim is properly focused upon unique and necessary features of the product, unnecessary details allow competitors to circumvent the patent by leaving out those details in their products. Remember, if a product lacks a single element recited in the claim, it does not infringe. Therefore, a claim should not require a bipolar junction transistor if any transistor, like a MOSFET, will function just as well.

Other aspects of the claim language should also be examined. Preferably, the claims describe the essence of the invention as accurately and precisely as possible. Ambiguities in the claims often provide fertile ground for competitors to argue that a patent's scope is too narrow or too broad. Either way, such ambiguities may lead to costly and lengthy litigation, regardless of the validity of the argument. It should be noted that claims are construed in light of the disclosure. This means that terms that may seem ambiguous at first may be defined in the disclosure, so the disclosure must be analyzed as well.

Many patents include claims that are drafted in a form requiring "means for" performing a specific function, commonly referred to as *means for* or *means-plus-function* clauses. This form carries particular significance, for such claims are construed to include only the corresponding structure, material or acts described in the specification or their equivalents. Consequently, any limitations that are expressly or implicitly included in the specification regarding the subject matter of the "means for" clause may be interpreted as restrictions, thus potentially limiting the scope of the patent.

39.3.3 The Prosecution History

During the prosecution of a patent, certain limitations in the claims may be relied upon by the applicant. In addition, claims may be amended or added. Although limitations and amendments often allow the patent to issue by distinguishing the claimed invention over the prior art, reliance upon such limitations may ultimately restrict the scope of the claims. An applicant's reliance on certain restrictions reinforces the significance of these limitations as crucial to the invention's patentability. By the express admission of the applicant, each of the elements relied upon during prosecution is a significant aspect of the invention, and a system lacking these characteristics is arguably beyond the scope of the patent.

The prosecution history is fairly easy to analyze. Copies of the prosecution histories for all U.S. patents are available through the U.S. Patent and Trademark Office (PTO). A review of the prosecution history will disclose any representations or amendments that were made during the prosecution that might affect the scope of the claims. For example, if during prosecution the patentee ascribes a certain meaning to a claim limitation, the patentee may later be bound to that meaning in litigation where another meaning would be desirable. Similarly, if an applicant amends the claims to overcome a rejection for obviousness, the party cannot later claim that the amendment added an unnecessary limitation.

Analysis of the prosecution history also provides information about how carefully the application was examined before a patent was allowed to issue. If the PTO carefully reviewed the application and addressed the important issues, it is less likely that a court would be willing to second guess the PTO and declare the patent invalid. The result is a stronger patent. On the other hand, if the application received only perfunctory examination, a competitor is more likely to find problems that the PTO missed. Consequently, careful scrutiny enhances the likelihood that a patent will be found valid and enforceable, for it is less likely that a challenger could find issues that had not already been addressed and ultimately found to be satisfied.

39.3.4 The Prior Art

Perhaps the most limiting factor in interpreting a claim is the prior art. In essence, the prior art comprises anything that was public knowledge before the time the invention was conceived, or anything that became public knowledge more than one year before the patent application was filed. The prior art includes material that was made public by the inventor more than one year before filing. The prior art defines the outer limits of the patent, for the patentee cannot "reinvent the wheel" and patent it. The prior art not only includes everything that was known at the relevant times, but encompasses all that would be "obvious" to one of ordinary skill in the field at the time of invention or filing.

The prior art not only limits the scope of claims, but may render claims invalid. A patent claim is invalid if the subject matter of the claim is publicly known or described in a printed publication before the inventor conceives it; if the subject matter of the claim is disclosed or offered for sale to the public more than one year prior to the filing date of the patent; or if the subject matter of the claim was "obvious" at the time the invention was made to a person having ordinary skill in the field. Any claims that describe such matter are invalid and cannot be used against a competitor. The validity of the other claims in the patent, however, remain valid and enforceable until they are shown to be otherwise. Thus, each and every claim must be analyzed to determine the overall potency of the patent.

A review of the prior art may vary in its thoroughness according to the importance of the patent at issue (or the size of an investment). An extremely thorough search of the prior art may uncover a large quantity of prior art material that might not have been available to the PTO, but might become available to a competitor. Any such material that was unavailable during the PTO's examination may affect the validity of the patent, for the new material might include information that would render the claims anticipated or obvious. Thus, the most thorough analysis of the patent requires an exhaustive search of the prior art to ensure that the prior art analysis is accurate.

The down side of such a search is that costs dramatically increase with the thoroughness of the search. At a point, it is not worth digging any deeper for an investment of a particular size and risk. That point is up to the judgment of the individual investor. In some situations, a simple review of the prior art cited in the prosecution history may be sufficient. In others, a complete and exhaustive review of the prior art may be required to satisfy the investor's due diligence needs.

39.3.5 Resolving Problems in the Claims

Occasionally, a review of the patent may determine that the claims are too narrow to cover the current product or a knockoff product of a competitor. In this situation, a company may be able to change the scope of the claims to include the latest or competitive product. Reissue proceedings allow claims to be tailored to a particular product or infringer. If successful, the reissued patent can be invaluable in securing a company's rights. A reissue involves resubmitting the patent application to the PTO for a second try at a new set of claims. The new claims cannot include anything that was not disclosed in the original application, and the scope of the claims can be broadened only for a period of two years from the date the original patent issued. After two years, the claims can only be narrowed or clarified without expanding their coverage.

In addition, if a competitor relies on the original patent claims and designs a product before the reissue is filed, the competitor may be awarded a limited license to continue selling the product. This limit is based on a concept referred to as "intervening rights," which allows competitors to rely upon issued patents until a reissue is filed.

Once in a while, prior art is discovered which might arguably affect a patent. Competitors are often fond of sending previously unknown prior art references to patent owners and claiming that the patent is invalid in view of the newly discovered prior art. If it appears that the competitor might be right, or could at least make it into a nasty court battle, the patentee has a couple of options. First, the patentee can try a reissue as described above. The reissue may allow the patentee to change the scope of the claims to avoid the new prior art, but still encompass the relevant products.

On the other hand, if it is simply a question of resolving whether the new prior art reference affects the validity of the patent, the patentee can petition the PTO for a reexamination of the patent. If the reexamination is granted, the patent application will be reexamined for patentability, but the analysis will include the new prior art. This is a somewhat risky proposition, for if the PTO decides against patentability, the patent terminates. But if the reexamination is favorable, it can be a powerful endorsement of the patent's validity. Reexamination has the added advantage that, unlike federal court proceedings, the patentee can argue its case without significant interference from competitors.

39.4 VALIDITY ISSUES

The starting point for evaluating the validity of a patent is determining whether the patent has ever been tested. An accused infringer typically attacks the validity of the patent. If the patent was found to be invalid, the inquiry stops. Once a patent has been adjudged invalid by a federal court and all appeals have been exhausted, it cannot be recovered. The patent is lost forever. On the other hand, if the patent was found to be valid, its validity can be challenged by the next infringer as well. But each time the patent's validity is successfully defended, it becomes more likely to be upheld by other courts, and become a more powerful competitive tool. Similarly, other challenges to a patent's validity and scope, like a reexamination proceeding in the PTO, often affect the perceived strength of the patent.

Under U.S. law, patents are accorded a strong presumption of validity. The relevant statute (35 U.S.C. §282) states:

> A patent shall be presumed valid. Each claim of a patent . . . shall be presumed valid independently of the validity of other claims; dependent . . . claims shall be presumed valid even though dependent upon an invalid claim. The burden of establishing invalidity of a patent or any claim thereof shall rest on the party asserting such invalidity.

A patent is valid unless (1) specific circumstances set forth in the statute occur, under which the invention is, in effect, deemed either to have already passed into the public domain, or to have become the property of another, or (2) it fails to meet the disclosure requirements of the statute with respect to the sufficiency of the patent specification and various formal requirements.

39.4.1 Timing and Procedural Requirements

A patent can also be rendered invalid if it can be shown that the invention was prematurely exploited. Under the public use or sale provisions of U.S. law, a patent may not be obtained if the claimed invention was "in public use or on sale in this country" more than one year prior to the application's filing date. If either of these events occurred, the patent is invalid. These requirements should be carefully investigated, for the PTO does not address these issues during the prosecution of the patent. Thus, if a mistake were made, it is unlikely to appear until it is too late.

To determine whether these criteria are satisfied, the dates of the first public use and the first offer for sale should be documented. Basically, the date of first public use is the date on which the invention or a device incorporating the invention was made available to the public. For many companies, this date coincides with a trade show or a similar event. Although test runs are not public uses, the test run must be truly for testing purposes, not simply verification that the invention is marketable.

Similarly, the "on sale" period is measured not from when the product is first sold, but when the product is first *offered* for sale. Even if the company has never sold a product, the patent can still be invalidated on these grounds. The investigation must determine when the initial offer sale was made; if more than one year passed between the initial offer and the filing of the patent application, the patent is invalid and worthless.

39.4.2 Statutory Disclosure Requirements

U.S. patent law (35 U.S.C. §112) also sets forth various formal disclosure requirements that must be complied with for a U.S. patent to be valid. These disclosure requirements generally comprise three individual areas: "description", "best mode", and "enablement". The description requirement requires the applicant to disclose a complete description of the system, including not only the structure of the invention, but "the process of making and using it". Similarly, the best mode requirement requires the inventor to disclose the best method of practicing the invention known at the time of filing. This requirement prevents an inventor from disclosing only prototype data that is outdated at the time of filing, or withholding information regarding particular components or the like that provide a particular and significant advantage over alternative components. Finally, the disclosure in the specification must be enabling to a person of ordinary skill in the field. Essentially, this means that the inventor must describe the invention in sufficient detail to allow his peers to make and use the invention without undue experimentation.

The sufficiency of the specification with respect to these requirements is determined as of the filing date of the application. In theory, an issued U.S. patent may be rendered partially or wholly invalid for failure to comply with the disclosure requirements. In practice, however, minor technical flaws typically are not fatal to patent validity.

Whether the enablement and description requirements are satisfied may usually be determined from the face of the patent. If the patent, including the written disclosure, drawings, and claims, includes a full description of the claimed invention, the description requirement is satisfied. Similarly, if a person of ordinary skill in the field could recreate the invention without significant difficulty by simply reading the patent, the enablement requirement is also fulfilled.

The best mode requirement is a bit trickier. The best mode requirement prevents inventors and companies from hiding the ball; the inventor is required to disclose the best known method of practicing the invention. This requirement prevents an inventor from disclosing an inferior version of the invention to throw competitors off the track. Because the government is granting an exclusive right to the invention to the patentee for 17 years, it insists on getting the best information possible. Failure to disclose the best mode results in invalidity.

Evaluating whether the best mode has been disclosed may be tricky because it is difficult to define "best mode". One mode may provide better or more reliable results, while others may be more economical. Typically, the best solution is to disclose the commercial version that is being marketed or is on the drawing board. Any intentional deception regarding claimed subject matter, however, may well lead to a verdict of invalidity.

It should be noted that each of these criteria is decided according to the inventor's knowledge at the time of filing. After the date of filing, the inventor can withhold all further information, even if he discovered a better mode the next day. This complicates the analysis, for the inventor's state of mind must be projected backwards, often over several years, to determine whether the invention disclosed was the best mode the inventor knew at the time of filing.

39.5 INEQUITABLE CONDUCT AND INVENTORSHIP

Inequitable conduct before the PTO presents a potential problem for every patent, though it is relatively uncommon, for a judgment of inequitable conduct renders the entire patent, not merely a few claims, unenforceable; the patent is useless. In essence, inequitable conduct amounts to intentionally deceiving the PTO. For example, every patent applicant is required to disclose everything within the applicant's knowledge that may be material to the patentability of the invention. If the applicant fails to mention a relevant prior art reference in its possession, the patent may well be held unenforceable for inequitable conduct. Any sort of materially deceitful or inequitable behavior by or on behalf of the applicant jeopardizes the enforceability of the patent.

In a similar vein, naming the wrong inventors can cause problems for a patent. In the United States, a patent is issued to the inventor or inventors. Anyone that contributed to the conception of the claimed invention is an inventor under U.S. law and must be named in the application. If someone did not contribute to the conception, he cannot be legally named as an inventor. This rule is inconsistent with those of many other countries, in which a research leader may take credit on a patent for ideas generated by a subordinate. Consequently, inventorship must be carefully considered, especially for inventions that originated in other countries.

An inaccurate list of inventors may endanger a patent's validity. Generally, where the list of inventors is inadvertently inaccurate, a court can correct it without any further consequence. On the other hand, if the party had reason to know that the list of inventors was inaccurate, the patent is invalid. For example, a party might leave an inventor off the list of inventors because he has recently departed the company on bad terms. If so, the company has shot itself in the foot, because the patent is invalid. Or, if another person is added to the list because he is the research team leader but had no part in the conception of the invention, the tribute to the added person's vanity will cost the company the patent.

Unfortunately, while these problems are rare, they are seldom detected until it is too late. Inequitable conduct and improper inventorship are understandably kept quiet until a thorough investigation, such as that associated with a lawsuit, uncovers the deceit. Consequently, little can be done other than to interview those involved, examine the file history for signs of problems, and hope for the best.

39.6 OWNERSHIP OF PATENT RIGHTS

Before relying upon the protection of a patent, a company must own the rights to the patent. Under U.S. law, all patents are originally the property of the inventor. Unless the inventor is under some preexisting obligation to transfer his rights to another party, he owns all rights in the patent. And like any other transfer of property, it is always best to get it in writing.

Preexisting obligations to transfer title to an invention frequently arise under two circumstances. First, the inventor may be obligated to transfer title to the invention because he is an employee and his job description includes inventing. For example, an in-house engineer employed to design systems is often legally obligated to transfer all interest in his inventions to his employer. A contract engineer, on the other hand, who is contracted for a particular job and is employed by another or by himself, assumes no such obligation. The dividing line between an employee and a contractor, however, is often hazy, making such distinctions dangerous to rely upon.

Second, transfer obligations may arise through contractual obligations, such as employment agreements and contracting agreements. Many of these contracts, especially employment agreements, contractually bind the employee to assign all inventions made in the course of employment to the company. These are often quite effective in preserving the company's rights in patents.

The best method of transferring title in an invention is to have the inventor execute an express assignment of the invention, including its title, a description, and the patent application serial number. This assignment should then be recorded in the U.S. Patent and Trademark Office Recording Office. When the assignment is recorded, its serves as a notice to the world that the patent is owned by the company. Failure to record an assignment in the PTO may result in another party claiming an interest in or full title to the patent. Thus, it is imperative to have the full chain of title recorded in the PTO to ensure clear ownership of the patent.

Another potential problem may arise with respect to inventions associated with a federal government contract. Some parts of the government, like NASA and the Department of Defense, have regulations and contractual provisions relating to ownership of technology developed or put into practice in conjunction with government contracts. These regulations and provisions vary according to which government branch is involved and the project characteristics. To establish clear ownership, however, any government interest must be examined closely in accordance with the appropriate regulations and the contract provisions.

39.7 CONCLUSION

Evaluation of a patent as an asset is a complicated but necessary process. The patent itself, its history, the product it protects, and competitors' products must all be considered to arrive at a useful conclusion. With this conclusion, the company is better equipped to evaluate its own competitive and legal position.

Ultimately, a useful patent is evaluated by somebody, whether it is the owner, a potential investor, or a hostile competitor. Analyzing a patent as an asset provides a company with insight regarding its legal position and the usefulness of the patent as a competitive tool. In addition, evaluation of the patent may identify problems early that might be remedied through reissue or reexamination. Consequently, the technology-oriented company that monitors its intellectual property assets will be ready for the challenges ahead.

INTELLECTUAL PROPERTY AUDITS AND AVOIDING LIABILITY FOR INFRINGEMENT OF THIRD PARTY RIGHTS

Michael A. Lechter

Michael A. Lechter, a member of the law firm of Meyer, Hendricks, Victor, Osborn & Maledon, P.A., in Phoenix, Arizona, specializing in intellectual property law is the coordinating editor of this book. A more complete biography is provided at the end of the book.

Abstract

This article introduces the concept of the intellectual property audit to maximize utilization of a company's intellectual property and minimize the likelihood of incurring liability for infringement of third party rights.

40.1 THE NATURE OF AN IP AUDIT

In many instances, intellectual property is one of a company's most valuable assets, if not its most valuable asset. Yet, while audits of tangible assets and liabilities are commonplace, focused audits of intellectual property assets and liabilities of a company extending beyond royalty payment compliance are still a relative rarity.

An intellectual property audit involves more than just compiling inventory of a company's intellectual property assets. It also involves determining potential liabilities that may be incurred from use of technology and other items that might be the subject of third party intellectual property rights. Up-to-date information on the company's intellectual property assets and potential liabilities can be invaluable to the proper management of a company.

Another important aspect of an intellectual property audit, however, is the development of systems and procedures for ensuring that the company's intellectual property is appropriately protected, and infringement of the third party intellectual property rights is avoided. Unless appropriate procedures are implemented, loss of rights and third party intellectual property claims can adversely impact the company.

Rights in intellectual property are often affected and liabilities created by various types of agreements. Obviously, the audit must consider agreements specifically related to transfer of rights (assignment, licenses, franchises, and technical assistance). However, certain other types of agreements, while not for the specific purpose of affecting intellectual property rights, may well affect intellectual property rights or create potential liabilities. Those agreements tend to relate to three broad categories of subject matter: internal relationships (employee, and noncompetition agreements); third party business relationships (confidentiality, consulting, development, maintenance and support, manufacturing, and joint venture agreements); and sales and market relationships (purchase, distribution, VAR, and OEM agreements). All such agreements should be reviewed and monitored for compliance.

40.2 SUGGESTED PROCEDURES

One of the functions of an intellectual property audit is to establish and monitor compliance with policies and procedures to ensure that intellectual property assets are maximized and potential liabilities minimized. Any procedures adopted by a company must be tailored to the particulars of that company. However, some general guidelines with respect to procedures respecting securing rights in technology and avoiding inadvertent infringement of third party rights are provided.

40.2.1 Securing and Maintaining Rights in Technology

40.2.1a Employee Nondisclosure and Nonuse Agreements

In general, an "employee" agreement respecting confidentiality and assignment of inventions should be obtained from each employee that may have access to confidential information (*e.g.*, proprietary know-how) or is in a position likely to generate technology.

40.2.1b Preliminary State of the Art Investigation

At the beginning of each new project or entry into a new field of endeavor, a preliminary investigation of the state of the art, and, in particular, issued patents should be conducted. This will provide an idea of the patents already held by others in the relevant area of technology, and can provide a starting point for research. It can also help identify potential infringement problems.

40.2.1c R&D Initially Trade Secret

Initially, all R&D should be maintained as a trade secret. Appropriate nondisclosure (confidentiality) agreements should be obtained from all third parties given access to confidential information (vendors and consultants and the like). Preferably, the agreements will also make it clear that all technology that is developed by the consultant or vendor during a project will be assigned to the company.

40.2.1d Maintain Documentation

Proper records relating to the developmental process should be maintained. The more information and documentation that can be shown, the more likely that the requisite conception, reduction to practice, and diligence for an early date of invention can be established. Detailed records of the development process also can be critical to defending against third party claims of trade secret, copyright and mask work infringement.

40.2.1e Timely Consideration of Patent Protection

The prospect of patent protection should be explored for each aspect or feature of a product that provides a competitive advantage in a marketplace. It is important to keep the potential consequences in mind when considering showing a product or offering it for sale. A patentability assessment should be performed, and patent application filed, if appropriate, before any public use or showing, publication, or offer for sale.

40.2.1f Patent Marking

All products should be periodically reviewed to determine the propriety of patent marking. Marking a product with the number of an applicable patent gives constructive notice of the patent to the world and avoids the requirement of showing actual notice of the infringement as a prerequisite to collecting damages. If more than a deminimus number of unmarked products are placed on the market by the patentee, or by an express or implied licensee, damages for infringement can be obtained only for use, manufacture and sales occurring after actual notice of infringement. A "patent pending" or "patent applied for" marking may be placed on products described and claimed in an application pending before the patent office. While a "patent pending" notice has no legal effect, it places potential competitors on notice that a patent may issue and tends to discourage them from investing in a similar product. Mismarking with either a "Patent Pending" or "Patent" notice is actionable under the patent statute.

40.2.2 Avoiding Potential Infringement of Third Party Intellectual Property Rights

In theory, the basic rule with respect to using or copying an aspect of a competitor's product is simple: absent an express or implied contractual obligation, a company is at liberty to use and copy any unpatented, uncopyrighted aspect that comes into a company's possession legally, as long as there is no likelihood that the public would be deceived or confused as to the source of a product. Practice, however, is another story. In many instances the incidence and outcome of intellectual property litigation is a function of the internal procedures of the contestants.

40.2.2a Avoiding Infringement of Third Party Trade Secret Rights

The analysis in determining whether any given information or technology constitutes a trade secret or is confidential is inevitably a fact-specific inquiry. However, a competitor's trade secret rights cannot prevent the company from independently developing information or technology or, for that matter, using or copying unpatented technology, if it is obtained legally and the company is not under any express or implied contractual obligation to the contrary.

40.2.2b Preventative Procedures May Be Adopted

1. Any competitor's materials that come into a company's possession should be reviewed for proprietary notices. While in many instances such material is in fact not "confidential" in view of lack of controls by the competitor, prudence may dictate discarding such materials.
2. Promulgate a policy statement directing employees not to use any potentially trade secret information (or at least to consult counsel prior to using).
3. Debrief any former employee of a competitor that is hired. It should be made clear that the company is not interested in using any confidential information of the new hire's previous employer.
4. Maintain detailed records of the development of products to prove that any potentially trade secret information that might have been acquired from a competitor was not incorporated in a company's products.

40.2.2c Avoiding Infringement of Third Party Patents

It is also possible that a competitor holds utility patents covering new and unobvious aspects of its products or design patents covering the appearance of its products. The scope of a utility patent is defined by the patent claims; a patent is infringed if an unlicensed product includes the equivalent of each and every element of any of the patent claims. Infringement exists even if the product has additional features or elements that are not included in the claim and even if those additional elements are in themselves patentable. In essence, a design patent is infringed if an unlicensed product is so similar in appearance to the patented design that a consumer, under normal market conditions, is likely to think them the same. Neither patented invention nor design need be actually copied from the patent or competitor's product for infringement to exist; independent development is no defense.

Since independent development is no defense to patent infringement, the following preventative procedures are suggested:

1. Prior to entering into any new product area, or initiating development of significant new features or aspects of a product, have a preliminary investigation performed to collect copies of any relevant patents.

2. Initiate an investigation of all known competitors to obtain copies of any patents they may hold.

3. Examine competitors' products for patent markings or reference to pending applications.

4. Maintain a continuing watch for patents issued to major competitors.

5. Consider having an extensive infringement investigation performed prior to introducing a significant new product. (A cost-benefit analysis should be performed in view of previous searching and knowledge of extant patents.)

6. If a potential infringement problem is identified, a formal invalidity/non infringement opinion from patent counsel should be obtained. If a company is found to infringe a patent of which it is aware, and did not obtain the opinion of a competent patent attorney, the infringement is likely to be considered willful, giving rise to potential liability for treble damages and the patentee's attorney's fees.

7. Develop the company's own portfolio of patents to facilitate cross-licensing in the event that the claims of a competitor's patent cannot be, or for some reason are not, avoided.

40.2.2d Avoiding Infringement of Third Party Copyrights

It is prudent to assume that a competitor holds a copyright on all of its "works of authorship", such as booklets, advertising brochures, artistic designs, maps and architectural blueprints, audio tapes, and records, and, at least to some extent, computer programs. However, copyright protection is of particularly limited scope:

> Copyright protection pertains only to the form of expression and not to substance (ideas, methods, systems, mathematical principles, formulas, and equations are expressly not copyrightable); and actual copying is a requisite element for infringement (independent development *is* a defense).

While independent development is a complete defense to a charge of copyright infringement, copying is presumed from "access" and "substantial similarity". Unfortunately, where there is substantial similarity, access is sometimes assumed by the courts merely by virtue of the fact that the copyrighted work was available in the marketplace. Where software is concerned, this can be problematical; similarity in software is sometimes the result of common conventions and practical and functional reasons. It is prudent that the development process be documented in depth so that the company will be able to prove that the work was in fact independently developed.

40.2.2e Avoiding Infringement of Third Party
Mask Work Registrations

To the extent that any product that the company might ultimately develop includes custom semiconductor chips, third party "mask work" protection may be applicable. A mask work registration, in essence, precludes the use of reproductions of the protected mask work to manufacture competing chips. However, the act protects only against outright copying, and expressly permits reverse engineering the chip for purposes of analysis and using any unpatented idea, principle, or technology embodied in the mask work.

Thus, as in the case of copyrights, independent development of mask work technologies is a complete defense and, as a matter of procedure, development should be fully documented.

40.3 CONCLUSION

An intellectual property audit can be an important tool for increasing a company's revenues. It can identify potentially licensable intellectual property of which the company was previously unaware with the ultimate result of increased licensing revenues to the company. It also can identify potential infringement of third party intellectual property rights before the company incurs any liability or, if liability cannot be avoided, in time to control or minimize the liability and perhaps avoid costly litigation. Additionally, contractual obligations can be identified to ensure compliance and, therefore, minimize potential disputes and liabilities. Perhaps most importantly, an intellectual property audit can serve as a vehicle for establishing procedures to ensure that intellectual property assets are protected and exploited to the fullest extent, and to ensure costly intellectual property liabilities and contractual disputes are avoided or minimized. Thus, if properly employed, an intellectual property audit can significantly and positively impact the company.

GLOSSARY

These explanations are not complete definitions but are intended as aids to understanding the terms used in this collection of papers.

Abandonment. The giving up of an invention or potential patent rights either voluntarily or through lack of diligence in completing the invention or through failure to respond adequately during Patent Office examination of the application for a patent.

Affidavit. A voluntary, written statement of facts made under oath.

Algorithm. A step-by-step procedure for solving a problem or accomplishing a desired result.

Application, patent. A legal petition that describes an invention sufficiently for others to practice it, consists of one or more figures, and specifies one or more claims.

Application, patent, continuation. A patent application, filed during the pendency of an earlier filed *parent* application, disclosing the same subject matter as in the parent application, and claiming priority based upon the earlier filed parent application. The continuation application is treated as if it were filed on the date that the parent application was filed.

Application, patent, continuation-in-part (CIP). Continuation-in-part application is an application filed during the pendency of a parent application, but includes new matter not described in the earlier filed parent application. Claims in the CIP application relating to the material described in the parent application are given the benefit of the parent application filing date. The claims directed to the new matter added to the application are given the filing date of the CIP application.

Art. A field or area of technology or technical data.

Assignment. A written transfer of property rights in an invention from the inventor (assignor) to someone else (assignee, which may be a corporation).

Best mode. The best way known by the inventor at the time of filing a patent application for carrying out or practicing the invention (*cf* preferred embodiment).

Claim. One or more statements at the end of a patent or application that precisely define the novel feature of the invention for which patent protection is granted or sought.

Classification. The numerical designation assigned a patent according to its subject matter, arranged according to broad fields of technology and divided into subclasses of narrower fields; used to file and retrieve patents.

Composition of matter. A mixture of two or more ingredients producing a final product having properties different from or in addition to those of the separate ingredients. This is one of the four classes of patentable subject matter.

Conception. The mental realization by an inventor of a means for solving a specific problem or performing a defined sequence of operations, creating a desired and useful result.

Copyright.   A statutory exclusive right to reproduce, prepare derivative works from and distribute copies of, automatically accorded to the author of original works of authorship. The copyright relates only to the expression, and not the substance, of the work of authorship.

Court of Appeals for the Federal Circuit.   The court in which most appeals from Patent Office decisions take place and which frequently interprets the patent laws.

Diligence.   Continuous activity or attentiveness in completing an invention (*cf* reduction to practice).

Disclosure.   A description or revelation of an invention, commonly the inventor's written statement of the subject matter of the invention and how it operates.

Doctrine of equivalents.   The basis of an inventor's protection from infringement by a product or process that does the same work in substantially the same way to accomplish substantially the same result as described in the patent.

European Patent Convention.   The agreement that established a European Patent Office in 1977 to examine applications (in English, French, or German) and issue patents that have the status of national patents in each member country that the applicant has designated.

Examiner.   An employee of the Patent Office who studies applications in detail to determine whether, in view of the applicable prior art, the applicant is entitled to a patent.

Filewrapper estoppel.   A doctrine that prevents the owner of a patent from interpreting the claims of the patent more broadly than was understood when the patent was granted. (The application file including all proceedings in the Patent Office is available to the public after a patent issues.)

Infringement.   The unauthorized making, using, or selling of a product or process that uses an invention protected by a patent.

Interference.   A legal proceeding in the Patent Office to decide the issue of priority between two or more inventors who claim substantially the same invention.

Invention, patentable.   Something conceived and developed that is new, useful, and unobvious and is within one of the four classes of statutory subject matter (see statutory classes).

License.   Authorization by the owner of a patent for someone else to make, use, or sell the protected invention.

Machine.   A device or apparatus, using or converting energy, that is a combination of elements which cooperate to perform a function; may be chemical, electrical, mechanical, or nuclear. This is one of the four classes of patentable subject matter.

Manufacture.   Any article made by man and not classified as a machine or a composition of matter. This is one of the four classes of patentable subject matter.

Mask work.   A statutory right to preclude others from copying the mask works (representation of the layout of a semiconductor chip) and using the copy in the manufacture of competing chips. To maintain the protection, the mask work must be registered with the Copyright Office within two years of its first commercial exploitation.

Official Gazette.   A weekly publication of the U.S. Patent and Trademark Office that identifies all patents issued that week, including a figure and the abstract or a representative claim.

Patent Cooperation Treaty.   A 1978 agreement under which inventors can file international applications in a member country and, after a preliminary search of prior art, have them forwarded to other member countries for independent determination of patentability.

Patent, design.   A patent covering an original ornamental design or configuration for an article of manufacture; issued for 3, 7, or 14 years at the option of the inventor.

Patent, plant. A patent covering a new, distinct, asexually reproducing plant; issued for 17 years.

Patent, utility. The most familiar type of patent, covering a new, useful, and unobvious process, machine, article of manufacture, or composition of matter; issued for 17 years.

Pendency. The period between the filing of a patent application and the issuing of a patent.

Preferred embodiment. The particular form in which the patent applicant discloses the invention, usually the most useful and practical form; synonymous with best mode.

Prior art. All of the pertinent and applicable public knowledge and experience that is known at the time a patent application is filed.

Priority. Where a patent application is treated as filed on the date of a prior (parent) application.

Process. A method or series of steps for producing a useful physical result. This is one of the four classes of patentable subject matter.

Prosecution. The essentially continuous series of actions and responses between the patent examiner and the inventor's patent agent or attorney after an application is filed.

Read on. A claim in a patent application that describes the elements of an existing product or process and the cooperative relationships among those elements is said to "read on" that product or process.

Reduction to practice, actual. The successful making and testing of an invention to prove its feasibility.

Reduction to practice, constructive. The filing of a patent application, which requires sufficient detail to instruct a person of ordinary skill in the art to practice the invention.

Search. An investigation of the applicable prior art in the field of an invention to determine whether it is new or has been anticipated.

Sight. The rectangular area of specified size that encloses figures of a patent drawing and from which other information is excluded.

Specification. The part of a patent application that fully describes the invention and how to make and use it, including the claims.

Statutory bar. Activities specified by law that preclude the granting of a patent, usually the activities of the patent applicant conducted more than one year before filing an application; for example, public use or sale of the invention, description in a printed publication, and patenting elsewhere.

Statutory classes. The 4 classes of invention that are patentable subject matter provided other requirements of the law are satisfied; see composition of matter, machine, manufacture, and process.

Trade secret. A formula, process, device, pattern, or other information that is intentionally kept secret (rather than being patented) for use in a business.

Trademarks. A trademark is any word, symbol, shape, or thing used to identify the source or origin of a product or service; used to distinguish the goods or services of one company from those of another.

"Working" a patent. Working a patent means, in general, to use the invention in a commercial context, *e.g.,* in a commercial product. The concept of "working" a patent is particularly important in countries other than the United States. Many countries make a patent subject to compulsory licensing (*i.e.,* the patent owner is required to grant licenses to others) if the patent is not "worked" within a predetermined period. The precise activities that constitute "working" vary from country to country.

ABOUT THE EDITOR

Michael A. Lechter is a partner specializing in intellectual property law with the law firm of Meyer, Hendricks, Victor, Osborn, & Maledon, P.A., in Phoenix, Arizona. He holds a Bachelor of Science in Electrical Engineering (High Honors, University of Maryland) and a Juris Doctorate (*cum laude,* Seton Hall). Mr. Lechter, with over 20 years experience in intellectual property practice, is the author of *The Intellectual Property Handbook* (Tech-Press, Inc., an affiliate of Meyer, Hendricks, 1994). He also has authored a number of articles, and has lectured extensively throughout the United States and the world on the subject of intellectual property law and, in particular, on the subjects of protecting software and semiconductor chips. He has, upon request of the House Judiciary Committee, submitted testimony to the Congress of the United States, and has participated in various United Nations and foreign government proceedings on intellectual property law and technology transfer.

INDEX

NOTE: Bold page numbers indicate figures, tables, and illustrations.